International B of Paremiography

Collections of Proverbs, Proverbial Expressions and Comparisons, Quotations, Graffiti, Slang, and Wellerisms

Wolfgang Mieder

"Proverbium"
in cooperation with the
Department of German and Russian

The University of Vermont
Burlington, Vermont
2011

Supplement Series

of

Proverbium
Yearbook of International Proverb Scholarship

Edited by Wolfgang Mieder

Volume 34

The cover illustration is a photograph
of Wolfgang Mieder's
International Proverb Archives

ISBN 978-0-9846456-0-2

Manufactured in the United States of America
by Queen City Printers Inc.
Burlington, Vermont

Table of Contents

Introduction

Some forty years ago, more precisely in 1968, I began assembling proverb collections from around the world while I also amassed studies on proverbs. Over the years I have published various paremiological bibliographies, with the most comprehensive being my two-volume *International Bibliography of Paremiology and Phraseology* (2009) that includes 10,027 titles. However, due to space limitations, I was not able to include my impressive library of 3,615 proverb collections, and it thus gives me much scholarly pleasure to present these paremiographical publications at this time. They represent the result of a dedicated and enthusiastic labor of love, so to speak. For over four decades I have spent time and private funds to amass this treasure that is part of my International Proverb Archives housed in part at the University of Vermont in Burlington, Vermont, and to a larger extent in my private library in our country home outside of Williston, Vermont. Numerous scholars from here and abroad have come to use my archives, and I obviously delight in having been able to establish these rich holdings of paremiological and paremiographical publications in order to serve scholars and students from everywhere.

As the first section of the present bibliography shows, there exist at least 140 bibliographies of proverb collections that I have been able to locate and acquire. Many of them are small and specific bibliographies that list collections for a particular language, culture, or subject matter. But there are, of course, also major international and interdisciplinary paremiographical publications, as for example Pierre-Alexandre Gratet-Duplessis, *Bibliographie parémiologique* (1847 [1969]), Wilfrid Bonser, *Proverb Literature. A Bibliography of Works Relating to Proverbs* (1930 [1967]), and Otto Moll, *Sprichwörterbibliographie* (1958). The latter bibliography with its almost nine thousand entries remains the *magnum opus*, but as is the case with all published bibliographies, it is very much out of date by now. This is also the case for another bibliography that I would like to single out in these short introductory comments. It is Ignace Bernstein's bibliophile two-volume *Catalogue des livres parémio-logiques composant la bibliothèque de Ignace Bernstein* (1900 [2003]) that I had the honor of reprinting a few years ago in Germany. Ignace Bernstein (1836-1909) was a well to do businessman at Warsaw for whom his paremiographical work was an avocation. He is rightfully remembered today for his massive collection *Jüdische Sprichwörter und Redensarten* (1908 [1969]), but it is his impressive paremiographical catalogue that has made him into one of my scholarly heroes. Having the means and above all interest in doing so, he was able to assemble 4,761 proverb collections that are now housed in the Biblioteka Jagiellońska of the University of Cracow in Poland. In fact, by the time of his death not quite ten years after the publication of the bibliography of his invaluable holdings, he had succeeded in purchasing 1,263 additional collections. Thus his private paremiographical library consists of 6,024 volumes, and as such it represents a national Polish treasure!

My own attempt to follow in the large footsteps of Ignace Bernstein has met with considerable success, but I must admit with all humility that he is the true master, surpassing by far the private paremiographical libraries of such other renowned proverb scholars as Matti Kuusi, Lutz Röhrich, Archer Taylor, Bartlett Jere Whiting, and others. But again, valuable as Bernstein's library of older proverb collections is, it is, together with the bibliographies by Gratet-Duplessis, Bonser, and Moll, seriously out of date and in need of updating. This is where my own private holdings come in, for while I have accumulated plenty of old collections from the sixteenth century on (often in the form of reprints), I have obviously been able to purchase or to obtain from fellow paremiographers especially such collections that have been published during the past hundred years. But there is another difference that I can mention with some satisfaction, for I have cast my net very wide including not only collections of proverbs, anti-proverbs, proverbial expressions, proverbial comparisons, and wellerisms but also books of quotations, graffiti, and slang that usually contain plenty of proverbial texts. But be that as it may, the 3,615 titles listed here are all in my possession and represent my sincere efforts in building a comprehensive library of collections. It will surprise nobody that my collection holdings are particularly rich in American, English, and German as well as primarily European publications. I am also well aware that there exist plenty of additional collections, and my bibliographical files contain many of them, but this bibliography only includes those publications that actually are part of my International Proverb Archives. I simply thought it would be of considerable interest to see what a modern scholar can do standing on the shoulders of the giants mentioned above. In addition, I hope that this bibliography will be of use to proverb scholars throughout the world. And as always I would be more than willing to make any collection available to fellow proverb scholars and students interested in proverbs.

The organization of the bibliography can easily be ascertained from the "Table of Contents". Following the first section of "Bibliographies", I present over two hundred "International Collections",

2

i.e., collections that contain texts from three or more languages or cultures. After this the consecutively numbered titles are grouped in alphabetically arranged sections according to languages, nationalities, or ethnicities. In order not to create too many sub-groups, I have combined all the "African Languages" and "Indian Languages" into one group each, with the individual languages being part of the subject index. Bilingual collections presented a special problem in deciding into which group to place them. Usually I chose the first language mentioned and placed the second language into the subject index at the end of the book. The subject index also includes significant keywords so that specialized collections of anti-proverbs, aphorisms, graffiti, legal proverbs, medical proverbs, proverbial comparisons, slang, somatisms, stereotypes, weather proverbs, wellerisms, etc. can easily be found. But there is considerable more information presented in the subject index, leading scholars or students to special collections on advertising, alcohol, animals, children, health, humor, love, media, music, names, obscenity, pedagogy, scatology, sexuality, sports, stereotypes, women, etc. There is also a name index that includes all the names of first, second, third and at times fourth authors. The entries themselves include precise page numbers and information as to pictorial illustrations.

During the more than four decades of my bibliographical activities I have benefited greatly from many colleagues and friends. While I cannot possibly thank them all individually here, I would like to acknowledge the following alphabetically-listed persons in particular for sending me their collections or for providing valuable information to me so that I could obtain them: Ahmad Abrishami (Tehran), Bendt Alster (Copenhagen), Shirley L. Arora (Los Angeles), Péter Barta (Budapest), Iwona Bartoszewicz (Wrocław), Dan Ben-Amos (Philadelphia), Simon J. Bronner (Middletown), George B. Bryan (Burlington), František Čermák (Prague), Maria Conca (Valencia), George Cotter (Debre Zeit), Heinrich L. Cox (Bonn), Carlos Alberto Crida Alvarez (Athens), Raymond Doctor (Pune), Aristeides Doulaveras (Zeuolatio-Korinthias), Charles Clay Doyle (Athens, Georgia), Alan Dundes (Berkeley), Peter Ďurčo (Bratislava), Sabine Fiedler (Leipzig), Teodor Flonta (Hobart), Czaba Földes (Veszprém), Erszébet and Tamás Forgács (Szeged), Temistocle Franceschi (Florence), Gabriela Funk (Ponta Delgada), Gabriel Gheorghe (Bucharest), Christian Grandl (Würzburg), Kazys Grigas (Vilnius), Peter Grzybek (Graz), Josep Guia (Valencia), Galit Hasan-Rokem (Jerusalem), Joseph Healey (Nairobi), Susanne Hose (Bautzen), José de Jaime Gómez (Valencia), José María de Jaime Lorén (Valencia), Georgi L. Kapchits (Moscow), Iver Kjaer (Birkerød), Jarmo Korhonen (Helsinki), Wacława Korzyn (Kraków),

Arvo Krikmann (Tartu), Matti Kuusi (Helsinki), Alejandro Lee (Los Angeles), Anna T. Litovkina (Szekszárd), Outi Lauhakangas (Helsinki), Démétrios Loukatos (Athens), S.D. Lourdu (Tirunelveli), Hans-Manfred Militz (Jena), Valerii M. Mokienko (St. Petersburg), Yoko Mori (Tokyo), Constantin Negreanu (Drobeta-Turnu-Severin), Timothy C. Nelson (Davos), Andreas Nolte (Burlington), Gyula Paczolay (Veszprém), Roumyana Petrova (Rousse), Elisabeth and Ilpo Piirainen (Steinfurt), Stanisław Prędota (Wrocław), Zuzana Profantová (Bratislava), Margit Raders (Madrid), Lutz Röhrich (Freiburg), Xesús Ferro Ruibal (Santiago de Compostela), Ingrid Schellbach-Kopra (Helsinki), Maria Helena Sampaio Sereno (Porto), Julia Sevilla Muñoz (Madrid), Danica Škara (Zadar), Rui João Baptista Soares (Tavira), Dumitru Stanciu (Bucharest), Alexandru Stanciulescu-Bîrda (Bârda), Kathrin Steyer (Mannheim), Emmanuel Strauss (Merstham), Grzegorz Szpila (Kraków), Katsuaki Takeda (Sapporo), Gerhard Uhlenbruck (Cologne), Peter Unseth (Dallas), Vilmos Voigt (Budapest), Monika and Harald Wallgrün (Ahrensburg), Harry Walter (Greifswald), Helmut Walther (Wiesbaden), Gerald Wanjohi (Nairobi), Jürgen Werner (Berlin), Fionnuala Carson Williams (Belfast), Barbara and Gerd Wotjak (Leipzig), Metin Yurtbasi (Ankara), and Francisco Zuluaga (Medellin).

Special thanks are due my good friend Hope Greenberg who once again has been of invaluable help in producing the name index and in formatting the final manuscript. As the production manager of *Proverbium* she has helped me with various projects for more than two decades. The same is true for Janet Sobieski, who as managing editor of *Proverbium* has also assisted me for more then twenty-five years with many of my projects, especially with the preparation of my annual bibliographies that are part of *Proverbium*. I cannot stress enough how special these two friends are to me, and I am so sad that Janet and her husband will be moving to Boise, Idaho, to be close to the rest of their family. Together Hope and Janet have made a big difference not only to me personally but also to my service for international paremiology and paremiography in general. They belong in the hall of fame of proverb scholarship, and in recognition and appreciation of their untiring efforts and generous support I would like to dedicate this bibliography to both of them with all good wishes and sincere thanks.

Summer 2011   Wolfgang Mieder

Bibliographies

1. Abrahams, Roger D. "On Proverb Collecting and Proverb Collections." *Proverbium*, no. 8 (1967), 181-184.

2. Adrianova-Peretts, V.P. "Iz istorii russkikh rukopisnykh sbornikov poslovits XVII-XVIII vv." *Stranitsky istorii russkoi literatury*. No editor given. Moskva: "Nauka", 1971. 24-36.

3. Aguerri Martínez, Ascensión, and Luis Barrio Cuenca-Romero. "José María Sbarbi en la Colección paremiológica. Libros impresos en el siglo XVIII." *Seminario Internacional: Colección paremiológica Madrid 1922-2007*. Eds. Carmen Lafuente Miño, Manuel Sevilla Muñoz, Fermín de los Reyes Gómez, and Julia Sevilla Muñoz. Madrid: Biblioteca Histórica Municipal de Madrid, 2007. 57-72. With 2 illustrations.

4. Aguerri Martínez, Ascensión, and Purificación Castro Gómez. "La Colección Paremiológica de Melchor García Moreno en la Biblioteca Histórica Municipal de Madrid." *Paremia*, 6 (1997), 25-30.

5. Arora, Shirley L. "A Critical Bibliography of Mexican American Proverbs." *Aztlán*, 13 (1982), 71-80.

6. Attal, Robert. "Bibliographie raisonnée des proverbes arabes et judéo-arabes du Maghreb." *Studies in Bibliography and Booklore*, 17 (1989), 43-54.

7. Bahder, Karl von. "Sprichwörter." In K. von Bahder, *Die deutsche Philologie im Grundriss*. Paderborn: Ferdinand Schöningh, 1883. 292-301.

8. Bárdosi, Vilmos, and Regina Hessky. "Phraseographie des Ungarischen." *Phraseologie. Ein internationales Handbuch zeitgenössischer Forschung*. Eds. Harald Burger, Dmitrij Dobrovol'skij, Peter Kühn, and Neal R. Norrick. Berlin: Walter de Gruyter, 2007. II, 1017-1026.

9. Bartlett, John. *Catalogue of a Choice and Valuable Collection of Rare Books of Proverbs and Emblems, Dance of Death, etc.* Boston: Little, Brown & Co., 1888. 45 pp.

10. Bernstein, Ignace. *Catalogue des livres parémiologiques composant la bibliothèque de Ignace Bernstein.* 2 vols. Varsovie: W. Drugulin, 1900; rpt. ed. Wolfgang Mieder. Hildesheim: Georg Olms, 2003. I, 560 pp.; II, 650 pp. With illustrations.

11. Bonser, Wilfrid. *Proverb Literature. A Bibliography of Works Relating to Proverbs. Compiled from Materials Left by the Late T.A.*

Stephens. London: William Glaisher, 1930; rpt. Nendeln / Liechtenstein: Kraus Reprint, 1967. 496 pp.

12. Bratu, Ion I. "Contributii la bibliografia paremiologiei românesti." *Proverbium Dacoromania*, 2 (1987), 47-52; and 3 (1988), 28-32.

13. Brückner, A. "Zur slavischen Parömiographie." *Archiv für slavische Philologie*, 18 (1896), 193-203.

14. Brunet, G. "Bibliographie des proverbes." *Bulletin du Bibliophile Belge*, 9 (1952), 233-240.

15. Buridant, Claude. "Sélection bibliographique: études sur les proverbes." *Revue des sciences humaines*, 41, no. 163 (1976), 431-436.

16. Carracedo, Leonor, and Elena Romero. "Refranes publicados por Ja'acob A. Yoná (edición concordada) y bibliografía del refranero sefardi." *Sefarad*, 41, no. 3 (1981), 389-560.

17. Chauvin, Victor. *Bibliographie des ouvrages arabes ou relatifs aux Arabes publiés dans l'Europe chrétienne de 1810 à 1885*. Volume I: *Les Proverbes*. Liège: Vaillant-Carmanne, 1892. 72 pp.

18. Chelmi, Evlampia. "El fondo griego de la Colección paremiológica (Biblioteca Histórica Municipal de Madrid)." *Seminario Internacional: Colección paremiológica Madrid 1922-2007*. Eds. Carmen Lafuente Miño, Manuel Sevilla Muñoz, Fermín de los Reyes Gómez, and Julia Sevilla Muñoz. Madrid: Biblioteca Histórica Municipal de Madrid, 2007. 155-174. With 1 illustration.

19. Cowie, Anthony P. "English Phraseology." *Phraseologie. Ein internationales Handbuch zeitgenössischer Forschung*. Eds. Harald Burger, Dmitrij Dobrovol'skij, Peter Kühn, and Neal R. Norrick. Berlin: Walter de Gruyter, 2007. II, 929-939.

20. de Caro, Francis (Frank) A., and William K. McNeil. *American Proverb Literature: A Bibliography*. Bloomington: Folklore Forum, Indiana University, 1971 (= *Folklore Forum, Bibliographic and Special Series*, No. 6). 81 pp.

21. Díaz Ferrero, Ana Maria. "Colecciones paremiológicas portuguesas." *Paremia*, 10 (2001), 57-65.

22. Doctor, Raymond D. "A Bibliography of Proverb Collections in Indian Languages." *Proverbium*, 21 (2004), 35-62.

23. Doyle, Charles Clay. "More Paremiological Publications by Archer Taylor." *Proverbium*, 8 (1991), 191-197.

24. Doyle, Charles Clay. "Collections of Proverbs and Proverb Dictionaries: Some Historical Observations on What's in Them and What's Not (With a Note on Current "Gendered" Proverbs)." *Phraseology and Culture in English*. Ed. Paul Skandera. Berlin: Walter de Gruyter, 2007. 181-203.

25. Eikelmann, Manfred. "Sprichwörtersammlungen (deutsche)." *Die deutsche Literatur des Mittelalters. Verfasserlexikon*. Eds. Burghart Wachinger, Gundolf Keil, Kurt Ruh, Werner Schröder, and Franz Josef Wortsbrock. Berlin: Walter de Gruyter, 1993. IX, cols. 162-179.

26. Eismann, Wolfgang, and Stefan Rittgasser. "Bibliographisches: Zur russischen Phraseologie." *Notizen und Materialen zur russischen Linguistik*. Ed. Gerd Freidhof. Frankfurt am Main: Kubon & Sagner, 1977. 182-201.

27. Fanfani, Massimo. "Phraseographie des Italienischen." *Phraseologie. Ein internationales Handbuch zeitgenössischer Forschung*. Eds. Harald Burger, Dmitrij Dobrovol'skij, Peter Kühn, and Neal R. Norrick. Berlin: Walter de Gruyter, 2007. II, 975-986.

28. Farø, Ken. "Danish Phraseography." *Phraseologie. Ein internationales Handbuch zeitgenössischer Forschung*. Eds. Harald Burger, Dmitrij Dobrovol'skij, Peter Kühn, and Neal R. Norrick. Berlin: Walter de Gruyter, 2007. II, 949-958.

29. Ferguson, Charles A., and John M. Echols. "Critical Bibliography of Spoken Arabic Proverb Literature." *Journal of American Folklore*, 65 (1952), 67-84. Also in *Structuralist Studies in Arabic Linguistics. Charles A. Ferguson's Papers, 1954-1994*. Eds. Kirk Belnap and Niloofar Haeri. Leiden: Brill, 1997. 151-174.

30. Filipenko, Tatjana, and Valerii M. Mokienko. "Phraseographie des Russischen." *Phraseologie. Ein internationales Handbuch zeitgenössischer Forschung*. Eds. Harald Burger, Dmitrij Dobrovol'skij, Peter Kühn, and Neal R. Norrick. Berlin: Walter de Gruyter, 2007. II, 998-1007.

31. Földes, Csaba. *Idiomatik / Phraseologie [Studienbibliographie]*. Heidelberg: Julius Groos, 1997. 53 pp.

32. Friesland, Carl. "Verzeichnis der seit 1847 erschienenen Sammlungen französischer Sprichwörter." *Zeitschrift für* *französische Sprache und Literatur*, 18 (1896), 221-237; 19 (1897), 122-123.

33. Friesland, Carl. "Französische Sprichwörter-Bibliographie. Verzeichnis der seit 1847 erschienenen Sammlungen französischer Sprichwörter." *Zeitschrift für französische Sprache und Literatur*, 28 (1905), 260-287.

34. Fumagalli, Giuseppe. "Bibliografia paremiologica italiana." *Archivio per lo studio delle tradizione popolari*, 5 (1886), 317-350 and 482-509; 6 (1887), 25-42 and 153-167.

35. Fumagalli, Giuseppe. "Nuovo contributo alla bibliografia paremiologica italiana." *Archivio per lo studio delle tradizione popolari*, 10 (1891), 210-227 and 332-342.

36. García Moreno, Melchor. *Catálogo Paremiológico*. Madrid: San Bernardo, 1918. 248 pp. With illustrations.

37. García Moreno, Melchor. *Extracto de Algunos Juicios acerca del Catálogo Paremiológico de Melchor García Moreno*. Madrid: Sociedad Española de Artes Gráficas, 1919. 37 pp.

38. García Moreno, Melchor. *Apendice al Catálogo Paremiológico*. Madrid: Miguel Servet, 1948. 71 pp.

39. García Moreno, Melchor. *Catálogo Paremiológico*. With an introduction by Francisco Calero. Madrid: Ollero & Ramos, 1995. 372 pp. With illustrations.

40. Goedeke, Karl. "Sprichwörter." In K. Goedeke. *Grundriss zur Geschichte der deutschen Dichtung aus den Quellen*. 2nd ed. Dresden: L. Ehlermann, 1886. II, 3-19.

41. Gratet-Duplessis, Pierre-Alexandre. *Bibliographie parémiologique*. Paris: Potier, 1847; rpt. Nieuwkoop: B. de Graaf, 1969. 520 pp.

42. Gratet-Duplessis, Pierre-Alexandre. *Catalogue des livres en partie rares et precieux composant la bibliothèque de Feu M. [Pierre-Alexandre] Gratet-Duplessis*. Paris: Potier, 1856. 150-179.

43. Grauls, Jan. "Een spreekwoordenbibliographie." *Volkskunde*, 61 (1960), 71-76.

44. Grzybek, Peter. "Bibliographie der Arbeiten G.L. Permjakovs." *Semiotische Studien zum Sprichwort. Simple Forms Reconsidered I*. Eds. P. Grzybek and Wolfgang Eismann. Tübingen: Gunter Narr, 1984. 203-214.

45. Haller, Joseph. *Altspanische Sprichwörter und sprichwörtliche Redensarten aus den Zeiten vor Cervantes.* 2 vols. Regensburg: G.J. Manz, 1883. I, 652 pp. (collection), II, 304 pp. (bibliography).

46. Hand, Wayland D. "Writings of Archer Taylor on Proverbs and Proverbial Lore." *Proverbium*, no. 15 (1970), 420-424.

47. Hanuš, Ignace Jan. *Literatura přislovnictví slovanského a německého.* Praze: Nákladem spisovatelovým, 1853; rpt. Leipzig: Zentralantiquariat der DDR, 1970. 152 pp.

48. Jaime Gómez, José de, and José María de Jaime Lorén. *Catálogo de la Exposición Bibliografía de Paremiológica Española.* Valencia: Instituto de Bachillerato "Fuente de San Luis," 1985. 12 pp. With illustrations.

49. Jaime Gómez, José de, and José María de Jaime Lorén. *Catalogo de Bibliografia Paremiologica Española.* Valencia: E.C.V.S.A., 1992. 234 pp. With illustrations.

50. Jaime Gómez, José de, and José María de Jaime Lorén. *Catálogo de Bibliografía Paremiológica Española.* Apendice 1. Valencia: DYNA, 1998. 107 pp.

51. Jente, Richard. "A Review of Proverb Literature Since 1920." *Corona. Studies in Celebration of the Eightieth Birthday of Samuel Singer.* Eds. Arno Schirokauer and Wolfgang Paulsen. Durham, North Carolina: Duke University Press, 1941. 23-44.

52. Kispál, Tamás. "Sprichwörtersammlungen." *Phraseologie. Ein internationales Handbuch zeitgenössischer Forschung.* Eds. Harald Burger, Dmitrij Dobrovol'skij, Peter Kühn, and Neal R. Norrick. Berlin: Walter de Gruyter, 2007. I, 414-423.

53. Klančar, Anthony J. "A Tentative Bibliography on the Slovene Proverb." *Journal of American Folklore*, 61 (1948), 194-200.

54. Konstantinova, Anna. "Russian Proverb Scholarship: A Bibliography of Candidacy and Doctorate Dissertations." *Proverbium*, 27 (2010), 425-450.

55. Korhonen, Jarmo. "Phraseographie des Finnischen." *Phraseologie. Ein internationales Handbuch zeitgenössischer Forschung.* Eds. Harald Burger, Dmitrij Dobrovol'skij, Peter Kühn, and Neal R. Norrick. Berlin: Walter de Gruyter, 2007. II, 1007-1017.

56. Kulišič, Spiro. "Ogled bibliografije nasin narodnin poslovica." *Bulletin du muse ethnographique de Beograd*, 5 (1930), 142-151.

9

57. Lafuente Niño, Carmen. *Colección paremiologica: Nuevas adquisiciones.* Madrid: Bibliotecca Histórica Municipal de Madrid, 1996. 57 pp.

58. Lafuente Niño, Carmen, Manuel Sevilla Muñoz, Fermín de los Reyes Gómez, and Julia Sevilla Muñoz (eds.). *Seminario Internacional: Colección paremiológica Madrid 1922-2007.* Madrid: Biblioteca Histórica Municipal de Madrid, 2007. 271 pp. With 20 illustrations.

59. Lengert, Joachim. *Romanische Phraseologie und Parömiologie: Eine teilkommentierte Bibliographie. (Von den Anfängen bis 1997).* 2 vols. Tübingen: Gunter Narr, 1999. 2132 pp.

60. Lengert, Joachim. "Phraseographie des Französischen." *Phraseologie. Ein internationales Handbuch zeitgenössischer Forschung.* Eds. Harald Burger, Dmitrij Dobrovol'skij, Peter Kühn, and Neal R. Norrick. Berlin: Walter de Gruyter, 2007. II, 958-975.

61. Lim, Kim Hui. "Malay Proverb Scholarship and Collections." *Proverbium*, 18 (2001), 185-203.

62. Loomis, C. Grant. "Bibliography of the Writings of Archer Taylor." *Humaniora. Essays in Literature, Folklore, Bibliography. Honoring Archer Taylor on His Seventieth Birthday.* Eds. Wayland D. Hand and Gustave Arlt. Locust Valley, New York: J.J. Augustin, 1960. 356-374.

63. Louis, Cameron. "Proverbs, Precepts, and Monitory Pieces." *A Manual of the Writings in Middle English 1050-1500.* Ed. Albert E. Hartung. New Haven, Connecticut: The Connecticut Academy of Arts and Sciences, 1993. Vol. 9, 2957-3048 (commentary), and 3349-3404 (bibliography).

64. Lubensky, Sophia, and Marjorie McShane. "Bilingual Phraseological Dictionaries." *Phraseologie. Ein internationales Handbuch zeitgenössischer Forschung.* Eds. Harald Burger, Dmitrij Dobrovol'skij, Peter Kühn, and Neal R. Norrick. Berlin: Walter de Gruyter, 2007. II, 919-928.

65. Luomala, Katharine. "A Bibliographical Survey of Collections of Hawaiian Sayings." *Proverbium*, 2 (1985), 279-306.

66. Mathews, Norris (ed.). *British Public Libraries. Reference Library. The Stuckey Lean Collection.* Bristol: John Wright, 1903. 73-123 (section II: "Proverbs").

67. Mayreder, C. "Die polyglotte Sprichwörterliteratur. Eine bibliographische Skizze, als Ergänzung zu M. [sic] Gratet-Duplessis': *Bibliographie parémiologique.*" *Rivista di Letteratura Popolare*, 1 (1877), 241-265.

68. Meier, John. "Sprichwörter." *Grundriss der germanischen Philologie*. Ed. Hermann Paul. Strassburg: Karl J. Trübner, 1893. II, 808-827 (2nd ed. 1901-1909), II, 1258-1281.

69. Mieder, Wolfgang. "International Bibliography of Explanatory Essays on Proverbs and Proverbial Expressions Containing Names." *Names*, 24 (1976), 253-304.

70. Mieder, Wolfgang. *International Bibliography of Explanatory Essays on Proverbs and Proverbial Expressions*. Bern: Herbert Lang, 1977. 146 pp.

71. Mieder, Wolfgang. "One Last Proverb Publication by Archer Taylor." *Journal of American Folklore*, 91 (1978), 970.

72. Mieder, Wolfgang. *Proverbs in Literature: An International Bibliography*. Bern: Peter Lang, 1978. 150 pp.

73. Mieder, Wolfgang. *International Proverb Scholarship: An Annotated Bibliography*. New York: Garland Publishing, 1982. 613 pp.

74. Mieder, Wolfgang. "Geschichte und Probleme der neuhochdeutschen Sprichwörterlexikographie." *Studien zur neuhochdeutschen Lexikographie*. Ed. Herbert Ernst Wiegand. Hildesheim: Georg Olms, 1984. V, 307-358 (= Germanistische Linguistik, 3-6 [1984], 307-358).

75. Mieder, Wolfgang. "International Bibliography of New and Reprinted Proverb Collections." *Proverbium*, 1 (1984), 251-271; 2 (1985), 373-378; 3 (1986), 421-430; 4 (1987), 361-368; 5 (1988), 213-218; 6 (1989), 273-279; 7 (1990), 299-303; 8 (1991), 279-284; 9 (1992), 323-327; 10 (1993), 361-364; 11 (1994), 333-342; 12 (1995), 411-420; 13 (1996), 411-420; 14 (1997), 471-486; 15 (1998), 477-487; 16 (1999), 453-465; 17 (2000), 493-500; 18 (2001), 477-485; 19 (2002), 477-487; 20 (2003), 487-494; 21 (2004), 471-485; 22 (2005), 477-484; 23 (2006), 477-485; 24 (2007), 473-481; 25 (2008), 461-469; 26 (2009), 473-480; 27 (2010), 451-462.

76. Mieder, Wolfgang. "International Proverb Scholarship: An Updated Bibliography." *Proverbium*, 1 (1984), 273-309; 2 (1985), 379-396; 3 (1986), 431-480; 4 (1987), 369-405; 5 (1988), 219-243; 6

(1989), 281-307; 7 (1990), 305-323; 8 (1991), 285-302; 9 (1992), 329-344; 10 (1993), 365-375; 11 (1994), 343-366; 12 (1995), 421-451; 13 (1996), 421-445; 14 (1997), 487-524; 15 (1998), 489-531; 16 (1999), 467-517; 17 (2000), 501-529; 18 (2001), 487-519; 19 (2002), 489-531; 20 (2003), 495-534; 21 (2004), 487-530; 22 (2005), 485-534; 23 (2006), 487-530; 24 (2007), 483-524; 25 (2008), 471-533; 26 (2009), 481-534; 27 (2010), 463-534.

77. Mieder, Wolfgang. *Investigations of Proverbs, Proverbial Expressions, Quotations and Clichés. A Bibliography of Explanatory Essays which Appeared in "Notes and Queries" (1849-1983)*. Bern: Peter Lang, 1984. 420 pp.

78. Mieder, Wolfgang. "Bibliography of Archer Taylor's Proverb Studies." In Archer Taylor. *The Proverb and An Index to "The Proverb"*. Hatboro, Pennsylvania: Folklore Associates, 1962. Copenhagen: Rosenkilde and Bagger, 1962. 328 pp. Rpt. ed. Wolfgang Mieder. Bern: Peter Lang, 1985. 381 pp. (bibliography, pp. XL-LIII).

79. Mieder, Wolfgang. "Das Sprichwörterbuch." *Wörterbücher. Ein internationales Handbuch zur Lexikographie*. Eds. Franz Josef Hausmann, Oskar Reichmann, Herbert Ernst Wiegand, and Ladislav Zgusta. Berlin: Walter de Gruyter, 1989. I, 1033-1044. Also in W. Mieder. *Sprichwort - Wahrwort!? Studien zur Geschichte, Bedeutung und Funktion deutscher Sprichwörter*. Frankfurt am Main: Peter Lang, 1992. 37-57.

80. Mieder, Wolfgang. "Seven Overlooked Paremiological Publications by Archer Taylor." *Proverbium*, 6 (1989), 187-190.

81. Mieder, Wolfgang. *International Proverb Scholarship: An Annotated Bibliography. Supplement I (1800-1981)*. New York: Garland Publishing, 1990. 453 pp.

82. Mieder, Wolfgang. "Prolegomena to Prospective Paremiography." *Proverbium*, 7 (1990), 133-144.

83. Mieder, Wolfgang. "Literaturverzeichnis zu Lutz Röhrichs *Lexikon*." In Lutz Röhrich. *Das große Lexikon der sprichwörtlichen Redensarten*. Freiburg: Herder, 1992. III, 1787-1834.

84. Mieder, Wolfgang. *International Proverb Scholarship: An Annotated Bibliography. Supplement II (1982-1991)*. New York: Garland Publishing, 1993. 945 pp.

85. Mieder, Wolfgang. *African Proverb Scholarship: An Annotated Bibliography*. Colorado Springs, Colorado: African Proverbs Project, 1994. 181 pp.

86. Mieder, Wolfgang. "Bartlett Jere Whiting's Proverb Publications." In Bartlett Jere Whiting. *"When Evensong and Morrowsong Accord": Three Essays on the Proverb*. Eds. Joseph Harris and W. Mieder. Cambridge, Massachusetts: Department of English and American Literature and Language, Harvard University, 1994. 115-130.

87. Mieder, Wolfgang. "Wellerism Bibliography." In W. Mieder and Stewart A. Kingsbury. *A Dictionary of Wellerisms*. New York: Oxford University Press, 1994. 153-166.

88. Mieder, Wolfgang. "A Bibliography of Proverbs in Russian Literature." *Proverbs in Russian Literature: From Catherine the Great to Alexander Solzhenitsyn*. Ed. Kevin J. McKenna. Burlington, Vermont: The University of Vermont, 1998. 99-112.

89. Mieder, Wolfgang. *Sprichwörter / Redensarten – Parömiologie [Studienbibliographie]*. Heidelberg: Julius Groos, 1999. 49 pp.

90. Mieder, Wolfgang. *International Proverb Scholarship: An Annotated Bibliography. Supplement III (1990-2000)*. New York: Peter Lang, 2001. 460 pp.

91. Mieder, Wolfgang. *International Bibliography of Paremiology and Phraseology*. 2 vols. Berlin: Walter de Gruyter, 2009. 1133 pp. I, A-M; II, N-Z (and indices).

92. Mieder, Wolfgang, and George B. Bryan. *Proverbs in World Literature: A Bibliography*. New York: Peter Lang, 1996. 305 pp.

93. Mieder, Wolfgang, and Janet Sobieski. *Proverb Iconography: An International Bibliography*. New York: Peter Lang, 1999. 225 pp. With 25 illustrations.

94. Mieder, Wolfgang, and Janet Sobieski. *Proverbs and the Social Sciences: An Annotated International Bibliography*. Baltmannsweiler: Schneider Verlag Hohengehren, 2003. 234 pp.

95. Moll, Otto. *Sprichwörterbibliographie*. Frankfurt am Main: Vittorio Klostermann, 1958. 630 pp.

96. Moon, Rosamund. "Phraseology in General Monolingual Dictionaries." *Phraseologie. Ein internationales Handbuch zeitgenössischer Forschung*. Eds. Harald Burger, Dmitrij Dobrovol'skij, Peter Kühn, and Neal R. Norrick. Berlin: Walter de Gruyter, 2007. II, 909-918.

97. Morawski, J. "Les recueils d'anciens proverbes français analysés et classés." *Romania*, 48 (1922), 481-558.

98. Müller, Peter O., and Kathrin Kunkel-Razum. "Phraseographie des Deutschen." *Phraseologie. Ein internationales Handbuch zeitgenössischer Forschung*. Eds. Harald Burger, Dmitrij Dobrovol'skij, Peter Kühn, and Neal R. Norrick. Berlin: Walter de Gruyter, 2007. II, 939-949.

99. Nikolaiéva, I. "Publications parémiologiques soviétiques (fin 1982-début 1985)." *Tel grain tel pain. Poétique de la sagesse populaire*. Ed. Grigorii L'vovich Permiakov. Moscou: Éditions du Progrès, 1988. 378-387.

100. Nkafu Nkemnkia, Martin. "Particular Bibliography of the African Proverbs." In M. Nkafu Nkemnkia. *African Vitalogy: A Step Forward in African Thinking*. Nairobi, Kenya: Paulines Publications in Africa, 1999. 233-239.

101. Nopitsch, Christian Conrad. *Literatur der Sprichwörter. Ein Handbuch für Literarhistoriker, Bibliographen und Bibliothekare*. Nürnberg: Ferdinand von Ebner, 1822 (2nd ed. 1833); rpt. Leipzig: Zentralantiquariat der DDR, 1974. 284 pp.

102. Ottow, A.M. "Beiträge zur Sprichwörterlitteratur [sic]." *Serapeum*, 28 (1867), 326-331.

103. Paczolay, Gyula. "Proverbs in Hungarian Literature: A Bibliography." *Proverbium*, 5 (1988), 207-211.

104. Pamies, Antonio. "Spanish Phraseography." *Phraseologie. Ein internationales Handbuch zeitgenössischer Forschung*. Eds. Harald Burger, Dmitrij Dobrovol'skij, Peter Kühn, and Neal R. Norrick. Berlin: Walter de Gruyter, 2007. II, 986-997.

105. Permiakov, Grigorii L'vovich. "Prilozhenie paremiologicheskie publikatsii 1975 - nachala 1982." *Paremiologicheskie issledovaniia*. Ed. G.L. Permiakov. Moskva: "Nauka", 1984. 300-318. Also in French as "Publications parémiologiques soviétiques (1975 - début 1982)," in *Tel grain tel pain. Poétique de la sagesse populaire*. Ed. G.L. Permiakov. Moscou: Éditions du Progrès, 1988. 364-378.

106. Pitrè, Giuseppe. *Bibliografia delle tradizioni popolari d'Italia*. Torino: Carlo Clausen, 1894. "Proverbi", pp. 177-257 and pp. 464-475.

107. Płaskowicka-Rymkiewicz, Stanisława. "Etat des recherches concernant la parémiographie et la parémiologie turques." *Rocznik orientalistyczny*, 28, no. 2 (1965), 59-74.

108. Prędota, Stanisław. "Ergänzungen zur Bibliographie der polnischen Parömiologie des 19. und 20. Jahrhunderts." *Proverbium*, 4 (1987), 345-360.

109. Prędota, Stanisław. "Zum modernen parömiologischen Handapparat." *Acta Universitatis Wratislaviensis*, no. 1061, *Anglica Wratislaviensia*, 17 (1991), 105-114.

110. Prędota, Stanisław. "Dictionaries of Proverbs." *A Practical Guide to Lexicography*. Ed. Piet van Sterkenburg. Amsterdam: John Benjamins, 2003. 94-101.

111. Röhrich, Lutz, and Wolfgang Mieder. *Sprichwort*. Stuttgart: Metzler, 1977. 137 pp. (section bibliographies throughout).

112. Ruiz Moreno, Rosa María. "Aproximación bibliográfica al refranero árabe." *Estudios de Asia y Africa*, 30, no. 2 (1995), 391-408.

113. Rupprecht, Karl. "Paroimiographoi." *Realencyclopädie der classischen Altertumswissenschaft*. Stuttgart: Metzler, 1949. XVIII, part 4, cols. 1735-1778.

114. Sardelli, María Antonella. "El fondo italiano de la Colección paremiológica (Biblioteca Histórica Municipal de Madrid)." *Paremia*, 15 (2006), 29-40.

115. Sbarbi, José María. *Monografía sobre los refranes, adagios y proverbios castellanos*. Madrid: Huérfanos, 1891. 412 pp.

116. Segre, Cesare. "I Proverbi." *Grundriss der romanischen Literaturen des Mittelalters*. Eds. Hans Robert Jauss and Erich Köhler. Heidelberg: Carl Winter, 1968 and 1970. VI, part 1, 102-108; part 2, 151-161.

117. Sereno, Maria Helena Sampaio. *Contributo para a história da paremiografia portuguesa*. Porto: Centro de Linguística da Universidade do Porto, 1999. 33 pp.

118. Sevilla Muñoz, Julia. "Fuentes paremiológicas francesas y españolas en el siglo XVI." *Revista de Filologia Románica*, 9 (1992), 103-123.

15

119. Sevilla Muñoz, Julia. "Fuentes paremiológicas francesas y españolas en la primera mitad del siglo XVII." *Revista de Filologia Románica*, 10 (1993), 357-369.

120. Sevilla Muñoz, Julia. "El fondo bibliográfico de Paremia: Wolfgang Mieder." *Paremia*, 3 (1994), 164-165.

121. Sevilla Muñoz, Julia. "La paremiologica española y los estudios bibliograficos." *Proverbium*, 12 (1995), 263-274.

122. Sevilla Muñoz, Julia. "El fondo francés de la Colección paremiológica (Biblioteca Histórica Municipal de Madrid)." *Paremia*, 15 (2006), 17-28.

123. Shurgaia, Tea. "General Review of Persian Paremiography." *Proverbium*, 22 (2005), 381-396.

124. Sternbach, L. "La parémiographie polonaise du XVII-e siècle." *Bulletin international de l'académie polonaise des sciences et des lettres*, no volume given, nos. 1-6 (1933), 111-117.

125. Stirling-Maxwell, Sir William. *An Essay Towards a Collection of Books Relating to Proverbs, Emblems, Apothegms, Epitaphs and Ana, Being a Catalogue of Those at Keir*. London: Privately Printed, 1860. 244 pp. (proverbs, pp. 1-107).

126. Sundwall, McKay. "The Writings of Bartlett Jere Whiting." *The Learned and the Lewed. Studies in Chaucer and Medieval Literature*. Ed. Larry D. Benson. Cambridge, Massachusetts: Harvard University Press, 1974. 389-402 (= *Harvard English Studies*, 5 [1974], 389-402).

127. Suringar, Willem Hendrik Dominikus. "Lijst van geschriften over de latijnsche spreekwoorden." *Tijdschrift voor de Nederlandsche Gymnasium*, no volume given (1861), 111-134.

128. Suringar, Willem Hendrik Dominikus. *Erasmus over nederlandsche spreekwoorden en spreekwoordelijke uitdrukkingen van zijnen tijd, uit 's mans "Adagia" opgezameld en uit andere, meest nieuwere geschriften opgehelderd*. Utrecht: Kemink, 1873. CIV pp. and 596 pp. (bibliography, pp. XV-CIV).

129. Taylor, Archer. "An Introductory Bibliography for the Study of Proverbs." *Modern Philology*, 30 (1932), 195-210. Also in A. Taylor. *Selected Writings on Proverbs*. Ed. Wolfgang Mieder. FFC 216. Helsinki: Suomalainen Tiedeakatemia, 1975. 180-194.

130. Taylor, Archer. "A Bibliographical Note on Wellerisms." *Journal of American Folklore*, 65 (1952), 420-421.

131. Taylor, Archer. "Investigations of English Proverbs, Proverbial and Conventional Phrases, Oaths and Clichés." *Journal of American Folklore*, 65 (1952), 255-265.

132. Tobias, Anton. "Beiträge zur Sprüchwörter-Litteratur." *Serapeum*, 29 (1868), 149-155 and 30 (1869), 336.

133. Vasconcellos, José Leite de. "Adagiarios." In J. Leite de Vasconcellos. *Ensaios Etnographicos*. 4 vols. Lisboa: Espozende, 1891-1910. I, 114-190 and 245-256.

134. Viellard, Stéphane. "Trois siècles de parémiographie russe." *Revue des études slaves*, 76, nos. 2-3 (2005), 181-189.

135. Wagner, Paul. "Karl Friedrich Wilhelm Wanders Arbeiten zur Sprichwörterkunde." *Karl Friedrich Wilhelm Wander 1803 bis 1879*. Ed. Ernst Eichler. Berlin: Volk und Wissen, 1954. 183-202.

136. Wander, Karl Friedrich Wilhelm. "Neueste Sprichwörter-Literatur." *Rheinische Blätter für Erziehung und Unterricht*, 7, no. 1 (1861), 45-60.

137. Wander, Karl Friedrich Wilhelm. "Literatur der lateinischen Sprichwörter." *Rheinische Blätter für Erziehung und Unterricht*, 12 (1863), 158-166.

138. Werner, Jürgen. "Sprichwortliteratur." *Zeitschrift für Volkskunde*, 57 (1961), 118-132; and 58 (1962), 114-129.

139. Wilson, F.P. "English Proverbs and Dictionaries of Proverbs." *The Library*, fourth series, 26 (1945), 51-71.

140. Zacher, Julius. *Die deutschen Sprichwörtersammlungen nebst Beiträgen zur Charakteristik der Meusebachschen Bibliothek. Eine bibliographische Skizze*. Leipzig: T.O. Weigel, 1852. 55 pp.

International Collections

141. Abasgulilev, Tofig. *English Proverbs with Their Azerbaijan and Russian Equivalents. Angliiskie poslovitsy i ikh azerbaidzhanskie i russkie ekvivalenty*. Baku: "Elm" Publishing House, 1981. 212 pp.

142. Abrishami, Ahmad. *A Dictionary of 800 Persian Proverbs with English and French Equivalents*. Tehran: Privately printed, 1994 (2nd ed. 1995). 144 pp.

143. Abrishami, Ahmad. *A Comparative Dictionary of 920 Persian Proverbs & Dictums with English, French, German & Spanish Equivalents*. Tehran: Homa Tej Typesetting, 1996. 272 pp.

144. Abu-Sharar, Hesham. *Refranes y dichos populares comparados: español – inglés – ruso – árabe*. Bellaterra: Universitat Autònoma de Barcelona, 1998. 153 pp.

145. Adeleye, Gabriel G., and Kofi Acquah-Dadzie. *World Dictionary of Foreign Expressions*. Wauconda, Illinois: Bolchazy-Carducci Publishers, 1999. 411 pp.

146. Andersen, Adi. *Deutsche Sprichwörter und Redensarten mit ihren englischen und französischen Gegenstücken*. Illustrations by Wolfgang Werkmeister. Hamburg: Matari Verlag, 1968. 93 pp.

147. Anonymous. *Ancient and Modern Familiar Quotations from the Greek, Latin, and Modern Languages. Translated into English and Occasionally Accompanied with Illustrations, Historical, Poetical, and Anecdotical*. Philadelphia: J.B. Lippincott, 1879. 527 pp.

148. Anonymous. *Proverbs From Around the World*. Illustrations by Kathy Davis. Lombard, Illinois: Great Quotations, 1991. 64 pp.

149. Anonymous. *Treasury of Love Proverbs from Many Lands*. Illustrations by Rosemary Fox. New York: Hippocrene Books, 1998. 119 pp.

150. Arsent'eva, E.F. et al. *Russko-anglo-nemetsko-turetsko-tatarskii frazeologicheskii slovar'*. Kazan': Izdatel'stvo Kazanskogo Gosudarstvennogo Universiteta, 2008. 719 pp.

151. Arthaber, Augusto. *Dizionario comparato di proverbi e modi proverbiali italiani, latini, francesi, spagnoli, tedeschi, inglesi e greci antichi con relativi indici sistematico-alfabetici*. Milano: Ulrico Hoepli, 1929; rpt. Milano: Ulrico Hoepli, 1986. 892 pp.

152. Bachmannová, Jarmila, and Valentin Suksov. *Jak se to řekne jinde. Česká přislovi a jejich jinojazyčné protějšky*. [As it is Told Elsewhere. Czech Proverbs and Their Equivalents in Foreign Languages]. Praha: Euromedia Group, 2007. 383 pp.

153. Balling, Adalbert Ludwig (ed.). *Zwischen den vier Meeren. Sprichwörter und Aphorismen aus der Dritten Welt*. Illustrations by Alexander J. Ultsch. Reimlingen/Nördlingen: Missionsverlag Mariannhill, 1978. 85 pp.

154. Balling, Adalbert Ludwig (ed.). *Weisheit der Völker. Sprichwörter und Aphorismen aus aller Welt*. Illustrations by Alexander J. Ultsch. Würzburg: Missionsverlag Mariannhill, 1981. 58 pp.

155. Bartsch, Ernst (ed.). *Wie das Land, so das Sprichwort. Sprichwörter aus aller Welt.* Illustrations by Christiane Baumgartner. Leipzig: VEB Bibliographisches Institut, 1989. 191 pp.

156. Benham, W. Gurney. *Putnam's Complete Book of Quotations, Proverbs and Household Words. A Collection of Quotations from British and American Authors, with Many Thousands of Proverbs, Familiar Phrases and Sayings, from All Sources, including Hebrew, Arabic, Greek, Latin, French, German, Italian, Spanish, and other Languages.* New York: G.P. Putnam's Sons, 1926. 1224 pp.

157. Bhalla, Jag. *"I'm not Hanging Noodles on Your Ears" and Other Intriguing Idioms from Around the World.* Illustrations by Julia Suits. Washington, D.C.: National Geographic Society, 2009. 266 pp.

158. Bilgrav, Jens Aage Stabell. *20,000 Proverbs, Sprichwörter, Proverbes, Ordspråk, Ordsprog.* Copenhagen: Hans Heide, 1985. 896 pp.

159. Bloch, Iwan. "Die Benennungen der Syphilis in der alten Welt." In I. Bloch. *Der Ursprung der Syphilis. Eine medizinische und kulturgeschichtliche Untersuchung.* Jena: Gustav Fischer, 1901. 297-304.

160. Boecklen, Adolf. *Sprichwörter in 6 Sprachen [Deutsch, Englisch, Französisch, Italienisch, Spanisch, Lateinisch].* Ed. Hermann Weller. 4th ed. Stuttgart: Ernst Klett, 1947. 190 pp.

161. Böhm, Richard et al. *Die Weisheit der Völker. Ausgewählte Sprichwörter.* Wiesbaden: Wiesbadener Graphische Betriebe, 1976. 128 pp.

162. Bohn, Henry G. *A Polyglot of Foreign Proverbs, Comprising French, Italian, German, Dutch, Spanish, Portuguese, and Danish, with English Translations & a General Index.* London: Henry G. Bohn, 1857; rpt. Detroit: Gale Research Company, 1968. 579 pp.

163. Bourgois, Lucien. *Kvarlingva Proverbaro (franca, angla, germana, esperanta).* Thaumiers, France: La Kancer Kliniko, 2000. 26 pp.

164. Brock, Suzanne. *Idiom's Delight. Fascinating Phrases and Linguistic Eccentricities. Spanish, French, Italian, Latin.* Illustrations by Laura Lou Levy. New York: Times Books, 1988. 158 pp.

165. Carbonell Basset, Delfín. *Diccionario panhispánico de refranes.* Barcelona: Herder, 2002. 527 pp.

166. Čelakovský, František Lanislav. *Mudrosloví národu slovanského ve přislovích.* Praha: Rivnáč, 1852. 644 pp. Rpt. Praha: Nakladatelstvi Vyšehrad, 1949. 822 pp. Partial reprint Praha: Československý Spisovatel, 1978. 308 pp.

167. Champion, Selwyn Gurney. *Racial Proverbs. A Selection of the World's Proverbs Arranged Linguistically with Authoritative Introductions to the Proverbs of 27 Countries and Races.* London: George Routledge, 1938; rpt. London: Routledge & Kegan, 1963. 767 pp.

168. Champion, Selwyn Gurney. *The Eleven Religions and Their Proverbial Lore.* New York: E.P. Dutton, 1945. 340 pp.

169. Champion, Selwyn Gurney. *War Proverbs and Maxims East and West.* London: Arthur Probsthain, 1945. 70 pp.

170. Champion, Selwyn Gurney, and Ethel Mavrogordato (eds.). *Wayside Sayings [of the World].* London: Duckworth, 1924. 284 pp.

171. Cibot, Pierre Martial. *Choix de maximes, pensées, et proverbes tirés de divers philosophes anciens et de différens peuples.* Londres: no publisher given, 1785. 284 pp. (miniature book).

172. Cohen, Israel. *Dictionary of Parallel Proverbs in English, German and Hebrew.* Tel Aviv: Machbarot Lesifrut Publishers, 1961 (in Hebrew). 620 pp.

173. Cordry, Harold V. *The Multicultural Dictionary of Proverbs. Over 20,000 Adages from More Then 120 Languages, Nationalities and Ethnic Groups.* Jefferson, North Carolina: McFarland, 1997. 406 pp.

174. Couzerau, Béatrice. *Auf ein Sprichwort! In a byword! En un proverbe! 333 Sprichwörter in drei Sprachen.* Reinbek: Rowohlt, 1997. 240 pp.

175. Cox, H.L. *Spreekwoordenboek in vier talen. Nederlands, Frans, Duits, Engels.* Utrecht/Antwerpen: Van Dale Lexicografie, 1988. 420 pp. With illustrations.

176. Cox, H.L. *Spreekwoordenboek in zes talen: Nederlands, Frans, Duits, Engels, Spaans, Latijn.* Utrecht/Antwerpen: Van Dale Lexicografie, 1994. 501 pp. With illustrations.

177. Cox, H.L. *Spreekwoordenboek: Nederlands, Fries, Afrikaans, Engels, Duits, Frans, Spaans, Latijn.* Utrecht/Antwerpen: Van Dale Lexicografie, 2000. 998 pp.

178. Cox, H.L., and Jurjen van der Kooi. *"Alle beetjes helpen" Nederlandse, Friese en Vlaamse wellerismen. Een compendium.* Groningen: Fries en Nedersaksisch Institut / Stichting FFYRUG, 2007. 398 pp.

179. Crida Álvares, Carlos Alberto, and Gerasimos Zoras. *Son paremias. Diccionario de concordancias paremiológicas griegas, españolas, italianas.* Athena: Efstathiadis Group, 2005. 158 pp.

180. Davidoff, Henry. *A World Treasury of Proverbs from Twenty-Five Languages.* New York: Random House, 1946. 526 pp.

181. Davis, Kathy (ill.). *Proverbs from Around the World: "The Road to a Friend's House is Never Long".* Lombard, Illinois: Great Quotations Publishing, 1991. 64 pp.

182. Davis, Kathy (ill.). *Proverbs from Around the World: "A Mile Walked With a Friend Contains Only a Hundred Steps".* Lombard, Illinois: Great Quotations Publishing, 1992. 64 pp.

183. Dennys, E.M. *Proverbs and Quotations of Many Nations.* London: Simpkin Marshall, 1890. 56 pp.

184. Draxe, Thomas. *Bibliotheca Scholastics Instructissima. Or, A Treatise of Ancient Adagies, and Sententious Pouerbes. Selected out of the English, Greeke, Latine, French, Italian and Spanish.* London: Ioann Billius, 1616; rpt. Norwood, New Jersey: Walter J. Johnson, 1976. 248 pp.

185. Dubrovin, M.I. *Illiustrirovannyi slovar' idiom na piati iazykakh: Russkii, angliiskii, frantsuzskii, ispanskii, nemetskii. A Picture Collection of Idioms in Five Languages: Russkii, English, Français, Español, Deutsch.* Illustrations by M. Skobelev. Moscow: "Rosman", 1997. 221 pp.

186. Dubrovin, M.I. *Illiustrirovannyi sbornik poslovitsy i pogovorok na piati iazykakh: Russkii, angliiskii, frantsuzskii, ispanskii, nemetskii. A Picture Collection of Proverbs and Sayings in Five Languages: Russkii, English, Français, Español, Deutsch.* Illustrations by A. Egorov. Moscow: "Rosman", 1998. 221 pp.

187. Düringsfeld, Ida von. *Das Sprichwort als Kosmopolit.* 3 vols. in one volume. Vol. 1: *Das Sprichwort als Philosoph.* Vol. 2: *Das Sprichwort als Praktikus.* Vol. 3: *Das Sprichwort als Humorist.*

Leipzig: Hermann Fries, 1866. Rpt. ed. Wolfgang Mieder. Hildesheim: Georg Olms, 2002. I, 160 pp.; II, 148 pp.; III, 173 pp. (introduction, I, pp. 5*-20*).

188. Düringsfeld, Ida von, and Otto von Reinsberg-Düringsfeld. *Sprichwörter der germanischen und romanischen Sprachen vergleichend zusammengestellt.* 2 vols. Leipzig: Hermann Fries, 1872-1875; rpt. Hildesheim: Georg Olms, 1973. I, 522 pp.; II, 638 pp.

189. Ehrlich, Eugene. *The Harper Dictionary of Foreign Terms.* New York: Harper & Row, 1987. 423 pp.

190. Esteban, José. *Refranero contra Europa.* Madrid: Ollero & Ramos, 1996. 78 pp.

191. Fattakhova, Nailia N., and Mariia A. Kul'kova. *Russko-nemetsko-tatarskii slovar' narodnykh primet.* Kazan': Shkola, 2006. 352 pp.

192. Finbert, Elian-J. *Dictionnaire des proverbes du monde.* Paris: Robert Laffont, 1965. 446 pp.

193. Flonta, Teodor. *Dicţionar englez-francez-român de proverbe echivalente. English-French-Romanian Dictionary of Equivalent Proverbs.* Bucureşti: Teopa, 1992. 304 pp.

194. Flonta, Teodor. *Dicţionar englez, spaniol, portughez, român de proverbe echivalente. English, Spanish, Portuguese, Romanian Dictionary of Equivalent Proverbs.* Bucureşti: Teopa, 1992. 399 pp.

195. Flonta, Teodor. *Dicţionar englez, italian, român de proverbe echivalente. English, Italian, Romanian Dictionary of Equivalent Proverbs.* Bucureşti: Teopa, 1993. 397 pp.

196. Flonta, Teodor. *Dio e il diavolo: Proverbi d'Europa in nove lingue.* Torino: Edizioni San Paolo, 1996. 128 pp.

197. Flonta, Teodor. *A Dictionary of English and Romance Languages Equivalent Proverbs.* Hobart, Tasmania: DeProverbio.com, 2001. 583 pp.

198. Flonta, Teodor. *God and the Devil: Proverbs in 9 European Languages.* Hobart, Tasmania: DeProverbio.com, 2002. 111 pp.

199. Földes, Csaba. *Magyar-német-orosz beszédfordulatok. A három nyelv azonas jelentésű állandósult szókapcsolatai.* Budapest Tankönyvkiadó, 1987. 171 pp.

200. Frackiewicz, Iwona. *Analoge Sprichwörter im Deutschen, Niederländischen und Polnischen*. Diss. Uniwersytet Wroclawski, 1987. 925 pp.

201. Frick, R. O. "Le peuple et la prévision du temps." *Schweizerisches Archiv für Volkskunde*, 26 (1926), 1-21, 89-100, 171-188, and 254-279. (weather proverbs).

202. Fritz, Karl August (ed.). *Weisheiten der Völker: Sprichwörter und Spruchweisheiten, Märchen und Mythen, Fabeln, Legenden und Poesie aus dem Orient, Asien, der Südsee, Amerika, Afrika und Europa*. Würzburg: Stürtz, 1998. 359 pp. With illustrations.

203. Fuller, Thomas. *Gnomologia; Adagies and Proverbs; Wise Sentences and Witty Sayings, Ancient and Modern, Foreign and British*. London: B. Barker, 1732; rpt. London: Thomas and Joseph Allman, 1816. 203 pp.

204. Gent, Nathaniel R. *Proverbs English, French, Dutch, Italian and Spanish*. London: Simon Miller, 1659. 151 pp.

205. Geyr, Heinz. *Sprichwörter und sprichwortnahe Bildungen im dreisprachigen Petersburger Lexikon von 1731*. Bern: Peter Lang, 1981. 234 pp.

206. Gheorghe, Gabriel. *Proverbele româneşti şi proverbele lumii romanice. Studiu comparativ*. Bucureşti: Editura Albatros, 1986. 423 pp.

207. Ghitescu, Micaela. *Novo dicionário de provérbios: Português, espanhol, francês, italiano, romeno*. Lisboa: Fim de Século Edições, 1992 (2nd ed. 1997). 202 pp.

208. Gleason, Norma. *Proverbs from Around the World. 1500 Amusing, Witty and Insightful Proverbs from 21 Lands and Languages*. New York: Citadel Press, 1992. 135 pp. With illustrations.

209. Gleason, Norma (ed.). *A Fool in a Hurry Drinks Tea with a Fork. 1047 Proverbs from Around the World*. New York: Citadel Press, 1994. 112 pp.

210. Gleason, Norma (ed.). *1001 Proverbs for Every Occasion. Wise Thoughts and Insightful Advice from Around the World*. New York: Citadel Press, 2001. 106 pp.

211. Gluski, Jerzy. *Proverbs, Proverbes, Sprichwörter, Proverbi, Proverbios, Poslovitsy. A Comparative Book of English. French, German, Italian, Spanish and Russian Proverbs with a Latin Appendix*. New York: Elsevier Publishing, 1971. 448 pp.

212. Gottschalk, Walter. *Die bildhaften Sprichwörter der Romanen.* 3 vols. Heidelberg: Carl Winter, 1935-1938. I, 279 pp.; II, 356 pp.; III, 468 pp.

213. Griffin, Albert Kirby. *Religious Proverbs: Over 1600 Adages from 18 Faiths Worldwide.* Jefferson, North Carolina: McFarland, 1991. 210 pp.

214. Grigas, Kazys. *Patarlių paralelés. Lietuvių patarlés su latvių, baltarusių, rusų, lenkų, vokiečių, anglų, lotynų, prancūzų, ispanų atitikmenimis.* Vilnius: Leidykla "Vaga", 1987. 663 pp.

215. Grunow, Alfred (ed.). *Weisheiten der Welt. Altertum und jüdische Geisteswelt.* Augsburg: Weltbild Verlag, 1987. 384 pp.

216. Grunow, Alfred (ed.). *Weisheiten der Welt. Europa und Neue Welt.* Augsburg: Weltbild Verlag, 1987. 392 pp.

217. Grunow, Alfred (ed.). *Weisheiten der Welt. Vorderer Orient, Indien und Ferner Osten.* Augsburg: Weltbild Verlag, 1987. 431 pp.

218. Guinzbourg, Lt. Colonel Victor S.M. de. *Wit and Wisdom of the United Nations. Proverbs and Apothegms on Diplomacy.* 2 vols. New York: Privately printed, 1961. I, 166 pp.; II, 355 pp.

219. Guinzbourg, Lt. Colonel Victor S.M. de. *Supplement: Wit and Wisdom of the United Nations or the Modern Machiavelli.* New York: Privately printed, 1965. 31 pp.

220. Guinzbourg, Lt. Colonel Victor S.M. de. *The Eternal Machiavelli in the United Nations World.* New York: Privately printed, 1969. 899 pp.

221. Guthke, Karl S. *Letzte Worte. Variationen über ein Thema der Kulturgeschichte des Westens.* München: C.H. Beck, 1990. 225 pp.

222. Guthke, Karl S. *Last Words: Variations on a Theme in Cultural History.* Princeton / New Jersey: Princeton University Press, 1992. 250 pp.

223. Herg, Emmi. *Deutsche Sprichwörter im Spiegel fremder Sprachen unter Berücksichtigung des Englischen, Französischen, Italienischen, Lateinischen und Spanischen.* Berlin: Walter de Gruyter, 1933. 130 pp.

224. Hiemer, Ernst. *Der Jude im Sprichwort der Völker.* Nürnberg: Der Stürmer Buchverlag, 1942. 210 pp. (anti-Semitic collection).

225. Holbek, Bengt, and Iørn Piø. *Allverdens ordsprog.* Oslo: Chr. Schibsteds, 1969. 219 pp.

226. Houghton, Patricia. *A World of Proverbs*. Poole, England: Blandford Press, 1981. Rpt. as *Book of Proverbs*. London: Cassell, 1994. 152 pp.

227. Howell, James. *Paroimiographia. Proverbs, or, Old Sayed Savves & Adages in English (or the Saxon Toung) Italian, French and Spanish whereunto the British, for their great Antiquity, and weight are added*. London: J.G., 1659. 229 pp.

228. Hürlimann, Martin. *Stimmen der Völker im Sprichwort*. Zürich: Atlantis, 1945. 184 pp.

229. Ilg, Gérard. *Proverbes français. Suivis des équivalents en allemand, anglais, espagnol, italien, néerlandais*. Amsterdam: Elsevier, 1960. 97 pp.

230. Iscla, Luis. *English Proverbs and Their Near Equivalents in Spanish, French, Italian and Latin*. New York: Peter Lang, 1995. 418 pp.

231. Jellinek, Ad. *Der jüdische Stamm in nichtjüdischen Sprichwörtern*. 2 vols. Wien: Waizner, 1881-1882. I, 43 pp.; II, 98 pp. (warns against such anti-Semitic stereotypes).

232. Jones, Hugh Percy. *Dictionary of Foreign Phrases and Classical Quotations, Comprising 14,000 Idioms, Proverbs, Maxims. Mottoes, ... in Latin, Greek, French, German, Portuguese, Italian, Spanish Alphabetically Arranged, with English Translations and Equivalents*. Edinburgh: John Grant, 1925; rpt. Edinburgh: Deacon, 1929. 532 pp.

233. Julliani, Le Seur. *Les proverbes Divertissants. Pour apprendre avec plus de facilité les Langues Françoises, Italiennes, et Espagnols*. Paris: Jean-Baptiste Loyson, 1641; rpt. ed. Mirella Conenna. Fasano, France: Schena-Nizet, 1990. 289 pp.

234. Kalma, Maurice. *Trésor des proverbs et locutions du monde*. Paris: Guy Le Prat, 1961. 243 pp.

235. Karagiorgos, Panos. *Greek Maxims and Proverbs with Their Counterparts in 5 Languages: English, French, German, Italian, Spanish*. Corfu, Greece: Apostrofos, 2000. 134 pp.

236. Kelly, Walter K. *A Collection of the Proverbs of All Nations. Compared, Explained, and Illustrated*. London: W. Kent, 1859; rpt. Andover, Massachusetts: Warren F. Draper, 1879; rpt. Darby, Pennsylvania: Folcroft Library Editions, 1972. Rpt. ed. Wolfgang Mieder. Burlington, Vermont: The University of Vermont, 2002. 232 pp. (introduction, pp. i-xiii).

237. Klein, Hans Wilhelm. *Die volkstümlichen sprichwörtlichen Vergleiche im Lateinischen und in romanischen Sprachen.* Diss. Universität Tübingen, 1936. Würzburg: Konrad Triltsch, 1936. 95 pp.

238. Knapp, Elisabeth. *Volkskundliches in den romanischen Wetterregeln.* Diss. Universität Tübingen, 1939. Tübingen: Karl Bölzle, 1939. 117 pp. (weather proverbs).

239. Krohn, Axel. *Tockene Hosen fangen keine Fische. Sprichwörter und Lebensweisheiten aus aller Welt.* Illustrations by Susanne Kracht. Reinbeck bei Hamburg: Rowohlt, 2010. 156 pp.

240. Kunitskaya-Peterson, Christina. *International Dictionary of Obscenities. A Guide to Dirty Words and Indecent Expressions in Spanish, Italian, French, German, Russian.* Oakland, California: Scythian Books, 1981. 93 pp.

241. Kuusi, Matti. *Regen bei Sonnenschein. Zur Weltgeschichte einer Redensart.* FFC 171. Helsinki: Suomalainen Tiedeakatemia, 1957. 420 pp. Italian translation by Maria Teresa Bizzarri. *La pioggia con il sole. Storia di un modo di dire nel mondo.* Bologna: Società editrice il Mulino, 1992-1994. (= *Quaderni di Semantica*, 13, no. 2 [1992], 279-327; 14, no. 1 [1993], 79-152; 14, no. 2 [1993], 249-331; 15, no. 1 [1994], 123-179; and 15, no. 2 [1994], 273-320).

242. Kuusi, Matti (in cooperation with Marje Joalaid, Elsa Kokare, Arvo Krikmann, Kari Laukkanen, Pentti Leino, Vaina Mälk, and Ingrid Sarv). *Proverbia septentrionalia. 900 Balto-Fimic Proverb Types with Russian, Baltic, German and Scandinavian Parallels.* FF Communications No. 236. Helsinki: Suomalainen Tiedeakatemia, 1985. 451 pp.

243. Lawson, James Gilchrist. *The World's Best Proverbs and Maxims.* New York: Grosset & Dunlap, 1926. 364 pp.

244. Legler, Erich. *Heiter-ernste Ehelogie in Sprichworten [sic] und Redenarten der Völker.* Ulm: Süddeutsche Verlagsanstalt, 1977. 24 pp.

245. Lehmann, Hedi. *Wer die Wahrheit sagt, muß ein schnelles Pferd haben. Spruchweisheiten aus aller Welt.* München: Deutscher Taschenbuch Verlag, 1993. 196 pp.

246. Ley, Gerd de. *International Dictionary of Proverbs.* New York: Hippocrene Books, 1998. 437 pp.

247. Lockridge, Norman (ed.). *World's Wit and Wisdom.* New York: Biltmore Publishing, 1945. 585 pp.

248. Ludwig, Gerda (ed.). *Kleine Spruchweisheiten aus aller Welt. 18 Farbpostkarten mit Texten.* Wörthersee bei München: Fotokunst Verlag Groh, 1985. 22 pp. (proverb postcards).

249. Mälk, Vaina. *Vadja vanosõnad eesti, soome, karala ja vene vastetega.* Tallinn: "Eesti Raamat", 1976. 404 pp.

250. Mälk, Vaina (in cooperation with Petõr Damberg, Elza Kokare, Arvo Krikmann, Lembit Vaba, Tiit-Rein Viitso, and Eduard Vääri). *Liivi vanasõnad – eesti, vadja ja läti vastetega.* 2 vols. Tallinn: "Eesti Raamat", 1981. I, 230 pp.; II, 253 pp.

251. Mälk, Vaina (in cooperation with Anne Hussar, Aime Kährik, Arvo Krikmann, and Tiit-Rein Viitso). *Vepsa vanasõnad: eesti, vadja, liivi, karjala ja vene vastetega.* 2 volumes. Tallinn: Eesti Teaduste Akadeemia – Keele ja Kirjanduse Institut, 1992. 681 pp.

252. Mapletoft, John. *Select Proverbs. Italian, Spanish, French, English, Scottish, British, etc. Chiefly Moral. The Foreign Languages done into English.* London: Monckton, 1707. 126 pp.

253. Martin, Walter. "Die Hand im Sprichwort der Völker." *Sprachpflege,* 17 (1968), 83-84.

254. Marvin, Dwight Edwards. *Curiosities in Proverbs. A Collection of Unusual Adages, Maxims, Aphorisms, Phrases and Other Popular Dicta from Many Lands.* 2 vols. New York: G.P. Putnam's Sons, 1916; rpt. Darby, Pennsylvania: Folcroft Library Editions, 1980. I, pp. 1-202; II, pp. 203-428.

255. Matras, Daniel. *Proverbes, sentences et mots dorez recüeillis Des Meilleurs Autheurs qui ont escrit de cette materie, en François, Danois, Italien & Allemand / Frantzøske, Danske, Italianiske oc Tydske Ordsprock oc Sententzer uddragen oc samlet ud aff de beste Scribenter some hafue skrefuet dm denne Materie.* Copenhague: Melch. Martzan, 1633. 265 pp. Rpt. ed Iver Kjaer. *Daniel Matras: Proverbes. Frantzøske. Danske. Italianiske oc Tydske Ordsprock oc Sententzer (1633).* København: C.A. Reitzel. 1981. 308 pp.

256. Mawr, E.B. *Analogous Proverbs in Ten Languages [English, Roumanian, French, German, Italian, Spanish, Dutch, Danish, Portuguese, Latin].* London: Elliot Stock, 1885. 113 pp.

27

257. McDonald, Julie Jensen. *Scandinavian Proverbs: Folk Wisdom from Denmark, Finland, Iceland, Norway and Sweden*. Illustrations by Esther Feske. Iowa City, Iowa: Penfield Press, 1985. 32 pp.

258. Micu, Anamaria, and Mioara Besoiu (eds.). *Proverbe, proverbs, proverbes*. Illustrations by Mariana Miertoiu. Deva, Romania: Editura Emia, 1999. 103 pp.

259. Middlemore, James. *Proverbs, Sayings and Comparisons in Various Languages*. London: Isbister, 1889. 458 pp.

260. Mieder, Wolfgang. *The Prentice-Hall Encyclopedia of World Proverbs*. Englewood Cliffs, New Jersey: Prentice-Hall, 1986; rpt. New York: MJF Books, 1996. 582 pp.

261. Mieder, Wolfgang. *Love: Proverbs of the Heart*. Illustrations by Kim S. Holtan. Shelburne, Vermont: New England Press, 1989. 80 pp. Translated into Chinese by Hu Xinnian. Urumchi: Xinjiang, 1991. 168 pp.

262. Mieder, Wolfgang. *Howl Like a Wolf: Animal Proverbs*. Illustrations by Chris Cart. Shelburne, Vermont: The New England Press, 1993. 95 pp.

263. Mieder, Wolfgang. *Illuminating Wit, Inspiring Wisdom: Proverbs from Around the World*. Paramus, New Jersey: Prentice Hall Press, 1998. 273 pp.

264. Mieder, Wolfgang. *Garden of Wisdom: A Collection of Plant Proverbs*. Illustrations by Elayne Sears. Shelburne, Vermont: The New England Press, 2000. 96 pp.

265. Mikić, Pavao, and Danica Škara. *Kontrastivni rječnik poslovica*. Zagreb: August Cesarec & Školska Knjiga, 1992. 389 pp.

266. Moritz, Lukas (ed.). *Die Sprichwörter der Welt*. Köln: Anaconda, 2006. 492 pp.

267. Muth-Schwering, Ursula. *Sprichwörter [aus aller Welt] für jeden Tag*. Freiburg: Herder, 1988. 123 pp.

268. Myers, Robert (ed.). *The Spice of Love. Wisdom and Wit about Love through the Ages*. Illustrations by John Trotta. Kansas City, Missouri: Hallmark Cards, 1968. 60 pp.

269. Newbern, John, and P.M. Rodebaugh (eds.). *Prixilated Proverbs of the World. Shafts that Drive Deep. You Can Laugh and Weep! Pointed Petards of 61. Countries*. Fort Worth, Texas: SRI Publishing Co., 1971. 128 pp.

270. Paczolay, Gyula. *Magyar-észt közmondások és szólások német, angol és latin megfelelöikkel. Ungari-eesti vanasõnu ja konekäände saksa. inglise ja ladina vastetega. [Dictionary of Hungarian-Estonian Proverbs with Their German. English and Latin Equivalents and Cheremis Appendix].* Veszprém-Budapest: VEAB-ELTE, 1985. 273 pp.

271. Paczolay, Gyula. *Magyar-észt-német-angol-finn-latin közmondások és szólások – c seremisz és zürjén függelékkel [A Comparative Dictionary of Hungarian-Estonian-German-English-Finnish and Latin Proverbs with an Appendix in Cheremis and Zyryan].* Veszprém: VEAB, 1985. 273 pp. (2nd ed. 1987) 300 pp.

272. Paczolay, Gyula. "Some Common Proverbs in Komi, Estonian and Hungarian and Their European Relationships." *Congressus Internationalis Fenno-Ugristarum 6, Studia Hungarica Syktyvkar 1985.* Eds. Istvan Dienes, Péter Domokos, Janos Kodolanyi, and Vilmos Voigt. Budapest: Nemzetközi Magyar Filologiai Tarsasag, 1985. 223-230.

273. Paczolay, Gyula. "European, Far-Eastern and Some Asian Proverbs." *Proverbium*, 10 (1993), 265-279.

274. Paczolay, Gyula. *European, Far-Eastern and Some Asian Proverbs. A Comparison of European, Chinese, Korean, Japanese, Vietnamese and Other Asian Proverbs.* Veszprém: Central Library of the University of Veszprém, 1994. 200 pp.

275. Paczolay, Gyula. "Korean, Chinese and Japanese Proverbs." *Tanulmányok a kultúraközi kommunikáció tárgyköréböl: Koreai nyelv és kultúra.* Ed. Gábor Osváth. Budapest: Külkereskedelmi Föiskola, 1995. 53-62.

276. Paczolay, Gyula. *Addenda to European, Far Eastern and Some Asian Proverbs: A Comparison of European, Chinese, Korean, Japanese, Vietnamese and Other Asian Proverbs with English, German and Hungarian Equivalents* (1994). Veszprém: Central Library of the University of Veszprém, 1996. 8 pp.

277. Paczolay, Gyula. "European Proverbs in Some Finno-Ugric Languages." *Congressus Octavus Internationalis Fenno-Ugristarum, Jyväskylä 10-15.8.1995. Pars V: Lexicologia & Onomastica.* Eds. Heikki Leskinen, Sándor Maticsák, and Tonu Seilenthal. Jyväskylä: Moderatores, 1996. 146-150.

278. Paczolay, Gyula. *European Proverbs in 55 Languages with Equivalents in Arabic, Persian, Sanskrit, Chinese and Japanese.*

Veszprém, Hungary: Veszprémi Nyomda, 1997; rpt. Hobart, Tasmania: DeProverbio.com, 2002. 527 pp.

279. Paczolay, Gyula. *Ezer magyar közmondás és szólás* – angol, észt, finn, német forditással és megfelelőkkel, latin forrásokkal. Budapest: Bárczi Géza Kiejtési Alapítvány, 2005. 138 pp.

280. Pereira Ginet, Tomás. "Fiando paremias: glosario paremiolóxico multilingüe galego, portugués, castelán, francés, italiano e inglés." *Cadernos de fraseoloxía galega*, 7 (2005), 191-223.

281. Permiakov, Grigorii L'vovich. *Iz'rannye poslovitsy i pogovorki naradov vostoka*. Moskva: Nauka, 1968. 376 pp.

282. Permiakov, Grigorii L'vovich. *Poslovitsy i pogovorki narodov vostoka. Sistematizirovannoe sobranie izrechenii dvukhsot narodov.* Moskva: Nauka, 1979. 671 pp.

283. Permiakov, Grigorii L'vovich. *Poslovitsy i pogovorki narodov vostoka.* Moskva: Nauka, 1979. 671 pp. Rpt. eds. E.M. Meletinsk and G.L. Kapchits. Moskva: Labirint, 2001. 624 pp.

284. Popovich, R.I. *Proverbe shi ziketor' francheze-moldovenesht'-ruse. Frantsuzsko-moldavsko-russkie poslovitsy i pogovorki / Proverbes et dictons français-moldaves-russes.* Kishinev: "Shtiintsa", 1986. 138 pp.

285. Quintão Duarte Silva, Helena Maria, and José Luís Quintão. *Dicionário de Provérbios: Alemão, Francês, Inglês, Português.* Lisboa: Escher, 1983 (2nd ed. 1990). 162 pp.

286. Radić, Tomislav. *Vox Populi: Zlatna knjiga poslovica svijeta.* Illustrations by Ivan Lacković Croata. Zagreb: Globus, 1989. 446 pp.

287. Rauch, Karl. *Sprichwörter der Völker.* Düsseldorf: Eugen Diederichs, 1963. 320 pp. Rpt. München: Deutscher Taschenbuch Verlag, 1975. 269 pp.

288. Rehbein, Detlev. *Spaß muß sein, sagte der Kater ... Sagwörter aus europäischen Sprachen.* Leipzig: VEB Bibliographisches Institut, 1990. 181 pp. (wellerisms).

289. Reinsberg-Düringsfeld, Otto von. *Die Frau im Sprichwort.* Leipzig: Hermann Fries, 1862. Rpt. ed. Wolfgang Mieder. Hildesheim: Georg Olms, 2009. 208 pp. (introduction, pp. 5*-39*).

290. Reinsberg-Düringsfeld, Otto von. *Internationale Titulaturen.* 2 vols. Leipzig: Hermann Fries, 1863. Rpt. in one volume ed. Wolfgang

Mieder. Hildesheim: Georg Olms, 1992. I, 166, II, 150 (introduction pp. 5*-35*).

291. Reinsberg-Düringsfeld, Otto von. *Das Wetter im Sprichwort.* Leipzig: Hermann Fries, I864; rpt. Leipzig: Zentralantiquariat der DDR, 1976. 216 pp. (weather proverbs).

292. Reinsberg-Düringsfeld, Otto von. *Das Kind im Sprichwort.* Leipzig: Hermann Fries, 1864. 105 pp.

293. Riley, Cindy. *Pearls in the Desert: Proverbs from Many Lands.* New York: April House, 1972. 48 pp.

294. Roback, Abraham Aaron. *A Dictionary of International Slurs.* Cambridge, Massachusetts: Sci-Art Publishers, 1944; rpt. Waukesha, Wisconsin: Maledicta Press, 1979. 394 pp.

295. Rosenzweig, Paul. *The Book of Proverbs; Maxims from East and West.* New York: Philosophical Library, 1965. 117 pp.

296. Sallinen, Pirkko. "Skandinavische Entsprechungen finnischer Wellerismen." *Proverbium*, no. 14 (1969), 390-395; and 15 (1970), 522-525.

297. Scheffler, Axel (ill.). *"Let Sleeping Dogs Lie" and Other Proverbs from Around the World.* Hauppauge, New York: Barron's Educational Series, 1997. 125 pp.

298. Schipper, Mineke. *Een goede vrouw is zonder hoofd. Europese spreekwoorden en zegswijzen over vrouwen.* Baarn: Ambo, 1993. 159 pp.

299. Schipper, Mineke. *"Eine gute Frau hat keinen Kopf". Europäische Sprichwörter über Frauen.* München: Deutscher Taschenbuch Verlag, 1996. 194 pp.

300. Schipper, Mineke. *"Never Marry a Woman with Big Feet". Women in Proverbs from Around the World.* New Haven, Connecticut: Yale University Press, 2003. 422 pp. New ed. Amsterdam: Amsterdam University Press, 2006. 350 pp.

301. Schipper, Mineke, and Angélica Dorfman. *En de boom blijft maar geven. Caribische en Latijns-Amerikaanse spreekwoorden en zegswijzen over vrouwen.* Baarn: Ambo, 1998. 176 pp.

302. Schmelz, Richard (ed.). *Sprichwörter, Proverbs, Poslovitsy, Przysłowia, Prislovi, Proverbes, Proverbios, Proverbia.* Illustrations by Rudolf Peschel. Berlin: Volk und Wissen Verlag, 1989. 124 pp.

303. Seiler, Friedrich. *Das deutsche Lehnsprichwort.* 4 vols. Halle: Verlag der Buchhandlung des Waisenhauses, 1921-1924; rpt. ed. Wolfgang Mieder. Hildesheim: Georg Olms, 2007. (= F. Seiler, *Die Entwicklung der deutschen Kultur im Spiegel des deutschen Lehnworts*, vols. 5-8). V, 305 pp.; VI, 202 pp.; VII, 65 pp.; VIII, 176 pp.

304. Sellner, Alfred. *Fremdsprachliche Redewendungen im Alltag. Sprichwörter, Floskeln, Phrasen, Formeln, Zitate, Sentenzen [Latein, Englisch, Französisch, Italienisch, Spanisch, Amerikanisch, Altgriechisch].* Wiesbaden: VMA-Verlag, 2008. 333 pp.

305. Senaltan, Semahat. "Türkische Entsprechungen zu germanisch-romanischen Sprichwörtern bei [Ida und Otto von Reinsberg] Düringsfeld." *Proverbium*, no. 13 (1969), 337-348.

306. Sevilla Muñoz, Julia, and Jesús Cantera Ortiz de Urbina (eds.). *877 refranes españoles con su correspondencia catalana, gallega, vasca, francesa e inglesa.* Madrid: Ediciones Internacionales Universitarias, 1998. 343 pp.

307. Sevilla Muñoz, Julia, and Jesús Cantera Ortiz de Urbina (eds.). *1001 refranes españoles con su correspondencia en ocho lenguas (alemán, árabe, francés, inglés, italiano, polaco, provenzal y ruso).* Madrid: Ediciones Internacionales Universitarias, 2001 (2nd ed. 2008). 438 pp.

308. Sevilla Muñoz, Julia, Jesús Cantera Ortiz de Urbina, Mercedes Burrel, Javier Calzacorta, and Germán Conde (eds.). *877 refranes españoles con su correspondencia catalana, gallega, vasca, francesa e inglesa.* Madrid: EUNSA, 2000. 357 pp.

309. Shearer, William J. *The Wisdom of the World, in Proverbs of All Nations.* New York: Richardson, Smith & Co., 1904. 224 pp.

310. Singer, Samuel. *Sprichwörter des Mittelalters.* 3 vols. Bern: Herbert Lang, 1944-1947. I, 198 pp.; II, 202 pp.; III., 162 pp.

311. Singer, Samuel, and Ricarda Liver (eds.). *Thesaurus proverbiorum medii aevi. Lexikon der Sprichwörter des romanischgermanischen Mittelalters.* 13 vols. Berlin: Walter de Gruyter, 1995. I, A-Birne, 488 pp.

312. Singer, Samuel, and Ricarda Liver (eds.). *Thesaurus proverbiorum medii aevi. Lexikon der Sprichwörter des romanischgermanischen Mittelalters. Quellenverzeichnis.* 13 vols. Eds. Werner Ziltener and Christian Hostettler. Berlin: Walter de Gruyter, 1996. No volume number given. 249 pp.

313. Singer, Samuel, and Ricarda Liver (eds.). *Thesaurus proverbiorum medii aevi*. *Lexikon der Sprichwörter des romanisch-germanischen Mittelalters*. 13 vols. Berlin: Walter de Gruyter, 1996. II, Bisam-erbauen, 484 pp.

314. Singer, Samuel, and Ricarda Liver (eds.). *Thesaurus proverbiorum medii aevi*. *Lexikon der Sprichwörter des romanisch-germanischen Mittelalters*. 13 vols. Berlin: Walter de Gruyter, 1996. III, Erbe-freuen, 496 pp.

315. Singer, Samuel, and Ricarda Liver (eds.). *Thesaurus proverbiorum medii aevi*. *Lexikon der Sprichwörter des romanisch-germanischen Mittelalters*. 13 vols. Berlin: Walter de Gruyter, 1997. IV, Freund-gewöhnen, 496 pp.

316. Singer, Samuel, and Ricarda Liver (eds.). *Thesaurus proverbiorum medii aevi*. *Lexikon der Sprichwörter des romanisch-germanischen Mittelalters*. 13 vols. Berlin: Walter de Gruyter, 1997. V, Gewohnheit-heilen, 476 pp.

317. Singer, Samuel, and Ricarda Liver (eds.). *Thesaurus proverbiorum medii aevi*. *Lexikon der Sprichwörter des romanisch-germanischen Mittelalters*. 13 vols. Berlin: Walter de Gruyter, 1998. VI, heilig-Kerker, 475 pp.

318. Singer, Samuel, and Ricarda Liver (eds.). *Thesaurus proverbiorum medii aevi*. *Lexikon der Sprichwörter des romanisch-germanischen Mittelalters*. 13 vols. Berlin: Walter de Gruyter, 1998. VII, Kern-Linie, 492 pp.

319. Singer, Samuel, and Ricarda Liver (eds.). *Thesaurus proverbiorum medii aevi*. *Lexikon der Sprichwörter des romanisch-germanischen Mittelalters*. 13 vols. Berlin: Walter de Gruyter, 1999. VIII, Linke-Niere, 484 pp.

320. Singer, Samuel, and Ricarda Liver (eds.). *Thesaurus proverbiorum medii aevi*. *Lexikon der Sprichwörter des romanisch-germanischen Mittelalters*. 13 vols. Berlin: Walter de Gruyter, 1999. IX, niesen-Schädlichkeit, 475 pp.

321. Singer, Samuel, and Ricarda Liver (eds.). *Thesaurus proverbiorum medii aevi*. *Lexikon der Sprichwörter des romanisch-germanischen Mittelalters*. 13 vols. Berlin: Walter de Gruyter, 2000. X, Schaf-sollen, 443 pp.

322. Singer, Samuel, and Ricarda Liver (eds.). *Thesaurus proverbiorum medii aevi*. *Lexikon der Sprichwörter des romanisch-*

germanischen Mittelalters. 13 vols. Berlin: Walter de Gruyter, 2001. XI, Sommer-Tröster, 460 pp.

323. Singer, Samuel, and Ricarda Liver (eds.). *Thesaurus proverbiorum medii aevi. Lexikon der Sprichwörter des romanischgermanischen Mittelalters*. 13 vols. Berlin: Walter de Gruyter, 2001. XII, trüb-weinen, 452 pp.

324. Singer, Samuel, and Ricarda Liver (eds.). *Thesaurus proverbiorum medii aevi. Lexikon der Sprichwörter des romanischgermanischen Mittelalters*. 13 vols. Berlin: Walter de Gruyter, 2002. XIII, Weinlese-zwölf, 476 pp.

325. Skuza, Sylwia. *Kobieta: matka, córka, panna, żona, teściowa, synowa i wdowa w przysłowiach polskich i włoskich*. Brzezia Łąka: Wydawnictwo Poligraf, 2010. 124 pp.

326. Soares, Rui J.B. *Provérbios Europeus. European Proverbs. Eurooppalaisia sananlaskuja*. Helsinki: Ibero-American Center, 2006. 93 pp.

327. Soares, Rui J.B. *Provérbios Europeus. European Proverbs. Przysłowia Europejskie*. Tavira: Tipografia Tavirense, 2008. 91 pp.

328. Soares, Rui J.B. *Provérbios Europeus. European Proverbs. Euroopa Vanasõnad*. Tavira: Tipografia Tavirense, 2009. 97 pp.

329. Spicker, Friedemann (ed.). *Aphorismen der Weltliteratur*. Stuttgart: Philipp Reclam, 1999. 344 pp. (2nd ed. 2009). 373 pp.

330. Stone, Jon R. *The Routledge Book of World Proverbs*. New York: Routledge, 2006. 519 pp.

331. Strafforello, Gustavo. *La sapienza del mondo ovvero dizionario universale dei proverbi di tutti i popoli*. 3 vols. Torino: Augusto Frederico Negro, 1883. I, A-E, 606 pp.; II, F-M, 670 pp.; III, N-Z, 782 pp.

332. Strauss, Emanuel. *Dictionary of European Proverbs*. 3 vols. London: Routledge, 1994. I-II, 1232 pp.; III, 789 pp. (bibliography and index).

333. Strauss, Emanuel. *Concise Dictionary of European Proverbs*. London: Routledge, 1998. 491 pp.

334. Suringar, Willem Hendrik Dominikus. *Erasmus over nederlandsche spreekwoorden en spreekwoordelijke uitdrukkingen van zijnen tijd, uit 's mans "Adagia" opgezameld en uit andere, meest nieuwere geschriften opgehelderd*. Utrecht: Kemink, 1873. CIV pp.

and 596 pp. (lists of Greek proverbs, pp. 517-521; Latin proverbs, pp. 521-543; Italian proverbs, pp. 543-546; French proverbs, pp. 546-551; Spanish proverbs, pp. 551-552; English proverbs, pp. 552-553; Danish proverbs, pp. 553-554; German proverbs, pp. 554-569; Westphalian proverbs, pp. 570-572; Dutch proverbs, pp. 572-593).

335. Swenson, Ann H. *Proverbs and Proverbial Expressions in English, in French, and in Italian.* Florence: Nerbini, 1931. 276 pp.

336. Świerczyńska, Dobrosława, and Andrzej Świerczyński. *Przysłowia w sześciu językach.* Illustrations by Blanka Łątka. Warszawa: Wydawnictwo Naukowe, 1995. 328 pp.

337. Świerczyńska, Dobrosława, and Andrzej Świerczyński. *Patarlių žodynas 9 kalbom.* Vilnius: Tyto alba, 2000. 413 pp.

338. Takashima, Taiji. *Közmondasok öt nyelven [Japanese, Hungarian, English, German, French].* Budapest: Primo Kiadó, 1991. 119 pp.

339. Tappe, Eberhard. *Germanicorum adagioroum cum latinis ac graecis collatorum, centuriae septem.* Straßburg: Vuendelini Rihelli, 1539, rpt. Hildesheim: Georg Olms, 2008. 282 pp.

340. Taylor, Archer. "Locutions for 'Never'." *Romance Philology*, 2 (1949), 103-134.

341. Thal, Hella (ed.). *Schmutzige Wörter: Internationale Lebenshilfe. Deutsch/Wienerisch – Französisch – Englisch / Amerikanisch – Italienisch – Portugiesisch – Spanisch – Türkisch. Schimpfwörter, Beleidigungen, Flüche. Internationale Verbal-Injurien.* Frankfurt am Main: Eichborn, 1987 (4th ed. 1996). 112 pp.

342. Tonn, Maryjane Hooper. *Proverbs to Live By. A Treasury of Timely Thoughts from Around the World.* Milwaukee, Wisconsin: Ideals Publishing Corporation, 1977. 64 pp. With illustrations.

343. Vlakhov, Sergei. *Sopostavitel'nyi slovar' poslovits. Bolgarskikh, russkikh, angliiskikh, frantsuzskikh, nemetskikh (i latinskikh).* Illustrations by Don'o Donev. Sofia: Izdatelstvo ETO, 1998. 276 pp.

344. Wahl, Moritz Callman. *Das Sprichwort der hebräisch-aramäischen Literatur mit besonderer Berücksichtigung des Sprichwortes der neueren Umgangssprachen. Ein Beitrag zur vergleichenden Parömiologie.* Leipzig: Oskar Leiner, 1871. 181 pp.

345. Wahl, Moritz Callman. *Das Sprichwort der neueren Sprachen. Ein vergleichend phraseologischer Beitrag zur deutschen Literatur.* Erfurt: Keyser, 1877. 86 pp.

346. Walter, Harry, Valerii M. Mokienko, Marc Ruiz-Zorrilla Cruzate, and Andrei Zainouldinov. *Russisch-Deutsch-Spanisches Wörterbuch aktueller Sprichwörter mit europäischen Parallelen*. Illustrations by Regina Walter. Greifswald: Ernst-Moritz-Arndt-Universität, 2009. 193 pp.

347. Ward, Caroline. *National Proverbs in the Principal Languages of Europe*. London: Parker, 1842. 176 pp.

348. Weininger, Simon. *Vielsprachige, komparative Sprichwörtersammlung*. Illustrations by Paul Fuchs. Jerusalem: Hamakor Press, 1992. 64 pp.

349. Wiznitzer, Manuel. *Bildliche Redensarten. Deutsch, Englisch, Französisch*. Stuttgart: Ernst Klett, 1975. 136 pp.

350. Yermoloff, Alexis. *Der Landwirtschaftliche Volkskalender*. Leipzig: F.A. Brockhaus, 1905. Rpt. ed. Wolfgang Mieder. Hildesheim: Georg Olms, 2010. 567 pp. (introduction, pp. 5*-30*). (weather proverbs).

351. Yoo, Young H. *Wisdom of the Far East. A Dictionary of Proverbs, Maxims, and Famous Classical Phrases of the Chinese, Japanese, and Korean*. Washington, D.C.: Far Eastern Research and Publications Center, 1972. 449 pp.

352. Yurtbaşi, Metin. *Turkish Proverbs and Their Equivalents in Fifteen Languages*. Illustrations by Sadik Pala. Istanbul: Serkon Etiket, 1996. 502 pp.

353. Zimmermann, Matthias. *Von nackten Rotkehlchen und furzenden Wölfen. Die witzigsten Redensarten unserer europäischen Nachbarn*. Berlin-Brandenburg: be.bra verlag, 2008. 139 pp.

354. Zolotnitskii, Isai. *Slovar' poslovits i pogovorok: Russkii-angliiskii-nemetskii-frantsuzskii-ispanskii-ital'ianskii-latinskii*. Ierusalim: Filobiblon, 2000. 248 pp.

355. Zona, Guy A. *"Eyes that See Do not Grow Old": The Proverbs of Mexico, Central and South America*. New York: Touchstone Book, 1996. 127 pp.

356. Zouogbo, Jean-Philippe. *Concepts et images parémiologiques: Étude de linguistique comparée allemande / français / bété*. Diss. Université de Strasbourg, 2005. 380 pp. With a separate German summary of 36 pp. (proverb index, pp. 316-369).

African Languages

357. Ademola, Lady Kofo. *African Proverbs*. Ibadan, Nigeria: Bookcraft, 1998. 58 pp.

358. Aden, Abdurahman H.H., and Irene Aden. *Murtidu waa Hodantinnimo: Maahmaahyada iyo Oraahda Soomaaliyeed / From the Soul of Nomads: Proverbs and Sayings of the Somalis / Aus der Seele der Hirten: Sprichwörter und Spruchweisheiten der Hirten*. Cologne: Omimee, Intercultural Publishers, 1995. Paris: Unesco Publishing, 1995. 159 pp. With illustrations.

359. Agbemenu, Cephas Yao. *A Collection of Ewe Proverbs*. Nairobi, Kenya: Privately Printed, 2010. 81 pp. With 100 illustrations.

360. Alagoa, E.J. *Noin Nengia, Bere Nengia: Nembe n'Akabu / More Days, More Wisdom: Nembe Proverbs*. Port Harcourt, Nigeria: University of Port Harcourt Press, 1986. 137 pp.

361. Amadiume, Solomon. *Ilu Ndi Igbo: A Study of Igbo Proverbs. Translation, Explanation and Usage (With a Comparison with some Hausa Proverbs)*. Enugu, Nigeria: Fourth Dimension Publishing Co., 1994. 100 pp.

362. Areje, Raphael Adekunle. *Yoruba Proverbs*. Ibadan, Nigeria: Daystar Press, 1985. 119 pp. With illustrations.

363. Avery-Coger, Greta Margaret Kay McCormick. *Indexes of Subjects, Themes, and Proverbs in the Plays of Wole Soyinka*. Diss. University of Colorado, 1980. 275 pp.

364. Babungu, Allan. *A Collection of Bembe Proverbs from the Democratic Republic of Congo*. Nairoibi, Kenya: African Proverbs Project, 2010. 16 pp.

365. Barra, G. *1000 Kikuyu Proverbs. With Translations and English Equivalents*. Nairobi, Kenya: Kenya Literature Bureau, 1939 (2nd ed. 1960). 123 pp.

366. Bonnet, Doris. *Le proverbe chez les Mossi du Yatenga (Haute Volta)*. Paris: Société d'Etudes Linguistiques et Anthropologigues de France, 1982. 193 pp.

367. Burton, Richard F. *Wit and Wisdom from West Africa; or, A Book of Proverbial Philosophy, Idioms, Enigams, and Laconisms*. London: Tinsley Brothers, 1865; rpt. New York: Negro Universities Press, 1969. 455 pp.

368. Cabakula, Mwamba. *Dictionnaire des proverbes africains.* Paris: L'Harmattan, 1992. 304 pp.

369. Campbell, Theophine Maria. *African and Afro-American Proverb Parallels.* M.A. Thesis University of California at Berkeley, 1975. 92 pp. (proverbs, pp. 72-87).

370. Chacha, Emmanuel P. *Collection of 104 Kuria Proverbs. Northwestern Tanzania Near Lake Victoria and Southwestern Kenya in East Africa.* Musoma, Tanzania: Maryknoll Language School, 1999. 32 pp.

371. Chesaina, Ciarunji. "Nthimo – Proverbs." In C. Chesaina. *Oral Literature of the Embu and Mbeere.* Nairobi, Kenya: East African Educational Publishers, 2000. 175-199.

372. Christaller, Johann Gottlieb. *A Collection of Three Thousand and Six Hundred Tshi Proverbs, in Use among the Negroes of the Gold Coast Speaking the Asante and Fante Language.* Basel: The Basel German Missionary Society, 1879. 152 pp. Rpt. as *Three Thousand Six Hundred Ghanian Proverbs (from the Asante and Fante Language).* Lewiston, New York: Edwin Mellen Press, 1990. 302 pp.

373. Crépeau, Pierre, and Simon Bizimana. *Proverbes du Rwanda.* Tervuren, Belgium: Musée Royal de l'Afrique Centrale, 1979. 800 pp.

374. Cribier, Jacqueline, Martine Dreyfus, and Mamadou Gueye. *Léébu: proverbes wolof.* Paris: edicef, 1986. 130 pp. With illustrations.

375. Dalfovo, Albert. *Lugbara Wisdom (Uganda/Zaire).* Illustrations by Paul Lubowa. Pretoria: University of South Africa Press, 1997. 152 pp.

376. Dogbeh, Lucia Isabelle. *Sprichwörter kontrastiv: Eine vergleichende Studie der Struktur und Funktion von Sprichwörtern im Deutschen und im Fon.* Bern: Peter Lang, 2000. 271 pp. (proverb index, pp. 261-271).

377. Farsi, S.S. *Swahili Sayings from Zansibar: Proverbs.* Nairobi, Kenya: East African Literature Bureau, 1958 (2nd ed. 1976). 52 pp.

378. Farsi, S.S. *Swahili Sayings from Zansibar: Riddles and Superstitions.* Nairobi, Kenya: East African Literature Bureau, 1958 (2nd ed. 1979). 37 pp.

379. Fátunmbi, Fá'lókun. *Ibà'ṣẹ Orìṣà: Ifà Proverbs, Folktales, Sacred History and Prayer.* Bronx, New York: Original Publications, 1994. 221 pp.

380. Gray, Ernest. "Some Proverbs of the Nyanja People [Zambia]." *African Studies*, 3, no. 3 (1944), 101-128.

381. Halemba, Andrzej. *Religious and Ethical Values in the Proverbs of the Mambwe People (Zambia)*. Warszawa: Oficyna Wydawniczo-Poligrafiszna "ADAM", 2005. 422 pp.

382. Healey, Joseph G. "Proverbs and Sayings: A Window into the African Christian World View." *Communicatio Socialis Yearbook*, 7 (1988), 53-76. Also published as a special issue of *Service*, no volume given, no. 3 (1988), 1-35.

383. Healey, Joseph G. "Using African Proverbs and Saying[s] to Promote Marriage Encounter." *Pastoral Orientation Service*, 4 (1992), 11-15.

384. Healey, Joseph G. *234 Misemo Kwenye Khanga za Afrika Mashariki (Sayings on East African Cloth)*. Dar es Salaam, Tanzania: Maryknoll Society, 1999. 17 pp.

385. Healey, Joseph G. *241 Misemo Kwenye Khanga za Afrika Mashariki (Sayings on East African Cloth)*. Dar es Salaam, Tanzania: Maryknoll Society, 2000. 17 pp.

386. Healey, Joseph G. (ed.). *Collection of, and Commentary on, 308 Sayings on East African Cloth (Misemo Kwenye Khanga za Afrika Mashariki)*. Dar es Salaam, Tanzania: Maryknoll Society, 2002. 24 pp.

387. Healey, Joseph G. (ed.). *Once Upon a Time in Africa. Stories of Wisdom and Joy*. Maryknoll, New York: Orbis Books, 2004. 144 pp. (with many proverbs).

388. Healey, Joseph G. (ed.). *Collection of, and Commentary on, 436 Sayings on East African Cloth (Misemo Kwenye Khanga na Vitenge vya Afrika Mashariki)*. Dar es Salaam, Tanzania: Maryknoll Society, 2005. 34 pp.

389. Herskovits, Melville J., and Sie Tagbwe. "Kru [African] Proverbs." *Journal of American Folklore*, 43 (1930), 225-293.

390. Herzog, George. *Jabo Proverbs from Liberia. Maxims in the Life of a Native Tribe*. London: Oxford University Press, 1936. 272 pp.

391. Hunzaye, Nasir Uddin, Yves-Charles Morin, and Etienne Tiffou. "Proverbes du Hounza." *Orbis: Bulletin international de documentation linguistique*, 33, nos. 1-2 (1984, published 1989), 239-251.

392. Igwe, G.E. *Onye Tūru Ikòrò wàa yà eze. A book of Igbo Proverbs*. Illustrations by Olu Byron. Ibadan, Nigeria: University Press Limited, 1986. 167 pp.

393. Kabale, Sim Kilosho. *Lega Proverbs (D.R. Congo)*. Nairobi, Kenya: African Proverbs Project, 2010. 31 pp.

394. Kabira, Wanjiku Mukabi, and Karega Mutahi. "Thimo Gikuyu Proverbs." In W.M. Kabira and K. Mutahi. *Gikuyu Oral Literature*. Nairobi, Kenya: East African Educational Publishers, 1988. 135-138.

395. Kapchits, Georgi L. *Somaliiskie poslovitsy i pogovorki na somaliiskom i russkom iazykakh s russkimi sootvetstviiami*. Moskva: Nauka, 1983. 284 pp.

396. Kapchits, Georgi L. *Qaamuuska maahmaahyada soomaaliyeed / The Dictionary of Somali Proverbs*. Moscow: "Vostochnaya Literatura" Publishers, 1998. 207 pp.

397. Kariuki, Joseph. *Hakuna matata. A Collection of Contemporary Nairobi Sayings with a Commentary*. Nairobi, Kenya: Privately printed, 2003. 27 pp.

398. Kariuki, Joseph. *Selected Justice and Peace Proverbs from the Horn of Africa and the Great Lakes Region*. Nairobi, Kenya: Privately Duplicated, 2005. 14 pp.

399. Kariuki, Joseph. *A Collection of Proverbs from the Kenyan Media*. Nairobi, Kenya: Privately Printed, 2007. 12 pp.

400. Katabarwa, Calvin C. *Hema Proverbs [Congo]*. Nairobi, Kenya: African Proverbs Project, 2010. 24 pp.

401. Knappert, Jan. "Rhyming Swahili Proverbs." *Afrika und Übersee*, 49 (1966), 59-68.

402. Knappert, Jan. *Proverbs from the Lamu Archipelago and the Central Kenya Coast*. Berlin: Dietrich Reimer, 1986. 127 pp.

403. Knappert, Jan. *The A-Z of African Proverbs*. London: Karnak House, 1989. 150 pp.

404. Knappert, Jan. *Swahili Proverbs*. Burlington, Vermont: The University of Vermont, 1997. 156 pp.

405. Korse, Piet. "Proverbs of Basankusu." *Annles Aequatoria*, 8 (1987), 365-372.

406. Kuria, Elizabeth Nafula. *African Proverbs on Food: Ninety-One (91) Proverbs from the Bukusu and Five (5) Proverbs from the Kikuyu in Kenya on Food.* Nairobi, Kenya: Department of Foods, Nutrition and Dietetics, Kenyatta University, 2002. 22 pp.

407. Kuusi, Matti. *Ovambo Proverbs with African Parallels.* FF Communications No. 208. Helsinki: Suomolainen Tiedeakatemia, 1970. 356 pp.

408. Kuusi, Matti. *Mustan Afrikan viisautta.* Illustrations by John Muafangejo. Porvoo: Werner Söderström, 1979. 93 pp.

409. Lange, Kofi Ron. *Dagban' Naha – Dagbani Proverbs.* Tamale, Ghana: Cyber Systems, 2006. 459 pp.

410. Leaver, K.D., and Cyril L. Sibusiso Nyembezi. "Proverbs Collected from the Amandebele [Southern Rhodesia]." *African Studies*, 5, no. 2 (1946), 136-139.

411. Leslau, Charlotte, and Wolf Leslau. *African Proverbs.* Illustrations by Jeff Hill. White Plains, New York: Peter Pauper Press, 1962 (2nd ed. 1985). 61 pp.

412. Leslau, Charlotte, and Wolf Leslau. *African Love Poems and Proverbs.* Photographs by Solomon M. Skolnick. White Plains, New York: Peter Pauper Press, 1995. 80 pp.

413. Ley, Gerd de. *African Proverbs.* New York: Hippocrene Books, 1999. 128 pp. With illustrations.

414. Lindfors, Bernth. "Chinua Achebe's Proverbs." *Nigerian Field*, 35 (1970), 180-185; 36 (1971), 45-48, 90-96 and 139-143.

415. Lupande, Joseph M., Albina Ambrose, and Makoye Lupande. *Tulibache Aba-Zinza Twimanye (Collection of 105 Zinza [Tanzania] Proverbs).* Mwanza: Privately printed, 2002. 12 pp.

416. Lupande, Joseph M., and Wilbard J. Lupande. *Zinza Proverbs.* Mwanza, Tanzania: Privately printed, 2000. 14 pp.

417. Madumulla, J.S. *Proverbs and Sayings: Theory and Practice. Hehe Proverbs with Kiswahili and English Translations.* Dar es Salaam: Institute of Kiswahili Research, University of Dar es Salaam, 1995. 170 pp. (proverbs, pp. 62-170).

418. Mayr, Fr. "Zulu Proverbs." *Anthropos*, 7 (1912), 957-963.

419. Mbonde, John P. *Wisdom from the Ngoni Proverbs.* Dar es Salaam: Privately printed, 2004. 70 pp.

420. Merriam, Alan P., Barbara W. Merriam, and Robert P. Armstrong. "Banyaruanda Proverbs." *Journal of American Folklore*, 67 (1954), 267-284.

421. Merrick, Captain G. *Hausa Proverbs*. London: Kegan, Paul, Trench, Trübner & Co., 1905; rpt. New York: Negro Universities Press, 1969. 113 pp.

422. Meyer, Gérard, Jean-Raphael Camara, and Fonsa Camara. *Proverbes malinké [Sénégal]*. Paris: edicef, 1985. 172 pp.

423. Miruka, Okumba. "Luo, Gikuyu, Yoruba, Acholi, Kalenjin, Luhyia, and Maasai Proverbs." In O. Miruka. *Studying Oral Literature*. Nairobi, Kenya: Akacia Stantex Publishers, 2000. 123-134.

424. Mitchison, Naomi, and Amos Kgamanyane Pilane. "The Bakgatla of South-east Botswana as Seen Through Their Proverbs." *Folklore* (London), 78 (1967), 241-268.

425. Mokitimi, 'Makali I. *The Voice of the People: Proverbs of the Basotho (Lesotho/South Africa)*. Pretoria: University of South Africa Press, 1997. 98 pp.

426. Monye, Ambrose A. *Proverbial Lore in Aniocha Oral Literature*. Diss. University of Nigeria at Nsukka, 1988. 726 pp. (proverb index, pp. 428-726),

427. Monye, Ambrose A. *Proverbs in African Orature: The Aniocha-Igbo Experience*. Lanham, Maryland: University Press of America, 1996. 211 pp. (proverb index, pp. 143-186).

428. Muranga, Manuel John Kamugisha. *Sprichwörter aus Uganda im europäischen Vergleich*. Frankfurt am Main: Peter Lang, 1997. 291 pp.

429. Murphy, William Peter. *A Semantic and Logical Analysis of Kpelle Proverb Metaphors of Secrecy*. Diss. Stanford University, 1976. 259 pp. (proverbs, pp. 174-204).

430. Mushi, Michael (ed.). *Collection of 100 Chagga (Tanzania) Sayings*. Arusha: Privately printed, 2005. 18 pp.

431. Mwela-Ubi, Kalunga. "Le proverbe taabwa [Zaire]." *Africa*, 35 (1980), 191-216.

432. Mweseli, Monica Nalyaka. *Art, Wit and Wisdom of African Proverbs: One Hundred Proverbs from the Babakusa of Western Kenya*. Nairobi, Kenya: University of Nairobi, 2001. 37 pp.

433. Ndunguru, Egino. *100 Matengo (Tanzania) Sayings and Proverbs*. Dar es Salaam: Privately printed, 2005. 42 pp.

434. Nestor, Hellen Byera. *500 Proverbs (Haya)*. Nairobi, Kenya: East African Literature Bureau, 1977. 95 pp. With illustrations.

435. Netaob, Alema (ed.). *My Favourite African Proverbs*. Ghana: no publisher given, 2000. 72 pp.

436. Ngoy Kasongo Kata, Mfum-wa-Mangi. "Les proverbes des Baluba-Shankadi: Mwana Maluba mu 'Kyondo'." *Problèmes sociaux zairois*, no volume goven, nos. 112-113 (1976), 5-29; nos. 114-115 (1976), 5-35

437. Nkumbulwa, Joseph, and Max Tertrais. *Collection of 197 Sumbwa Proverbs. Geita/Kahama Districts Around the Southern Part of Lake Victoria in Western Tanzania*. Mwanza, Tanzania: Sukoma Cultural Centre, 1999. 48 pp.

438. Nkumbulwa, Joseph, and Max Tertrais. *Balongo, Tanzania Proverbs*. Dar es Salaam: Privately printed, 2002. 100 pp.

439. Nkumbulwa, Joseph, and Max Tertrais. *Collection of 186 Proverbs of the Kishubi Language of North-West Tanzania*. Bujora, Mwanza: Cultural Center of Bujora, 2005. 63 pp.

440. Nkumbulwa, Joseph, and Max Tertrais. *198 Proverbs of the Kishubi Language from the North-West of Tanzania*. Bujora, Mwanza: Bujora Museum, 2006. 68 pp.

441. Nyakundi, Evans K. *The Gusii Proverbs*. Nairobi, Kenya: Hekima College, 2001. 41 pp.

442. Nyakundi, Evans K. *Which Way to Evangelization in Africa? The Gusii Proverbs: In English Translation With Explanation and Scriptural Parallel*. Dar es Salaam: Maryknoll Society, 2004. 130 pp.

443. Nyandwi, Jean (ed.). *Collection of 100 Rundi (Burundi) Proverbs*. Nairobi, Kenya: Privately printed, 2003. 29 pp.

444. Nyembezi, Cyril L. Sibusiso. *Zulu Proverbs*. Johannesburg: Witwatersrand University Press, 1963. 250 pp.

445. Odaga, Asenath Bole. *Luo Sayings [from Kenya]*. Kisumu, Kenya: Lake Publishers & Enterprises, 1995. 80 pp.

446. Ojoade, J. Olowo. "Some Mbembe Proverbs." *The Nigerian Field*, 43 (1978), 64-71.

447. Ojoade, J. Olowo. "Some Ilaje Wellerisms." *Folklore* (London), 91 (1980), 63-71.

448. Ojoade, J. Olowo. "Some Itsekiri Proverbs." *The Nigerian Field*, 45 (1980), 91-96.

449. Ojoade, J. Olowo. "African Sexual Proverbs: Some Yoruba Examples." *Folklore* (London), 94, no. 2 (1983), 201-213.

450. Opoku, Kofi Asare. *Hearing and Keeping. Akan Proverbs.* Preotria: University of South Africa Press, 1997. 163 pp.

451. Owomoyela, Oyekan. *A Ki i. Yorùbá Proscriptive and Prescriptive Proverbs.* Lanham, Maryland: University Press of America, 1988. 388 pp.

452. Owomoyela, Oyekan. *Yoruba Proverbs.* Lincoln, Nebraska: University of Nebraska Press, 2005. 502 pp.

453. p'Bitek, Okot. *Acholi Proverbs.* Nairobi, Kenya: Heinemann Kenya Ltd., 1985. 38 pp.

454. Pachocinski, Ryszard. *Proverbs of Africa. Human Nature in the Nigerian Oral Tradition.* St. Paul, Minnesota: Professors World Peace Academy, 1996. 434 pp.

455. Pampalk, José. *Nzerumbawiri. Provérbios Sena: Dinamizar o desenvolvimento comunitario o valorizando a literatura oral.* Maputo, Moçambique: Paulinas, 2003. 160 pp. (2nd ed. 2008. 224 pp.

456. Paqué, Ruprecht. *Auch schwarze Kühe geben weiße Milch. Spruchweisheit aus Afrika.* Illustrations by Heiner Rothfuchs. Mainz: Matthias-Grünewald-Verlag, 1976. 46 pp.

457. Penfield, Joyce. *Communicating with Quotes: The Igbo Case.* Westport, Connecticut: Greenwood Press, 1983. 138 pp. (proverb index, pp. 111-120).

458. Petro, Makuru S. *Collection of 10 Ngoreme Proverbs, 1 Song and 2 Stories (Northwestern Tanzania).* Dar es Salaam: Privately printed, 2000. 20 pp.

459. Rattray, R. Sutherland. *Ashanti Proverbs. The Primitive Ethics of a Savage People.* Oxford: Clarendon Press, 1916; rpt. Oxford: Clarendon Press, 1981. 190 pp.

460. Ries, Hubert (ed.). *Ebenholz. Afrikanische Sprichwörter.* Illustrations by Günther Stiller. Frankfurt am Main: Bauer, 1967. 26 pp.

461. Rodegem, F. *Paroles de sagesse au Burundi*. Leuven: Peeters, 1983. 499 pp.

462. Scheven, Albert. "Politics in Swahili Porverbs." *Ufahamu: Journal of the African Activist Association*, 8, no. 1 (1977), 95-105.

463. Scheven, Albert. *Swahili Proverbs. Nia zikiwa moja, kilicho mbali huja*. Washington, D.C.: University Press of America, 1981. 586 pp.

464. Schipper, Mineke. *Source of All Evil: African Proverbs and Sayings on Women*. London: Allison and Busby, 1991. Chicago: Ivan R. Dee, 1991. Rpt. Nairobi, Kenya: Phoenix Publishers, 1992. 97 pp.

465. Schlee, Günther, and Karaba Sahado. *Rendille Proverbs in Their Social and Legal Context*. Köln: Rüdiger Köppe, 2002. 192 pp.

466. Seitel, Peter. *Proverbs and the Structure of Metaphor Among the Haya of Tanzania*. Diss. University of Pennsylvania, 1972. 258 pp. (index of Haya and Swahili proverbs, pp. iv-viii).

467. Sheba, Laide. *Yorùbá Proverbs with Feminine Lexis*. Ibadan, Nigeria: Spectrum Books, 2006. 131 pp.

468. Shongolo, Abdullahi A., and Günther Schlee. *Boran Proverbs in Their Cultural Context*. Köln: Rüdiger Köppe, 2007. 139 pp.

469. Simmons, Donald C. "Oron Proverbs [Nigeria]." *African Studies*, 19, no. 3 (1960), 126-137.

470. Simmons, Donald C. and Lydia F. Akesson. "Fifteen Nzima Proverbs." *Folklore* (London), 76 (1965), 262-265.

471. Stenstrom, Oscar Sten Paul. *Proverbs of the Bakongo [Congo]*. Diss. Hartford Seminary Foundation, 1948. 582 pp.

472. Sumbwa, Nyambe. *Zambian Proverbs*. Lusaka, Zambia: Zambia Printing Company, 1993. 84 pp.

473. Sybertz, Donald, and Joseph G. Healey (eds.). *Kugundua Mbegu za Injili: Kitabu ch Pili. Hekima ya Kisukuma na Lugha Mbalimbali juu ya Familia*. Peramiho, Tanzania: Benedictine Publications Ndanda, 1993. (2nd ed. 1999). 124 pp. With illustrations.

474. Vedder, H. "Die Spruchweisheit und Sprichwörter der Bergdama [Afrika]." In H. Vedder. *Die Bergdama*. Hamburg: L. Friederichsen, 1923. 49-61 and 106-131 (collection).

475. Vidal, O.E. "[Yoruba Proverbs]." In Samuel Crowther. *A Grammar and Vocabulary of the Yoruba Language*. London: Seeleys, 1852. 17-37.

476. Wanjohi, Gerald Joseph. *The Wisdom and the Philosophy of the Gikuyu Proverbs*. Nairobi, Kenya: Paulines Publications Africa, 1997. 271 pp. (proverb index, pp. 231-251).

477. Wanjohi, Gerald Joseph. *Under One Roof: Gikuyu Proverbs Consolidated*. Nairobi, Kenya: Paulines Publications, 2001. 238 pp.

478. Wannyn, Robert L. *Les proverbes anciens du Bas-Congo notés en 1936 dans la langue orale*. 2 vols. Bruxelles: Editions du Vieux Planquesaule, 1983 and 1988. I, 107 pp.; II, 72 pp. With illustrations.

479. Warren, D.M., Tijani Abioye-Salami, and Mary S. Warren. "Yoruba Terms Denoting Individual and Social Shortcomings." *Maledicta*, 3 (1979), 39-54.

480. Weier, Hans-Ingolf. *Luba – Sprichwörter: Übersetzte, erweiterte und überarbeitete Ausgabe einer anonymen Sammlung aus Zaire*. 2 vols. Köln: Rüdiger Köppe Verlag, 1992. 841 pp.

481. Whitting, Charles Edward Jewel. *Hausa and Fulani Proverbs*. Lagos: Government Printer, 1940; rpt. Farnborough, Hants: Gregg Press, 1967. 192 pp.

482. Witte, P.A. "Sprichwörter der Ewhe-Neger, Gẽ-Dialekt (Togo), Westafrika." *Anthropos*, 12-13 (1917-1918), 58-83.

483. Yankah, Kwesi. *The Proverb in Context of Akan Rhetoric*. Diss. Indiana University, 1985. 455 pp. Also as *The Proverb in the Context of Akan Rhetoric. A Theory of Proverb Praxis*. Bern: Peter Lang, 1989. 313 pp. With illustrations. (proverb index, pp. 261-300).

484. Zona, Guy A. *"The House of the Heart is Never Full" and Other Proverbs of Africa*. New York: Touchstone, 1993. 128 pp.

Afrikaans

485. Botha, R.P., G. Kroes, and C.H. Winckler. *Afrikaanse idiome en ander vaste uitdrukkings*. Kaapstad: Southern Boekuitgewers, 1994. 432 pp.

486. Combrink, Johan. *Daar is 'n spreekwoord wat sê ... uit ander tale en uit Afrikaans*. Pretoria: J.L. van Schaik, 1993. 173 pp.

487. Schipper, Mineke. *Een vrouw is als de aarde. Afrikaanse spreekwoorden en zegswijzen over vrouwen.* Baarn: Ambo, 1994. 138 pp.

488. Weyers, Susan Paramore. *The Evergreen South African Diary.* Pretoria: Paramore Diary Company, 1991. 370 pp. With illustrations. (proverbs for each day).

Albanian

489. Guli, Meri. *A Comparative Study of Anglo-American and Albanian Proverbs.* Diss. Universität Graz, 2006. 318 pp. (comparative proverb index, pp. 130-247; and proverbs of Latin origin, pp. 292-318).

American

490. Adams, Owen S. "Traditional Proverbs and Sayings from California." *Western Folklore*, 6 (1947), 59-64.

491. Adams, Owen S. "More California Proverbs." *Western Folklore*, 7 (1948), 136-144.

492. Adams, Ramon F. *Western Words: A Dictionary of the American West.* Norman, Oklahoma: University of Oklahoma Press, 1968. Rpt. as *The Cowboy Dictionary: The Chin Jaw Words and Whing-Ding Ways of the American West.* New York: Perigee Books, 1993. 355 pp.

493. Adler, Bill (ed.). *The Uncommon Wisdom of Ronald Reagan. A Portrait in His Own Words.* Boston: Little, Brown and Company, 1996. 166 pp.

494. Allen, Harold B. "Hunting for Minnesota Proverbs." *Minnesota History*, 27 (1946), 33-36.

495. Alstad, Ken. *Savvy Sayin's. Lean & Meaty One-Liners.* Illustrations by Frederic Remington & Charles M. Russell. Tucson, Arizona: Ken Alstad Co., 1986 (6th ed. 1990). 167 pp.

496. Alstad, Ken. *Savvy Sayin's. True Wisdom from the Real West.* Fort Worth, Texas: Whippersnap Press, 2004. 95 pp. With illustrations.

497. Ammer, Christine. *The American Heritage Dictionary of Idioms.* Boston: Houghton Mifflin Company, 1997. 729 pp.

498. Anderson, William C., Bart Andrews, and Scott Anderson. *Different Spokes for Different Folks.* San Diego, California: Serendipity Publishing, 1973. 46 pp. With illustrations. (anti-proverbs).

499. Andrews, Malachi, and Paul T. Owens. *Black Language.* Los Angeles, California: Seymour-Smith, 1973 (2nd ed. 1976). 150 pp.

500. Anonymous. "Proverbs and Phrases [from Massachusetts]." *Journal of American Folklore*, 5 (1892), 60.

501. Anonymous. *Boston Post Proverb Book. Containing all the Proverbs, Wise Sayings, Epigrams, etc. used in Boston Post Proverb Contests after October 1, 1904.* Boston: Post Publishing Co., 1904. 58 pp.

502. Anonymous. "Indian Proverbs [from Oklahoma]." *Journal of American Folklore*, 19 (1906), 173-174.

503. Anonymous. "Pennsylvania-German Proverbs." *Penn-Germania*, 7 (1906), 265.

504. Anonymous. *Book of Proverbs.* Compiled for the Toledo-News-Bee Proverb Contest. St. Louis, Missouri: Monroe Publishing Co., 1907. 61 pp.

505. Anonymous. *Proverbs from the Almanac of one Richard Saunders (Benjamin Franklin).* New York: Duffield, 1908. 26 pp.

506. Anonymous. *Proverb Book Compiled by the "Boston American" for the $10,000 Prize Contest.* New York: McConnell, ca. 1913. 79 pp.

507. Anonymous. "Proverbs and Sayings [from New York]." *New York Folklore Quarterly*, 2 (1946), 219-220.

508. Anonymous. *Ben Franklin's Wit & Wisdom.* Illustrations by Joseph Crawhall. White Plains, New York: Peter Pauper Press, 1960. 62 pp.

509. Anonymous. "Perverted Proverbs." *Western Folklore*, 20 (1961), 200.

510. Anonymous. "Parodied Proverbs from Idaho." *Western Folklore*, 24 (1965), 289-290.

511. Anonymous. "Some Wellerisms from Idaho." *Western Folklore*, 25 (1966), 34.

512. Anonymous. *Official CB Dictionary. Latest Terms & Definitions of Citizens Band Jargon.* New York: Book Craft-Guild, 1976. 140 pp.

513. Anonymous. *"I Speak English Yet". A Collection of Amusing Pennsylvania Dutch Expressions.* Gettysburg, Pennsylvania: Dutchcroff, 1992. 16 pp.

514. Anthony, Robert. *Think Big. A "Think" Collection.* New York: Berkeley Books, 1999. 312 pp. (aphorisms and anti-proverbs).

515. Archer, Fred. *Country Sayings.* Wolfeboro Falls, New York: A. Sutton, 1991. 105 pp.

516. Arora, Shirley L. "Some Spanish Proverbial Comparisons from California." *Western Folklore*, 20 (1961), 229-237.

517. Arora, Shirley L. "Spanish Proverbial Exaggerations from California." *Western Folklore*, 27 (1968), 229-253; 30 (1971), 105-118.

518. Arora, Shirley L. *Proverbial Comparisons and Related Expressions in Spanish. Recorded in Los Angeles, California.* Berkeley, California: University of California Press, 1977. 521 pp.

519. Atkinson, Mary Jourdan. "Familiar Sayings of Old Time Texans." *Rainbow in the Morning.* Ed. J. Frank Dobie. Austin, Texas: Texas Folklore Society, 1926; rpt. Dallas, Texas: Southern Methodist University Press, 1975. 78-92 (not identical to next entry).

520. Atkinson, Mary Jourdan. "Familiar Sayings of Old-Time Texans." *Texas Folk and Folklore.* Eds. Mody C. Boatright, Wilson M. Hudson, and Allen Maxwell. Dallas, Texas: Southern Methodist University Press, 1954 (2nd ed. 1965). 213-218. (not identical to previous entry).

521. Aurand, Ammon Monroe. *Quaint Idioms and Expressions of the Pennsylvania Germans.* Lancaster, Pennsylvania: Aurand Press, 1939. 32 pp.

522. Aurand, Ammon Monroe. *Wit and Humor of the Pennsylvania Germans.* Lancaster, Pennsylvania: Aurand Press, ca. 1940. 32 pp.

523. Austin, Mary. "Sayings." *Virginia Quarterly Review.* 9 (1933), 574-577.

524. Ayers, Edward L. (ed.). *"A House Divided ...": A Century of Great Civil War Quotations.* New York: John Wiley & Sons, 1997. 258 pp.

525. Ayres, Alex (ed.). *The Wit and Wisdom of Abraham Lincoln.* New York: Meridian, 1992. 222 pp.

526. Ayres, Alex (ed.). *The Wisdom of Martin Luther King, Jr. An A-to-Z Guide to the Ideas and Ideals of the Great Civil Rights Leader.* New York: Meridian, 1993. 274 pp.

527. Ayres, Alex (ed.). *The Wit and Wisdom of Eleanor Roosevelt.* New York: Meridian, 1996. 242 pp.

528. Bachelder, Louise (ed.). *Abraham Lincoln: Wisdom & Wit.* Illustrations by Jeff Hill. Mount Vernon, New York: Peter Pauper Press, 1965. 61 pp.

529. Baldwin, L. Karen. "A Sampling of Housewives' Proverbs and Proverbial Phrases from Levittown, Pennsylvania." *Keystone Folklore Quarterly*, 10 (1965), 127-148.

530. Barbour, Frances M. "Some Foreign Proverbs in Southern Illinois." *Midwest Folklore*, 4, no. 3 (1954), 161-164.

531. Barbour, Frances M. *Proverbs and Proverbial Phrases of Illinois.* Carbondale, Illinois: Southern Illinois University Press, 1965. 213 pp.

532. Barbour, Frances M. *A Concordance to the Sayings in Franklin's "Poor Richard".* Detroit: Gale Research Company, 1974. 245 pp.

533. Barnes-Harden, Alene L. "Proverbs, Folk Expressions and Superstitions." In A.L. Barnes-Harden. *African American Verbal Arts: Their Nature and Communicative Interpretation (A Thematic Analysis).* Diss. University of New York at Buffalo, 1980. (proverbs, pp. 57-80).

534. Barrick, Mac E. "Proverbs and Sayings from Cumberland County [Pennsylvania]." *Keystone Folklore Quarterly*, 8 (1963), 139-203.

535. Barrick, Mac E. "Popular Comparisons and Similes." *Keystone Folklore Quarterly*, 10 (1965), 3-34.

536. Barrick, Mac E. "Proverbs and Sayings from Gibbsville, Pa. John O'Hara's Use of Proverbial Materials." *Keystone Folklore Quarterly*, 12 (1967), 55-80.

537. Barrick, Mac E. "Early Proverbs from Carlisle, Pennsylvania (1788-1821)." *Keystone Folklore Quarterly*, 13 (1968), 193-217.

538. Barrick, Mac E. "[George Frederick] Ruxton's Western Proverbs." *Western Folklore*, 34 (1975), 215-225.

539. Barrick, Mac E. "Proverbs." In M.E. Barrick. *German-American Folklore*. Little Rock, Arkansas: August House, 1987. 36-46.

540. Bartlett, John Russell. *The Dictionary of Americanisms*. New York: Bartlett & Welford, 1849; rpt. New York: Crescent Books, 1989. 412 pp.

541. Baughman, Ernest W. "Folk Sayings and Beliefs." *The New Mexico Folklore Record*, 9 (1954-1955), 23-27.

542. Beilenson, Evelyn L., and Ann Tenenbaum. *Wit and Wisdom of Famous American Women*. Illustrations by Fran Waldmann. White Plains, New York: Peter Pauper Press, 1986. 64 pp.

543. Beilenson, Evelyn L., and Ann Tenenbaum. *Wit and Wisdom of Famous American Women*. White Plains, New York: Peter Pauper Press, 1995. 64 pp. With illustrations. (different from previous entry).

544. Benardete, Doris (ed.). *Mark Twain. Wit and Wisecracks*. Illustrations by Henry R. Martin. Mount Vernon, New York: Peter Pauper Press, 1961. 61 pp.

545. Bender, Texas Bix. *Don't Squat with Yer Spurs on! A Cowboy's Guide to Life*. 2 vols. Salt Lake City, Utah: Peregrine Smith Books, 1992 and 1997. I, 138 pp.; II, 128 pp. With illustrations.

546. Bernstein, R. B. (ed.). *The Wisdom of John and Abigail Adams*. New York: MetroBooks, 2002. 138 pp.

547. Berrey, Lester V., and Melvin van den Bark. *The American Thesaurus of Slang. A Complete Reference Book of Colloquial Speech*. New York: Thomas Y. Crowell, 1942. 1174 pp.

548. Bethea, Audley Wheeler. *Little Gnome Facts. To Say the Least and Make Most of It*. Illustrations by John Lara. Austin, Texas: Quip-Wit Press, 1991. 120 pp. (anti-proverbs).

549. Billings, Josh (pseud. Henry Wheeler Shaw). *Josh Billings, His Sayings*. New York: Carleton, 1866. 232 pp. With illustrations.

550. Billings, Josh (pseud. Henry Wheeler Shaw). *America's Phunniest Phellow Josh Billings. The Delightful, Funny Stories & Sayings of Our Wisest American Humorist*. Ed. James E. Myers. Springfield, Illinois: Lincoln-Herndon Press, 1986. 235 pp. With illustrations.

551. Bitting, Carrie V. "Proverbs." *Pennsylvania Dutchman*, 1, no. 25 (1950), 3.

552. Blair, Marion E. "The Prevalence of Older English Proverbs in Blount County, Tennessee." *Tennessee Folklore Society Bulletin*, 4 (1938), 1-24.

553. Blank, Steven C. "Partial Glossary of American Food/Agricultural Clichés, Colloquialisms, Sayings, Etc." In S.C. Blank. *The End of Agriculture in the American Portfolio*. Westport, Connecticut: Quorum Books, 1998. 197-200.

554. Bloch, Arthur. *Murphy's Law and Other Reasons Why Things Go Wrong*. Los Angeles, California: Price, Stern, Sloan Publishers, 1979. 94 pp. With illustrations.

555. Bloch, Arthur. *Murphy's Law. Book Two. More Reasons Why Things Go Wrong*. Los Angeles, California: Price, Stern, Sloan Publishers, 1982. 94 pp. With illustrations.

556. Bloch, Arthur. *Murphy's Law. Book Three. Wrong Reasons Why Things Go More*. Los Angeles, California: Price, Stern, Sloan Publishers, 1982. 93 pp. With illustrations.

557. Blue, John S. *Hoosier Tales and Proverbs*. Rensselaer, Indiana: J. S. Blue, 1982. 93 pp.

558. Boatner, Maxine Tull, and John E. Gates. *A Dictionary of American Idioms for the Deaf*. West Hartford, Connecticut: American School for the Deaf, 1966. Also as *A Dictionary of American Idioms*. Woodbury, New York: Barron's Educational Series, 1975. 392 pp.

559. Bohle, Bruce (ed.). *The Home Book of American Quotations*. New York: Dodd, Mead & Company, 1967; rpt. New York: Gramercy Publishing Company, 1986. 512 pp.

560. Boritt, Gabor S. (ed.). *Of the People, by the People, for the People, and Other Quotations by Abraham Lincoln*. New York: Columbia University Press, 1996. 162 pp.

561. Boshears, Frances, and Herbert Halpert. "Proverbial Comparisons from an East Tennessee County." *Tennessee Folklore Society Bulletin*, 20 (1954), 27-41.

562. Boswell, George. "Folk Wisdom in Northeastern Kentucky." *Tennessee Folklore Society Bulletin*, 33 (1967), 10-17.

563. Boudreaux, Anna Mary. "[French] Proverbs, Metaphors and Sayings of the Kaplan Area." *Louisiana Folklore Miscellany*, 3 (1970), 16-24.

564. Bradley, F.W. "South Carolina Proverbs." *Southern Folklore Quarterly*, 1 (1937), 57-101.

565. Brendel, John. "Proverbs." *Pennsylvania Dutchman*, 1, no. 10 (1949), 2; and 1, no. 11 (1949), 2.

566. Brendle, Thomas R., and William S. Troxell (eds.). *Pennsylvania German Folk Tales, Legends, Once-Upon-a-Time Stories, Maxims, and Sayings*. Norristown, Pennsylvania: Pennsylvania German Society, 1944. 85-89 (proverbs).

567. Brewer, J. Mason. "Old-Time Negro Proverbs." *Spur-of-the-Cock*. Ed. J. Frank Dobie. Austin, Texas: Texas Folklore Society, 1933; rpt. Dallas, Texas: Southern Methodist University Press, 1965. 101-105; rpt. in *Texas Folk and Folklore*. Eds. Mody C. Boatright, Wilson M. Hudson, and Allen Maxwell. Dallas, Texas: Southern Methodist University Press, 1954. 219-223; rpt. *Mother Wit from the Laughing Barrel. Readings in the Interpretation of Afro-American Folklore*. Ed. Alan Dundes. Englewood Cliffs, New Jersey: Prentice Hall, 1973. 246-250.

568. Brewer, J. Mason. "Proverbs." In J.M. Brewer. *Negro Folklore*. Chicago: Quadrangle Books, 1968. 311-325.

569. Brewster, Paul G. "Folk 'Sayings' from Indiana." *American Speech*, 14 (1939), 261-268; and 16 (1941), 21-25.

570. Brookhiser, Richard. *Rules of Civility. The 110 Precepts that Guided Our First President [George Washington] in War and Peace*. New York: The Free Press, 1997. 90 pp. With illustrations.

571. Brunvand, Jan Harold. *A Dictinary of Proverbs and Proverbial Phrases from Books Published by Indiana Authors before 1890*. Bloomington, Indiana: University of Indiana Press, 1961. 168 pp.

572. Bryan, George B., and Wolfgang Mieder. *The Proverbial Eugene O'Neill: An Index to Proverbs in the Works of Eugene Gladstone O'Neill*. Westport, Connecticut: Greenwood Press, 1995. 365 pp.

573. Bryan, George B., and Wolfgang Mieder. "The Proverbial Carl Sandburg (1878-1967). An Index of Folk Speech in his American Poetry." *Proverbium*, 20 (2003), 15-49.

574. Buehler, Allan M. "Proverbs and Sayings in Pennsylvania German and the English Translations." In A.M. Buehler. *The Pennsylvania German Dialect and the Autobiography of an Old Mennonite.* Cambrudge, Ontario: Privately printed, 1977. 34-36.

575. Burrell, Brian. *The Words We Live By: The Creeds, Mottoes, and Pledges that Have Shaped America.* New York: The Free Press, 1997. 367 pp.

576. Bynum, Joyce L. "Syriac Proverbs from California." *Western Folklore,* 31 (1972), 87-101.

577. Caldwell, George S. (ed.). *Good Old Harry. The Wit and Wisdom of Harry S. Truman.* New York: Hawthorn, 1966. 96 pp.

578. Canterbury, E. Betty. *Cliff Hangers and Down to Earth Sayings by Abe Lincoln and Other Common Folk.* Illustrations by Lloyd Ostendorf. Springfield, Illinois: Phillip H. Wagner, 1991. 77 pp.

579. Carruth, Gorton, and Eugene Ehrlich. *The Harper Book of American Quotations.* New York: Harper & Row, 1988. 821 pp.

580. Cassell, Clark. *President Reagan's Quotations.* Washington, D.C.: Braddock Publications, 1984. 148 pp.

581. Cassidy, Frederic G., and Joan Houston Hall. *Dictionary of American Regional English.* Cambridge, Massachusetts: Harvard University Press, 1985-2002. I, A-C, 903 pp.; II, D-H, 1175 pp.; III, S-O, 927 pp.; IV, P-Sk, 1014 pp.; V (not yet published).

582. Chapman, Robert L. *Thesaurus of American Slang.* New York: Harper & Row, 1989. 489 pp.

583. Chertok, Harvey, and Martha Torge (eds.). *Quotations from Charlie Chan.* New York: Golden Press, 1968. 51 pp. With illustrations. (anti-proverbs).

584. Chiu, Tony (ed.). *Ross Perot in His Own Words.* New York: Warner Books, 1992. 189 pp.

585. Ciardi, John. *A Browser's Dictionary and Native's Guide to the Unknown American Language.* New York: Harper & Row, 1980. 429 pp.

586. Clark, J.D. "Similes from the Folk Speech of the South: A Spplement to [Frank J.] Wilstach's Compilation [*A Dictionary of Similes.* Boston: Little, Brown & Company, 1916]." *Southern Folklore Quarterly,* 4, no. 4 (1940), 205-226.

587. Cleary, Kristen Marée (ed.). *Native American Wisdom.* New York: Fall River Press, 1996. 64 pp. With illustrations.

588. Cobos, Rubén. *Refranes: Southwestern Spanish Proverbs.* Santa Fe, New Mexico: Museum of New Mexico Press, 1985. 180 pp.

589. Cobos, Rubén. "New Mexican Spanish Proverbs." *Perspectives in Mexican American Studies,* 1 (1988), 47-54.

590. Coffin, Tristram P., and Hennig Cohen (eds.). "Proverbs." In T.P. Coffin and H. Cohen (eds.). *Folklore in America.* Garden City, New York: Doubleday, 1966. 141-151.

591. Coghlan, Evelyn. "Ethnic Proverbs in New Jersey." *New Jersey Folklore,* 1 (1976), 3-27.

592. Cole, Arthur H. *The Charming Idioms of New England. An Essay Upon Their Significance, Together with a Compilation of Those Current in the Region Around 1900.* Freeport, Maine: The Bond Wheelwright Company, 1961. 52 pp.

593. Collis, Harry. *American English Idioms. Understanding and Speaking English Like an American.* Illustrations by Mario Risso. Lincolnwood, Illinois: Passport Books, 1986. 121 pp.

594. Collis, Harry. *101 American English Proverbs. Understanding Language and Culture Through Commonly Used Sayings.* Illustrations by Mario Risso. Lincolnwood, Illinois: Passport Books, 1992. 105 pp.

595. Collis, Harry. *101 American English Proverbs [with Korean Translations].* Illustrations by Mario Risso. Seoul, Korea: Compass Publishing, 2004. 239 pp.

596. Conlin, Joseph R. *The Morrow Book of Quotations in American History.* New York: William Morrow, 1984. 352 pp.

597. Coonley, Prentiss L. (ed.). *Analects.* Washington, D.C.: Prentiss Coonley, 1963. 60 pp. (quotations and aphorisms).

598. Costello, Robert B. (ed.). *American Expressions: A Thesaurus of Effective and Colorful Speech.* New York: McGraw-Hill Book Company, 1981. 172 pp.

599. Covell, Charles H. *Diamonds and Nuggets, Polished and in the Rough, Gathered from American Minds.* Worcester, Massachusetts: Gilbert G. Davis, 1898. 415 pp.

600. Cox, Ernest. "Rustic Imagery in Mississippi Proverbs." *Southern Folklore Quarterly*, 11 (1947), 263-267.

601. Cutting, Edith E. "Weather-Lore; Proverbial Sayings." In E.E. Cutting. *Lore of an Adirondack County*. Ithaca, New York: Cornell University Press, 1944. 29-35.

602. Dalzell, Tom (ed.). *The Routledge Dictionary of Modern American Slang and Unconventional English*. New York: Routledge, 2009. 1104 pp.

603. Dance, Daryl C. "A Potpourri: Miscellaneous Black Folklore." In D.C. Dance. *Suckin' and Jivin'. Folklore from Contemporary Black Americans*. Bloomington, Indiana: Indiana University Press, 1978. 306-324.

604. Daniel, Jack L. *The Wisdom of Sixth Mount Zion [Baptist Church] from The Members of Sixth Mount Zion and Those Who Begot Them [African American Proverb Collection]*. Pittsburgh, Pennsylvania: University of Pittsburgh, College of Arts and Sciences, 1979. 21 pp.

605. De Jong, Benjamin R. *Uncle Ben's Instant Clip-Quotes*. Grand Rapids, Michigan: Baker Book House, 1985. 127 pp. (anti-proverbs).

606. Décharné, Max. *Straight from the Fridge, Dad. A Dictionary of Hipster Slang*. New York: Broadway Books, 2000. 192 pp.

607. Dickson, Paul. *Slang! Topic-by-Topic Dictionary of Contemporary American Lingoes*. New York: Pocket Books, 1990. 295 pp.

608. Dickson, Paul. *War Slang: Fighting Words and Phrases of Americans from the Civil War to the Gulf War*. New York: Pocket Books, 1994. 403 pp.

609. Dickson, Paul. *Slang. The Topical Dictionary of Americanisms*. New York: Walker, 2006. 418 pp.

610. Dieffenbach, Victor C. "Proverbs." *Pennsylvania Dutchman*, 2, no. 5 (1950), 2.

611. Diggs, Anita Doreen (ed.). *Talking Drums: An African-American Quote Collection*. New York: St. Martin's Griffin, 1996. 178 pp.

612. Dinwiddie-Boyd, Elza (ed.). *In Our Own Words: A Treasury of Quotations from the African-American Community*. New York: Avon Books, 1996. 410 pp.

613. Donadio, Stephen, Joan Smith, Susan Mesner, and Rebecca Davison (eds.). *The New York Public Library Book of Twentieth-Century American Quotations*. New York: Warner Books, 1992. 622 pp.

614. Donovan, Robert J. (ed.). *The Words of Harry S. Truman*. New York: Newmarket Press, 1984; rpt. New York: Barnes & Noble, 1994. 112 pp.

615. Drysdale, William (ed.). *Proverbs from Plymouth Pulpit Selected from the Writings and Sayings of Henry Ward Beecher*. New York: D. Appleton, 1887. 230 pp.

616. Ducovny, Amram M. *(ed.). The Wisdom of Spiro T. Agnew*. Illustrations by Peter Green. New York: Ballantine Books, 1969. 64 pp.

617. Dundes, Alan, and Carl R. Pagter (eds.). *Urban Folklore from the Paperwork Empire*. Austin, Texas: American Folklore Society, 1975. 223 pp. With illustrations.

618. Dundes, Alan, and Carl R. Pagter (eds.). *When You're Up to Your Ass in Alligators ... More Urban Folklore from the Paperwork Empire*. Detroit, Michigan: Wayne State University Press, 1987. 271 pp. With illustrations.

619. Dundes, Alan, and Carl R. Pagter (eds.). *Never Try to Teach a Pig to Sing. Still More Urban Folklore from the Paperwork Empire*. Detroit, Michigan: Wayne State University Press, 1991. 433 pp.

620. Dundes, Alan, and Carl R. Pagter (eds.). *Sometimes the Dragon Wins. Yet More Urban Folklore from the Paperwork Empire*. Syracuse, New York: Syracuse University Press, 1996. 366 pp.

621. Dundes, Alan, and Carl R. Pagter (eds.). *Why Don't Sheep Shrink When It Rains? A Further Collection of Photocopier Folklore*. Syracuse, New York: Syracuse University Press, 2000. 332 pp.

622. Eble, Connie. *College Slang 101. A Definitive Guide to Words, Phrases and Meanings They Don't Teach in English Classes*. Illustrations by Felipe Galindo. Georgetown, Connecticut: Spectacle Lane Press, 1989. 95 pp.

623. Eddins, A.A. "Grandma's Sayings." *Texas Folk and Folklore*. Eds. Mody C. Boatright, Wilson M. Hudson, and Allen Maxwell. Dallas, Texas: Southern Methodist University Press, 1954 (2nd ed. 1965). 218-219.

624. Eisiminger, Sterling. "A Glossary of Ethnic Slurs in American English." *Maledicta*, 3 (1979), 153-174.

625. Eli, Quinn (ed.). *African-American Wisdom. A Book of Quotations and Proverbs*. Philadelphia: Running Press, 1996. 128 pp. (miniature book).

626. Elizabeth, Mary. *American Slang Dictionary and Thesaurus*. New York: Barron's Educational Series, 2009. 596 pp.

627. Emrich, Duncan. "Proverbs and Proverbial Speech." In D. Emrich. *Folklore on the American Land*. Boston: Little, Brown and Company, 1972. 60-89.

628. Engelbreit, Mary (ill.). *A Good Marriage*. Kansas City, Missouri: Andrews and McMeel, 1992. 28 pp.

629. Engelbreit, Mary (ill.). *Life Is Just a Chair of Bowlies*. Kansas City, Missouri: Andrews and McMeel, 1992. 32 pp.

630. Engelbreit, Mary (ill.). *The Wit and Whimsy of Mary Engelbreit*. Kansas City, Missouri: Andrews and McMeel, 1997. 120 pp.

631. England, George Allen. "Rural Locutions of Maine and Northern New Hampshire." *Dialect Notes*, 4, no. 2 (1914), 67-83.

632. Ewing, Ida. *Cow Pie Ain't No Dish You Take to the County Fair and Other Cowboy Facts of Life*. Illustrations by Jim Willoughby. Phoenix, Arizona: Arizona Highways, 1997. 144 pp.

633. Eyre, Richard. *Don't Just Do Something, Sit There. New Maxims to Refresh and Enrich Your Life*. New York: Fireside Books, 1995. 175 pp. (anti-proverbs).

634. Faden, I.B. *How America Speaks and Writes. A Dictionary of American Idioms with a Norwegian Vocabulary*. Oslo: H. Aschehoug, 1949. 360 pp.

635. Farrell, Orin J. "Proverbs." *Pennsylvania Dutchman*, 1, no. 23 (1950), 2.

636. Farries, Helen. *A Sampler of Proverbs: A Collection of Familiar and Less Familiar Proverbs Done in Stitchery*. Illustrations by Sandy Eylar. Anaheim, California: Buzza-Cardoza, 1970. 25 pp.

637. Farwell, Harold F., and J. Karl Nicholas (eds.). *Smoky Mountain Voices: A Lexicon of Southern Appalachian Speech Based on the Research of Horace Kephart*. Lexington, Kentucky: The University Press of Kentucky, 1993. 191 pp.

638. Federer, William J. *America's God and Country. Encyclopedia of Quotations*. St. Louis, Missouri: Amerisearch, 2000. 845 pp.

639. Fehrenbacher, Don E., and Virginia Fehrenbacher. *Recollected Words of Abraham Lincoln*. Stanford, California: Stanford University Press, 1996. 592 pp.

640. Feibleman, James Kern. *New Proverbs for Our Day*. New York: Horizon Press, 1978. 127 pp. (anti-proverbs).

641. Fink, Paul. *Bits of Mountain Speech Gathered Between 1910 and 1965 Along the Mountains Bordering North Carolina and Tennessee*. Boone, North Carolina: The Appalachian Consortium, 1974. 31 pp.

642. Flexner, Stuart Berg. *I Hear America Talking. An Illustrated Treasury of American Words and Phrases*. New York: Van Nostrand Reinhold Company, 1976. 505 pp. With Illustrations.

643. Flexner, Stuart Berg. *Listening to America: An Illustrated History of Words and Phrases from our Lively and Splendid Past*. New York: Simon and Schuster, 1982. 591 pp. With illustrations.

644. Flexner, Stuart Berg, and Anne H. Soukhanov. *Speaking Freely: A Guided Tour of American English from Plymouth Rock to Silicon Valley*. New York: Oxford University Press, 1997. 472 pp. With illustrations.

645. Fogel, Edwin Miller. *Proverbs of the Pennsylvania Germans*. Lancaster, Pennsylvania: Pennsylvania-German Society, 1929. 222 pp. Rpt. ed. C. Richard Beam. Millersville, Pennsylvania: Center for Pennsylvania German Studies, Millersville University, 1995. 171 pp.

646. Fogel, Edwin Miller. *Proverbs of the Pennsylvania Germans*. Lancaster, Pennsylvania: Pennsylvania-German Society, 1929. 222 pp. Rpt. ed. Wolfgang Mieder. Bern: Peter Lang, 1995. 268 pp.

647. Ford, Paul Leicester (ed.). T*he Prefaces, Proverbs, and Poems of Benjamin Franklin. Originally Printed in "Poor Richard's Almanacs" 1733-1758*. New York: G.P. Putnam's Sons, 1890. 288 pp.

648. Foss, William O. (ed.). *First Ladies Quotation Book. A Compendium of Provocative, Tender, Witty and Important Words from the Presidents' Wives*. New York: Barricade Books, 1999. 305 pp.

649. Franke, David (ed.). *Quotations from Chairman Bill. The Best of Wm.F. Buckley, Jr.* New Rochelle, New York: Arlington House, 1970; rpt. New York: Pocket Books, 1971. 326 pp.

650. Franklin, Benjamin. *Poor Richard: The Almanacks for the Years 1733-1758. By Richard Saunders.* Introduction by Van Wyck Brooks. Illustrations by Norman Rockwell. New York: Limited Editions Club, 1964; rpt. New York: Bonanza Books, 1979. 300 pp.

651. Freeman, Criswell. *Wisdom Made in America. Common Sense and Uncommon Genius from 101 Great Americans.* Nashville, Tennessee: Walnut Grove Press, 1995. 153 pp.

652. Frome, Keith Weller (ed.). *"Hitch Your Wagon to a Star" And Other Quotations by Ralph Waldo Emerson.* New York: Columbia University Press, 1996. 130 pp.

653. Frost, Elizabeth. *The Bully Pulpit. Quotations from America's Presidents.* New York: Facts on File, 1988. 282 pp.

654. Gabel, Marie. "Proverbs of Volga German Settlers in Ellis County." *Heritage of Kansas*, 9, nos. 2-3 (1976), 55-58.

655. Giloi, Dietlinde. *American Talk. Die typischen Redensarten. Ein fröhliches Lehrbuch.* Illustrations by "Much". Frankfurt am Main: Eichborn, 1991. 63 pp.

656. Glazer, Mark. *Flour From Another Sack & Other Proverbs, Folk Beliefs, Tales. Riddles & Recipes. A Collection of [Mexican American] Folklore from the Lower Rio Grande Valley of Texas.* Edinburg, Texas: Pan American University Press, 1982 (2nd ed.1984). 225 pp.

657. Glazer, Mark. *A Dictionary of Mexican American Proverbs.* Westport, Connecticut: Greenwood Press, 1987. 347 pp.

658. Glick, David I. *Proverbs of the Pennsylvania Dutch.* Smoketown, Pennsylvania: Brookshire, 1972. 64 pp.

659. Glickman, Ken. *Deaf Proverbs: A Proverbial Professor's Points to Ponder.* Silver Springs, Maryland: DEAFinitely Yours Studio, 1999. 250 pp. (anti-proverbs).

660. Goldin, Hyman E. *Dictionary of American Underworld Lingo.* New York: Twayne, 1950. 327 pp.

661. Goldman, Alex J. *The Truman Wit.* New York: The Citadel Press, 1966. 88 pp.

662. Graffagnino, J. Kevin, and H. Nicholas Muller (eds.). *The Quotable Ethan Allen*. Barre, Vermont: Vermont Historical Society, 2005. 70 pp.

663. Griessman, Gene. *The Words Lincoln Lived By. 52 Timeless Principles to Light Your Path*. New York: Fireside, 1997. 144 pp.

664. Groom, Winston. *Gumpisms. The Wit and Wisdom of Forrest Gump*. New York: Pocket Books, 1994. 88 pp.

665. Gross, Anthony. *The Wit and Wisdom of Abraham Lincoln*. New York: Barnes & Noble, 1992. 224 pp.

666. Guzzetta-Jones, Angeline, Joseph Antinoro-Polizzi, and Carl Zollo. *Diceva la Mia Honna ... [My Grandmother Used to Say ...]*. Rochster, New York: Flower City Printing, 1972. 40 pp.

667. Guzzetta-Jones, Angeline, Joseph Antinoro-Polizzi, and Carl Zollo. *We Remember ... A Collection of 200 Years of Golden Sayings of Some of the Ethnic Groups that Made America Great*. Rochester, New York: Flower City Priunting, 1975. 54 pp. With illustrations.

668. Haan, Marina N., and Richard B. Hammerstrom. *Graffiti in the Big Ten*. Madison, Wisconsin: Brown House Galleries, 1980. 161 pp.

669. Hall, Terry, and Gregg Stebben. *Cowboy Wisdom*. New York: Warner Books, 1995. 148 pp. With illustrations.

670. Halpert, Herbert. "Proverbial Comparisons from Idaho Territory." *Western Folklore*, 6 (1947), 379-380.

671. Halpert, Herbert. "Proverbial Comparisons from West Tennessee." *Tennessee Folklore Society Bulletin*, 17 (1951), 49-61; and 18 (1952), 15-21.

672. Halpert, Herbert. "Some Wellerisms from Kentucky and Tennessee." *Journal of American Folklore*, 69 (1956), 115-122.

673. Hamilton, Kim, and Dana Holcomb. "Old Time Expressions [of the Appalachian Area]." *Foxfire*, 13 (1979), 69-72.

674. Hand, Wayland D. "Perverted Proverbs." *Western Folklore*, 27 (1968), 263-264. (anti-proverbs).

675. Hanford, G.L. "Metaphor and Simile in American Folk-Speech." *Dialect Notes*, 5 (1918-1927), 149-180; and 289-291 (addenda from B.Q. Morgan).

676. Hannaford, Peter (ed.). *The Quotable Calvin Coolidge: Sensible Words for a New Century*. Bennington, Vermont: Images from the Past, 2001. 183 pp.

677. Hardie, Margaret. "Proverbs and Proverbial Expressions Current in the United States East of the Missouri and North of the Ohio Rivers." *American Speech*, 4 (1929), 461-472.

678. Harmon, Marion F. "Old Sayings." In M.F. Harmon. *Negro Wit and Humor*. Louisville, Kentucky: Harmon Publishing Co., 1914. 121-122.

679. Harnsberger, Caroline Thomas. *Treasury of Presidential Quotations*. Chicago: Follett Publishing Co., 1964. 419 pp.

680. Heinlein, Robert A. *The Notebooks of Lazarus Long*. Illustrations by D.F. Vassallo. New York: G.P. Putnam's Sons, 1978. 63 pp. (aphorisms and anti-proverbs).

681. Hendricks, George D. "Texas Wellerisms." *Journal of American Folklore*, 69 (1956), 356.

682. Hendricks, George D. "Texas Folk Similes." *Western Folklore*, 19 (1960), 245-262.

683. Hendricks, George D. "Texas Folk Proverbs." *Western Folklore*, 21 (1962), 92.

684. Hendrickson, Robert. *Whistlin' Dixie: A Dictionary of Southern Expressions*. New York: Facts on File, 1992. 251 pp.

685. Hendrickson, Robert. *Happy Trails. A Dictionary of Western Expressions*. New York: Facts on File, 1994. 274 pp.

686. Hendrickson, Robert. *Yankee Talk: A Dictionary of New England Expressions*. New York: Facts on File, 1996. 255 pp.

687. Hendrickson, Robert. *Mountain Range. A Dictionary of Expressions from Appalachia to the Ozarks*. New York: Facts on File, 1997. 147 pp.

688. Hendrickson, Robert. *New Yawk Tawk. A Dictionary of New York City Expressions*. New York: Facts on File, 1998. 181 pp.

689. Hendrickson, Robert. *American Regionalisms. Local Expressions from Coast to Coast*. New York: Facts on File, 2000. 786 pp.

690. Hertzog, Phares H. "Proverbial Comparisons, Proverbs, Beliefs, Sayings, and Advice." *Pennyslvania Dutch Folklore*. Ed.

Elmer L. Smith. Lebanon, Pennsylvania: Applied Arts Publishers, 1960. 38-42.

691. Hertzog, Phares H. "Proverbs, Sayings, and Advice." In P.H. Hertzog. *The Favorite Songs, Sayings and Stories of a Pennsylvania Dutchman*. Lebanon, Pennsylvania: Applied Arts Publishers, 1966. 32-34.

692. Herzig, Tina, and Horst Herzig (eds.). *Weisheiten der Indianer*. Photographs by Christian Heeb. Würzburg: Flechsig, 2005. 40 pp.

693. Hines, Donald M. "Wry Wit and Frontier Humor – The Wellerism in the Inland Pacific Northwest." *Southern Folklore Quartely*, 35 (1971), 15-26.

694. Hirsch, E.D. *Cultural Literacy. What Every American Needs to Know*. With an Appendix "What Literate Americans Know" by E.D. Hirsch, Joseph Kett, and James Trefil. Boston: Houghton Mifflin Co., 1987. 251 pp.

695. Hirsch, E.D., Joseph Kett, and James Trefil. *The Dictionary of Cultural Literacy: What Every American Needs to Know*. Boston: Houghton Mifflin Co., 1988. 586 pp. (proverbs, pp. 46-57; idioms, pp. 58-80).

696. Hoffman, W.J. "Folk-Lore of the Pennsylvania Germans." *Journal of American Folklore*, 2 (1889), 191-202 (proverbs, pp. 197-202).

697. Holder, R.W. *A Dictionary of American and British Euphemisms*. Bath: Bath University Press, 1987. Rpt. as *The Faber Dictionary of Euphemisms*. London: Faber and Faber, 1989. 408 pp.

698. Hollenbach, Ida V. "Proverbs." *Pennsylvania Dutchman*, 2, no. 1 (1950), 2.

699. Horne, Abraham Reeser. "Shprich-Werder: Proverbs in Use Among Pennsylvania Germans." In A.R. Horne. *Pennsylvania German Manuel for Pronouncing, Speaking and Writing English. A Guide Book for Schools and Families*. Kutztown, Pennsylvania: Urick & Gehring, 1875. 31-36.

700. Horne, Abraham Reeser. "Proverb and Sayings of the Pennsylvania-Germans." *Pennsylvania-German Society Proceedings*, 2 (1892), 47-54.

701. Horne, Abraham Reeser. "Schrpichwadde." *A Pennsylvania German Anthology*. Ed. Earl C. Haag. Selinsgrove, Pennsylvania: Susquehanna University Press, 1988. 85-86.

702. Hoskins, Lotte (ed.). *"I Have a Dream": The Quotations of Martin Luther King Jr..* New York: Grosset & Dunlap, 1968. 154 pp.

703. Hubbard, Elbert. *Elbert Hubbard's Scrap Book Containing the Inspired and Inspiring Selections, Gathered During a Life Time of Discriminating Reading for His Own Use.* New York: William H. Wise, 1923. 240 pp.

704. Hubbard, Elbert. *A Thousand & One Epigrams and The Roycroft Shop: A History.* East Aurora, New York: The Roycrofters, 1911. Rpt. ed Nancy Hubbard Brady. Englewood Cliffs, New Jersey: Prentice-Hall, 1973. 238 pp.

705. Hughes, Muriel J. "Vermont Dialect Expressions." *Vermont History*, 19 (1951), 81-84.

706. Hughes, Muriel J. "Vermont Proverbial Comparisons and Similes." *Vermont History*, 26 (1958), 257-293.

707. Hughes, Muriel J. "A Word-List from Vermont." *Vermont History*, 27 (1959), 123-167.

708. Hughes, Muriel J. "Vermont Proverbs and Proverbial Sayings." *Vermont History*, 28 (1960), 113-142 and 200-230.

709. Hummerding, Pearl. *Grandma Always Said ... The Little Book of Farm Country Wisdom.* Photographs by J.C. Allen. Stillwater, Minnesota: Voyageur Press, 2001. 108 pp.

710. Hurd, Charles. *A Treasury of Great American Quotations.* New York: Hawthorn Books, 1964. 319 pp.

711. Hyatt, Harry Middleton. *Folk-Lore from Adams County Illinois.* New York: Memoirs of the Alma Egan Hyatt Foundation, 1935. 723 pp. (primarily weather proverbs and superstitions).

712. Irwin, Godfrey (ed.). *American Tramp and Underworld Slang.* New York: Sears Publishing Company, 1931; rpt. Detroit: Gale Research Company, 1971. 264 pp.

713. Jente, Richard. "German Proverbs Collected in Los Angeles." *California Folklore Quarterly*, 4 (1945), 432-434.

714. Jordan, Gilbert J. "Proverbs, Admonitions, and Picturesque Expressions." In G.J. Jordan. *German Texana: A Bilingual Collection of Traditional Materials.* Austin, Texas: Eakin Press, 1980. 124-135.

715. Joseph, Michael (ed.). *"Man Is the Only Animal that Blushes …or Needs to": The Wisdom of Mark Twain*. Los Angeles, California: Stanyan Books, 1970. 51 pp. With illustrations.

716. Kacirk, Jeffrey. *Informal English: Puncture Ladies, Egg Harbors, Mississippi Marbles, and Other Curious Words and Phrases of North America*. New York: Touchstone, 2005. 239 pp. With illustrations.

717. Kammerer, Kristen, and Bridget Snyder. *Wisdom from the Walls: The Greatest Graffiti Ever Scrawled*. New York: Boulevard Books, 1995. 83 pp.

718. Kammerman, Roy. *Poor Richard's [Nixon] Watergate*. Los Angeles, California: Price, Stern, Sloan Publishers, 1973. 60 pp. With Illustrations.

719. Kandel, Howard. *The Power of Positive Pessimism. Proverbs for Our Times*. Illustrations by Frank Page. Los Angeles: Price, Stern, Sloan Publishers, 1964 (9th ed. 1976). 44 pp. (anti-proverbs).

720. Kelly-Gangi, Carol (ed.). *Essential African American Wisdom*. New York: Fall River Press, 2009. 143 pp.

721. Kerschen, Lois. *American Proverbs About Women: A Reference Guide*. Westport, Connecticut: Greenwood Press, 1998. 200 pp.

722. Keyes, Ralph (ed.). *The Wit & Wisdom of Harry Truman. A Treasury of Quotations, Anecdotes, and Observations*. New York: HarperCollins, 1995. 200 pp.

723. Kieffer, Jarold. *What Are Those Crazy Americans Saying? An Easy Way to Understand Thousands of American Expressions*. Fairfax, Virginia: Kieffer Publications, 1989 (2nd ed. 1990; 3rd ed. 1998). 472 pp.

724. Kin, David (pseud. David George Plotkin). *Dictionary of American Maxims*. New York: Philosophical Library, 1955. 597 pp.

725. Kin, David (pseud. David George Plotkin). *Dictionary of American Proverbs*. New York: Philosophical Library, 1955. 286 pp.

726. Kloberdanz, Timothy J., and Rosalinda Kloberdanz. "'Wolgadeitsch ili Kauderwelsch?': Volga German Folk Speech." In T.J. and R. Kloberdanz. *Thunder on the Steppe. Volga German Folklife in a Changing Russia*. Lincoln, Nebraska: American Historical Society of Germans from Russia, 1993 (3rd ed. 2001). 94-118.

727. Klöker, Ralf (ed.). *Don't Say It ... Spray It. American Graffiti*. Illustrations by Peter Balassa. Münster: F. Coppenrath, 1985. 81 pp.

728. Knecht, George. "Proverbs." *Pennsylvania Dutchman*, 1, no. 13 (1949), 2; and 1, no. 14 (1949), 2.

729. Knortz, Karl. "Amerikanische Sprichwörter und Redensarten." In K. Knortz. *Folkloristische Streifzüge*. Oppeln: Georg Maske, 1899. 210-223.

730. Knortz, Karl. "Proverbs; Folk Speech and Slang; Folk Similes, Metaphors, Curses, Exclamations, and Sayings; Tongue Twisters and Words Which Can Be Read Backwards." In Eleonore Schamschula. *A Pioneer of American Folklore: Karl Knortz and His Collections*. Moscow, Idaho: University of Idaho Press, 1996. 237-272.

731. Koch, William E. "Wellerisms from Kansas." *Western Folklore*, 18 (1959), 180; and 19 (1960), 196.

732. Koch, William E. "Proverbs and Riddles." *Kansas Folklore*. Eds. Samuel J. Sackett and W.E. Koch. Lincoln, Nebraska: University of Nebraska Press, 1961. 87-88 and 90-103.

733. Kossman, Leonid. *1000 American Idioms and Their Russian Equivalents / 1000 Amerikanskikh vyrazhenii i ikh russkie sootvetstviia*. New York: Russian Phototypesetting Corporation, 1979. 79 pp.

734. Kossman, Leonid. *American Slang Terms and Colloquialisms. A Practical Manual for Russian Speakers / Amerikanskie slengovye i razgovornye vyrazheniia. Prakticheskoe posobie dlia govoriashchikh po-russki*. New York: Privately printed, 1987. 85 pp.

735. Langer, Howard J. *American Indian Quotations*. Westport, Connecticut: Greenwood Press, 1996. 260 pp.

736. Leibenguth, Albert. "Proverbs." *Pennsylvania Dutchman*, 1, no. 8 (1949), 2.

737. Lenz, Peter, and Aurora Lucy Lenz-Watson (eds.). *Lost & Forgotten Maine-New England Folk & Literary Sayings, Expressions, Terms, Wit, Wisdom, Charm & History*. Norway, Maine: Peter Lenz, 2000. 102 pp.

738. Leonhardt, Wolfram, and Susan Rambow. *Amerikanisch im Alltag. Alphabetisch geordnetes Nachschlagewerk von amerikanischen Sentenzen, Sprichwörtern, Phrasen, Floskeln, Redewendungen, Zitaten und Formeln*. Wiesbaden: VMA-Verlag, 1989. 128 pp.

739. Lewis, Gerald E. *How to Talk Yankee*. Illustrations by Tim Sample. Thorndike, Maine: Thorndike Press, 1986. 57 pp.

740. Lewis, Edward, and Jack Belck (eds.). *The Living Words of Abraham Lincoln*. Kansas City, Missouri: Hallmark Editions, 1967. 62 pp.

741. Lewis, Edward, and Robert Myers (eds.). *A Treasury of Mark Twain. The Wit and Wisdom of a Great American Writer*. Illustrations by James Parkinson. Kansas, Missouri: Hallmark Editions, 1967. 60 pp.

742. Lewis, Edward, and Richard Rhodes (eds.). *John F. Kennedy. Words to Remember*. Kansas City, Missouri: Hallmark Editions, 1967. 59 pp. With illustrations.

743. Lichty, Verna, and Nancy Martin. "Pennsylvania German Sayings." *Journal of the Center for Pennsylvania German Studies*, 8, no. 2 (2001), 18-19.

744. Lighter, Jonathan E. (ed.). *Random House Historical Dictionary of American Slang*. 2 vols. New York: Random House, 1994 and 1997. I, A-G, 1006 pp.; II, H-O, 736 pp. (3rd vol. never appeared)

745. Liu, Paul, and Robert Vasselli. *Proverbial Twists: Modern Day Updates to Some of the World's Most Famous Proverbs and Quotes*. Highland Park, New Jersey: Johanne Inc., 1996. 158 pp. (anti-proverbs).

746. Loomis, C. Grant. "Traditional American Word Play: Wellerisms or Yankeeisms." *Western Folklore*, 8 (1949), 1-21.

747. Loomis, C. Grant. "Traditional American Wordplay: The Epigram and Perverted Proverbs." *Western Folklore*, 8 (1949), 348-357.

748. Loomis, C. Grant. "Wellerisms in California Sources." *Western Folklore*, 14 (1955), 229-245.

749. Loomis, C. Grant. "American Pre-Weller Wellerisms." *Western Folklore*, 16 (1957), 51-52.

750. Loomis, C. Grant. "Proverbs in Business." *Western Folklore*, 23 (1964), 91-94.

751. Loomis, C. Grant. "Proverbial Phrases in Journalistic Wordplay." *Western Folklore*, 23 (1964), 187-189.

752. Lopez, Benjamin. *Dichos Folklóricos*. Texas City, Texas: College of the Mainland, 1978. 35 pp.

753. Lott, Noah. *Silly Syclopedia [sic]*. Illustrations by Louis F. Grant. New York: G.W. Dillingham, 1905. 159 pp. (anti-proverbs).

754. Mabry, Edward Loughlin. *Photo Finish*. Chicopee, Massachusetts: Pond-Ekberg Company, 1986. 95 pp. (aphorisms and anti-proverbs).

755. Macon, John Alfred. "Aphorisms [Proverbs] from the [Slave] Quarters." In J.A. Macon. *Unce Gabe Tucker; or Reflections, Song, and Sentiment in the Quarters*. Philadelphia: Lippincott, 1883. 131-147.

756. Mahoney, Kathleen (ed.). *Simple Wisdom: Shaker Sayings, Poems, and Songs*. Photographs by Lilo Raymond. New York: Viking Studio Books, 1993. 96 pp.

757. Maitland, James. *The American Slang Dictionary. Embodying All American and English Slang Phrases in Current Use, with Their Derivation and Philology*. Chicago: R.J. Kittredge, 1891. 308 pp.

758. Major, Clarence. *Dictionary of Afro-American Slang*. New York: International Publishers, 1970. 127 pp.

759. Major, Clarence. *Juba to Jive. A Dictionary of African-American Slang*. New York: Penguin Books, 1994. 548 pp.

760. Makkai, Adam. *A Dictionary of American Idioms*. New York: Barron's Educational Series, 1987. 398 pp.

761. Makkai, Adam. *Handbook of Commonly Used American Idioms*. Woodbury, New York: Barron's Educational Series, 1984. 296 pp.

762. Malone, Kemp. "Negro Proverbs from Maryland." *American Speech*, 4 (1929), 285.

763. Marcus, Eric (ed.). *Pessimisms. Famous (and not so Famous) Observations, Quotations, Thoughts, and Ruminations on What to Expect When You're Expecting the Worst*. New York: CDS Books, 2003. 160 pp. With illustrations. (anti-proverbs).

764. Mathews, Mitford M. *A Dictionary of Americanisms on Historical Principles*. Chicago: University of Chicago Press, 1951 (4th impression 1966). 1946 pp.

765. Mathews, Mitford M. *Americanisms: A Dictionary of Selected Americanisms on Historical Principles*. Chicago: University of Chicago Press, 1966. 304 pp.

766. McCleary, John Bassett. *The Hippie Dictionary. A Cultural Encyclopedia (and Phraseicon) of the 1960s and 1970s.* Berkeley, California: Ten Speed Press, 2004. 704 pp.

767. McIntyre, Gail (ed.). *Our Book of Proverbs (1993).* By the Second Grade Rochester Elementary School. Rochester, Vermont: Rochester Elementary School, 1993. 18 pp. (varied proverbs by children).

768. McNeil, William K. "Folklore from Big Flat, Arkansas, Part III: Proverbs and Proverbial Phrases." *Mid-American Folklore,* 12 (1984), 27-30.

769. Mead, Jane Thompson. "Proverbs: Sayings from Westfield, Chautauqua Co." *New York Folklore Quarterly,* 10 (1954), 226-227.

770. Meredith, Mamie. "Prairie Schooner Slogans." *American Speech,* 7 (1932), 172-174.

771. Mickenberg, Risa (ed.). *Taxi Driver Wisdom.* Photographs by Joanne Dugan. San Francisco: Chronicle Books, 1996. 171 pp.

772. Mieder, Wolfgang. *Talk Less and Say More: Vermont Proverbs.* Illustrations by Mary Azarian. Shelburne, Vermont: The New England Press, 1986. 64 pp.

773. Mieder, Wolfgang. *As Sweet as Apple Cider. Vermont Expressions.* Illustrations by Mary Azarian. Shelburne, Vermont: The New England Press, 1988. 72 pp.

774. Mieder, Wolfgang. *American Proverbs: A Study of Texts and Contexts.* Bern: Peter Lang, 1989. 394 pp. With illustrations.

775. Mieder, Wolfgang. *Yankee Wisdom: New England Proverbs.* Illustrations by Elayne Sears. Shelburne, Vermont: The New England Press, 1989. 72 pp.

776. Mieder, Wolfgang. *As Strong as a Moose: New England Expressions.* Illustrations by Elayne Sears. Shelburne, Vermont: The New England Press, 1997. 87 pp.

777. Mieder, Wolfgang. *The Proverbial Abraham Lincoln: An Index to Proverbs in the Works of Abraham Lincoln.* New York: Peter Lang, 2000. 209 pp.

778. Mieder, Wolfgang. *"No Struggle, No Progress". Frederick Douglass and His Proverbial Rhetoric for Civil Rights.* New York: Peter Lang, 2001. 532 pp. (proverb index, pp. 105-532)

779. Mieder, Wolfgang. *"Yes We Can". Barack Obama's Proverbial Rhetoric.* New York: Peter Lang, 2009. 362 pp. (proverb index, pp. 161-344).

780. Mieder, Wolfgang. *"Making a Way Out of No Way". Martin Luther King's Sermonic Proverbial Rhetoric.* New York: Peter Lang, 2010. 559 pp. (proverb index, pp. 207-541).

781. Mieder, Wolfgang, and George B. Bryan. *The Proverbial Harry S. Truman: An Index to Proverbs in the Works of Harry S. Truman.* New York: Peter Lang, 1997. 247 pp.

782. Mieder, Wolfgang, Stewart A. Kingsbury, and Kelsie B. Harder (eds.). *A Dictionary of American Proverbs.* New York: Oxford University Press, 1992. Paperback edition New York: Oxford University Press, 1996. 726 pp.

783. Miller, Donald L. *From George ... to George. 200 Years of Presidential Quotations.* Washington, D.C.: Braddock Communications, 1989. 156 pp. With illustrations.

784. Miller, Peter (ed.). *Yankee Weather Proverbs.* Illustrations by Christine Gerrish. Waterbury, Vermont: Vermont People Books, 1992. 56 pp. (miniature book).

785. Miller, Peter (ed.). *Yankee Weather Proverbs.* Illustrations by Daryl V. Storrs. Colbyville, Vermont: Silver Print Press, 2004. 88 pp.

786. Mintz, Morton (ed.). *Quotations from President Ron [Reagan].* New York: St. Martin's Press, 1986. 58 pp.

787. Mitchell, Roger. "Farm Talk from Marathon County." *Midwestern Journal of Language and Folklore*, 10, nos. 1-2 (1984), 146-167; rpt in *Wisconsin Folklore*. Ed. James P. Leary. Madison, Wisconsin: University of Wisconsin Press, 1998. 89-105.

788. Mitchener, Joseph J. *River Dance Rhyme.* Salinas, California: River Dance Society, 1990. 56 pp. (miniature book). (aphorisms and anti-proverbs).

789. Molera, Frances M. "California Spanish Proverbs." *Western Folklore*, 6, no. 1 (1947), 65-67.

790. Montana, Gladiola. *Never Ask a Man the Size of His Spread: A Cowgirl's Guide to Life.* With illustrations by Bonnie Cazier, Thomas J. Sanker, and Will James. Salt Lake City, Utah: Peregrine Smith Books, 1993. 138 pp.

791. Monteiro, George. "Proverbs and Proverbial Phrases of the Continental Portuguese [in the United States]." *Western Folklore*, 22 (1963), 19-45.

792. Monteiro, George. "As palavras são como as cerejas: umas puxam as outras. Proverbs of Mainland Portuguese in the United States." *Revista de Etnografia*, 11, no. 21 (1968), 33-68.

793. Mook, Maurice A. "Northwestern Pennsylvania Wellerisms." *Journal of American Folklore*, 70 (1957), 183-184.

794. Moore, Gary. *Spiritual Investments: Wall Street Wisdom from the Career of Sir John Templeton*. Radnor, Pennsylvania: Templeton Foundation Press, 1998. 121 pp.

795. Mullane, Deirdre (ed.). *Words to Make My Dream Children Live. A Book of African American Quotations*. New York: Anchor Books, 1995. 531 pp.

796. Mumford, Ethel Watts, Oliver Merford, and Addison Mizner. *The Revived Cynic's Calendar! The Ax to the Axiom!* San Francisco: Paul Elder, 1917. No pp. (many parodied proverbs).

797. Munro, Pamela (ed.). *Slang U. Official Dictionary of College Slang*. New York: Harmony Books, 1989. 244 pp.

798. Nussbaum, Stan. *The ABC of American Culture: First Steps toward Understanding the American People through Their Common Sayings and Proverbs*. Colorado Springs, Colorado: Global Mapping International, 1998. 55 pp.

799. Nussbaum, Stan. *American Cultural [and Proverbial] Baggage. How to Recognize and Deal with It*. Maryknoll, New York: Orbis Books, 2005. 160 pp.

800. Odell, Ruth. "Nebraska Smart Sayings." *Southern Folklore Quarterly*, 12 (1948), 185-195.

801. Otis, Harry B. (ed.). *Simple Truths. The Best of "The Cockle Bur". A Collection of Wit, Wisdom, Humor and Beauty*. Illustrations by Larri Munderloh. Kansas City, Missouri: Andrews and McMeel, 1990. 250 pp.

802. Parks, Taylor E., and Lois F. Parks (eds.). *Memorable Quotations of Franklin D. Roosevelt*. New York: Thomas Y. Crowell, 1965. 276 pp.

803. Pearce, Helen. "Folk Sayings in a Pioneer Family of Western Oregon." *California Folklore Quarterly*, 5 (1946), 229-242.

804. Pearce, T.M. "The English Proverb in New Mexico." *California Folklore Quartely*, 5 (1946), 350-354.

805. Pérez, Soledad. "Dichos from Austin [Texas]." *Texas Folk and Folklore*. Eds. Mody C. Boatright, Wilson M. Hudson, and Allen Maxwell. Dallas, Texas: Southern Methodist University Press, 1954. 223-229.

806. Perkins, Anne E. "Vanishing Expressions of the Maine Coast." *American Speech*, 3 (1927), 134-141.

807. Person, Henry. "Proverbs and Proverbial Lore from the State of Washington." *Western Folklore*, 17 (1958), 176-185.

808. Pierron, Louis. "Deutsche Sprichwörter: German Sayings in Milwaukee." *Wisconsin Folklore*. Ed. James P. Leary. Madison, Wisconsin: University of Wisconsin Press, 1998. 42-48 (rpt. from an unpublished report of 1936).

809. Platt, Suzy. *Respectfully Quoted: A Dictionary of Quotations from the Library of Congress*. Washington, D.C.: Congressional Quarterly, 1992. Rpt. as *Respectfully Quoted: A Dictionary of Quotations*. New York: Barnes & Noble, 1993. 520 pp.

810. Polve, Adella. "Utah Folksay." *Utah Humanities Review*, 1 (1947), 300-301.

811. Porter, Kenneth. "Some Central Kansas Wellerisms." *Midwest Folklore*, 8 (1958), 158-160.

812. Pound, Louise. "Proverbs and Phrases [from Massachusetts]." *Journal of American Folklore*, 5 (1892), 60.

813. Pound, Louise. "American Euphemisms for Dying, Death, and Burial. An Anthology." *American Speech*, 11, no. 3 (1936), 195-202.

814. Powers, Nick. *Barefoot in Boogar Hollow: Yestiday's Sayin's to Liv [sic] by Today*. Illustrations by William Powers. Lindale, Georgia: Country Originals, 1971. 48 pp.

815. Prahlad, Sw. Anand (Dennis Folly). *African-American Proverbs in Context*. Jackson, Mississippi: University of Mississippi Press, 1996. 306 pp. (proverb index, pp. 204-260).

816. Prahlad, Sw. Anand (Dennis Folly). *Reggae Wisdom: Proverbs in Jamaican Music*. Jackson, Mississippi: University Press of Mississippi, 2001. 302 pp. (proverb index, pp. 234-273).

817. Preston, Dennis R. "Proverbial Comparisons from Southern Indiana." *Orbis: Bulletin international de documentation linguistique*, 24 (1975), 72-114.

818. Price, Barbara Wells (ed.). *Early American Wisdom: Good Thoughts from Yesterday to Think about Today*. Illustrations by Susan Tinker. Kansas City, Missouri: Hallmark, 1974. 44 pp.

819. Price-Thompson, Tracy, and TaRessa Stovall (eds.). *Proverbs for the People. An Anthology of Contemporary African-American Stories*. New York: Kensington Publishing, 2003. 494 pp. (56 short stories based on proverbs).

820. Ramirez, Manuel D. "Italian Folklore from Tampa, Florida: Proverbs." *Southern Folklore Quarterly*, 13 (1949), 121-132.

821. Randolph, Vance, and George P. Wilson. *Down in the Holler: A Gallery of Ozark Folk Speech*. Norman, Oklahoma: University of Oklahoma Press, 1953. 314 pp. (sayings and wisecracks pp. 172-222).

822. Rawson, Hugh, and Margaret Miner. *The Oxford Dictionary of American Quotations*. New York: Oxford University Press, 2006. 898 pp.

823. Read, Allen Walker. *Classic American Graffiti*. Paris: Privately printed, 1935; rpt. Waukesha, Wisconsin: Maledicta Press, 1977. 83 pp.

824. Reagan, Michael (ed.). *In the Words of Ronald Reagan. The Wit, Wisdom, and Eternal Optimism of America's 40th President*. Nashville, Tennessee: Thomas Nelson, 2004. 209 pp.

825. Reitman, Judith (ed.). *American Proverbs*. Illustrations by Barbara Smolover. New York: Hippocrene Books, 2000. 107 pp.

826. Robertson, James I. (ed.). *Stonewall Jackson's Book of Maxims*. Nashville, Tennessee: Cumberland House, 2002. 144 pp.

827. Rogak, Lisa (ed.). *Barack Obama in His Own Words*. New York: Carroll & Graf, 2007. 169 pp.

828. Roger, E.G. "Popular Sayings of Marshall County [Tennessee]." *Tennessee Folklore Society Bulletin*, 15 (1949), 70-75.

829. Rosenberger, Jesse Leonard. "Proverbs and Superstitions." *The Pennsylvania Germans*. Chicago: University of Chicago Press, 1923. 127-138.

830. Rosten, Leo. *Rome Wasn't Burned in a Day. The Mischief of Language.* Illustrations by Rob't Day. Garden City, New York: Doubleday, 1972. 189 pp. (anti-proverbs).

831. Roth, Herb (ed.). *Poor Richard's Almanack. Being the Choicest Morsels of "Wisdom", Written During the Years of the Almanack's Publication, By that Well-known "Savant", Dr. Benjamin Franklin of Philadelphia.* Mount Vernon, New York: Peter Pauper Press, 1936 (2nd ed. 1980). 77 pp.

832. Rowsome, Frank. *The Verse by the Side of the Road. The Story of the Burma-Shave Signs and Jingles.* Illustrations by Carl Rose. Brattleboro, Vermont: Stephen Greene Press, 1965. 121 pp. (collection of texts, pp. 71-121).

833. Russell, Thomas Herbert (ed.). *The Sayings of Poor Richard: Wit, Wisdom and Humor of Benjamin Franklin in the Proverbs and Maxims of Poor Richard's Almanacks for 1733 to 1758.* Chicago: Veterans fo Foreign Wars of the United States, 1926. 39 pp. Rpt. Chicago: E.T. Kelly, 1926. 47 pp.

834. Safian, Louis A. *The Book of Updated Proverbs.* New York: Abelard-Schuman, 1967. 64 pp. (anti-proverbs).

835. Sandburg, Carl. "Nut Proverbs and Folk Ways and Says." *Fables, Foibles, and Foobles by Carl Sandburg.* Ed. George Hendrick. Illustrations by George Hendrick. Urbana, Illinois: University of Illinois Press, 1988. 109-120. (proverbs and anti-proverbs).

836. Schmidt, Curt E. "Sprichwörter (Proverbs – Adages)." In C.E. Schmidt. *Oma & Opa: German-Texas Pioneers.* New Braunfels, Texas: Folkways Publishing, 1975. 53-57.

837. Schulz, Charles M. (ill.). *Snoopy's Philosophy.* Kansas City, Missouri: Hallmark, 1967. 48 pp. (comics).

838. Schutz, Stephen (ed.). *Poor Richard's Quotations: Being a Collection of Quotations from Poor Richard Almanacks, Published by Benjamin Franklin in the Years of Our Lord, 1733 though 1758.* Boulder, Colorado: Blue Mountain Arts, 1975. 77 pp. With illustrations.

839. Seely, Hart (ed.). *Pieces of Intelligence. The Existential Poetry of Donald H. Rumsfeld.* New York: The Free Press, 2003. 118 pp.

840. Settel, T.S. (ed.). *The Quotable Harry S Truman*. Anderson, South Carolina: Droke House, 1967; rpt. New York: Berkley Publishing Corp., 1975. 186 pp.

841. Shaffer, J. Frank. *Frankly Speaking*. Atlanta, Georgia: Gunter Publishing, 1994. 105 pp. With Illustrations. (aphorisms and anti-proverbs).

842. Shankle, George Earlie. *American Mottoes and Slogans*. New York: The H.W. Wilson Company, 1941. 183 pp.

843. Shaw, Susanna (ed.). *Women in the John. A Collection of Graffiti from the Women's Room*. Berkeley, California: Creative Arts Book, 1980. 64 pp.

844. Shelton, Ferne (ed.). *Pioneer Superstitions. Old-Timey Signs and Sayings*. Collected by Helen K. Moore. High Point, North Carolina : Hutcraft, 1969. 24 pp.

845. Shelton, Ferne (ed.). *Pioneer Proverbs. Wit and Wisdom From Early America*. Collected by Mary Turner. High Point, North Carolina: Hutcraft, 1971. 24 pp.

846. Shoemaker, Henry Wharton, *Scotch-Irish and English Proverbs and Sayings of the West Branch Valley of Central Pennyslvania*. Reading, Pennsylvania: Reading Eagle Press, 1927. 24 pp.

847. Shoemaker, William P. "Proverbs." *Pennsylvania Dutchman*, 1, no. 9 (1949), 2.

848. Slung, Michele. *Momilies. As My Mother Used to Say ....* New York: Ballantine Books, 1985 (4th ed. 1986). 88 pp. With illustrations. (aphorisms and anti-proverbs).

849. Slung, Michele. *More Momiles. As My Mother Used to Say ....* New York: Ballantine Books, 1986. 88 pp. With illustrations. (aphorisms and anti-proverbs).

850. Slung, Michele. *Momiles & More Momilies. As My Mother Used to Say….* New York: Ballantine Books, 1987. 180 pp. With illustrations. (aphorisms and anti-proverbs).

851. Smith, Diann Sutherlin. *Down-Home Talk: An Outrageous Dictionary of Colorful Expressions*. Illustrated by Elwood H. Smith. New York: Collier, 1988. 84 pp.

852. Smith, Morgan, and A.W. Eddins. "Wise Saws from Texas." *Straight Texas*. Eds. J. Frank Dobie and Mody C. Boatright. Dallas,

Texas: Southern Methodist University Press, 1937; rpt. Hatboro, Pennsylvania: Folklore Associates, 1966. 239-244.

853. Smith, Norman A. "Proverbs." *Pennsylvania Dutchman*, 1, no. 12 (1949), 2.

854. Smith, Elmer L. "Proverbs and Sayings – Weather Lore." *Pennsylvania Dutch Folklore*. Ed. E.L. Smith. Lebanon, Pennsylvania: Applied Arts Publishers, 1960. 22-24.

855. Smith, Elmer L. (ed.). *American Proverbs, Maxims & Folk Sayings*. Lebanon, Pennsylvania: Applied Arts Publishers, 1968 (9th printing, 1994). 34 pp. With illustrations.

856. Smitherman, Geneva. *Talkin and Testifyin. The Language of Black America*. Detroit: Wayne State University Press, 1986. 285 pp. (proverbs pp. 245-246).

857. Smitherman, Geneva. *Black Talk: Words and Phrases from the Hood to the Amen Corner*. Boston: Houghton Mifflin Company, 1994. 243 pp.

858. Snapp, Emma Louise. "Proverbial Lore in Nebraska." *University of Nebraska Studies in Language, Literature, and Criticism*, 13 (1933), 51-112.

859. Snavely, Elmer S. "Proverbs." *Pennsylvania Dutchman*, 1, no. 7 (1949), 2.

860. Spalding, Henry D. "Proverbs, Folk Talk and Superstitions." *Encyclopedia of Black Folklore and Humor*. Ed. H.D. Spalding. Middle Village, New York: Jonathan David, 1972. 530-541.

861. Spears, Richard A. *Essential American Idioms*. Lincolnwood, Illinois: National Textbook Company, 1990 (2nd ed. 1996). 247 pp.

862. Spears, Richard A. *Forbidden American English. A Serious Compilation of Taboo American English*. Lincolnwood, Illinois: National Textbook Company, 1990; rpt. Lincolnwood, Illinois: Passport Books, 1995. 225 pp.

863. Spears, Richard A. *NTC's Dictionary of American English Phrases*. Lincolnwood, Illinois: National Textbook Company, 1995. 559 pp.

864. Spears, Richard A. *Hip and Hot! A Dictionary of 10,000 American Slang Expressions*. New York: Gramercy Books, 1998. 555 pp.

865. Spears, Richard A., and Linda Schinke-Llano (eds.). *NTC's American Idioms Dictionary*. Lincolnwood, Illinois: National Textbook Company, 1987. 463 pp.

866. Sperber, Hans, and Travis Trittschuh. *American Political Terms. An Historical Dictionary*. Detroit: Wayne State University Press, 1962. 516 pp.

867. Stark, Judith. *Priceless Proverbs ... from the Tongue of the Young*. Los Angeles, California: Price, Stern, Sloan, 1982. 76 pp. With illustrations. (anti-proverbs).

868. Steiner, Paul (ed.). *The [Adlai] Stevenson Wit & Wisdom. The Wise and Humorous Words of a Distinguished American*. New York: Pyramid Books, 1965. 126 pp. With illustrations.

869. Still, James. *The Wolfpen Notebooks. A Record of Appalachian Life*. Lexington, Kentucky: University Press of Kentucky, 1991. 179 pp. (sayings on pp. 43-143).

870. Stoudt, John Baer. "Weather-Prognostications and Superstitions among the Pennsylvania Germans." *Pennsylvania-German*, 6 (1905), 328-335; and 7 (1906), 242-243.

871. Sullivan, Andrew, and Jacob Weisberg (eds.). *Bushisms. President George Herbert Walker Bush, in His Own Words*. New York: Workman Publishing, 1992. 87 pp. With Illustrations.

872. Sunners, William (ed.). *American Slogans*. New York: The Paebar Company, 1949. 345 pp.

873. Swope, Pierce E. "Proverbs." *Pennsylvania Dutchman*, 1, no. 24 (1950), 2.

874. Taft, Michael. "Proverbs in the Blues: How Frequent is Frequent?" *Proverbium*, 11 (1994), 227-258.

875. Taylor, Archer. *Proverbial Comparisons and Similes from California*. Berkeley, California: University of California Press, 1954. 97 pp.

876. Taylor, Archer. "A Curious List of Americanisms." *American Speech*, 30 (1955), 151-152.

877. Taylor, Archer. "Proverbial Materials in Edward Eggleston *The Hoosier Schoolmaster*." *Studies in Honor of Stith Thompson*. Ed. G.W. Edson Richmond. Bloomington, Indiana: Indiana University Pess, 1957. 262-270.

878. Taylor, Archer. "Americanisms Current in 1845." *Western Folklore*, 17 (1958), 280-281.

879. Taylor, Archer. "More Proverbial Comparisons from California." *Western Folklore*, 17 (1958), 12-20.

880. Taylor, Archer. "Proverbs and Proverbial Phrases in the Writngs of Mary N. Murfree." *Tennessee Folklore Society Bulletin*, 24 (1958), 11-50.

881. Taylor, Archer. "Proverbial Comparisons and Similes in [James Still's] *On Troublesome Creek*." *Kentucky Folklore Record*, 8 (1962), 87-96.

882. Taylor, Archer. "A Few Additional Nineteenth-Century American Proverbs." *North Carolina Folklore*, 13, nos. 1-2 (1965), 37-38.

883. Taylor, Archer, and C. Grant Loomis. "California Proverbs and Sententious Sayings." *Western Folklore*, 10 (1951), 248-249.

884. Taylor, Archer, and Bartlett Jere Whiting. *A Dictionary of American Proverbs and Proverbial Phrases, 1820-1880*. Cambridge, Massachusetts: Harvard University Press, 1958. 418 pp.

885. Thompson, Harold W. "Proverbs." In H.W. Thompson. *Body, Boots & Britches. Folktales, Ballads and Speech from Country New York*. Philadelphia: J.B. Lippincott, 1940; rpt. New York: Dover, 1962; rpt. New York: Syracuse University Press, 1979. 540 pp. (proverbs pp. 481-504).

886. Thompson, Harold W. "Proverbs and Sayings." *New York Folklore Quarterly*, 5 (1949), 230-235 and 296-300.

887. Thurston, Helen M. "Sayings and Proverbs from Massachusetts." *Journal of American Folklore*, 19 (1906), 122.

888. Tidwell, James N. "Wellerisms in *Alexander's Weekly Messenger* [Philadelphia], 1837-1839." *Western Folklore*, 9 (1950), 257-262.

889. Titus, Charles H. "Political Maxims." *California Folklore Quarterly* (= *Western Folklore*), 4 (1945), 377-389.

890. Troyer, Lester O. "Some Proverbs from the Ohio Amish." *Der Reggeboge: Journal of the Pennsylvania German Society*, 27, no. 1 (1993), 24.

891. Tuleja, Tad. *Book of Popular Americana*. New York: Macmillan, 1994. 451 pp.

892. Wagner, Joh. Jacob. *Moralische Probirsteine aus Nord-America oder 800 englische Sentenzen, Denkübungen und Sittensprüche zur Unterhaltung und Belehrung*. Lindenfels: Joh. Jacob Wagner, 1854. 85 pp.

893. Wakefield, Edward. "Wisdom of Gombo [French-based Creole Proverbs from Louisiana]." *The Nineteenth Century*, 30 (1891), 575-582.

894. Weaver, Nevilee Maass. *Rezepte: German-Texan Culinary Art. When Everything Was "Hausgemacht"*. Austin, Texas: Eakin Press, 1999. 128 pp. (with many German/English proverbs).

895. Weigel, Lawrence A. "German Proverbs from Around Fort Hays, Kansas. Courtesy S.J. Sackett." *Western Folklore*, 18 (1959), 98.

896. Weisberg, Jacob (ed.). *George W. Bushisms. The Slate Book of the Accidental Wit and Wisdom of Our Forty-third President*. New York: Fireside, 2001. 96 pp. With illustrations.

897. Weller, Tom. *Minims [sic] or, Man Is the Only Animal Around That Wears Bow Ties*. Boston: Houghton Mifflin Company, 1982. 110 pp. With illustrations. (anti-proverbs).

898. Welsch, Roger L. "Sayings, Proverbs, and Beliefs." *A Treasury of Nebraska Pioneer Folklore*. Ed. Roger L. Welsch. Lincoln, Nebraska: University of Nebraska Press, 1966. 266-280.

899. Wentworth, Harold, and Stuart Berg Flexner. *Dictionary of American Slang*. New York: Thomas Y. Crowell, 1960. 669 pp. Revised ed. New York: Thomas Y. Crowell, 1975. 766 pp.

900. Wentworth, Harold, and Stuart Berg Flexner. *The Pocket Dictionary of American Slang*. New York: Pocket Books, 1968. 414 pp.

901. White, Vallie Tinsley. "Proverbs and Picturesque Speech from Clairborne Parish, Louisiana." *Louisiana Folklore Miscellany*, 2, no. 1 (1962), 85-87.

902. Whiting, Bartlett Jere. "American Wellerisms of the Golden Age." *American Speech*, 20 (1945), 2-11.

903. Whiting, Bartlett Jere. "Proverbial Sayings from *Fisher's River, North Carolina* [by Harden E. Taliaferro]." *Southern Folklore Quarterly*, 11 (1947), 173-185.

904. Whiting, Bartlett Jere. "Lowland Scots and Celtic Proverbs in North Carolina." *Celtic Studies*, 1 (1949), 116-127.

905. Whiting, Bartlett Jere. "Proverbs and Proverbial Sayings [from North Carolina]." *The Frank C. Brown Collection of North Carolina Folklore*. Ed. Newman Ivey White. 7 vols. Durham, North Carolina: Duke University Press, 1952. I, 329-501.

906. Whiting, Bartlett Jere. "Proverbs in Cotton Mather's *Magnalia Christi Americana*." *Neuphilologische Mitteilungen*, 73 (1972), 477-484.

907. Whiting, Bartlett Jere. *Early American Proverbs and Proverbial Phrases*. Cambridge, Massachusetts: Harvard Universlty Press, 1977. 555 pp.

908. Whiting, Bartlett Jere. *Modern Proverbs and Proverbial Sayings*. Cambridge, Massachusetts: Harvard University Press, 1989. 710 pp.

909. Wilder, Roy. *You All Spoken Here*. Illustrations by Glen Rounds. New York: Viking, 1984. 215 pp.

910. Wilgus, D.K. "Proverbial Material from the Western Kentucky Folklore Archive." *Kentucky Folklore Record*, 6 (1960), 47-49.

911. Williams, Derek A. *The Proverbial Zora Neale Hurston: A Study of Texts and Contexts*. Diss. Emory University, 1997. 311 pp. (proverb index, pp. 260-299).

912. Williams, Michael G. *Modern Proverbs*. Bountiful, Utah: Horizon Publishers, 1990. 176 pp. (aphorisms and anti-proverbs).

913. Willson, Frederick Newton. *Paraphrased Proverbs*. Princeton, New Jersey: Graphics Room Edition, 1933. 55 pp. (anti-proverbs).

914. Winick, Stephen D. *The Proverb Process: Intertextuality and Proverbial Innovation in Popular Culture*. Diss. University of Pennsylvania, 1998. 360 pp. With illustrations. (proverb index to Gary Larson's *The Far Side* cartoons, pp. 304-318).

915. Woods, Henry F. *American Sayings: Famous Phrases, Slogans, and Aphorisms*. New York: Duell, Sloan and Pearce, 1945. 310 pp. Revised ed. New York: Perma Giants, 1950. 312 pp.

916. Work, Monroe N. "Geechee [Sea Islands off the Coast of South Carolina] and Other Proverbs." *Journal of American Folklore*, 32 (1919) 441-442.

917. Wortman, Art (ed.). *Will Rogers: Wise and Witty Sayings*. Kansas City, Missouri: Hallmark Editions, 1969. 62 pp. With illustrations.

918. Wu, S.M. (ed.). *The Wit and Wisdom of Benjamin Franklin*. Illustrations by Paul Hoffman. New York: Barnes & Noble, 1995. 87 pp.

919. Yates, Irene. "A Collection of Proverbs and Proverbial Sayings from South Carolina Literature." *Southern Folklore Quarterly*, 11 (1947), 187-199.

920. Yoder, Jacob H. "Proverbial Lore from Hegins Valley [Pennsylvania]." *Pennsylvania Dutchman*, 3, no. 16 (1952), 3.

921. Youngquist, Mary J., and Harry W. Hazard. "Malaproverbs." *Word Ways*, 8 (1975), 255 (anti-proverbs),

922. Zona, Guy A. *"The Soul Would Have no Rainbow, if the Eyes Had no Tears" – and Other Native American Proverbs*. New York: Touchstone Books, 1994. 128 pp.

Arabic Languages

923. Abdelkafi, Mohamed. *One Hundred Arabic Proverbs from Libya*. London: Vernon & Yates, 1968. 100 pp.

924. Al-Amily, Hussain Mohammed. *The Book of Arabic Wisdom. Proverbs & Anecdotes*. Northampton, Massachusetts: Interlink Books, 2005. 199 pp.

925. Arnander, Primrose, and Ashkhain Skipwith (eds.). *The Son of a Duck is a Floater and Other Arab Sayings with English Equivalents*. Illustrations by Kathryn Lamb. London: Stacey International, 1985. 90 pp.

926. Bailey, Clinton. *A Culture of Desert Survival. Bedouin Proverbs from Sinai and the Negev*. New Haven, Connecticut: Yale University Press, 2004. 478 pp.

927. Bobzin, Hartmut (ed.). *1001 Alt-arabische Sprichwörter*. Deutsch von Friedrich Rückert. Wiesbaden: Otto Harrassowitz, 1988. 119 pp.

928. Böhm, Richard. *Die Weisheit der Völker. I. Sprüche der Araber*. Wiesbaden: Wiesbadener Graphische Betriebe, 1960. 25 pp.

929. Brunner, Hellmut. "Sprichwörter." In H. Brunner. *Altägyptische Weisheit. Lehren für das Leben*. Zürich: Artemis, 1988. 421-422.

930. Burckhardt, John Lewis. *Arabic Proverbs, or the Manners and Customs of the Modern Egyptians, Illustrated from Their Proverbial Sayings Current in Cairo.* London: John Murray, 1830; rpt. with the title *Arabic Proverbs.* Mineola, New York: Dover Publications, 2004. 283 pp.

931. Burckhardt, Johann Lewis. *Arabische Sprüchwörter oder die Sitten und Gebräuche der neueren Ägypter erklärt aus den zu Kairo umlaufenden Sprüchwörtern.* Deutsch mit einigen Anmerkungen und Registern von H.G. Kirmβ. Weimar: Verlag des Landes-Industrie-Comptoirs, 1834. 396 pp.

932. Dévényi, Kinga. "Omani Proverbs: Date Palms and Dates." *Essays in Honor of Alexander Fodor.* Eds. K. Dévényi and Tamás Iványi. Budapest: Eötvös Loránd University, 2001. 29-46.

933. Elkhadem, Saad. *Egyptian Proverbs and Popular Sayings.* Fredericton, New Brunswick: York Press, 1987. 28 pp.

934. Elkhadem, Saad. *Old Arabic Sayings, Similes, and Metaphors.* Fredericton, New Brunswick: York Press, 1991. 58 pp.

935. Elkhadem, Saad. *Life is Like a Cucumber: Colloquial Egyptian Proverbs, Coarse Sayings and Popular Expressions.* Fredericton, New Brunswick: York Press, 1993. 161 pp.

936. Freya, Anis. *A Dictionary of Modern Lebanese Proverbs.* Beirut: Librairie du Liban, 1974. 748 pp.

937. Goitein, S.D.F. *Jemenica: Sprichwörter und Redensarten aus Zentral-Jemen mit zahlreichen Sach- und Worterklärungen.* Leiden: E.J. Brill, 1970. 194 pp.

938. Hankí, Joseph. *Arabic Proverbs With Side by Side English Translations.* New York: Hippocrene Books, 1998. 129 pp.

939. Lane-Poole, Stanley (ed.). *Sayings of Mohammed.* Illustrations by Boyd Hanna. Mount Vernon, New York: Peter Pauper Press, 1958. 61 pp.

940. Lunde, Paul, and Justin Wintle. *A Dictionary of Arabic and Islamic Proverbs.* London: Routledge & Kegan Paul, 1984. 158 pp.

941. Mahgoub, Fatma Mohammed. *A Linguistic Study of Cairene Proverbs.* Bloomington, Indiana: Indiana University Press, 1968. 141 pp. (proverbs, pp. 57-127).

942. Mannai, Ali Shabeeb al-. "A Selection of Qatari Proverbs in Arabic." *Al-Ma'thurat Al-Sha'biyyah*, 59-60 (2000), 7-29 (Arabic section), 26 (English section; abstract).

943. Meaini, Amado M. *Spaziergang durch den Garten der arabischen Sprichwörter und Weisheiten*. Hamburg: Helmut Buske, 1987. 71 pp.

944. Müller, Kathrin. *"Da war ihm, als müsse er fliegen vor Freuden"*. *"Tausendundeine Nacht" als Fundus für arabische Phraseologie*. München: Verlag der Bayerischen Akademie der Wissenschaften, 2001. 199 pp. (texts, pp. 51-110).

945. Noueshi, Mona Rashad. *[Deutsch-Arabisches] Wörterbuch: Idiome*. Kairo: Arab Bookshop, 1986. 135 pp.

946. Ould Mohamed-Babá, Ahmed-Salem. "Refranero en dialecto árabe hassaniyyä." *Anaquel de Estudios Árabes*, 7 (1996), 145-240.

947. Ould Mohamed-Babá, Ahmed-Salem. "Hagäytak ma gäytak." *Anaquel de Estudios Árabes*, 8 (1997), 179-205.

948. Ould Mohamed-Babá, Ahmed-Salem. "Otros refranes en dialecto hassaniyyä." *Anaquel de Estudios Árabes*, 9 (1998), 97-128.

949. Ould Mohamed-Babá, Ahmed-Salem. "Los berberismos del dialecto árabe hassaniyyä de el-Geblä / Berberisms in el-Geblä Hassaniyyä Arab Dialect." *Anaquel de Estudios Árabes*, 15 (2004), 175-184.

950. Rübesamen, Anneliese (ed.). *Arabische Weisheit*. München: F.A. Herbig, 1985. 159 pp.

951. Ruiz Moreno, Rosa Maria. *Egipto y su sabiduria popular: el refranero*. Jaén: Universidad de Jaén, 1999. 370 pp.

952. Schmidt, Jean-Jacques (ed.). *Maxi proverbes arabes*. Paris: Marabout, 2003. 383 pp.

953. Sellheim, Rudolf. "Arabische Sprichwörter und Weisheitssprüche von jugendlicher Kalligraphenhand aus der ersten Hälfte des 7. / 13. Jahrhunderts." *Oriens*, 35 (1996), 111-142.

954. Shehab El-Din, Tahia. "Ancient Egyptian Proverbs." *Annales du Service des Antiquités de l'Égypte*, 66 (2001), 157-171.

955. Sima, Alexander. "101 Sprichwörter und Redensarten im Mehri-Dialekt von Hawf." *Zeitschrift für arabische Linguistik*, 44 (2005), 71-93.

956. Socin, Albert. *Arabische Sprichwörter und Redensarten.* Tübingen: Laupp, 1878; rpt. Schaan, Liechtenstein: Sändig, 1982. 56 pp.

957. Webster, Sheila K. *The Shadow of a Noble Man: Honor and Shame in Arabic Proverbs.* Diss. Indiana University, 1984. 222 pp. (proverb index, pp. 198-209).

958. Westermarck, Edward. *Wit and Wisdom in Morocco: A Study of Native Proverbs.* London: George Routledge, 1930. New York: Horace Liveright, 1931; rpt. New York: AMS Press, 1980. 448 pp.

959. Yetiv, Isaac. *1,001 Proverbs from Tunisia.* Washington, D.C.: Three Continents Press, 1987. 152 pp.

Aramaic

960. Lewin, Moses. *Aramäische Sprichwörter und Volkssprüche. Ein Beitrag zur Kenntnis eines ostaramäischen Dialekts sowie zur vergleichenden Parömiologie.* Diss. Universität Erlangen, 1895. Berlin: H. Itzkuwski, 1895. 55 pp.

961. Lindenberger, James Miller. *The Aramaic Proverbs of Ahiqar.* Diss. Johns Hopkins University, 1974. 579 pp.

Argentine

962. Moya, Ismael. *Refranero. Refranes, proverbios, adagios, frases proverbiales, modismos refranescos, giros y otras formas paremiológicas tradicionales en la república argentina.* Buenos Aires: Imprenta de la Universidad, 1944. 669 pp. (proverbs, pp. 247-657).

963. Pérez Bugallo, Rubén, Adriana Speranza, and Marcelo A. Pagliaro. *Refranero tradicional argentino.* Buenos Aires: Del Sol, 2004. 141 pp.

Armenian

964. Karapetiana, G.O. *Armianskie poslovitsy i pogovorki.* Moskva: Nauka, 1973. 264 pp.

965. Manuelian, P.M. *Seven Bites From a Raisin. Proverbs from the Armenian.* Illustrations by Suzanne Anoushian Froundjian. New York: Ararat Press, 1980. 109 pp.

966. Sakayan, Dora. *Armenian Proverbs: A Paremiological Study with an Anthology of 2,500 Armenian Folk Sayings Selected and*

Translated into English. Delmar, New York: Caravan Books, 1994. 477 pp.

967. Sakayan, Dora. *Armenische Sprichwörter*. Wiesbaden: Otto Harrassowitz, 2001. 262 pp.

Australian

968. Bowles, Colin. *G'Day! Teach Yourself Australian in 20 Easy Lessons*. Illustrations by Louis Silvestro. North Ryde, New South Wales: Angus & Robertson, 1986. 118 pp.

969. Jonsen, Helen. *Kangaroo's Comments and Wallaby's Words. The Aussie Word Book*. Illustrations by John Colquhoun. New York: Hippocrene Books, 1988. 168 pp. Revised ed. 1999. 184 pp.

970. Lambert, James (ed.). *Macquarie Book of Slang. Australian Slang in the Noughties*. Sydney: The Macquarie Library, 1996 (revised ed. 2000). 276 pp.

971. Pinkney, Maggie (ed.). *Great Aussie Slang*. Illustrations by Geoff Hocking. Noble Park, Victoria: The Five Mile Press, 1999. 300 pp.

972. Wilkes, G.A. *A Dictionary of Australian Colloquialisms*. Sydney: Sydney University Press, 1978. 370 pp. (2nd ed. 1985) 362 pp.; 4th ed. Oxford: Oxford University Pess, 1996. 426 pp.

Austrian

973. Hörmann, Ludwig von. *Volkstümliche Sprichwörter und Redensarten aus den Alpenländern*. Leipzig: Liebeskind, 1891. 165 pp. (miniature book). Rpt. Innsbruck: Edition Löwenzahn, 1994. 158 pp.

974. Hörmann, Ludwig von. *Volkstümliche Sprichwörter und Redensarten aus den Alpenländern*. Stuttgart: J.G. Cotta, 1913. 165 pp.

975. Peyerl, Elke. *Zwillingsformeln in der österreichischen Alltagssprache*. Wien: Infothek, 2008. 156 pp.

976. Skupy, Hans-Horst (ed.). *Österreich Brevier. Aphorismen und Zitate von Altenberg bis Zweig*. Illustrations by Wilfried Zeller-Zellenberg. Wien: Amalthea, 1983. 208 pp.

977. Solman, Joseph. *Mozartiana: Two Centuries of Notes, Quotes and Anecdotes about Wolfgang Amadeus Mozart*. New York: Vintage Books, 1990. 201 pp. With illustrations.

978. Thiele, Johannes (ed.). *Das österreichische Zitatenlexikon.* Graz: Styria, 2001. 328 pp.

979. Trojer, Johann. "Redensarten aus Osttirol. Der verbale Vergleich im Dialekt von Villgraten." *Österreichische Zeitschrift für Volkskunde*, 77 (1974), 1-24.

980. Welzig, Werner (ed.). *Wörterbuch der Redensarten zu der von Karl Kraus 1899 bis 1936 herausgegebenen Zeitschrift "Die Fackel".* Wien: Verlag der Österreichischen Akademie der Wissenschaften, 1999. 1055 pp.

Azerbaijani

981. Daneshgar, Shahyar. *Azerbaijani Proverbs: Collection and Analysis (Formal and Thematic).* Diss. Indiana University, 1995. 371 pp.

Babylonian

982. Langdon, S. "Babylonian Proverbs." *American Journal of Semitic Languages and Literatures*, 28 (1912), 217-243. With 10 illustrations.

983. Lutz, H.F. "Babylonian Proverbs." *University of California Chronicle*, 35 (1933), 38-54.

Barbadian

984. Blackman, Margot. *Bajan [Barbadian] Proverbs.* Illustrations by Virgil Broodhagen. Montreal: Cedar Press, 1982 (7th ed. 2001). 18 pp.

Basque

985. Gárate, Gotzon. *Euskal Atsotitzak / Basque Proverbs.* Bilbo: Gero Euskal Liburuak, 1995. 159 pp.

Belgian

986. Collot, Joseph et al. "Enquête concernant les proverbes météorologiques wallons de la région de Neufchâteau." *Les Cahiers Wallons*, 42 (1979). 254-263.

987. Léonard, Lucien. "Comparaisons traditionelles en namurois." *Les Dialectes de Wallonie*, 6 (1978), 107-126; and 7 (1979), 31-42.

988. Mandos, Hein, and Miep Mandos-van de Pol. *De Brabantse spreekwoorden: Uitdrukkingen in Brabant gebruikt en opgetekend.* Waalre: Hein Mandosstichting, 1988. 631 pp. With illustrations.

989. Tibau, Georges. "Zestig Vlaamse weerspreuken onder de loep van de statistiek." *Volkskunde*, 75 (1974), 135-139; and 78 (1977), 33-59. (weather proverbs).

Biblical

990. Anonymous. *Berühmte Bibelzitate.* Wiesbaden: Vertriebsgesellschaft Modernes Antiquariat, 1981. 286 pp.

991. Anonymous. *Proverbs of Solomon, Son of David, King of Israel. Sprüche Salomos, des Sohnes David, des Königs von Israel. Proverbes de Salomon, fils de David, roi d'Israël.* Jerusalem: Korén Publishers, 1997. 54 pp.

992. Anonymous. *A Family Treasure of [Bible] Proverbs.* New York: Simon & Schuster, 1998. 77 pp. With 48 illustrations.

993. Buchna, Jörg. *Alle Jubeljahre ist nicht der wahre Jakob. Biblische Redewendungen.* Norden: Selbstverlag, 2003. 96 pp.

994. Buchna, Jörg. *Schwarzen Schafen geht ein Licht auf. Biblische Redewendungen.* Norden: Selbstverlag, 2004. 95 pp.

995. Buchna, Jörg. *Ein Unschuldslamm im siebten Himmel. Biblische Redewendungen.* Norden: Selbstverlag, 2006. 127 pp.

996. Csizmadia, Károly. *Bibliai eredetű szállóigék, szólásmondások, közmondások.* Györ: A Hazafias Népfront Györ-Sopron megyei bizottsága, 1987. 237 pp.

997. Ehrlich, Eugene, and David H. Scott. *Mene, Mene, Tekel. A Lively Lexicon of Words and Phrases from the Bible.* New York: HarperCollins, 1990. 306 pp.

998. Fulghum, Walter B. *A Dictionary of Biblical Allusions in English Literature.* New York: Holt, Rinehart and Winston, 1965. 291 pp.

999. Grünberg, Paul. *Biblische Redensarten. Eine Studie über den Gebrauch und Missbrauch der Bibel in der deutschen Volks- und Umgangssprache.* Heilbronn: Henninger, 1888. 68 pp.

1000. Haefeli, Leo. *Sprichwörter und Redensarten aus der Zeit Christi.* Luzern: Räber, 1934. 71 pp.

1001. Hinds, Arthur. *The Complete Sayings of Jesus Christ.* Radford, Virginia: Wilder Publications, 2008. 248 pp.

1002. Jüchen, Aurel von. *Gott begegnet dir alle Tage, wenn du ihn nur grüßen möchtest. Christliche Sprichwörter neu bedacht.* Illustrations by Kurt Schmischke. Hamburg: Agentur des Rauhen Hauses, 1980. 48 pp.

1003. Kidner, Frank Derek. *The Proverbs [Bible]. An Introduction and Commentary.* London: Tyndale Press, 1964. 192 pp.

1004. Krauss, Heinrich. *Geflügelte Bibelworte: Das Lexikon biblischer Redensarten.* München: C.H. Beck, 1993. 276 pp.

1005. Loukatos, Démétrios. *La Bible dans le parler proverbial du peuple grec.* Diss. Faculté des Lettres l'Université de Paris, 1950. 304 pp.

1006. Loukatos, Démétrios. "Locutions proverbiales du peuple grec venant des épitres de Saint Paul." *L'Hellenisme contemporain,* 2nd series, 5, no. 3 (1951), 247-257.

1007. Loukatos, Démétrios. "L'Évangile de Saint Luc dans le parler proverbial du peuple grec." *Benetia,* no volume given (1974), 41-57.

1008. Mayotte, Ricky Alan. *The Complete Jesus.* South Royalton, Vermont: Steerforth Press, 1997. 269 pp. (teachings on proverbs, pp. 87-141).

1009. Mead, Frank. *The Encyclopedia of Religious Quotations.* Westwood, New Jersey: Fleming H. Revell, 1965. 534 pp.

1010. Mieder, Wolfgang. *Not By Bread Alone: Proverbs of the Bible.* Illustrations by Mary Azarian. Shelburne, Vermont: The New England Press, 1990. 79 pp. Translated into Chinese by Xinnian Hu. Urumchi: Xinjiang, 1995. 240 pp.

1011. Miller, Cynthia L. "Translating Proverbs [Proverbs 10.1-31.9] by Topics." *The Bible Translator,* 57, no. 4 (2006), 170-194.

1012. Mokienko, Valerii M., G.A. Lilich, and O.I. Trofimkina. *Tolkovyi slovar' bibleiskikh vyrazhenii i slov: Oklo 2000 edinits.* Moskva: Astrel', 2010. 639 pp.

1013. Peterson, Eugene H. (ed.). *Proverbs [The Book of Proverbs].* Colorado Springs, Colorado: NavPress, 2004. 107 pp.

1014. Pfeffer, J. Alan. "Das biblische Zitat im Volksmund der Germanen und Romanen." *Teilnahme und Spiegelung. Festschrift für Horst Rüdiger.* Eds. Beda Allemann and Erwin Koppen. Berlin: Walter de Gruyter, 1975. 99-111.

1015. Schmoldt, Hans. *Reclams Lexikon der Bibelzitate.* Stuttgart: Philipp Reclam, 2002. 336 pp.

1016. Scholasticus, Ph. *Das deutsche Sprichwort im Dienste des Religions-Unterrichts in der Volksschule. Geordnet nach den 10 Geboten Gottes und den 7 Bitten des Vater unser.* Würzburg: F. Bucher, 1883. 218 pp.

1017. Schulze, Carl. "Deutsche Sprichwörter auf biblischem Grunde." *Archiv für das Studium der neueren Sprachen und Literaturen,* 28 (1860), 129-148.

1018. Schulze, Carl. *Die biblischen Sprichwörter der deutschen Sprache.* Göttingen: Vandenhoeck & Ruprecht, 1860; rpt. ed. Wolfgang Mieder. Bern: Peter Lang, 1987. 202 pp. (introduction, pp. I-LVIII).

1019. sB.Y. *The Anchor Bible. Proverbs. Ecclesiastes. Introduction, Translation and Notes.* Garden City, New York: Doubleday, 1965. 257 pp.

1020. Söhns, Franz. "Die Bibel und das Volk. Eine Sammlung von Worten, Redewendungen, Bildern und sprichwörtlichen Redensarten, welche die Sprache unseres Volkes der Bibel entlehnt hat." *Zeitschrift für den deutschen Unterricht,* 4 (1890), 9-29.

1021. Steger, Heribert. *333 biblische Redensarten.* Augsburg: Pattloch, 1998. 344 pp.

1022. Steger, Heribert. *Das A und O einer Sache: 100 Gedichte zu 99 sprichwörtlichen Redensarten biblischen Ursprungs.* Nürnberg: Eigenverlag, 1998. 41 pp.

1023. Steger, Heribert. *Ein Buch mit sieben Siegeln? 300 Bibelquizfragen und Antworten zu 99 biblischen Redewendungen im Alltag.* Nürnberg: Eigenverlag, 1998. 41 pp.

1024. Steger, Heribert. *Nicht von gestern sein: 99 biblische Redewendungen im Alltag.* Nürnberg: Eigenverlag, 1998. 208 pp. With illustrations.

1025. Stevenson, Burton Egbert. *The Home Book of Bible Quotations.* New York: Harper & Brothers, 1949. 645 pp.

1026. Walter, Harry, Ewa Komorowska, and Agnieszka Krzanowska. *Deutsch-polnisches Wörterbuch biblischer Phraseologismen mit historisch-etymologischen Kommentaren. Niemiecko-polski słownik frazeologii biblijnejz komentarzem historyczno-etymologicznym.* Szczecin: Daniel Krzanowski, 2010. Greifswald: Ernst-

Moritz-Arndt-Universität, 2010. 349 pp. (German title and phrases, everything else in Polish).

1027. Walter, Harry, and Valerii M. Mokienko. *Deutsch-russisches Wörterbuch biblischer Phraseologismen. Mit historisch-etymologischen Kommentaren.* Greifswald: Ernst-Moritz-Arndt-Universität, 2009. 199 pp.

1028. Weckmann, Berthold (ed.). *Alles Gute kommt von oben. Biblische Sprichwörter.* Kevelaer: Butzon & Bercker, 1993. 95 pp. (miniature book).

Bosnian

1029. Suljkić, Hifzija. *Poslovice. (Riječi treba mjeriti, a ne brojati).* Tuzla, Bosnia: no publisher given, 1996. 69 pp. With illustrations.

Brazilian

1030. Cascudo, Luís da Câmara. *Locuções tradicionais no Brasil.* Rio de Janeiro: Campanha de Defesa de Folclore Brasileiro, 1970 (2nd ed. 1977). 236 pp.

1031. Monteiro, George. "Brazil, 1969: A Sampling of New World Proverbs." *Proverbium,* no. 15 (1970), 503-504.

1032. Peixoto, Alfrânio. "Adagios brasileiros." A. Peixoto. *Missangas: Poesia e folklore.* São Paulo: Companhia Editora Nacional, 1931. 61-106.

1033. Valle, Alvaro. *À noite todos os gatos são pardos: Antologia de provérbios.* Rio de Janeiro: Léo Christiano, 1996. 272 pp.

Bulgarian

1034. Baerlein, Henry. *The Shade of the Balkans. Being a Collection of Bulgarian Folk-Songs and Proverbs.* London: Nutt, 1904; rpt. New York: R. West, 1977. 328 pp.

1035. Nicoloff, Assen. "Proverbs, Riddles, and Conjuration." In A. Nicoloff. *Bulgarian Folklore.* Cleveland, Ohio: Privately printed, 1983. 237-273 (proverbs).

1036. Simeonova, Ruska. *Deutsche und bulgarische Sprichwörter und Antisprichwörter / Nemski i bulgarski poslovitsi i antiposlovitsi.* Plovdid: Koala Press, 2009. 239 pp.

1037. Stoikova, Stefana. *Bulgarski poslovitsi i pogovorki*. Sofiia: Kolibri, 2007. 430 pp.

1038. Vlakhov, Sergei. *Angliiski poslovitsi (za izuchavashchite chuzhdi ezitsi v bulgarskite uchilishcha)*. Sofia: Izdatelstvo ETO, 1999. 96 pp.

Burmese

1039. Pe, Hla. *Burmese Proverbs*. London: John Murray, 1962. 114 pp.

Canadian

1040. Casselman, Bill. *Canadian Sayings. 1,200 Folk Sayings Used by Canadians*. Toronto: McArthur & Company, 1999. 133 pp.

1041. Casselman, Bill. *Canadian Sayings 2. 1,000 Folk Sayings Used by Canadians*. Toronto: McArthur & Company, 2002. 161 pp.

1042. Colombo, John Robert. *Colombo's Little Book of Canadian Proverbs, Graffiti, Limericks & Other Vital Matters*. Edmonton, Alberta: Hurtig, 1975. 143 pp.

1043. Colombo, John Robert. "Canadian Slurs, Ethnic and Other." *Maledicta*, 3 (1979), 182-184.

1044. Colombo, John Robert. *The Dictionary of Canadian Quotations*. Toronto: Stoddard, 1991. 671 pp.

1045. Coté, Jean. *Expressions populaires québécoises*. Outremont, Québec: Les Editions Quebecor, 1995. 141 pp.

1046. DesRuisseaux, Pierre. *Le livre des proverbes québécois*. Montréal: Editions Hurtubise, 1978. 219 pp.

1047. DesRuisseaux, Pierre. *Le livre des expressions québécoises*. Montréal: Editions Hurtubise, 1979. 278 pp.

1048. DesRuisseaux, Pierre. *Dictionnaire des expressions québécoises*. Québec: Bibliothèque québécoise, 1990. 446 pp.

1049. DesRuisseaux, Pierre. *Dictionnaire des proverbes québécois*. Montréal: Éditions de l'Hexagone, 1991. 287 pp.

1050. Devine, Patrick Kevin. *Devine's Folk Lore of Newfoundland in Old Words, Phrases and Expressions, Their Origin and Meaning*. St. John's, Newfoundland: Robinson, 1937; rpt. St. John's, Newfoundland: Memorial University of Newfoundland, Folklore and Language Publications, 1997. 81 pp. With Illustrations.

1051. Dunn, Charles W. "Gaelic Proverbs in Nova Scotia." *Journal of American Folklore*, 72 (1959), 30-35.

1052. Friesen, Victor Carl. "Maxims [Proverbs], [Proverbial] Comparisons, and Other [Proverbial] Expressions." In V.C. Friesen. *The Windmill Turning: Nursery Rhymes, Maxims, and Other Expressions of Western Canadian Mennonites*. Edmonton, Alberta: University of Alberta Press, 1988. 88-115.

1053. Lacey, Gary. "Folk Sayings from Lunenberg County [Nova Scotia]." *Lunenberg County Folklore and Oral History: Project '77*. Ed. Laurie Lacey. Ottowa: National Museums of Canada, 1979. 87-89.

1054. Morison, O. "Tsimshian Proverbs [British Columbia]." *Journal of American Folklore*, 2 (1889), 285-286.

1055. Proteau, Lorenzo. *La parlure québécoise*. Boucherville, Québec: Les Éditions franco-québécoises, 1982. 230 pp.

1056. Thiessen, Jack. "Sprichwörter im Niederdeutsch der kanadischen Mennoniten." *Niederdeutsches Jahrbuch*, 91 (1968), 109-120.

1057. Young, Kathleen E., and Elizabeth L. Mapplebeck. "Proverbial Sayings." *A Folklore Sampler from the Maritimes with a Bibliographical Essay on the Folktale in English*. Ed. Herbert Halpert. St. Johns, Newfoundland: Memorial University of Newfoundland Folklore and Language Publications for the Centre of Canadian Studies, 1982. 117-137.

Celtic

1058. Carmichael, Alexander. *Das Kreuz in der Sonne. Altkeltische Sprüche und Gebete*. München: Kaiser, 1978. 79 pp. With illustrations.

1059. O'Donnell, James. *Celtic Proverbs in Irish and English*. Illustrations by Brian Fitzgerald. Belfast: Appletree Press, 1996. 60 pp.

Chechen

1060. Lawson, JonArno, and Amjad Jaimoukha. "Proverbs and Sayings." *The Chechens. A Handbook*. Ed. Amjad Jaimoukha. London: RoutledgeCurzon, 2008. 241-248.

Cheremis

1061. Roberts, Warren. "The [Cheremis] Proverb." *Studies in Cheremis Folklore*. Ed. Thomas A. Sebeok. Bloomington, Indiana: Indiana University Press, 1952. I, 118-169.

Chinese

1062. Anonymous. *Chinese Proverbs*. Los Angeles, California: Quon-Quon Company, 1944. 20 pp. (miniature book).

1063. Anonymous. *Chinese Proverbs from Olden Times*. Mount Vernon, New York: Peter Pauper Press, 1956. 62 pp. With illustrations.

1064. Anonymous. *100 Common Chinese Idioms and Set Phrases*. Beijing: Sinolingua, 1999. 202 pp.

1065. Berg, Dagmar von (ed.). *Chinesische Weisheiten*. München: Wilhelm Heyne, 1978 (7th ed. 1983). 74 pp. With illustrations.

1066. Chen, Berta Alicia (ed.). *Proverbios Chinos*. Panamá: CMC Publishing, 2000. 61 pp. With illustrations.

1067. Chinnery, John D. *Corresponding English & Chinese Proverbs & Phrases*. Beijing: New World Press, 1984 (2nd ed. 1989). 258 pp.

1068. Clements, Jonathan. *The Little Book of Chinese Proverbs*. New York: Paragon, 2001; rpt. New York: Barnes & Noble Books, 2003. 255 pp.

1069. Confucius. *The Sayings of Confucius. The Teaching of China's Greatest Sage*. Ed. James R. Ware. New York: Mentor Books, 1955. 128 pp.

1070. Confucius. *The Analects of Confucius*. Translated into Modern Chinese by Bao Shixiang. Translated into English by Lao Am. Shandong: Shandong Friendship Press, 1992. 369 pp.

1071. Debon, Günther. *Chinesische Weisheit*. Stuttgart: Philipp Reclam, 1993. 263 pp. (proverbs, pp. 205-234). With illustrations.

1072. Eberhard, Wolfram. "Pekinger Sprichwörter." *Baessler-Archiv*, 24 (1941), 1-43. The introduction to this collection also in English in W. Eberhard. *Studies in Chinese Folklore and Related Essays*. Bloomington, Indiana: Indiana University Press, 1970. 173-176.

1073. Hart, Henry H. *Seven Hundred Chinese Proverbs*. Palo Alto, California: Stanford University Press, 1937; London: Humphrey Milford, 1937. 89 pp.

1074. Hart, Henry H. *700 chinesische Sprichwörter*. Unter Benutzung der englischen Übersetzung von Henry H. Hart ins Deutsche übertragen von M. von Wyss-Vögtlin. Zürich: Rascher, 1942; rpt. Zürich: Racher, 1965. 106 pp.

1075. He Jing-jiang, Zhang Xiu-Fang. *Xinhua Chengyu Cidian [A New Dictionary of Chinese Proverbs]*. Changchun: Jilin Daxue Chubanshe, 1993. 980 pp. (in Chinese).

1076. Herrmann, Konrad. *Chinesische Sprichwörter. Reiskörner fallen nicht vom Himmel*. Leipzig: Gustav Kiepenheuer, 1984; Wiesbaden: Vertriebsgesellschaft Modernes Antiquariat, 1984. 207 pp. With illustrations.

1077. Hettinger, Eugen (ed.). *Springs of Oriental Wisdom*. New York: Herder Book Center, 1964. 42 pp. (miniature book).

1078. Huanyou, Huang. *Chinese Proverbs, Quotations, and Fables*. Felinfach, Wales: Llanerch Publishers, 1998. 188 pp.

1079. Lau, Theodora. *Best-Loved Chinese Proverbs*. New York: HarperCollins, 1995. 180 pp.

1080. Lin, Marjorie, and Leonard Schalk (eds.). *Dictionary of 1000 Chinese Proverbs*. New York: Hippocrene Books, 1998. 200 pp.

1081. Lohmann, Heinz. *Der Frosch am Grunde des Brunnens. Geschichten von chinesischen Sprichwörtern*. Münster: Waxmann, 1990. 58 pp. With illustrations.

1082. McCunn, Ruthanne Lum. *Chinese Proverbs*. Illustrations by You Shan Tang. San Francisco: Chronicle Books, 1991. 58 pp.

1083. McCunn, Ruthanne Lum. *Chinese Proverbs*. Illustrations by Hu Yong Yi. San Francisco: Chronicle Books, 2002. 80 pp.

1084. Merwin, W.S. *Asian Figures*. New York: Atheneum, 1971 (4th 1986). 99 pp.

1085. Osterbrauck, Cornelia. *Fernöstliche Weisheiten*. Illustrations by Sabine Wittmann. München: Compact/Minipräsent Verlag, 1996. 253 pp. (miniature book).

1086. Plopper, Clifford Henry. *Chinese Religion Seen Through the Proverb*. Shanghai: China Press, 1926; rpt. New York: Paragon Book Reprint Corporation, 1969. 381 pp. With illustrations.

1087. Rohsenow, John S. *A Chinese-English Dictionary of Enigmatic Folk Similes*. Tucson, Arizona: University of Arizona Press, 1991. 324 pp. With illustrations.

1088. Rohsenow, John S. *ABC Dictionary of Chinese Proverbs*. Honolulu, Hawaii: University of Hawaii Press, 2001. 239 pp.

1089. Rottauscher, Anna von. *Zündet man Kerzen an, so erhält man Licht. Weisheiten der alten Chinesen*. Salzburg: Verlag das Bergland-Buch, 1978. 104 pp. With illustrations.

1090. Schipper, Mineke, and Sanjukta Gupta. *Een wenkbrauw als een wilgeblad. Aziatische spreekwoorden en zegswijzen over vrouwen*. Baarn: Ambo, 1995. 167 pp.

1091. Sheng-qing, Gu. *Sprichwörter und Lehrgeschichten der Chinesen*. Köln: Eugen Diederichs, 1985. 144 pp. With illustrations.

1092. Smith, Arthur H. *Proverbs and Common Sayings from the Chinese*. Shanghai: American Presbyterian Mission Press, 1914; rpt. New York: Paragon and Dover, 1965. 403 pp.

1093. Sun, C.C. *As the Saying Goes: An Annotated Anthology of Chinese and Equivalent English Sayings and Expressions, and an Introduction to Xiēhòuyŭ (Chinese Wit)*. St. Lucia, Queensland: University of Queensland Press, 1981. 685 pp.

1094. Tan, Situ. *Best Chinese Idioms. Chinese-English*. Hong Kong: Hai Feng Publishing Co., 1984 (5th ed. 1989). 322 pp.

1095. Turnitz, Georg von. *Weisheit des Ostens*. München: Wilhelm Heyne, 1982. 74 pp. With illustrations.

1096. Wood, Robert (ed.). *Echoes from the Orient: Wisdom of Lao-Tse. With Parallels from Western Thought*. Kansas City, Missouri: Hallmark Cards, 1972. 46 pp. With illustrations.

1097. Zona, Guy A. *If You Have Two Loaves of Bread, Sell One and Buy a Lily and Other Proverbs of China*. New York: Touchstone, 1997. 124 pp.

Chuvash

1098. Bläsing, Uwe. *Tschuwaschische Sprichwörter und sprichwörtliche Redensarten*. Wiesbaden: Otto Harrassowitz, 1994. 849 pp.

1099. Yüge, Nuri. "Einige Bemerkungen über tschuwaschische Sprichwörter." *Zeitschrift der Morgenländischen Gesellschaft*, 130 (1980), 453-457.

Colombian

1100. Bedoya, Luis Iván et al. *Refranes y dichos*. Medellín, Colombia: Universidad de Antioquia, 1996. 417 pp.

1101. García, Carlos. *Diccionario de locuciones del habla de Antioquia*. Medellín, Colombia: Universidad de Antioquia, 1991. 151 pp.

1102. García, Carlos. "Fraseologismos autóctonos en el habla popular de Antioquia." *Lingüistíca y Literatura*, 18, no. 31 (1997), 118-127.

1103. García, Carlos, and César Muñoz. *Refranero Antioqueño*. Medellin, Colombia: Universidad de Antioquia, 1996. 292 pp.

1104. Soto Posada, Gonzalo. *Los refranes en el derecho y el derecho en los refranes*. Medellín, Colombia: Editorial Universidad Pontificia Bolivariana, 1997. 66 pp.

1105. Soto Posada, Gonzalo. *Los refranes en la medicina y la medicina en los refranes*. Medellín, Colombia: Editorial Universidad Pontificia Bolivariana, 2000. 156 pp. With illustrations.

Corsican

1106. Arrighi, Paul. *Le livre des dictons corses: 500 dictons et surnoms collectifs sur 300 localités de l'Ile, commentés et traduits*. Toulouse: Privat, 1976. 123 pp.

Creole

1107. D'iachkova, M.V. *Poslovitsy i pogovorki s'erraleonskikh krelov na iazykakh krio i russkom*. Moskva: Nauka, 1977. 103 pp.

1108. Hearn, Lafcadio. *"Gombo Zhèbes": Little Dictionary of Creole Proverbs, Selected from Six Creole Dialects. Translated into French and into English, with Notes, Complete Index to Subjects and Some Brief Remarks upon the Creole Idioms of Louisiana*. New York: Will H. Coleman, 1885. 42 pp.

1109. Young, Colville N. *Creole Proverbs of Belize*. Belize: National Printers, 1980 (2nd ed. 1988). 37 pp.

Croatian

1110. Matković, Dinko. "Poslovice Vrboske." *Čakavska rič*, 27, no. 1 (1999), 79-95.

1111. Miholek, Vladimir. "Đurđevečke narodne poslovice." *Kaj*, 38, nos. 1-2 (2005), 109-114.

Cuban

1112. Sanchez-Boudy, José. *Diccionario de refranes populares cubanos*. Miami, Florida: Universal Miami, 2000. 171 pp.

Czech

1113. Asala, Joanne (ed.). *Czech Proverbs*. Iowa City, Iowa: Penfield Press, 1994. 64 pp.

1114. Bittnerová, Dana, and Franz Schindler. *Česka přísloví. Soudobý stav konce 20. století*. Praha: Karolinum, 1997. 315 pp.

1115. Čermák, František, Jiri Hronek, and Jaroslav Machač (eds.). *Slovnik české frazeologie a idiomatiky*. 4 vols. Praha: Vydala Academia, 1983-1994. I, 492 pp.; II, 511 pp.; III, 757 pp.; IV, 634 pp.

1116. Martin, Pat (ed.). *Czechoslovak Wit and Wisdom*. Iowa City, Iowa: Penfield Press, 1984. 40 pp.

1117. Munzar, Jan. *Medardova kápě: Aneb pranostiky očima meteorologa*. Praha: Horizont, 1986. 238 pp. (weather proverbs).

Danish

1118. Enevoldsen, Poul. *"Hans Thomissøns Ordsprog" [c. 1600/1650] og Poul Enevoldsen: Farrago[1607]*. Ed. John Kousgård Sørensen. København: C.A. Reitzel, 1977. 184 pp.

1119. Kjaer, Iver. "Wellerisms in Earlier Danish Tradition." *Proverbium*, no. 16 (1971), 579-582.

1120. Kjaer, Iver, and Bengt Holbek. *Ordsprog i Danmark. 4000 ordsprog fra skrift og tale gennem 600 år*. København: Jørgen Paludans, 1973. 336 pp.

1121. Kjaer, Iver, John Kousgård Sørensen, and Niels Werner Frederiksen (eds.). *Problemata et Proverbia moralia (København 1611 og 1624). Hans Chr. Sthens Ordsprog (Efter tabt Cod. Hamb. theol. 2090a,8)*. København: C.A. Reitzel, 1987. 290 pp.

1122. Låle, Peder. *Adagia Danica et Latina*. København: Gotfred af Ghemen, 1508 ff. Rpt. eds. Iver Kjaer and Erik Petersen. *Peder Låles Ordsprog. (1508. 1515. 1626)*. 2 vols. København: C.A. Reitzel, 1979. I, 436 pp.; II, 328 pp

1123. McDonald, Julie Jensen. *Danish Proverbs*. Illustrations by Esther Feske. Iowa City, Iowa: Penfield Press, 1993. 51 pp.

1124. Sørensen, John Kousgård (ed.). *Samlinger fra 17. århundrede*. København: C.A. Reitzel, 1980. 177 pp.

1125. Syv, Peder. *Danske Ordsproge*. Kiøbenhafn: Christian Geertz, 1682. 594 pp. Rpt. eds. Iver Kjaer and John Kousgård Sørensen. *Peder Syv: Danske Ordsproge (1682)*. København: C.A. Reitzel. 1983. 594 pp.

1126. Thomissøn, Hans. *"Hans Thomissøns Ordsprog" [c. 1600/1650] og Poul Enevoldsen: Farrago[1607]*. Ed. John Kousgård Sørensen. København: C.A. Reitzel, 1977. 184 pp.

Dutch

1127. Acker, Achille van. *De duivel in spreekwoord en gezegde*. Kortrijk-Heule: UGA, 1977. 208 pp.

1128. Acker, Achille van. *Het verleden in spreekwoord en gezegde*. Kortrijk-Heule: UGA, 1977. 365 pp.

1129. Adsiz, Sahir. *Nederlandse en Turkse zegswijzen / Hollandaca-Türkçe atasözleri ve deyimler sözlüğü*. Utrecht: Prisma, 1992. 422 pp.

1130. Albers, Gerard. *How Do We Say It? 500 Dutch Sayings, Expressions, Phrases and Quotations*. Holland, Michigan: Gerard Albers, 1986. 36 pp.

1131. Andrews, Oscar. *Dutch Song (Perverted Proverbs)*. Words and music by Oscar Andrews; arranged by O.W. Lane. Boston: Oliver Ditson, 1883. 5 pp.

1132. Andriessoon, Symon. *Duytsche Adagia ofte Spreecwoorden*. Antwerpen: Heynrick Alssens, 1550. 103 pp. In Facsimile, Transcription of the Dutch Text and English Translation. Rpt. ed. Mark A. Meadow and Anneke C.G. Fleurkens, with two introductory essays by S.A.C. Dudok van Heel and Herman Roodenburg. Hilversum: Verloren, 2003. 334 pp.

1133. Broek, Marinus A. van den. *De spreekwoorden van Jacob Cats*. Antwerpen: C. de Vries-Brouwers, 1998. 179 pp. With illustrations.

1134. Broek, Marinus A. van den. *Alcoholisch Spreekwoordenboek. Spreekwoorden, zegswijzen en zeispreuken in alcoholisch perspectief bijeengebracht en verklaard*. Antwerpen: L.J. Veen, 2000. 111 pp.

1135. Broek, Marinus A. van den. *Erotisch Spreekwoordenboek. Spreekwoorden en zegswijzen*. Antwerpen: L.J. Veen, 2002. 127 pp.

1136. Cock, Alfons de. *Spreekwoorden en zegswijsen afkomstig van oude gebruiken en volkszeden*. Gent: Ad. Hoste, 1905. 421 pp.

1137. Cox, H.L., and Stanisław Prędota. *Nederlands-Pools spreekwoordenboek / Niderlandzko-polski słownik przysłów*. Wrocław: Wydawnictwo Uniwersytetu Wrocławskiego, 1997. 328 pp. With illustrations.

1138. Czochralski, Jan, and Stanisław Prędota. *Podręczny niderlandzko-polski słownik fraseologiczny / Nederlands-Pools frazeologisch handwoordenboek*. Wrocław: Wydawnictwo Uniwersytetu Wrocławskiego, 1992. 221 pp.

1139. Dundes, Alan, and Claudia A. Stibbe. *The Art of Mixing Metaphors. A Folkloristic Interpretation of the "Netherlandish Proverbs" by Pieter Bruegel the Elder*. FFC 230. Helsinki: Suomalainen Tiedeakatemia, 1981. 71 pp. With 5 illustrations.

1140. Eeden, Ed van. *Deltas groot spreekwoordenboek voor het hele gezin*. Aartselaar: Deltas, 1989. 249 pp.

1141. Frijlink, H. "Samwelleriana." *Het Leeskabinet*, no volume given, no. 2 (1856), 155-158; and no volume given, no. 2 (1863), 139-141 (wellerisms).

1142. Grauls, Jan. *De spreekwoorden van Pieter Bruegel den Oude (1527 [sic] - 1569) verklaard*. Antwerpen: Gevaert, 1937. Also in English as *The Proverbs of Pieter Bruegel the Elder (1527 [sic] - 1569) Explained*. Translated by Rob. Roemans and Hilda van Assche. Antwerpen: Gevaert, 1938. 11 pp. And in German as *Die Sprichwörter Pieter Bruegels des Älteren (±1527- 1569)*. Antwerpen: Gevaert, 1938. 11 pp. With 1 illustration.

1143. Grauls, Jan. *Volkstaal en Volksleven in het werk van Pieter Bruegel*. Antwerpen: N.V. Standaard-Boekhandel, 1957. With 22 illustrations.

1144. Harrebomée, Pieter Jacob. *Spreekwoordenboek der Nederlandsche Taal.* 3 vols. Utrecht: Kemink, 1858-1870; rpt. in one volume Amsterdam: Van Hoeve, 1980. I, LXXIX + XV and 463 pp.; II, LXXX and 517 pp.; III, CCCXVIII and 494 pp.

1145. Heusinkveld, Holly Flame, and Jean Caris-Osland. *Dutch Proverbs.* Illustrations by Sally Haugen DeReus. Iowa City, Iowa: Penfield Press, 1996. 63 pp.

1146. Hoefnagels, Peter. *Onbekende spreekwoorden en zegswizen. De ontdekking van onbekende zegswijzen en hun verklaringen.* Illustrations by Len Munnik. Amsterdam: Assen, 1977. 58 pp.

1147. Hoffmann von Fallersleben, August Heinrich. "Altniederländische Sprichwörter nach der ältesten Sammlung [*Proverbia communia*]." *Horae Belgicae*, 9 (1854), 1-59.

1148. Jente, Richard (ed.). *Proverbia communia. A Fifteenth Century Collection of Dutch Proverbs Together with the Low German Version.* Bloomington, Indiana: Indiana University Press, 1947. 334 pp.

1149. Kiriş, Mehmet. *Uitdrukkingen- en spreekwoordenboek: Nederlands-Turks / Turks-Nederlands.* Nijmegen: Etnicom, 1992. 754 pp.

1150. Kruyskamp, C. *Allemal Mensen ... Apologische Spreekwoorden.* 's-Gravenhage: Martinus Nijhoff, 1947. 94 pp. Revised 3rd ed. 1965. 150 pp. (wellerisms).

1151. Laan, K. ter. *Nederlandse spreekwoorden, spreuken en zegswijzen.* Amsterdam: Elsevier, 1979. 433 pp. With illustrations.

1152. Ley, Gerd de. *Dictionary of 1000 Dutch Proverbs.* New York: Hippocrene Books, 1998. 142 pp.

1153. Mesters, G.A. *Spreekwoordenboek.* Utrecht: Prisma, 1966 (20th printing 1995). 192 pp.

1154. Prędota, Stanisław, and Marijke Mooijaart. *Reyer Gheurtz' "Adagia" [1552], hs. Gent, Universiteitsbibliotheek, Res. 524².* Wrocław: Wydawnictwo Uniwersytetu Wrocławskiego, 2009. 282 pp.

1155. Prędota, Stanisław, and Siegfried Theissen. *Nederlandse en Poolse fraseologismen en spreekwoorden / Niderlandzkie i polskie frazeologizmy oraz przysłowia.* Wrocław: Wydawnictwo Uniwersytetu Wrocławskiego, 1997. 182 pp.

1156. Prędota, Stanisław, and P.G.J. van Sterkenburg (eds.). *Nederduytse spreekwoorden (1601), hs. Krakau, Biblioteka Jagiellońska 2812 I.* Wrocław: Wydawnictwo Uniwersytetu Wrocławskiego, 2000. 140 pp.

1157. Rehbein, Detlev. *Tür zu, die Heiden kommen. Sprichwörter aus den Niederlanden.* 4the ed. Berlin: Union Verlag, 1984. Rpt. as *Das Glück kommt im Schlaf. Sprichwörter aus den Niederlanden.* Berlin: Union Verlag, 1985. Hanau: Werner Dausien, 1985. 132 pp. With illustrations.

1158. Spaan, Gerrit van. *Lyste van spreek-woorden, op verscheyde voorvallen toepasselijk.* Arabien: Zeg-Waardt, 1708. Rpt. ed. Rietje van Vliet. Leiden: Astraea, 1997. 32 pp. (wellerisms).

1159. Stoett, F.A. *Nederlandsche spreekwoorden, spreekwijzen, uitdrukkingen en gezegden.* Zutphen: J.W. Thieme, 1901. 744 pp. Revised 4th ed. in 2 vols. Zutphen: J.W. Thieme, 1924-1925. I, 582 pp.; II, 639 pp.

1160. Stoett, F.A. *Nederlandse spreekwoorden en gezegden verklaard en vergeleken met die in het Frans, Duits en Engels.* Ed. C. Kruyskamp. Zutphen: W.J. Thieme, 1974. 379 pp.

1161. Vliet, Rietje van (ed.). *Lyste van spreek-woorden [1708?].* Leiden: Astraea, 1997. 32 pp. (wellerisms).

1162. Zeeman, C.F. *Nederlandsche spreekwoorden, spreekwijzen, benamingen en volksuitdrukkingen, aan den Bijbel ontleend.* Dordrecht: J.R. Revers, 1877 (2nd ed.1888). 539 pp.

English

1163. Abel, Alison M. *Make Hay While the Sun Shines. A Book of Proverbs.* Illustrations by Shirley Hughes. London: Faber and Faber, 1977; rpt. London: Faber and Faber, 1981. 46 pp. Rpt. again London: Faber and Faber, 1998. 40 pp. (children's book).

1164. Ackerman, Robert J. *A Husband's Little Black Book. Common Sense, Wit and Wisdom for a Better Marriage.* Deerfield Beach, Florida: Health Communications, 1994. 157 pp.

1165. Adams, Abby (ed.). *An Uncommon Scold. Words to Live by.* New York: Fireside, 1994. 268 pp. With illustrations.

1166. Adler, Bill (ed.). *The Churchill Wit.* New York: Coward-McCann, 1965. 86 pp. With illustrations.

1167. Adler, Bill (ed.). *First, Kill All the Lawyers. Legal Proverbs, Epitaphs, Jokes, and Anecdotes.* Illustrations by Richard Zorn. New York: Citadel Press, 1994. 147 pp.

1168. Adler, Mortimer J., and Charles Van Doren. *Great Treasury of Western Thought. A Compendium of Important Statements on Man and His Institutions by the Great Thinkers in Western History.* New York: R.R. Bowker Company, 1977. 1771 pp.

1169. Agel, Jerome, and Walter D. Glanze. *Cleopatra's Nose, the Twinkie Defense, & 1500 Other Verbal Shortcuts in Popular Parlance.* New York: Prentice Hall Press, 1990. 266 pp.

1170. Aik, Kam Chuan. *Dictionary of Proverbs.* Singapore: Federal Publications, 1988. 310 pp.

1171. Albiński, Jacek. *English Proverbs and Sayings. Przysłowia i porzekadła angielskie.* Tychy: Odon, 1991. 174 pp.

1172. Alexander, James. *The World's Funniest Proverbs.* Cheam, Surrey: Crombie Jardine, 2004. 162 pp. (anti-proverbs).

1173. Ali, Ahmed F., and Omar Au Nuh. *The Modern English-Somali Phrase Book.* Muqdisho: Wakaaladda Madbacadda Qaranka, 1975. 94 pp. (proverbs on pp. 88-91).

1174. Allibone, S. Austin. *Prose Quotations from Socrates to Macaulay. With Indexes. Authors 544; Subjects 571; Quotations 8810.* Philadelphia: J.B. Lippincott, 1905. 764 pp.

1175. Almond, Jordan. *Why Do We Say It? The Stories Behind the Words, Expressions and Clichés We Use.* Secaucus, New Jersey: Castle Books, 1985. Rpt. as *Dictionary of Word Origins. A History of the Words, Expressions, and Clichés We Use.* Secaucus, New Jersey: Citadel Press, 1997. 286 pp.

1176. Aman, Reinhold (ed.). *How Do They Do It? A Collection of Wordplays Revealing the Sexual Proclivities of Man and Beast.* Waukesha, Wisconsin: Maledicta Press, 1983. 64 pp.

1177. Amgart, O. (ed.). *The Proverbs of Alfred. An Amended Text.* Lund: Gleerup, 1978. 30 pp.

1178. Ammer, Christine. *It's Raining Cats and Dogs ... And Other Beastly Expressions.* New York: Paragon House, 1989. 247 pp.

1179. Ammer, Christine. *Have a Nice Day – No Problem! A Dictionary of Clichés.* New York: Dutton, 1992. 454 pp.

1180. Ammer, Christine. *Seeing Red or Tickled Pink: Color Terms in Everyday Language*. New York: Dutton, 1992. 215 pp.

1181. Ammer, Christine. *Southpaws & Sunday Punches and Other Sporting Expressions*. New York: Plume, 1993. 262 pp.

1182. Andrews, Robert. *The Routledge Dictionary of Quotations*. London: Routledge & Kegen Paul, 1987. 343 pp.

1183. Andrews, Robert. *The Columbia Dictionary of Quotations*. New York: Columbia University Press, 1993. 1092 pp.

1184. Anglund, Joan Walsh (ill.). *A Pocketful of Proverbs*. New York: Harcourt, Brace & World, 1964. 28 pp. (miniature book).

1185. Anonymous. *A Treasury of Table Talk*. Edinburgh: William P. Nimmo, 1868. 128 pp.

1186. Anonymous. *Toasts and Maxims. A Book of Humour to Pass the Time*. New York: R.F. Fenno, 1908. 110 pp. With illustrations.

1187. Anonymous. *Origin of Things Familiar. Sketches on the Origin of Common Things, Prevalent Beliefs, Everyday Words and Phrases, Familiar Signs and Symbols and Current Customs*. Cincinnati, Ohio: United Book Corporation, 1934. 286 pp.

1188. Anonymous. *The Wisdom of the Ages. A Collection of Proverbs Illustrated Photographically which, during the Period of 1936 to 1946, formed the Basis for the Advertising of Textile Machine Works*. Reading, Pennsylvania: Textile Machine Works, 1946. 105 pp. With illustrations.

1189. Anonymous. *Proverbs for Daily Living*. Illustrations by Johannes Troyer. Mount Vernon, New York: Peter Pauper Press, 1949. 60 pp.

1190. Anonymous. *Book of Proverbs and Epigrams*. New York: Ottenheimer, 1954. 143 pp.

1191. Anonymous. *Treasury of Proverbs and Epigrams*. New York: Avenel Books, 1954. 133 pp.

1192. Anonymous. *Vest Pocket Book of Proverbs and Epigrams*. Baltimore, Maryland: I. & M. Ottenheimer, 1954. 202 pp.

1193. Anonymous. *Treasury of Familiar Quotations*. New York: Avenel Books, 1955. 251 pp.

1194. Anonymous. *Lasting Ideas: Some Expressions on the Art of Persuasion. Wise and Witty Enough to Endure*. Pleasantville, New

York: The Reader's Digest Association, 1956. 44 pp. With illustrations.

1195. Anonymous. *Salty Sayings from Cynical Tongues.* Illustrations by Henry R. Martin. Mount Vernon, New York: Peter Paul Press, 1959. 60 pp.

1196. Anonymous. *Thoughts for a Good Life.* Illustrations by Ruth McCrea. Mount Vernon, New York: Peter Pauper Press, 1959. 60 pp.

1197. Anonymous. *Love is Like the Wonder of a Flower.* Kansas City, Missouri: Hallmark, ca. 1968. 8 pp. (miniature book).

1198. Anonymous. *Great "Quotes" from Great Women!* Lombard, Illinois: Great Quotations, 1984. 75 pp.

1199. Anonymous. *Friendship. A Bouquet of Quotes.* Philadelphia: Running Press, 1989. 93 pp. (miniature book).

1200. Anonymous. *Quotable Women: A Collection of Shared Thoughts.* Philadelphia: Running Press, 1989. 92 pp. (miniature book).

1201. Anonymous. *Love. Quotations from the Heart.* Philadelphia: Running Press, 1990. 88 pp.

1202. Anonymous. *The Quotable Woman.* Philadelphia: Running Press, 1991. 192 pp.

1203. Anonymous. *Dictionary of Phrase and Fable.* London: Bloomsbury Books, 1994. 252 pp.

1204. Anonymous. *Dictionary of Proverbs.* London: Bloomsbury Books, 1994. 256 pp.

1205. Anonymous. *"Bringing Home the Bacon" and "Cutting the Mustard": The Origins & Meanings of the Food We Speak.* Oxford: Past Times, 2000. Edison, New Jersey: Castle Books, 2002. 191 pp. With illustrations.

1206. Anonymous. *Salt of the Earth. Origins and Meanings of Country Sayings.* Westbury, Wiltshire: The National Trust, 2002. 143 pp.

1207. Anonymous. *Swinging the Lead & Spiking His Guns: Military & Naval Expressions and Their Origins.* Edison, New Jersey: Castle Books, 2002. 190 pp. With illustrations.

1208. Anonymous. *The Little Book of Proverbs and Sayings. Taken from the "Oxford Advanced Learner's Dictionary"*. Oxford: Oxford University Press, 2006. 24 pp.

1209. Anton, Jim. *The Sense and Nonsense of Proverbs*. Illustrations by Jean Anton. New York: Sterling Publishing, 1993. 128 pp.

1210. Apperson, G.L. *English Proverbs and Proverbial Phrases: A Historical Dictionary*. London: J.M. Dent, 1929; rpt. Detroit: Gale Research Co., 1969. Rpt. as *The Wordsworth Dictionary of Proverbs*. Ware, Hertfordshire: Wordsworth Editions, 1993. 721 pp.

1211. Auden, W.H., and Louis Kronenberger. *The Viking Book of Aphorisms. A Personal Selection*. New York: Viking Press, 1962. 405 pp.; rpt. New York: Dorset Press, 1981. 431 pp.

1212. Augarde, Tony. *The Oxford Dictionary of Modern Quotations*. Oxford: Oxford University Press, 1991. 371 pp.

1213. Ayto, John. *Euphemisms: Over 3,000 Ways to Avoid Being Rude or Giving Offence*. London: Bloomsbury, 1993. 332 pp.

1214. Ayto, John, and John A. Simpson. *The Oxford Dictionary of Modern Slang*. Oxford: Oxford University Press, 1992. 299 pp.

1215. B., R.T. (ed.) *The Oxford Dictionary of Quotations*. 3rd ed. Oxford: Oxford Univerity Press, 1979. 907 pp. (1st ed. 1941), 879 pp.; (2nd ed. 1953), 1003 pp.; (4th ed. 1992), 1061 pp.; (5th ed. 1999), 1136 pp.

1216. Bachelder, Louise (ed.). *Flower Thoughts*. Illustrations by Eric Carle. Mount Vernon, New York: Peter Pauper Press, 1967. 62 pp.

1217. Bachelder, Louise (ed.). *Time for Reflection*. Illustrations by Pat Stewart. Mount Vernon, New York: Peter Pauper Press, 1968. 62 pp. (quotations).

1218. Bachelder, Louise (ed.). *Little Things*. Illustrations by Pat Stewart. Mount Vernon, New York: Peter Pauper Press, 1969. 62 pp. (quotations).

1219. Backer, Theodore B. *A Compact Anthology of Bartlett's Quotations*. Middle Village, New York: Jonathan David, 1974. 176 pp.

1220. Baggini, Julian. *Should You Judge This Book by Its Cover? 100 Fresh Takes on Familiar Sayings and Quotations*. Berkeley, California: Counterpoint, 2010. 223 pp.

1221. Bailey, Nathan. *Divers Proverbs with Their Explication & Illustration*. Illustrations by Allen Lewis. London: E. Bell, 1721; rpt. New Haven, Connecticut: Yale University Press, 1917. 83 pp.

1222. Bailey, Nathan. *Dictionarium Britannicum: Or a More Compleat Universal Etymological English Dictionary Than any Extant*. London: T. Cox, 1730; rpt. Hildesheim: Georg Olms, 1969. 702 pp.

1223. Bailey, Nathan. *Old English Proverbs. Collected by Nathan Bailey, 1736, Edited from His "Dictionarium Britannicum or a More Compleat Universal Etymological English Dictionary"*. Eds. John Ettlinger and Ruby Day. Metuchen, New Jersey: Scarecrow Press, 1992. 163 pp.

1224. Baldwin, Robert, and Ruth Paris. *The Book of Similes*. Illustrations by David Austin. London: Routledge & Kegan Paul, 1982. 149 pp.

1225. Barber, David W. (ed.). *Quotable Sherlock*. Illustrations by Sidney Paget. Toronto: Quotable Books, 2001. 118 pp.

1226. Barber, John W. *The Hand Book of Illustrated Proverbs. Comprising also a Selection of Approved Proverbs of Various Nations and Languages, Ancient and Modern. Interpreted with Numerous Engravings and Descriptions*. New Haven, Connecticut: Justus H. Bradley & John W. Barber, 1855. New York: George F. Tuttle, 1856; rpt. Ann Arbor, Michigan: University of Michigan Library, 2009. 252 pp.

1227. Barnette, Martha. *Dog Days and Dandelions. A Lively Guide to the Animal Meanings Behind Everyday Words*. New York: St. Martin's Press, 2003. 194 pp.

1228. Barten, John. *A Select Collection of English and German Proverbs, Proverbial Expressions, and Familiar Quotations with Translations / Ausgwählte Sammlung Englischer u. Deutscher Sprichwörter, sprichwörtlicher Redensarten und Citate mit Übersetzungen*. Hamburg: Conrad Kloss, 1896. 323 pp.

1229. Bartlett, John. *A Collection of Familiar Quotations, with Complete Indices of Authors and Subjects*. Cambridge, Massachusetts: John Bartlett, 1855. Facsimile Edition. New York: Philosophical Library, 1958. 295 pp.

1230. Bartlett, John. *A Collection of Familiar Quotations, with Complete Indices of Authors and Subjects*. New edition [2 nd ed.]. Cambridge, Massachusetts: John Bartlett, 1856. 358 pp.

1231. Bartlett, John. *A Collection of Familiar Quotations, with Complete Indices of Authors and Subjects.* 3rd ed. Cambridge, Massachustters: John Bartlett, 1860. 446 pp.

1232. Bartlett, John. *Familiar Quotations: Being an Attempt to Trace to Their Source Passages and Phrases in Common Use; Chiefly from English Authors.* 4th ed. Boston: Little, Brown, and Company, 1867. 480 pp. (plus 16 pp. addenda).

1233. Bartlett, John. *Familar Quotations: Being an Attempt to Trace to Their Source Passages and Phrases in Common Use.* 5th ed. Boston: Little, Brown, and Company, 1868. 778 pp.

1234. Bartlett, John. *Familiar Quotations: Being an Attempt to Trace to Their Source Passages and Phrases in Common Use.* 7th ed. Boston, Little, Brown, and Company, 1879. 864 pp.

1235. Bartlett, John. *The Shakespeare Phrase Book.* Boston: Little, Brown, and Company, 1881. 1034 pp.

1236. Bartlett, John. *Familiar Quotations: Being an Attempt to Trace to Their Sources Passages and Phrases in Common Use.* 8th ed. Boston: Little, Brown, and Company, 1882. 904 pp.

1237. Bartlett, John. *Familiar Quotations. Being an Attempt to Trace to Their Source Passages and Phrases in Common Use.* Author's Edition. London: George Routledge, 1889. 524 pp.

1238. Bartlett, John. *Familiar Quotations: A Collection of Passages, Phrases, and Proverbs Traced to Their Sources in Ancient and Modern Literature.* 9th ed. Boston: Little, Brown, and Company, 1906. 1158 pp.

1239. Bartlett, John. *Familiar Quotations: A Collection of Passages, Phrases, and Proverbs Traced to Their Sources in Ancient and Modern Literature.* Ed. Nathan Haskell Dole. 10th ed. New York: Blue Ribbon Books, 1914. New York: Halcyon House, 1914. 1454 pp.

1240. Bartlett, John. *Familiar Quotations. A Collection of Passages, Phrases, and Proverbs Traced to Their Sources in Ancient and Modern Literature.* Eds. Christopher Morley and Louella D. Everett. 11th ed. Boston: Little, Brown, and Company, 1941. 1578 pp.

1241. Bartlett, John. *Familar Quotations: A Collection of Passages, Phrases, and Proverbs Traced to Their Sources in Ancient and Modern Literature.* Eds. Christopher Morley and Louella D. Everett. 12th ed. Boston: Little, Brown, and Company, 1949. 1831 pp.

1242. Bartlett, John. *The Shorter Bartlett's Familiar Quotations.* Ed. Kathleen Sproul. New York: Permabook, 1953 (10th printing 1960). 500 pp.

1243. Bartlett, John. *Familiar Quotation: A Collection of Passages, Phrases, and Proverbs Traced to Their Sources in Ancient and Modern Literature.* [Ed. Emily Morison Beck]. 13th ed. Boston: Little, Brown, and Company, 1955. London: Macmillan, 1957. 1614 pp.

1244. Bartlett, John. *A Collection of Familiar Quotations.* Facsimile Edition. New York: Philosophical Library, 1965; rpt. Secaucus, New Jersey: Citadel Press, 1983. 126 pp.

1245. Bartlett, John. *Familiar Quotations. A Collection of Passages, Phrases and Proverbs Traced to Their Sources in Ancient and Modern Literature.* Ed. Emily Morison Beck. 14th ed. Boston: Little, Brown, and Company, 1968. 1750 pp.

1246. Bartlett, John. *Familar Quotations: A Collection of Passages, Phrases, and Proverbs Traced to Their Sources in Ancient and Modern Literature.* Ed. Emily Morison Beck. 15th ed. Boston: Little, Brown, and Company, 1980.

1247. Bartlett, John. *Familiar Quotations. A Collection of Passages, Phrases, and Proverbs Traced to Their Sources in Ancient and Modern Literature.* Ed. Justin Kaplan. 16th ed. Boston: Little, Brown and Co., 1992. 1405 pp.

1248. Bartlett, John. Familiar Quotations. A Collection of Passages, Phrases, and Proverbs Traced to Their Sources in Ancient and Modern Literature. Ed. Justin Kaplan. 17th ed. Boston: Little, Brown and Company, 2002. 1431 pp.

1249. Barwick, Dee Danner. *Great Words of Our Time. Memorable Thoughts of Famous Men and Women of the 20th Century.* Kansas City, Missouri: Hallmark Cards, 1970. 62 pp. With illustrations.

1250. Baughman, M. Dale. *Educator's Handbook of Stories, Quotes, and Humor.* Englewood Cliffs, New Jersey: Prentice-Hall, 1963. 340 pp.

1251. Baz, Petros D. *A Dictionary of Proverbs. With a Collection of Maxims, Phrases, Passages, Poems and Anecdotes from Ancient and Modern Literature.* New York: Philosophical Library, 1963. 169 pp.

1252. Beal, George. *Fun with English Proverbs*. Illustrations by Peter Stevenson. London: Chambers, 1995. 32 pp.

1253. Bear, John. *The World's Worst Proverbs*. Illustrations by Ed Powers. Los Angeles, California: Price, Stern, Sloan Publishers, 1976. 46 pp. (anti-proverbs).

1254. Becker, Sven, Adnan Jelali, and Cheri Booth. *Idioms. Lexikon der englischen Redewendungen*. Eltville am Rhein: Bechtermünz, 1988. 511 pp.

1255. Beeton, Samuel Orchat. "Pictorial Proverbs [as Picture Riddles]." In S.O. Beeton. *Drawing-Room Plays, Acting Charades, Riddles, Enigmas, Rebuses, etc*. London: Ward, Lock and Co., ca. 1880-1890. 106-115 (pictures) and 138-139 (key).

1256. Beilenson, Evelyn L., and Sharon Melnick (eds.). *Words on Women*. White Plains, New York: Peter Pauper Press, 1987. 64 pp. With illustrations.

1257. Beilenson, John P. *Proverbs for Daily Living*. White Plains, New York: Peter Pauper Press, 1992. 80 pp. (miniature book).

1258. Berger, Terry (ed.). *Garden Proverbs*. Philadelphia: Running Press, 1984. 127 pp. (miniature book).

1259. Berger, Terry (ed.). *Garden Proverbs*. Illustrations by Diane Bigda. Philadelphia: Running Press, 2005. 127 pp. (miniature book). (not identical with previous entry).

1260. Berlitz, Charles. "The Local Coloring of Proverbs." In C. Berlitz. *Native Tongues*. New York: Grosset and Dunlap, 1982. 199-205.

1261. Berman, Louis A. *Proverb Wit & Wisdom: A Treasury of Proverbs, Parodies, Quips, Quotes, Clichés, Catchwords, Epigrams and Aphorisms*. New York: Perigee Book, 1997. 522 pp.

1262. Bertram, Anne. *NTC's Dictionary of Folksy, Regional, and Rural Sayings*. Ed. Richard A. Spears. Lincolnwood, Illinois: NTC Publishing Group, 1996. 381 pp.

1263. Bertram, Anne. *Aw, Shucks! The Dictionary of Country Jawing*. Lincolnwood, Illinois: NTC Publishing Group, 1997. Also as *In a Pig's Eye. The Dictionary of Country Jawing*. New York: Gramercy Books, 1998. 383 pp.

1264. Bertram, Anne, and Richard A. Spears (eds.). *NTC's Dictionary of Proverbs and Clichés*. Lincolnwood, Illinois: National Textbook Company, 1993. 321 pp.

1265. Bertram, Anne, and Richard A. Spears. *Dictionary of Folksay, Regional, and Rural Sayings*. Lincolnwood, Illinois: National Textbook Company, 1996. 381 pp.

1266. Bettmann, Otto L. *A Word from the Wise. A Sufficiency of Quotes & Images to Brighten Your Day*. New York: Harmony Books, 1977. 117 pp. With illustrations.

1267. Bickerstaff, H. George. *So Well Expressed*. Salt Lake City, Utah: Bookcraft, 1964. 124 pp.

1268. Blackwood, Margaret (ed.). *The Monstrous Regiment. A Book of Aphorisms*. London: Andre Deutsch, 1990. 158 pp. With illustrations.

1269. Bloem, Diane. *A Woman's Workshop on Proverbs. Leader's Manual*. Grand Rapids, Michigan: Zondervan Publishing House, 1978. 137 pp.

1270. Bloem, Diane. *A Woman's Workshop on Proverbs. Student's Manual*. Grand Rapids, Michigan: Zondervan Publishing House, 1978. 111 pp.

1271. Blumberg, Dorothy Rose. *Whose What? Aaron's Beard to Zorn's Lemma*. New York: Holt, Rinehart and Winston, 1969. 183 pp.

1272. Bohn, Henry G. *A Hand-Book of Proverbs Comprising an Entire Republication of Ray's Collection of English Proverbs, with His Additions from Foreign Languages*. London: Henry G. Bohn, 1855; rpt. London: Bell & Daldy, 1870; rpt. New York: AMS Press, 1968. 583 pp.

1273. Boller, Paul F., and John George. *They Never Said It: A Book of Fake Quotes, Misquotes, and Misleading Attributions*. Oxford: Oxford University Press, 1989. 159 pp.

1274. Booth, Cheri. *Idioms. Lexikon der englischen Redewendungen. Englisch-Deutsch*. Eltville am Rhein: Bechtermünz, 1988. 511 pp

1275. Booth, Cheri, and Christian Gerritzen. *Slang. Lexikon der englischen Umgangssprache. Englisch-Deutsch*. Eltville am Rhein: Bechtermünz, 1989. 508 pp.

1276. Bradley, John P., Leo F. Daniels, and Thomas C. Jones. *The International Dictionary of Thoughts*. Chicago: J.G. Ferguson, 1969. 1146 pp.

1277. Brady, John. "Collection of [English] Proverbs [Explained]." In J. Brady. *Varieties of Literature; Being, Principally, Selections from the Portfolio of the Late John Brady, Esq.* Ed. John Henry Brady. London: George B. Whittaker, 1826. 1-63 and 285-291 (index).

1278. Brandreth, Gyles. *Famous Last Words and Tombstone Humor.* New York: Sterling Publishing Co., 1989. 128 pp.

1279. Braude, Jacob M. *Speaker's Encyclopedia of Stories, Quotations and Anecdotes.* Englewood Cliffs, New Jersey: Prentice-Hall, 1955. 476 pp.

1280. Braude, Jacob M. *Braude's Handbook of Stories for Toastmasters and Speakers.* Englewood Cliffs, New Jersey: Prentice-Hall, 1957. 468 pp.

1281. Braude, Jacob M. *Complete Speaker's and Toastmaster's Library.* 8 vols. Englewood Cliffs, New Jersey: Prentice-Hall, 1965. I, 110 pp. (*Speech Openers and Closers*); II, 121 pp. (*Business and Professional Pointmakers*); III, 123 pp. (*Definitions and Toasts*), IV, 123 pp. (*Human Interest Stories*); V, 120 pp. (*Origins and Firsts*); VI, 124 pp. (*Proverbs, Epigrams, Aphorisms, Sayings, and Bon Mots*); VII, 123 pp. (*Remarks of Famous People*); VIII, 117 pp. (*Rhyme and Verse, to Help Make a Point*).

1282. Brennan-Nelson, Denise. *My Momma Likes to Say.* Illustrations by Jane Monroe Donovan. Chelsea, Michigan: Sleeping Bear Press, 2003. 32 pp. (children's book of proverbs and phrases).

1283. Brennan-Nelson, Denise. *My Teacher Likes to Say.* Illustrations by Jane Monroe Donovan. Chelsea, Michigan: Sleeping Bear Press, 2004. 32 pp. (children's book of proverbs and phrases).

1284. Brennan-Nelson, Denise. *My Grandma Likes to Say.* Illustrations by Jane Monroe Donovan. Chelsea, Michigan: Sleeping Bear Press, 2007. 32 pp. (children's book of proverbs and phrases).

1285. Breton, Nicholas. *Crossing of Proverbs: Crosse-Answers and Crosse-Humours.* 2 parts. London: John Wright, 1616. I, 10 pp.; II, 24 pp. Also in Nicholas Breton. *The Works in Verse and Prose.* Ed. Alexander B. Grosart. 2. vols. Edinburgh: Edimburgh University Press, 1879; rpt. Hildesheim: Georg Olms, 1969. II,e, 12 pp.

1286. Brewer, Ebenezer Cobham. *Dictionary of Phrase and Fable.* London: Cassell, 1870. Philadelphia: Claxton, Remsen, and Haffelfinger, 1870. 979 pp. Revised Centenary Edition. Ed. Ivor H. Evans. New York: Harper & Row, 1970. 1175 pp. (14th ed. 1989) 1220 pp.

1287. Brewer, Ebenezer Cobham. *Brewer's Dictionary of 20th-Century Phrase and Fable*. Eds. David Pickering, Alan Isaacs, and Elizabeth Martin. Boston: Houghton Mifflin Co., 1992 (1st ed. 1870). 662 pp.

1288. Brewer, Ebenezer Cobham. *Brewer's Dictionary of Modern Phrase & Fable*. Ed. Adrian Room. London: Cassell, 2000. 773 pp.

1289. Bronner, Michael A. *Bronner's Rhyming Phrases Dictionary*. Chicago, Illinois: New Edge Publishing Company, 2000. 324 pp.

1290. Brown, H. Jackson. *A Father's Book of Wisdom*. Nashville, Tennessee: Rutledge Hill Press, 1988 (2nd ed. 1990). 159 pp.

1291. Brown, H. Jackson. *Life's Little Instruction Book: Suggestions, Observations, and Reminders on How to Live a Happy and Rewarding Life*. 2 vols. Nashville, Tennessee: Rutledge Hill Press, 1991 and 1993. I, 160 pp.; II, 156 pp. (anti-proverbs).

1292. Brown, H. Jackson. *Live and Learn and Pass It on. People Age 5 to 95 Share What They've Learned about Successful Living*. Nashville, Tennessee: Rutledge Hill Press, 1991. 160 pp. With illustrations.

1293. Brown, H. Jackson (ed.). *Wit and Wisdom from the Peanut Butter Gang [i.e., children]*. Nashville, Tennessee: Rutledge Hill Press, 1994. 128 pp. With illustrations.

1294. Brown, Marshall. *Wit and Wisdom of Proverbial Philosophy. Odd Comparisons*. Philadelphia: J.B. Lippincott, 1884. 326 pp.

1295. Brown, Marshall. *Sayings that Never Grow Old. Wit and Humor of Well-known Quotations*. Boston: Small, Maynard & Company, 1918. 354 pp.

1296. Browning, D.C. *Everyman's Dictionary of Quotations and Proverbs*. London: J.M. Dent, 1951; rpt. London: J.M. Dent, 1969. 766 pp.

1297. Browning, D.C. *Everyman's Dictionary of Quotations and Proverbs*. London: Octopus Books, 1982. London: Chancellor Press, 1988. 745 pp.

1298. Browning, D.C. *The Complete Dictionary of Shakespeare Quotations*. London: New Orchard Editions, 1991. 560 pp.

1299. Bryan, George B. *Black Sheep, Red Herrings, and Blue Murder: The Proverbial Agatha Christie*. Bern: Peter Lang, 1993. 482 pp.

1300. Bryan, George B. "The Proverbial Sherlock Holmes [Arthur Conan Doyle]: An Index to Proverbs in the Holmesian Canon." *Proverbium*, 13 (1996), 47-68.

1301. Bryan, George B. "The Proverbial W.S. Gilbert: An Index to Proverbs in the Works of [William S.] Gilbert and [Arthur] Sullivan." *Proverbium*, 16 (1999), 21-35.

1302. Bryan, George B. "An Unfinished List of Anglo-American Proverb Songs." *Proverbium*, 18 (2001), 15-56.

1303. Bryan, George B. "Proverbial Titles of Dramas." *Proverbium*, 19 (2002), 65-74.

1304. Bryan, George B., and Wolfgang Mieder. *The Proverbial Charles Dickens: An Index to Proverbs in the Works of Charles Dickens*. New York: Peter Lang, 1997. 319 pp.

1305. Bryan, George B., and Wolfgang Mieder. *A Dictionary of Anglo-American Proverbs and Proverbial Phrases Found in Literary Sources of the Nineteenth and Twentieth Centuries*. New York: Peter Lang, 2005. 871 pp.

1306. Buchanan, Anne Christian, and Debra K. Klingsporn (eds.). *100 Voices. Words that Shaped Our Souls / Wisdom to Guide Our Future*. Bloomington, Minnesota: FrontPorch Books, 1999. 159 pp.

1307. Byrne, Robert. *The Other 637 Best Things Anybody Ever Said*. New York: Atheneum, 1984. 161 pp. With illustrations.

1308. Byrne, Robert. *The 2,548 Best Things Anybody Ever Said*. New York: Galahad Books, 1996. 633 pp.

1309. Cader, Michael, and Lisa Cader. *"But I Wouldn't Want to Live There!" Wicked Wisdom from Seasoned Travelers*. Illustrations by Sarah McMenemy. Philadelphia: Running Press, 1993. 160 pp.

1310. Camp, Wesley D. *Unfamiliar Quotations from 2000 B.C. to the Present*. Englewood Cliffs, New Jersey: Prentice Hall, 1990. 470 pp.

1311. Campbell, Hannah. *Why Did They Name It...? The Story Behind the Stories of the Brand Names that Have Become House Hold Words throughout the World*. New York: Fleet Publishing Corporation, 1964. 207 pp. With illustrations.

1312. Carleton, George Washington. *Carleton's New Handbook of Popular Quotations*. New York: G.W. Carleton, 1900. 500 pp.

1313. Carnahan, Mary (ed.). *In Praise of Moms*. Illustrated by Eliza Gran. Kansas City, Missouri: Andrews McMeel Publishing, 1998. 80 pp. (miniature book).

1314. Carothers, Gibson, and James Lacey. *Dictionary of Colorful Phrases*. New York: Sterling Publishing, 1979. 88 pp. With illustrations.

1315. Carr, Edwin Hamlin. *Putnam's Minute-a-Day Phrase-Maker. A Handbook of 4900 Allied Phrases*. New York: G.P. Putnam's Sons, 1928. 331 pp.

1316. Chamberlain, Alexander F. "Proverbs in the Remaking: Some Scientific Commonplaces." *Journal of American Folklore*, 17 (1904), 161-170 and 268-278.

1317. Chant, Steve (ed.). *(Un)Conventional Wisdom*. Burlington, Vermont: University Graphics & Printing, 1995. 32 pp. With Illustrations.

1318. Chapman, Bruce. *Why Do We Say Such Things? Stories Behind the Words We Use*. New York: Miles-Emmett, 1947. 286 pp.

1319. Cheales, Alan B. *Proverbial Folk-Lore*. London: Simpkin, Marshall & Co., 1874; rpt. Folcroft: Folcroft Library Editions, 1976. 173 pp.

1320. Chieger, Bob, and Pat Sullivan. *Inside Golf. Quotations on the Royal and Ancient Game*. New York: Atheneum, 1985. 271 pp.

1321. Childers, Evelyn Jones. *Kiss a Mule, Cure a Cold. Omens, Signs and Sayings*. Illustrations by Tim Lee. Atlanta. Georgia: Peachtree Publishers, 1988. 122 pp.

1322. Chiu, Kwong Ki. *A Dictionary of English Phrases with Illustrative Sentences*. New York: A.S. Barnes, 1881; rpt. Detroit: Gale Research Company, 1971. 915 pp.

1323. Christy, Robert. *Proverbs, Maxims and Phrases of All Ages. Classified Subjectively and Arranged Alphabetically*. 2 vols. New York: G.P. Putnam's Sons, 1887; rpt. Detroit: Gale Research Company, 1974; rpt. Norwood, Pennsylvania: Norwood Editions, 1977. I, 665 pp; II, 602 pp. (both volumes bound in one).

1324. Clairborne, Robert. *Loose Cannons & Red Herrings. A Book of Lost Metaphors*. New York: W.W. Norton, 1988. 254 pp.

1325. Clarke, John. *Paroemiologia Anglo-Latina in usum scholarum concinnata. Or Proverbs English, and Latine.* London: Felix Kyngston, 1639. 336 pp.

1326. Cohen, J.M., and M.J. Cohen. *The Penguin Dictionary of Quotations.* Middlesex, England: Penguin, 1960. 664 pp.

1327. Cohen, J.M., and M.J. Cohen. *The Penguin Dictionary of Modern Quotations.* Harmondsworth, England: Penguin, 1971. 366 pp. 2nd ed. Middlesex, England: Penguin, 1980. 496 pp.

1328. Cohen, J.M., and John Major. *History in Quotations.* London: Cassell, 2004. 1008 pp.

1329. Cole, Sylvia, and Abraham H. Lass. *The Dictionary of 20th-Century Allusions.* New York: Fawcett Gold Medal, 1991. 302 pp.

1330. Collison, Robert, and Mary Collison. *Dictionary of Foreign Quotations.* New York: Facts on File, 1980. 407 pp.

1331. Conklin, George W. *Who Said That? Being the Sources of Famous Sayings.* Chicago: George W. Ogilvie, 1906. 193 pp.

1332. Conny, Beth Mende (ed.). *Winning Women. Quotations on Sports, Health & Fitness.* White Plains, New York: Peter Pauper Press, 1993. 64 pp.

1333. Cook, Alexandra, and Verva Carter. *Mother Tried to Tell Me ... and I Just Wouldn't Listen.* Otillia, Canada: Periwinkle. 1982. 72 pp.

1334. Copeland, Lewis. *Popular Quotations for All Uses.* Garden City, New York: Doubleday, 1961. 560 pp.

1335. Cotgrave, Randle. *A Dictionarie of the French and English Tongues.* London: Adam Islip, 1611; rpt. Hildesheim: Georg Olms, 1970. 968 pp.

1336. Cowan, E. *Fractured Proverbs and Twisted Thoughts.* New York: 1st Books Library, 2001. 197 pp. (anti-proverbs).

1337. Cowan, Frank. *Dictionary of the Proverbs and Proverbial Phrases of the English Language Relating to the Sea.* Greenesburgh, Pennsylvania: Oliver, 1894. 144 pp.

1338. Cowie, Anthony P., and R. Mackin. *Oxford Dictionary of Current Idiomatic English.* Vol. 1. *Verbs with Prepositions & Particles.* London: Oxford University Press, 1975. 396 pp.

1339. Cowie, Anthony P., R. Mackin, and I. R. McCaig . *Oxford Dictionary of Current Idiomatic English*. Vol. 2. *Phrase, Clause & Sentence Idioms*. Oxford: Oxford University Press, 1983. 685 pp.

1340. Craig, Doris. *Catch Phrases, Clichés and Idioms. A Dictionary of Familiar Expressions*. Jefferson, North Carolina: McFarland, 1990. 232 pp.

1341. Crawley, Tony (ed.). *Chambers Film Quotes*. Edinburgh: Chambers, 1991; rpt. as *The Wordsworth Dictionary of Film Quotations*. Ware, Hertfordshire: Wordsworth, 1994. 296 pp.

1342. Crystal, David, and Hilary Crystal. *Words on Words. Quotations About Language and Languages*. Chicago: University of Chicago Press, 2000. 580 pp.

1343. Curran, Peter. *Proverbs in Action*. Illustrations by Roy Gale. Hove, Sussex: Editype, 1972. 53 pp.

1344. Cusick, Rick. *The Proverbial Bestiary*. Illustations by Warren Chappell. Woolwich, Maine: TBW Books, 1982. 62 pp.

1345. Czarnomski, F.B. (ed.). *The Eloquence of Winston Churchill*. New York: Signet Key Books, 1957. 200 pp.

1346. Daintith, John et al. (eds.). *The Macmillan Dictionary of Quotations*. New York: Macmillan, 1987. 790 pp.

1347. Daintith, John et al. (eds.). *Who Said What When. A Chronological Dictionary of Quotations*. London: Bloomsbury Publishing, 1988; New York: Hippocrene Books, 1991. 437 pp.

1348. Dalbiac, Philip Hugh. *A Dictionary of Quotations*. London: Thomas Nelson, 1909. 535 pp.

1349. Dale, Rodney (ed.). *The Wordsworth Dictionary of Sayings – Usual and Unusual*. Ware, Hertfordshire: Wordsworth Reference, 2007. 286 pp.

1350. DalzellA, Tom (ed.). *The Slang of Sin*. Illustrations by Istvan Banyai. Springfield, Massachusetts: Merriam-Webster, 1998. 385 pp.

1351. Davidoff, Henry. *The Pocket Book of Quotations*. New York: Pecket Book, 1942. 481 pp. (2nd ed. 1952). 480 pp.

1352. Denham, M.A. *A Collection of Proverbs and Popular Sayings Related to the Seasons, the Weather, and Agricultural Pursuits*. London: T. Richards, 1846. 73 pp.

1353. Dent, Robert W. *Shakespeare's Proverbial Language. An Index.* Berkeley, California: University of California Press, 1981. 289 pp.

1354. Dent, Robert W. *Proverbial Language in English Drama Exclusive of Shakespeare, 1495-1616. An Index.* Berkeley, California: University of California Press, 1984. 797 pp.

1355. Dickens, Charles Cedric, and Alan S. Watts (eds.). *The Sayings of Charles Dickens.* London: Gerald Duckworth, 1995. 64 pp.

1356. Dobson, Austin. *Proverbs in Porcelain.* Illustrations by Bernard Partridge. London: Kegan Paul, Trench, Trübner, & Co., 1893. 113 pp. (six "proverbe dramatique" in English translation).

1357. Donald, Graeme. *The Dictionary of Modern Phrase.* London: Simon & Schuster, 1994. 343 pp.

1358. Donald, Graeme. *Sticklers, Sideburns & Bikinis. The Military Origins of Everyday Words and Phrases.* Oxford: Osprey Publishing, 2008. 280 pp.

1359. Douglas, Charles Noel. *Forty-Thousand Sublime and Beautiful Thoughts.* 2 vols. New York: The Christian Herald, 1904; rpt. as *Forty Thousand Quotations, Prose and Poetical.* New York: Halcyon House, 1940. 2008 pp.

1360. Doyle, Charles Clay. "On 'New' Proverbs and the Conservativeness of Proverb Dictionaries." *Proverbium*, 13 (1996), 69-84. Also in *Cognition, Comprehension, and Communication: A Decade of North American Proverb Studies (1990-2000).* Ed. Wolfgang Mieder. Baltmannsweiler: Schneider Verlag Hohengehren, 2003. 85-98. (with lists of modern Anglo-American proverbs).

1361. Dunn, Jerry. *Idiom Savant: Slang as It Is Slung.* New York: Henry Holt, 1997. 296 pp.

1362. Dunwoody, H.H.C. *Weather Proverbs.* Washington, D.C.: Government Printing Office, 1883. 148 pp.

1363. Dykes, Oswald. *Moral Reflections Upon Select English Proverbs: Familiarly Accommodated to the Humour and Manners of the Present Age.* London: H. Meere, 1708. 280 pp.

1364. Eames, Alan D. *A Beer Drinker's Companion. 5000 Years of Quotes and Anecdotes.* Harvard, Massachusetts: Ayers Rock Press, 1986. 145 pp.

1365. Edwards, Tryon. *A Dictionary of Thoughts, Being a Cyclopedia of Laconic Quotations from the Best Authors of the World, Both Ancient and Modern.* Detroit: F.B. Dickerson, 1914. 678 pp. and xxxiv pp. (authors' reference index). Also as *The New Dictionary of Thoughts. A Cyclopedia of Quotations.* New York: Classic Publishing, 1936; rpt. New York: Standard Book Company, 1954. 746 pp. and xxxiv pp. (authors' reference index).

1366. Edwards, Tryon. *Useful Quotations. A Cyclopedia of Quotations.* Eds. C.N. Catrevas and Jonathan Edwards. New York: Grosset & Dunlap, 1936. 734 pp. and xxxiv pp. (authors' reference index).

1367. Ely, Virginia. *I Quote. A Collection of Ancient & Modern Wisdom & Inspiration.* New York: George W. Stewart, 1947. 404 pp.

1368. Engelmann, Larry. *They Said That! The Wit and Wisdom of Modern Celebrity Culture.* Los Angeles, California: Renaissance Books, 2000. 317 pp.

1369. Engeroff, Karl, and Cicely Lovelace-Käufer. *An English-German Dictionary of Idioms. Idiomatic and Figurative English Expressions with German Translations.* München: Max Hueber, 1959 (5th ed. 1975). 313 pp.

1370. Esar, Evan. *Esar's Comic Dictionary.* New York: Harvest House, 1943. 313 pp.

1371. Esar, Evan. *20,000 Quips & Quotes. A Treasury of Witty Remarks, Comic Proverbs, Wisecracks, and Epigrams.* Garden City, New York: Doubleday, 1968; rpt. New York: Barnes & Noble, 1995. 908 pp.

1372. Evans, Bergen. *Dictionary of Quotations.* New York: Avenel Books, 1968. 832 pp.

1373. Ewart, James. *Dictionary of British Slang and Colloquial Expressions.* Lincolnwood, Illinois: NTC Publishing Group, 1997. 573 pp.

1374. Ewart, Neil. *Everyday Phrases. Their Origins and Meanings.* Poole, Dorset: Blandford Press, 1983; rpt. London: Cassell, 1991. 162 pp.

1375. Exley, Helen (ed.). *Mother Quotations. A Collection of Beautiful Paintings and the Best Mother Quotes.* New York: Exley Giftbooks, 1993. 57 pp. With illustrations.

1376. Faber, Harold. *The Book of Laws.* New York: Times Books, 1979. 113 pp.

1377. Fadiman, Clifton (ed.). *The Little, Brown Book of Anecdotes.* Boston: Little, Brown and Company, 1985. 751 pp.

1378. Fakih, Kimberly Olsen. *Off the Clock: A Lexicon of Time Words and Expressions.* New York: Ticknor & Fields, 1995. 123 pp. With illustrations.

1379. Farkas, Anna. *The Oxford Dictionary of Catchphrases.* Oxford: Oxford University Press, 2002. 357 pp.

1380. Farman, John. *You Can't Tell a Rook [sic] by Its Cover. Unreliable Proverbs.* London: Pan Books, 1989. 63 pp. With illustrations. (anti-proverbs).

1381. Farmer, John Stephen, and William Ernest Henley. *Slang and Its Analogues Past and Present. A Dictionary, Historical and Comparative, of the Heterodox Speech of All Classes of Society for More Than Three Hundred Years. With Synonyms in English, French, German, etc.* 7 vols. London: Printed for subscribers only, 1890-1904. Rpt. ed. Theodore M. Bernstein. New York: Arno Press, 1970. I, A – Bye, 405 pp.; II, Cab – Fizzle, 406 pp.; III, Fla – Hyps, 387 pp.; IV, Ice – My, 399 pp.; V, Nab – Razzle, 381 pp.; VI, Reaches – Stozzle, 378 pp.; VII, Strada – Zu, 380 pp.

1382. Feldman, David. *Who Put the Butter in Butterfly? And Other Fearless Investigations into Our Illogical Language.* Illustrations by Kassie Schwan. New York: Harper & Row, 1989. 209 pp.

1383. Fergusson, Rosalind. *The Facts on File Dictionary of Proverbs.* New York: Facts on File Publications, 1983. Also as *The Penguin Dictionary of Proverbs.* New York: Penguin Books, 1983. 331 pp.

1384. Fielding, Thomas (pseud. John Wade). *Select Proverbs of All Nations: Illustrated with Notes and Comments. To which is Added a Summary of Ancient Pastimes, Holidays, and Customs; with an Analysis of the Wisdom of the Ancients, and of the Fathers of the Church.* London: Longman 1824. 215 pp. Rpt. as *Select Proverbs of All Nations: with Notes and Comments. A Summary of Ancient Pastimes, Holidays and Customs; with An Analysis of the Ancients, and of the Fathers of the Church.* Baltimore, Maryland: W.B. Cram, 1831. 280 pp.

1385. Fielding, Thomas (pseud. John Wade). *Select Proverbs of All Nations. Pastimes, Holidays, and Customs of Olden Times. Wise*

Sayings and Maxims of the Ancient Fathers, and the Economy of Life. By an Ancient Bramin. Dayton, Ohio: More, Clarke & Company, 1854. 384 pp.

1386. Fischer, Katrin. *Reclams Lexikon der Shakespeare-Zitate.* Stuttgart: Philipp Reclam, 2002. 399 pp.

1387. Fitzhenry, Robert I. (ed.). *The Fitzhenry & Whiteside Book of Quotations. Revised and Enlarged.* Toronto: Fitzhenry & Whiteside, 1986. Rpt. as *Barnes & Noble Book of Quotations. Revised and Enlarged.* New York: HarperCollins Publishers, 1987. 412 pp.

1388. Flavell, Linda, and Roger Flavell. *Dictionary of Idioms and Their Origins.* London: Kyle Cathie, 1992. 216 pp.

1389. Flavell, Linda, and Roger Flavell. *Dictionary of Proverbs and Their Origins.* London: Kyle Cathie, 1993; rpt. New York: Barnes & Noble, 1997. 273 pp.

1390. Flesch, Rudolf. *The Book of Unusual Quotations.* New York: Harper & Brothers, 1957. 338 pp.

1391. Flexner, Stuart Berg, and Doris Flexner. *Wise Words and Wives' Tales. The Origins, Meanings and Time-Honored Wisdom of Proverbs and Folk Sayings, Olde [sic] and New.* New York: Avon Books, 1993. 218 pp.

1392. Florio, John. *His Firste Fruites: which Yeelde Familiar Speech, Merie Prouerbes, Wittie Sentences, and Golden Sayings. Also a Perfect Induction to the Italian, and English Tongues.* London: Thomas Dawson, 1578; rpt. New York: Da Capo Press, 1969. 163 leaves (Italian-English proverbs).

1393. Florio, John. *Second Frvtes, to Be Gathered of Twelue Trees, of Diuers but Delightsome Tastes to the Tongues of Italians and Englishmen.* 2 parts. London: Thomas Woodcock, 1591; rpt. New York: Da Capo Press, 1969. I, 207 (Italian-English proverbs); II, 218 pp. (Italian proverbs).

1394. Fogg, Walter. *One Thousand Sayings of History Presented as Pictures in Prose.* New York: Grosset & Dunlap, 1929. 919 pp.

1395. Fonseca, José da, and Pedro Carolino. *English as She is Spoke or A Jest in Sober Earnest.* New York: D. Appleton, 1883. 60 pp.

1396. Forbes, Malcolm S. (ed.). *The Forbes Scrapbook of Thoughts on the Business of Life.* New York: B.C. Forbes & Sons Publishing Co., 1984. 546 pp.

1397. Förster, Max. "Das elisabethanische Sprichwort nach Th. Draxe's *Treasurie of Ancient Adagies* (1616)." *Anglia*, 42 (1919), 361-424.

1398. Frank, Leonard Roy. *Influencing Minds. A Reader in Quotations.* Portland, Oregon: Feral House, 1995. 245 pp.

1399. Frank, Leonard Roy. *Random House Webster's Quotationary: The Authoritative Source for over 20,000 Quotations.* New York: Random House, 2001. 1040 pp.

1400. Franklyn, Julian. *A Dictionary of Rhyming Slang.* London: Routledge, 1960. 202 pp.

1401. Fraser, Betty (ill.). *First Things First: An Illustrated Collection of Sayings – Useful and Familiar for Children.* New York: Harper & Row, 1990. 32 pp. (children's book).

1402. Freeman, Criswell (ed.). *The Golfer's Book of Wisdom. Common Sense and Uncommon Genius from 101 Golfing Legends.* Nashville, Tennessee: Walnut Grove Press, 1995. 148 pp.

1403. Freier, George D. *Weather Proverbs: How 600 Proverbs, Sayings and Poems Accurately Explain Our Weather.* Tucson, Arizona: Fisher Books, 1992. Rpt. as *The Wonder of Weather. 600 Proverbs, Sayings, Facts and Folklore About the Always Unpredictable Weather.* New York: Gramercy Books, 1999. 214 pp.

1404. Frieser, Walter. *Das Sprichwort in den dramatischen Werken John Lyly's. Zugleich ein Beitrag zur Geschichte des englischen Sprichworts.* Diss. Universität Leipzig, 1920. 205 pp.

1405. Frost-Knappman, Elizabeth, and David S. Shrager. *A Concise Encyclopedia of Legal Quotations.* New York: Barnes and Noble, 2003. 390 pp.

1406. Fuller, Edmund (ed.). *Thesaurus of Epigrams.* New York: Crown Publishers, 1943. 382 pp.

1407. Fuller, Edmund (ed.). *4800 Wisecracks, Witty Remarks, and Epigrams for All Occasions.* New York: Avenel Books, 1980. 338 pp.

1408. Funk, Charles Earle. *A Hog on Ice and Other Curious Expressions.* New York: Harper & Row, 1948. 214 pp. Rpt. New York: Warner, 1972. 239 pp. Rpt. New York: Harper Colophon Books, 1985. 214 pp.

1409. Funk, Charles Earle. *Thereby Hangs a Tale. Stories of Curious Word Origins.* New York: Harper & Row, 1950; rpt. New York: Harper Colophon Books, 1985. 303 pp.

1410. Funk, Charles Earle. *Heavens to Betsy! and Other Curious Sayings.* New York: Harper & Row, 1955. 224 pp. Rpt. New York: Warner, 1972. 255 pp. Rpt. New York: Harper & Row, 1986. 224 pp.

1411. Funk, Charles Earle. *Horse Feathers and Other Curious Words.* New York: Harper & Row, 1958; rpt. New York: Harper & Row, 1986. 240 pp.

1412. Funk, Charles Earle. *2107 Curious Word Origins, Sayings & Expressions from "White Elephants" to a "Song and a Dance".* New York: Galahad Books, 1993. 988 pp. (Based on Funk's earlier volumes *A Hog on Ice and Other Curious Expressions* [1948], *Thereby Hangs a Tale* [1950], *Heavens to Betsy!* [1955], and *Horse Feathers and Other Curious Words* [1958]).

1413. Gallo, Rudy (ill.). *The Book of Illustrated Proverbs.* Cambridge, Maryland: Golden Seal Press, 1996. 255 pp.

1414. Garriott, Edward B. *Weather Folk-Lore and Local Weather Signs.* Washington: Government Printing Office, 1903; rpt. Detroit, Michigan: Grand River Books, 1971. 153 pp.

1415. Garrison, Webb. *Why You Say It. The Fascinating Stories Behind Over 600 Everyday Words and Phrases.* Nashville, Tennessee: Rutledge Hill Press, 1992. 356 pp.

1416. Gash, Amy (ed.). *What the Dormouse Said. Lessons for Grown-ups from Children's Books.* Illustrations by Pierre Le-Tan. Chapel Hill, North Carolina: Algonquin Books, 1999. 146 pp.

1417. Gerbert, Manfred, and Peter Zimmermann. *Idiomatische Redewendungen Englisch-Deutsch.* Leipzig: VEB Verlag Enzyklopädie, 1987. 271 pp.

1418. Gerhard, Hartwig. *Der "Liber Proverbiorum" des Godefrid von Winchester.* Diss. Universität Würzburg, 1971. Würzburg: Selbstverlag, 1974. 130 pp.

1419. Ginsburg, Susan. *Family Wisdom. The 2,000 Most Important Things Ever Said About Parenting, Children, and Family Life.* New York: Columbia University Press, 1996. 315 pp.

1420. Goldsmith, Warren H. *Crumbs of Commonsense. An Odd Venture to Help You Get the Habit of Thinking*. Boston: Wright and Potter, 1928. 320 pp.

1421. Goldstein, Sharon (ed.). *The Merriam-Webster Dictionary of Quotations*. Springfield, Massachusetts: Merriam-Webster, 1992. 501 pp.

1422. Gomes, Hélio. *Quality Quotes*. Milwaukee, Wisconsin: ASQC Quality Press, 1996. 249 pp.

1423. Goodman, Ted (ed.). *The Forbes Book of Business Quotations. 14,173 Thoughts on the Business of Life*. New York: Black Dog & Leventhal Publishers, 1997. 992 pp.

1424. Graffagnino, J. Kevin (ed.). *Only in Books. Writers, Readers, & Bibliophiles on Their Passion*. Madison, Wisconsin: Madison House, 1996. 266 pp. With illustrations.

1425. Green, Joanne, and John D.A. Widdowson. *Traditional English Language Genres [Proverbial Usage, Traditional Sayings and Expressions, Rhymes and Riddles, Blason populaire, Language of Children's Traditional Play and Games]. Continuity and Change, 1950-2000*. 2 vols. Sheffield: The National Centre for English Cultural Tradition, University of Sheffield, 2003. 712 pp.

1426. Green, Jonathon. *Slang Through the Ages*. Lincolnwood, Illinois: NTC Publishing Group, 1997. 393 pp.

1427. Gregorich, Barbara. *Waltur [sic] Buys a Pig in a Poke and Other Stories*. Illustrations by Kristin Sorra. Boston, Massachusetts: Houghton Mifflin, 2006. 54 pp. (proverb stories for children).

1428. Gregorich, Barbara. *Waltur [sic] Paints Himself into a Corner and Other Stories*. Illustrations by Kristin Sorra. Boston, Massachusetts: Houghton Mifflin, 2007. 48 pp. (proverb stories for children).

1429. Grocott, John C. *Familiar Quotations with Parallel Passages from Various Writers*. With an Appendix Containing Quotations from American Writers by Anna L. Ward. London: George Routledge, 1890. 699 pp.

1430. Grose, Francis. *A Classical Dictionary of the Vulgar Tongue*. London: S. Hooper, 1785. 182 pp.; 3rd ed. London: Hooper & Wigstead, 1796. 244 pp.; rpt. with a preface and "A Sketch of the Life & Works of Francis Grose [1731?-1791] by Eric Partridge. London:

Scholartis Press, 1931. 396 pp.; rpt. New York: Barnes & Noble, 1963; rpt. once again New York: Dorset Press, 1992. 396 pp.

1431. Grose, Francis. *Dictionary of the Vulgar Tongue*. London: C. Chappel, 1811; rpt. London: Bibliophile Books, 1984. 224 pp.

1432. Gross, John. *The Oxford Book of Aphorisms*. Oxford: Oxford University Press, 1983. 383 pp.

1433. Grothe, Mardy. *"Never Let a Fool Kiss You or a Kiss Fool You": Chiasmus and a World of Quotations That Say What They Mean and Mean What They Say*. New York: Viking Penguin, 1999. 126 pp. With illustrations.

1434. Grothe, Mardy. *Oxymoronica. Paradoxical Wit and Wisdom from History's Greatest Wordsmiths*. New York: HarperCollins, 2004. 246 pp.

1435. Grothe, Mardy. *Ifferisms. An Anthology of Aphorisms that Begin with the Word "If"*. New York: HarperCollins, 2009. 326 pp.

1436. Guinagh, Kevin. *Dictionary of Foreign Phrases and Abbreviations*. New York: H.W. Wilson, 1965; rpt. New York: Pocket Book, 1966. 320 pp.

1437. Gulland, Daphne M., and David G. Hinds-Howell. *The Penguin Dictionary of English Idioms*. Harmondsworth, Middlesex: Penguin Books, 1986. 300 pp.

1438. Gvardzhaladze, I.S., and D.I. Mchedlishzili. *Angliiskie poslovitsi i pogovorki*. Moskva: Vysshaia shkola, 1971. 77 pp.

1439. Hale, Sarah Josepha. *A Complete Dictionary of Poetical Quotations: Comprising the Most Excellent and Appropriate Passages in the Old British Poets; with Choice and Copious Selections from the Best Modern British and American Poets*. Philadelphia: Lippincott, Grambo & Co., 1854. 576 pp.

1440. Hand, Wayland D. "A Dictionary of Words and Idioms Associated with Judas Iscariot." *University of California Publications in Modern Philology*, 24, no. 3 (1942), 289-356.

1441. Hanger, Charles Henry. *Proverbial and Moral Thoughts*. London: James Cornish, 1857. 204 pp.

1442. Hardwick, Michael, and Mollie Hardwick. "A Sampler of Quotations." In M. and M. Hardwick. *The Charles Dickens Companion*. London: John Murray, 1965. 173-228.

1443. Hardwick, Michael and Mollie Hardwick. "Quotations." In M. and M. Hardwick. *The Charles Dickens Encyclopedia*. New York: Charles Scribner's Sons, 1973. 239-521.

1444. Hargrave, Basil. *Origins and Meanings of Popular Phrases and Names. Including Those which Came into Use During the Great War*. London: T. Werner Laurie, 1925; rpt. Detroit: Gale Research Company, 1968. 376 pp.

1445. Harter, Jim. *Thoughts on Success. Thoughts and Reflections from History's Great Thinkers*. New York: American Heritage, 1995. 150 pp. With Illustrations.

1446. Harvey, Sir Paul. *The Oxford Dictionary of English Proverbs*. 2nd ed. Oxford: Clarendon Press, 1948. 740 pp. 1st ed. by William George Smith. With an introduction and index by Janet E. Heseltine. Oxford: Clarendon Pess, 1935. 644 pp. 3rd ed. revised by F.P. Wilson. Oxford: Clarendon Press, 1970. 930 pp.

1447. Hayward, Arthur L. "Familiar Sayings; Wellerisms; Wisdom from Mrs. Gamp." In A.L. Hayward. *The Dickens Encyclopaedia*. Hamden, Connecticut: Archon Books, 1968. 171-172, 173-174, 175.

1448. Hazlitt, W. Carew. *English Proverbs and Proverbial Phrases, Collected from the Most Authentic Sources, Alphabetically Arranged and Annotated*. London: J.R. Smith, 1869. 505 pp. Rev. ed. London: Reeves and Turner, 1907; rpt. Detroit: Gale Research Company, 1969. 580 pp.

1449. Henderson, B.L.K. *A Dictionary of English Idioms*. Vol. 1: *Verbal Idioms*. Vol. 2: *Colloquial Phrases*. London: James Blackwood, 1937. I, 352 pp.; II, 408 pp.

1450. Henderson, George Surgeon. *The Popular Rhymes. Sayinqs and Proverbs of the County of Berwick*. Newcastle-on-Tyne: For the author, 1856; rpt. Darby, Pennsylvania: Folcroft Library Editions, 1977. 184 pp.

1451. Hendrickson, Robert. *Animal Crackers. A Bestial Lexicon*. New York: Penguin Books, 1983. 239 pp.

1452. Hendrickson, Robert. *Salty Words*. New York: Hearst Marine Books, 1984. 224 pp.

1453. Hendrickson, Robert. *The Facts on File Encyclopedia of Word and Phrase Origins*. New York: Facts on File Publications, 1987. 581 pp.

1454. Hendyng. *The Proverbs of Hendyng.* In *Reliquiae antiquae. Scraps from Ancient Manuscripts Illustrating Chiefly Early English Literature and the English Language.* Eds. Thomas Wright and James O. Halliwell. London: William Pickering, 1841; rpt. New York: AMS Press, 1966. I, 109-116, 193-194, and 256-257.

1455. Henry, Lewis C. *Five Thousand Quotations for all Occasions.* Garden City, New York: Doubleday, 1945. 346 pp.

1456. Henschel, F. A *Collection of Anglicisms, Germanisms and Phrases of the English and German Languages / Sammlung von Anglicismen, Germanismen und Redensarten der englischen und deutschen Sprache.* Berlin: F. Henschel, 1871. 244 pp.

1457. Herbert, George. *Outlandish Proverbs.* London: Humphrey Blunden, 1640; rpt. London: T. Garthwait, 1651. In *Musarum Deliciae; or, The Muses Recreation, Containing Severall Pieces of Poetique Wit.* Ed. John Mennes. London: John Camden Hotten, 1947. II, 483-525.

1458. Herbert, George. *Outlandish Proverbs.* London: Humphrey Blunden, 1640; rpt. ed. Gordon Jackson. Lincoln, Great Britain: Asgill Press, 2001. 43 pp.

1459. Heuber, Hans-Georg. *Talk One's Head Off. Ein Loch in den Bauch reden. Englische Redewendungen und ihre deutschen "opposite numbers".* Illustrations by Birgit Rieger. Reinbek: Rowohlt, 1982. 119 pp.

1460. Heywood, John. *The Proverbs of John Heywood. Being the "Proverbs" of that Author Printed 1546.* Ed. Julian Sharman. London: George Bell, 1874; rpt. Darby, Pennsylvania: Folcroft Library Editions, 1972. 173 pp.

1461. Heywood, John. *A Dialogue Conteynyng the Number of the Effectuall Prouerbes in the Englishe Toungue, Compact in a Matter Concernynge Two Maner of Maryyages. With One Hundred of Epigrammes: and Three Hundred of Epigrammes upon Three Hundred Prouverbes: and a Fifth Hundred of Epigrams. Wherevnto Are Now Newly Added a Syxt Hundred of Epigrams.* London: Thomas Powell, 1562. Rpt. as *The Proverbs, Epigrams, and Miscellanies of John Heywood. With an Index, Note-Book, and Word-List.* Ed. John S. Farmer. London: Early English Drama Society, 1906; rpt. New York: Banes & Noble, 1966. 466 pp.

1462. Heywood, John. *John Heywood's "A Dialogue of Proverbs".* Ed. Rudolph E. Habenicht. Berkeley, California: University of California Press, 1963. 300 pp.

1463. Hill, Wayne F., and Cynthia J. Öttchen. *Shakespeare's Insults for Lawyers.* Illustrations by Tom Lulevitch. New York: Clarkson N. Potter, 1996. 80 pp.

1464. Holder, R.W. *A Dictionary of Euphemisms.* Oxford: Oxford University Press, 1995. 470 pp.

1465. Holt, Alfred H. *Phrase Origins. A Study of Familiar Expressions.* New York: Thomas Y. Crowell, 1936. 328 pp.

1466. Holt, Alfred H. *Phrase and Word Origins. A Study of Familiar Expressions.* Revised ed. New York: Dover, 1961. 254 pp.

1467. Hood, Edwin Paxton. *The World of Proverb and Parable. With Illustrations from History, Biography, and the Anecdotal Table-Talk of All Ages. With an Introductory Essay on the Historic Unity of the Popular Proverb and Tale in All Ages.* London: Hodder and Stoughton, 1885. 563 pp

1468. Hook, Donald D., and Lothar Kahn. *Book of Insults & Irreverent Quotations.* Middle Village, New York: Jonathan David, 1980. 268 pp.

1469. House, Jack (ed.). *Winston Churchill: His Wit and Wisdom.* London: Collins, 1965; rpt. London: Hyperion Books, 1990. 149 pp.

1470. Howard, Philip. *Winged Words.* New York: Oxford University Press, 1988. 292 pp.

1471. Hoyt, Jehiel Keeler. *The Cyclopedia of Practical Quotations: English, Latin and Modern Foreign Languages.* New York: Funk & Wagnalls, 1892 (12th ed. 1894). 899 pp.

1472. Hoyt, Jehiel Keeler. *The Cyclopedia of Practical Quotations: English, Latin and Modern Foreign Languages.* Revised ed. New York: Funk & Wagnalls, 1896. 1178 pp.

1473. Hughes, Shirley (ill.). *"Make Hay While the Sun Shines": A Book of Proverbs.* London: Faber and Faber, 1977; rpt. London: Faber and Faber, 1998. 40 pp. (children's book).

1474. Hughes, Shirley (ill.). *"Over the Moon": A Book of Sayings.* London: Faber and Faber, 1980; rpt. London: Faber and Faber, 1998. 40 pp.

1475. Humes, James C. *The Wit and Wisdom of Winston Churchill. A Treasury of More Than 1,000 Quotations and Anecdotes*. New York: HarperCollins, 1994. 234 pp.

1476. Humphreys, William Jackson. *Weather Proverbs and Paradoxes*. Baltimore, Maryland: William & Wilkins, 1923. 126 pp. With illustrations.

1477. Hyamson, Albert M. *A Dictionary of English Phrases*. New York: E.P. Dutton, 1922; rpt. Detroit: Gale Research Company, 1970. 365 pp.

1478. Hyman, Dick. *Crazy Laws*. Illustrations by Tom Eaton. New York: Scholastic, 1976. 90 pp.

1479. Hyman, Dick. *More Crazy Laws*. Illustrations by Don Orehek. New York: Scholastic, 1992. 94 pp.

1480. Hyman, Robin (ed.). *The Pan Dictionary of Famous Quotations*. London: Pan Books, 1989. 688 pp.

1481. Ichikawa, Sanki, Takuji Mine, Ryoichi Inui, Kenzo Kihara, and Shiro Takaha (eds.). *The Kenkyusha Dictionary of Current English Idioms*. Tokyo: Kenkyusha, 1964. 849 pp.

1482. Inwards, Richard. *Weather Lore: A Collection of Proverbs, Sayings, and Rules Concerning the Weather*. London: Elliot Stock, 1893. rpt. London: Senate, 1994. 190 pp.

1483. Isil, Olivia A. *"When a Loose Cannon Flogs a Dead Horse There's the Devil to Pay": Seafaring Words in Everyday Speech*. Camden, Maine: International Marine, 1996. 134 pp. With illustrations.

1484. Jack, Albert. *Red Herrings & White Elephants. The Origins of the Phrases We Use Every Day*. New York: HarperCollins, 2004. 256 pp.

1485. Jacobson, John D. *Eatioms. A Short Salmagundi of Phrases, Metaphors, and Bon Mots that Are Irresistable Food for Thought*. New York: Laurel, 1993. 196 pp.

1486. Jagendorf, Moritz A. "Apples in Life and Lore." *New York Folklore Quarterly*, 18 (1962), 273-283.

1487. James, Ewart. *NTC's Dictionary of British Slang and Colloquial Expressions*. Lincolnwood, Illinois: NTC Publishing Group, 1996. 573 pp.

1488. Jay, Antony. *The Oxford Dictionary of Political Quotations.* Oxford: Oxford University Press, 1996. 515 pp.

1489. Jeffares, A. Norman, and Martin Gray (eds.). *A Dictionary of Quotations.* New York: HarperCollins, 1995; rpt. New York: Barnes & Noble, 1997. 1027 pp.

1490. Jente, Richard. "The Proverbs of Shakespeare with Early and Contemporary Parallels." *Washington University Studies, Humanistic Series*, 13, no. 2 (1926), 391-444.

1491. Jernigan, Kenneth. *The Bell, the Clapper, and the Cord: Wit and Witticism.* Baltimore, Maryland: National Federation of the Blind, 1994. 88 pp.

1492. Jernigan, Kenneth. *Wit and Witticism. The Second Time Around.* Baltimore, Maryland: National Federation of the Blind, 1996. 88 pp.

1493. Johnson, Albert. *Common English Proverbs.* London: Longmans, Green & Co., 1954. 122 pp.

1494. Johnson, Albert. *Common English Sayings.* London: Longmans, Green & Co., 1958. 152 pp.

1495. Johnson, Sterling. *English as a Second F*cking Language. How to Swear Effectively, Explained in Detail with Numerous Examples Taken from Everyday Life.* Pacific Grove, California: ESFL University Press, 1995. 88 pp.

1496. Kaufman, Lois L. (ed.). *Bringing Up Baby. A Witty Look at Child Rearing.* White Plains, New York: Peter Pauper Press, 1989. 64 pp. With illustrations.

1497. Keitges, John. *Proverbs and Quotations for School and Home.* Chicago: A. Flanagan, 1905. 105 pp.

1498. Kenin, Richard, and Justin Wintle (eds.). *The Dictionary of Biographical Quotation of British and American Subjects.* New York: Alfred A. Knopf, 1978. 860 pp.

1499. Ker, John Bellenden. *An Essay on the Archaeology of Our Popular Phrases, and Nursery Rhymes.* London: Longman, Rees, Brown, Green, & Co., 1835. 290 pp.

1500. Keyes, Ralph. *"Nice Guys Finish Seventh": False Phrases, Spurious Sayings, and Familiar Misquotations.* New York: HarperCollins, 1992. 273 pp.

1501. Keyes, Ralph. *The "Quote" Verifier. Who Said What, Where, and When.* New York: St. Martin's Griffin, 2006. 389 pp.

1502. King, John. "A Collection of [English-German] Proverbs." In J. King. *The True English Guide for Germans.* London: J. Nourse, 1758. 269-294.

1503. King, John. "English and German Phrases and Idioms." In J. King. *The True English Guide for Germans.* London: J. Nourse, 1758. 254-268.

1504. King, Kevin. *The Big Picture. Idioms as Metaphors.* Boston: Houghton Mifflin Company, 1999. 194 pp. With illustrations.

1505. Kingsbury, Stewart A., Mildred E. Kingsbury, and Wolfgang Mieder. *Weather Wisdom: Proverbs, Superstitions, and Signs.* New York: Peter Lang, 1996. 486 pp.

1506. Kipfer, Barbara Ann. *Phraseology. Thousands of Bizarre Origins, Unexpected Connections, and Fascinating Facts About English's Best Expressions.* Naperville, Illinois: Sourcebooks, 2008. 301 pp.

1507. Kirkpatrick, Betty. *Clichés. Over 1500 Phrases Explored and Explained.* New York: St. Martin's Griffin, 1999. 207 pp.

1508. Kirkpatrick, E.M., and C.M. Schwarz (eds.). *Dictionary of Idioms.* Edinburgh: W & R Chambers, 1982; rpt. Singapore: Federal Publications, 1989. Rpt. as *The Wordsworth Dictionary of Idioms.* Ware, Hertfordshire: Wordsworth Editions, 1993. 432 pp.

1509. Klein, Allen. *Winning Words. Quotations to Uplift, Inspire, Motivate and Delight.* New York: Portland House, 2002. 443 pp.

1510. Kleiser, Grenville. *Fifteen Thousand Useful Phrases.* New York: Funk & Wagnalls, 1917. 453 pp.

1511. Kleiser, Grenville. *Similes and Their Use.* New York: Grosset & Dunlap, 1925. 381 pp.

1512. Kneen, Maggie (ill.). *"Too Many Cooks .." and Other Proverbs.* New York: Green Tiger Press, 1992. 26 pp. (children's book).

1513. Knowles, Elizabeth (ed.). *The Oxford Dictionary of Phrase, Saying, & Quotation.* Oxford: Oxford University Press, 1997. 694 pp.

1514. Knowles, Elizabeth (ed.). *The Oxford Dictionary of Quotations.* 5th ed. Oxford: Oxford University Press, 1999. 1136 pp. (1st ed. 1941), 879 pp.; (2nd ed. 1953), 1003 pp.; (3rd ed. 1979), 907 pp.; (4th ed. 1992), 1061 pp.

1515. Knowles, Elizabeth. *Little Oxford Dictionary of Proverbs.* Oxford: Oxford University Press, 2009. 500 pp.

1516. Knox, D.B. *Children's Funny Sayings. An Amusing Book for Everybody.* New York: E.P. Dutton, 1925. 206 pp.

1517. Kohl, Ida, and J.G. Kohl. "Eine kleine Sammlung häufig wiederkehrender englischer Redensarten." In I. and J.G. Kohl. *Englische Skizzen.* 2 vols. Dresden: Arnold, 1845. II, 203-211.

1518. Kohn, Alfie. *You Know What They Say ... The Truth about Popular Beliefs.* New York: HarperCollins, 1990. 236 pp.

1519. Komarov, A.S. *Angliiskie poslovitsy, pogovorki i krylatye vyrazheniia. Uchebnoe posobie.* Moskva: Prospekt, 2005. 76 pp.

1520. Korach, Myron, and John B. Mordock. *Common Phrases and Where They Come From.* Guilford, Connecticut: The Lyons Press, 2001. 200 pp.

1521. Kövecses, Zoltán, Marianne Tóth, and Bulcsú Babarci. *A Picture Dictionary of English Idioms.* Volume 2: *Human Relations.* Illustrations by Bulcsá Babarci. Budapest: Eötvös University Press, 1997. 173 pp.

1522. Küffner, Georg M. *Die Engländer im Sprichwort.* Ludwigshafen: Weiß & Hameier, 1916. 46 pp.

1523. Kunin, A.V. *Anglo-russkii frazeologicheskii slovar'.* Moskva: Gosudarstvennoe Izdatel'stvo Inostrannykh i Natsional'nykh Slovarei, 1956. 1456 pp.

1524. Kuskovskaya, S. *English Proverbs and Sayings.* Minsk: Vysheishaya Shkola, 1987. 253 pp.

1525. Lamb, G.F. *Animal Quotations.* Illustrations by William Rushton. Harlow, Essex: Longman Group, 1985. 198 pp.

1526. Landy, Eugene E. *The Underground Dictionary.* New York: Simon and Schuster, 1971. 206 pp.

1527. Lean, Vincent Stuckey. *Lean's Collectanea: Collections of Vincent Stuckey Lean of Proverbs (English & Foreign), Folk Lore, and Superstitions, also Compilations towards Dictionaries of Proverbial Phrases and Words, Old and Disused.* Ed. T.W. Williams. 5 vols. Bristol: J.W. Arrowsmith, 1902-1904; rpt. Detroit: Gale Research Company, 1969. Rpt. as *Lean's Collectanea: Encyclopedia* *of Proverbs.* Bristol: Thoemmes Press, 2000. I, 509 pp,; II,1, 477 pp.; II,2, 463 pp.; III, 512 pp.; IV, 481 pp.

1528. Lederer, Richard. *The Play of Words [Metaphors, Clichés, Proverbs, etc.]. Fun & Games for Language Lovers.* Illustrations by Bernie Cootner. New York: Pocket Books, 1990. 274 pp.

1529. Lee, Albert. *Weather Proverbs. Being an Illustrated Practical Volume Wherein Is Contained Unique Compilation and Analysis of the Facts and Folklore of National Weather Prediction.* Garden City, New York: Doubleday & Company, 1976; rpt. Garden City, New York: Dolphin Books, 1977. 180 pp.

1530. Leedy, Loreen, and Pat Street. *There's a Frog in My Throat! 440 Animal Sayings a Little Bird Told Me.* Illustratations by Loreen Leedy. New York: Scholastic Inc., 2003. 48 pp.

1531. Lemon, Mark (ed.). *The Jest Book. The Choicest Anecdotes and Sayings.* Cambridge: Sever and Francis, 1865. 389 pp.

1532. Leventhal, Sallye (ed.). *Notations: Quotations on Music.* New York: Barnes & Noble, 2003. 89 pp.

1533. Levinson, Leonard Louis. *The Left Handed Dictionary.* London: Collier-Macmillan, 1963. 255 pp.

1534. Lewin, Esther, and Albert E. Lewin. *The Thesaurus of Slang.* New York: Facts on File Publications, 1988. Rpt. as *The Random House Thesaurus of Slang.* New York: Random House, 1989. 435 pp.

1535. Lewis, Alec (ed.). *The Quotable Quotations Book.* New York: Thomas Y. Vrowell, 1980. 333 pp.

1536. Ley, Gerd de, and David Potter (eds.). *"Do Unto Others ... Then Run": A Little Book of Twisted Proverbs.* London: Prion Books, 2001. 125 pp. (miniature book). (anti-proverbs).

1537. Lindup, Rowland. *The Little Book of Wit & Wisdom from Old Amos.* Skipton, North Yorkshire: Dalesman, 2003. 126 pp. (miniature book). (cartoons with anti-proverbs)..

1538. Linfield, Jordan L., and Joe Kay. *"Your Mother Wears Army Boots!" A Treasure Trove of Insults, Slurs and Putdowns.* New York: Avon Books, 1992. 282 pp.

1539. Lister, Ronald, and Klemens Veth. *Treffsicher in Englisch: Englische Idiomatik zum Lernen, Üben und Nachschlagen.* Berlin: Langenscheidt, 1999. 320 pp.

1540. Litovkina, Anna T., and Wolfgang Mieder. *"Old Proverbs Never Die, They Just Diversify": A Collection of Anti-Proverbs*. Illustrations by Olga Mirenska. Burlington, Vermont: The University of Vermont, 2006. Veszprém: The Pannonian University of Veszprém, 2006. 405 pp.

1541. Loomis, C. Grant. "Wellerisms in *Punch*." *Western Folklore*, 14 (1955), 110-113.

1542. Lucas, Edward Verrall. "Daughters of Experience [Proverbs]." In E.V. Lucas. *Turning Things Over. Essays and Fantasies*. New York: E.P. Dutton, 1929; rpt. New York: Books for Libraries Press, 1970. 146-156.

1543. Lurie, Charles N. *Everyday Sayings. Their Meanings Explained, Their Origins Given*. New York: G.P. Putnam's Sons, 1928; rpt.Detroit: Gale Research Company, 1968. 360 pp.

1544. Lyman, Darryl. *The Animal Things We Say*. Middle Village, New York: Jonathan David, 1983. 258 pp.

1545. Lyman, Darryl. *Dictionary of Animal Words and Phrases*. Middle Village, New York: Jonathan David, 1994. 280 pp.

1546. Lytle, Clyde Francis (ed.). *Leaves of Gold. An Anthology of Prayers, Memorable Phrases, Inspirational Verse and Prose*. Williamsport, Pennsylvania: Coslett, 1938 (2nd ed. 1948), 200 pp.

1547. Maaβ, M. "39 Old Similes aus den *Pickwick Papers* von Charles Dickens." *Archiv für das Studium der neueren Sprachen und Literaturen*, 41 (1867), 207-215.

1548. MacHale, Des. *Ultimate Wit. A Treasury of Even More of the Cleverest Things Ever Said on Any Subject*. New York: Barnes & Noble, 2006. 320 pp.

1549. Macrone, Michael. *Brush Up Your Shakespeare!* Illustrations by Tom Lulevitch. New York: Harper & Row, 1990. 235 pp.

1550. Macrone, Michael. *Animalogies. "A Fine Kettle of Fish" and 150 Other Animal Expressions*. Illustrations by Thorina Rose. New York: Doubleday, 1995. 150 pp.

1551. Maggio, Rosalie (ed.). *Quotations on Education*. Paramus, New Jersey: Prentice Hall, 1997. 180 pp.

1552. Mair, James Allan. *A Handbook of Proverbs, Mottoes, Quotations and Phrases*. London: Routledge, 1874. 505 pp.

1553. Mann, Leonard. *A Bird in the Hand: And the Stories Behind 250 Other Common Expressions*. New York: Prentice Hall, 1994. 262 pp.

1554. Manser, Martin H. *Get to the Roots: A Dictionary of Word & Phrase Origins*. New York: Avon Books, 1990. 254 pp.

1555. Manser, Martin H., and Rosalind Fergusson. *The Facts on File Dictionary of Proverbs. Meanings and Origins of More Than 1,500 Popular Sayings*. New York: Checkmark Books, 2002. 440 pp.

1556. Margolin, Robert (ed.). *The Little Pun Book*. Mount Vernon, New York: Peter Pauper Press, 1960. 61 pp.

1557. Marsh, John B. *Familiar Proverbial and Select Sayings from Shakspere [sic]*. London: Simpkin, Marshall, and Co., 1863. 162 pp.

1558. Martin, Thomas L. *Malice in Blunderland*. New York: McGraw-Hill, 1973. 143 pp.

1559. Marvin, Dwight Edwards. *The Antiquity of Proverbs. Fifty Familiar Proverbs and Folk Sayings with Annotations and Lists of Connected Forms, Found in All Parts of the World*. New York: G.P. Putnam's Sons, 1922

1560. Mateaux, Clara. *Old Proverbs with New Pictures*. Illustrations by Lizzie Lawson. London: Cassell, 1881; rpt. New York: Merrimack Publishing, ca. 1980. 16 pp. (children's book).

1561. Matthewman, Lisle de Vaux. *Completed Proverbs*. Pictured by Clare Victor Dwiggins. Philadelphia: H.T. Coates, 1904. 100 pp. With 100 illustrations.

1562. McCormick, Malachi. *A Collection of English Proverbs*. New York: The Stone Street Press, 1982. 50 pp.

1563. McDonald, James. *Dictionary of Obscenity and Taboo*. London: Sphere Books, 1988; rpt. Ware, Hertfordshire: Wordsworth Editions, 1996. 168 pp.

1564. McFadden, Tara Ann (ed.). *Home. A Little Book of Comfort*. Philadelphia: Running Press, 1996. 127 pp. (miniature book).

1565. McKenzie, Carol. *Quotable Sex*. New York: St. Martin's Press, 1992. 208 pp.

1566. McKenzie, E.C. *Mac's Giant Book of Quips & Quotes*. Grand Rapids, Michigan: Baker Book House, 1980. 581 pp.

1567. McKernan, Maggie (ed.). *The Sayings of Jane Austen*. London: Duckworth, 1993. 64 pp.

1568. McLellan, Vern. *Proverbs for People. Illustrated.* Illustrations by Nate Owens. Eugene, Oregon: Harvest House Publishing, 1983. 158 pp. (anti-proverbs).

1569. McLellan, Vern. *The Complete Book of Practical Proverbs & Wacky Wit*. Whaton, Illinois: Tyndale House Publishers, 1996. 251 pp. With illustrations.

1570. McMahon, Sean (ed.). *A Book of Irish Quotations*. Springfield, Illinois: Templegate Publishers, 1984. 231 pp.

1571. McPhee, Nancy (ed.). *The Book of Insults, Ancient & Modern*. New York: St. Martin's Press, 1978; rpt. New York: Penguin Books, 1980; rpt. New York: Barnes & Noble, 1994. 160 pp.

1572. Mencken, H.L. *A New Dictionary of Quotations on Historical Principles from Ancient and Modern Times*. New York: Alfred A. Knopf, 1942 (2nd ed. 1960). 1347 pp.

1573. Meyer-Werfel, Fred (ed.). *Save Water, Bath with a Friend. Sponti-Sprüche – Englisch*. Photographs by Chris Wróblewski. Frankfurt am Main: Eichborn, 1985. 69 pp. (anti-proverbs).

1574. Mieder, Wolfgang. *English Proverbs*. Stuttgart: Philipp Reclam, 1988. 151 pp.

1575. Mieder, Wolfgang. *Salty Wisdom: Proverbs of the Sea*. Illustrations by Mary Azarian. Shelburne, Vermont: The New England Press, 1990. 64 pp.

1576. Mieder, Wolfgang (ed.). *English Expressions*. Stuttgart: Philipp Reclam, 1992. 147 pp.

1577. Mieder, Wolfgang. "Welleristic Addenda to the *Dictionary of Wellerisms* [New York: Oxford University Press, 1994; eds. Wolfgang Mieder and Stewart A. Kingsbury]." *Proverbium*, 14 (1997), 187-217.

1578. Mieder, Wolfgang (ed.). *Wisecracks! Fractured Proverbs*. Illustrations by Elayne Sears. Shelburne, Vermont: The New England Press, 2003. 96 pp.

1579. Mieder, Wolfgang, and George B. Bryan. *The Proverbial Winston S. Churchill: An Index to Proverbs in the Works of Sir Winston Churchill*. Westport, Connecticut: Greenwood Press, 1995. 448 pp.

1580. Mieder, Wolfgang, and Stewart A. Kingsbury (eds.). *A Dictionary of Wellerisms*. New York: Oxford University Press, 1994. 206 pp.

1581. Mieder, Wolfgang, and Anna Tóthné Litovkina. *Twisted Wisdom: Modern Anti-Proverbs*. Burlington, Vermont: The University of Vermont, 1999. 254 pp. With illustrations.

1582. Miner, Margaret, and Hugh Rawson (eds.). *The New International Dictionary of Quotations*. New York: Dutton, 1993. 480 pp.

1583. Mingo, Jack, and John Javna. *Primetime Proverbs. The Book of TV Quotes*. New York: Harmony Books, 1989. 255 pp. With illustrations.

1584. Montapert, Alfred Armand. *Distilled Wisdom*. Englewood Cliffs, New Jersey: Prentice-Hall, 1964. 355 pp.

1585. Monteiro, George. "Derisive Adjectives: Two Notes and a List." *Western Folklore*, 34 (1975), 244-246.

1586. Moorhead, J.K., and Charles Lee. *A Dictionary of Quotations and an Alphabet of Proverbs*. 2 vols. London: J.M. Dent, 1928. I, 380 pp.; II, 444 pp. (alphabetical proverbs, II, 1-216).

1587. Morgan, Frances Elnora Williams. *Proverbs from Four Didactic Works of the Thirteenth Century*. Diss. University of Kentucky, 1968. 492 pp.

1588. Morris, William, and Mary Morris. *Dictionary of Word and Phrase Origins*. 2 vols. New York: Harper & Row, 1962-1967. I, 376 pp.; II, 297 pp.

1589. Munro, Angus. *Englisch im Alltag. Alphabetisch geordnetes Nachschlagewerk von englischen Sentenzen, Sprichwörtern, Phrasen, Floskeln, Redewendungen, Zitaten und Formeln*. Wiesbaden: VMA-Verlag, 1988. 128 pp.

1590. Murphy, Edward F. *The Crown Treasury of Relevant Quotations*. New York: Crown Publishers, 1978. Rpt. as *Webster's Treasury of Relevant Quotations*. New York: Greenwich House, 1983. 658 pp.

1591. Murphy, Edward F. *2,715 One-Line Quotations for Speakers, Writers & Raconteurs*. New York: Crown Publishers, 1981; rpt. New York: Bonanza Books, 1989. 216 pp.

1592. Nares, Robert. *A Glossary of Words, Phrases, Names and Allusions in the Works of English Authors Particularly of Shakespeare and His Contemporaries*. London: George Routledge, 1905; rpt. London: Gale Research Company, 1966. 982 pp.

1593. Neaman, Judith S., and Carole G. Silver. *Kind Words. A Thesaurus of Euphemisms*. New York: McGraw-Hill, 1985. 371 pp.

1594. Necker, Claire. *The Cat's Got Your Tongue*. Metuchen, New Jersey: The Scarecrow Press, 1973. 172 pp.

1595. Newlin, George. "Indexes of Words and Phrases." In G. Newlin, *Every Thing in Dickens: Ideas and Subjects Discussed by Charles Dickens in His Complete Works. A Topicon*. Westport, Connecticut: Greenwood Press, 1996. 1039-1072.

1596. Notley, David (ed.). *Winston Churchill Quotations*. Whitefriars: Jarrold Publishing, 1997. 42 pp. With illustrations.

1597. Nowlan, Robert A., and Gwendolyn L. Nowlan. *A Dictionary of Quotations and Proverbs about Cats and Dogs*. Jefferson, North Carolina: McFarland, 2001. 197 pp.

1598. O'Byrne, Lorraine. *What Is It? A Gallery of Historic Phrases*. Erin, Ontario: The Boston Mills Press, 1977. 48 pp. With illustrations.

1599. O'Connor, Gemma. *"Hell!" said the Duchess or First Lines*. Illustrations by Wendy Shea. Dublin: Wolfhound Press, 1985. 96 pp.

1600. O'Leary, C.F. *Proverbs and Proverbial Phrases*. St. Louis, Missouri: B. Herder, 1907. 195 pp.

1601. Ohrbach, Barbara Milo (ed.). *Food for the Soul. Delicious Thoughts to Nourish Mind and Heart*. New York: Clarkson Potter, 1996. 64 pp.

1602. Opalenko, M.E. *The New English Learner's Dictionary of Modern Phraseology / Novyi uchebnyi slovar' frazeologii sovremennogo angliiskogo iazyka*. Moskva: Tsentrpoligraf, 2004. 351 pp.

1603. Orben, Robert. *2000 New Laughs for Speakers. The Ad-Libber's Handbook*. New York: Gramercy Publishing, 1978. 216 pp.

1604. Page, Robin. *Weather Forecasting: The Country Way*. Illustrations by Thomas Bewick. London: Davis-Poynter, 1977. New

York: Summit Books, 1977. 56 pp. Rpt. Harmondsworth, England: Penguin Books, 1981. 71 pp.

1605. Palmatier, Robert A. *Speaking of Animals: A Dictionary of Animal Metaphors.* Westport, Connecticut: Greenwood Press, 1995. 472 pp.

1606. Panati, Charles. *Words to Live By: The Origins of Conventional Wisdom and Commonsense Advice.* New York: Penguin Books, 1999. 416 pp. With illustrations.

1607. Parkinson, Judy. *Catchphrase, Slogan and Cliché. The Origins and Meanings of Our Favourite Expressions.* London: Michael O'Mara Books, 2003. 179 pp. With illustrations.

1608. Partington, Angela (ed.). *The Oxford Dictionary of Quotations.* 4th ed. Oxford: Oxford University Press, 1992. 1061 pp. (1st ed. 1941), 879 pp.; (2nd ed. 1953), 1003 pp.; (3rd ed. 1979), 907 pp.; (5th ed. 1999), 1136 pp.

1609. Partnow, Elaine. *The Quotable Woman: An Encyclopedia of Useful Quotations Indexed by Subject and Author – 1800-1975.* Los Angeles, California: Corwin Books, 1977. 539 pp.

1610. Partnow, Elaine. *The New Quotable Woman. Completely Revised and Updated.* New York: Facts on File, 1992. 714 pp.

1611. Partridge, Eric. *Slang To-Day and Yesterday. With a Short Historical Sketch; and Vocabularies of English, American, and Asustralian Slang.* London: Routledge & Kegan Paul, 1933 (3rd ed. 1950; 4th ed. 1970; rpt. 1979). 476 pp.

1612. Partridge, Eric. *A Dictionary of Slang and Unconventional English.* New York: Macmillan, 1937. 999 pp.; (5 th ed. 1961) 1352 pp.; (7th ed. 1970) 1528 pp.

1613. Partridge, Eric. *A Dictionary of Clichés.* London: George Routledge, 1940 (5th ed. 1978). 261 pp.

1614. Partridge, Eric. *Smaller Slang Dictionary.* New York: Dorset Press, 1961. 204 pp.

1615. Partridge, Eric. *A Dictionary of Catch Phrases. British and American, from the Sixteenth Century to the Present Day.* New York: Stein and Day, 1977. 278 pp. Revised edition ed. Paul Beale. Lanham, Maryland: Scarborough House, 1992. 384 pp.

1616. Peake, Mervyn (ill.). *Figures of Speech.* London: V. Gollancz, 1954; rpt. Cambridge, Massachusetts: Candlewick Press, 2003. 60 pp.

1617. Pearl, Anita. *The Jonathan David Dictionary of Popular Slang*. Middle Village, New York: Jonathan David, 1980. 191 pp.

1618. Pearson, Rosemary. *Idioms*. Singapore: Federal Publications, 1989. 204 pp.

1619. Peers, John, and Gordon Bennett (eds.). *1,001 Logical Laws, Accurate Axioms, Profound Principles, Trusty Truisms, Homey Homilies, Colorful Corollaries, Quotable Quotes, and Rambunctious Ruminations for All Walks of Life*. Illustrations by George Booth. Garden City, New York: Doubleday, 1979; rpt. New York: Fawcett Gold Medal, 1988. 189 pp.

1620. Peter, Laurence J. *Peter's Quotations: Ideas for Our Time*. New York: William Morrow, 1977. 540 pp.; rpt. New York: Bantam Books, 1979. 579 pp.

1621. Peterson, Gail. *Proverbs to Live by. Timeless Words of Wit and Wisdom*. Kansas City, Missouri: Hallmark Cards, 1968 (2nd ed. 1975). 48 pp.

1622. Peterson, Gail. *Proverbs to Live By. Truths that Live in Words*. Illustrations by Fritz Kredel. Kansas City, Missouri: Hallmark Editions, 1968. 60 pp. (not identical with previous entry).

1623. Petty, Jo (ed.). *Apples [Quotations] of Gold*. Norwalk, Connecticut: C.R. Gibson, 1962. 86 pp.

1624. Pfeffer, Karl. *Das Elisabethanische Sprichwort in seiner Verwendung bei Ben Jonson*. Diss. Universität Gießen, 1933. Gießen: Richard Glagow, 1933. 193 pp. (proverb index, pp. 58-180).

1625. Phillips, Bob. *Phillips' Book of Great Thoughts and Funny Sayings*. Wheaton, Illinois: Tyndale House, 1993. 343 pp.

1626. Phythian, B.A. (ed.). *Guide to English Idioms*. London: Hodder and Stoughton, 1973; rpt. Singapore: Federal Publications, 1988. 321 pp.

1627. Pickering, David. *Dictionary of Proverbs*. London: Cassell, 1997. 297 pp.

1628. Pine, L.G. *A Dictionary of Mottoes*. London: Routledge & Kegan Paul, 1983. 303 pp.

1629. Pinette, Roger G. *On Modes of Communication. Other Modes of Conveyance. Featuring Popular Figures of Speech, A Glossary of Metaphors, Familiar Similes, Facets of Communica-*

tion, Communication Stimuli. Philadelphia: Xlibris Corporation, 2009. 213 pp.

1630. Pinette, Roger G. *On Modes of Communication. Popular Figures of Speech, A Glossary of Metaphors, Familiar Similes, Facets of Communication, Communication Stimuli.* LaVergne, Tennessee: Xlibris Corporation, 2009. 219 pp.

1631. Pitts, Arthur William. J*ohn Donne's Use of Proverbs in His Poetry*. Diss. Louisiana State University, 1966. 213 pp.

1632. Pollock, Carl Arthur (ed.?). *The Oxford Dictionary of Quotations*. 2nd ed. Oxford: Oxford University Press, 1953. 1003 pp. (1st ed. 1941), 879 pp.; (3rd ed. 1979), 907 pp.; (4th ed. 1992), 1061 pp.; (5th ed. 1999), 1136 pp.

1633. Powell, Michael. *100 Pretentious Proverbs*. London: Prion Books, 2002. 191 pp. With illustrations. (anti-proverbs).

1634. Powers, George W. *Handy Dictionary of Prose Quotations*. New York: Thomas Y. Crowell, 1901. 364 pp.

1635. Priest, William L. *"Swear Like a Trooper": A Dictionary of Military Terms and Phrases*. Charlottesville, Virginia: Rockbridge, 2000. 232 pp.

1636. Prochnow, Herbert V. *The Public Speaker's Treasure Chest*. New York: Harper & Brothers, 1942. 413 pp. Revised ed. with Herbert V. Prochnow, Jr. New York: Harper & Row, 1964. 516 pp.

1637. Prochnow, Herbert V. *Speaker's Handbook of Epigrams and Witticisms*. Blackpool, England: A. Thomas, 1955. 332 pp.

1638. Prochnow, Herbert V., and Herbert V. Prochnow, Jr. *A Dictionary of Wit, Wisdom, and Satire*. New York: Harper & Row, 1962; rpt. New York: Popular Library, 1964. 285 pp.; rpt. Edison, New Jersey: Castle Books, 2005. 243.

1639. Prochnow, Herbert V., and Herbert V. Prochnow, Jr. *The Toastmaster's Treasure Chest*. New York: Harper & Row, 1979. 470 pp.

1640. Ramsey, Betty Jo (ed.). *The Little Book of Famous Insults*. Illustrations by Fritz Kredel. Mount Vernon, New York: Peter Pauper Press, 1964. 60 pp.

1641. Ratcliffe, Susan (ed.). *The Oxford Dictionary of Phrase, Saying, and Quotation*. 2nd ed. (1st ed. by Elizabeth Knowles, 1997). Oxford: Oxford University Press, 2002. 696 pp.

1642. Ratcliffe, Susan. *Little Oxford Dictionary of Quotations.* Oxford: Oxford University Press, 1994 (4th ed. 2008). 477 pp.

1643. Rawson, Hugh. *Wicked Words: A Treasury of Curses, Insults, Put-Downs, and Other Formerly Unprintable Terms from Anglo-Saxon Times to the Present.* New York: Crown Publishers, 1989. 435 pp.

1644. Rawson, Hugh. *Devious Derivations. Popular Misconceptions and More Than 1000 True Origins of Common Words and Phrases.* New York: Crown Publishers, 1994; rpt. Edison, New Jersey: Castle Books, 2002. 245 pp.

1645. Rawson, Hugh. *Dictionary of Euphemisms and Other Doubletalk: Being a Compilation of Linguistic Fig Leaves and Verbal Flourishes for Artful Users of the English Language.* New York: Crown Publishers, 1995. 463 pp.

1646. Ray, John. *A Compleat Collection of English Proverbs; Also the most celebrated Proverbs of the Scotch, Italian, French, Spanish, And other Languages. The Whole Methodically Digested and Illustrated with Annotations, and proper Explications. By the late Rev. and Learned J. Ray. To which is added (Written by the same Author) A Collection of English Words Not Generally Used [...].* The Fourth Edition. London: W. Otridge, 1768. 319 pp. and 150 pp. (one of my personal treasures – W.M.).

1647. Rees, Nigel. *Graffiti Lives, O.K.* London: Unwin Paperbacks, 1979. 96 pp.

1648. Rees, Nigel. *"Quote ... Unquote."* New York: St. Martin's Press, 1979. 96 pp.

1649. Rees, Nigel. *Sayings of the Century. The Stories Behind the Twentieth Century's Quotable Sayings.* London: George Allen and Unwin, 1984. 270 pp.

1650. Rees, Nigel. *The Joy of Clichés: A Complete User's Guide.* London: Guild Publishing, 1984. 159 pp.

1651. Rees, Nigel. *A Who's Who of Nicknames.* London: George Allen & Unwin, 1985. 194 pp.

1652. Rees, Nigel. *Why Do We Say ... ? Words and Sayings and Where They Come From.* Poole, Dorset: Blandford Press, 1987. 224 pp.

1653. Rees, Nigel. *Why Do We Quote?* London: Blandford Press, 1989. 232 pp.

1654. Rees, Nigel. *Dictionary of Popular Phrases*. London: Bloomsbury, 1990. Also as *Dictionary of Catch Phrases*. London: Bloomsbury, 1994. 277 pp.

1655. Rees, Nigel. *Dictionary of Phrase & Allusion*. London: Bloomsbury, 1991. 358 pp.

1656. Rees, Nigel. *The Phrase that Launched 1,000 Ships*. New York: Dell Publishing, 1991. 244 pp.

1657. Rees, Nigel. *Epitaphs: A Dictionary of Grave Epigrams and Memorial Eloquence*. New York: Carroll & Graf, 1993. 276 pp.

1658. Rees, Nigel. *"As We Say in Our House": A Book of Family Sayings*. London: Robson Books, 1994. 159 pp.

1659. Rees, Nigel. *Brewer's Quotations. A Phrase and Fable Dictionary*. London: Cassell, 1994. 397 pp.

1660. Rees, Nigel. *Dictionary of Catch Phrases*. London: Bloomsbury, 1994. 277 pp.

1661. Rees, Nigel. *Dictionary of Catchphrases*. London: Cassell, 1995. 230 pp.

1662. Rees, Nigel. *Phrases and Sayings*. London: Bloomsbury, 1995. 531 pp.

1663. Rees, Nigel. *Cassell Dictionary of Clichés*. London: Cassell, 1996. 288 pp.

1664. Rees, Nigel. *Cassell Companion to Quotations*. London: Cassell, 1997. 640 pp.

1665. Rees, Nigel. *Dictionary of Slogans*. Glasgow: HarperCollins, 1997. 285 pp.

1666. Rees, Nigel. *Cassell's Humorous Quotations*. London: Cassell, 2001. 912 pp.

1667. Rees, Nigel. *A Man about a Dog. Euphemisms and Other Examples of Verbal Squeamishness*. London: Collins, 2006. 417 pp.

1668. Rees, Nigel. *A Word in Your Shell-like. 6,000 Curious & Everyday Phrases Explained*. London: HarperCollins, 2006. 768 pp.

1669. Reisner, Robert. *Graffiti. Two Thousand Years of Wall Writing*. New York: Cowles Book Company, 1971. 204 pp. With illustrations. (collection, pp. 119-202),

1670. Reisner, Robert, and Lorraine Wechsler. *Encyclopedia of Graffiti*. New York: Galahad Books, 1980. 403 pp.

1671. Richmond, Arthur (ed.). *Modern Quotations for Ready Reference*. New York: Dover Publications, 1947. 502 pp.

1672. Richter, Alan. *Sexual Slang. A Compendium of Offbeat Words and Colorful Phrases from Shakespeare to Today*. New York: Harper Perennial, 1993. 250 pp.

1673. Ridout, Ronald, and Clifford Witting. *English Proverbs Explained*. London: Pan Books, 1967; rpt. London: Pan Books, 1969 and 1979. 223 pp.

1674. Ridout, Ronald, Clifford Witting, Zhong Lin, and Lianxiang Lin. *English Proverbs Explained and Their Chinese Counterparts*. Taipei, Taiwan: Crane, 1983. 609 pp.

1675. Ringo, Miriam. *Nobody Said It Better! 2700 Wise & Witty Quotations About Famous People*. Chicago: Rand McNally, 1980. 382 pp.

1676. Ritter, Michael (ed.). *Great Women and Their Words of Wisdom*. Glendale Heights, Illinois: Great Quotations Publishing Company, 1996. 63 pp.

1677. Rittersbacher, Christa. *Frau und Mann in der sprichwörtlichen Weltanschauung Großbritanniens und Amerikas*. Diss. Universität Heidelberg, 2000. 297 pp. Also as *Frau und Mann im Sprichwort. Einblicke in die sprichwörtliche Weltanschaung Großbritanniens und Amerikas*. Heidelberg: Das Wunderhorn, 2002. 332 pp. (proverb index, pp. 306-330).

1678. Roberts, Kate Louise. *Hoyt's New Cyclopedia of Practical Quotations*. New York: Funk & Wagnalls, 1922. 1343 pp.

1679. Rogers, James. *The Dictionary of Clichés*. New York: Facts on File Publications, 1985. 305 pp.

1680. Roman, Christian (ed.). *Love Makes the World Go Up and Down. Englische Sprüche aus der Beziehungskiste*. Illustrations by Stano Kochan. Frankfurt am Main: Eichborn, 1986. 68 pp. (antiproverbs).

1681. Roman, Christian (ed.). *All We Need is Love – All You Get is Video. Englische Schülersprüche*. Illustrations by Klaus Puth. Frankfurt am Main: Eichborn, 1987. 68 pp. (anti-proverbs).

1682. Room, Adrian. *Bloomsbury Dictionary of Dedications*. London: Bloomsbury, 1990. Rpt. as *Tuttle Dictionary of Dedications*. Rutland, Vermont: Charles E. Tuttle, 1992. 354 pp.

1683. Rosenthal, Beatrice. *Webster's Dictionary of Familiar Quotations*. New York: Galahad Books, 1974; rpt. New York: Ottenheimer Publishers, 1980. 256 pp.

1684. Rosenthal, Peggy, and George Dardess. *Every Cliché in the Book*. Illustrations by Peter LaVigna. New York: William Morrow, 1987. 219 pp.

1685. Rosten, Leo. *Infinite Riches. Gems from a Lifetime of Reading*. New York: McGraw-Hill, 1979. 588 pp.

1686. Rowinski, Kate (ed.). *The Quotable Cook*. New York: The Lyons Press, 2000. 232 pp.

1687. Roylance, William H. *I shoulda Said ... A Treasury of Insults, Put-Downs, Boasts, Praises, Witticisms, Wisecracks, Comebacks and Ad-Libs*. West Nyack, New York: Parker, 1973. 227 pp.

1688. Royle, Trevor. *A Dictionary of Military Quotations*. New York: Simon & Schuster, 1989. 210 pp.

1689. Rubin, Bonnie Miller. *Fifty on Fifty. Wisdom, Inspiration, and Reflections on Women's Lives Well Lived*. New York: Warner Books, 1998. 159 pp. With illustrations.

1690. Runes, Dagobert D. *Treasury of Thought. Observations Over Half a Century*. New York: Philosophical Society, 1966. 395 pp.

1691. Rutledge, Leigh W. *Unnatural Quotations. A Compendium of Quotations by, for, or about Gay People*. Boston, Massachusetts: Alyson Publications, 1988. 182 pp. With illustrations.

1692. Safian, Louis A. *2,000 Insults for all Occasions*. New York: Citadel Press, 1965. 224 pp. Rpt. New York: Pocket Books, 1966. 241 pp.

1693. Safian, Louis A. *The Giant Book of Insults*. New York: Castle Books, 1967. 416 pp.

1694. Safire, William. *Safire's Political Dictionary. An Enlarged, Up-to-Date Edition of "The New Language of Politics"*. New York: Random House, 1968 (2nd ed. 1972; 3rd ed. 1978). 846 pp.

1695. Safire, William, and Leonard Safir [*sic*] (eds.). *Words of Wisdom. More Good Advice*. New York: Simon and Schuster, 1989. 432 pp.

1696. Sarnoff, Jane, and Reynold Ruffins. *Words: A Book about the Origins of Everyday Words and Phrases*. New York: Charles Scribner's Sons, 1981. 64 pp. With illustrations.

1697. Schlim, Cora A. *Wit 'n Wisdom*. Durham, North Carolina: Durham Technical Institute, 126 pp.

1698. Schmidt, J.E. *Cyclopedic Lexicon of Sex. Exotic Practices, Expressions, Variations of the Libido*. New York: Brussel & Brussel, 1967. Rpt. as *Lecher's Lexicon. An A-Z Encyclopedia of Erotic Expressions and Naughty Bits*. New York: Bell Publishing Company, 1984. 389 pp.

1699. Scott, John. *Treasured Volume of Thoughts. An Anthology*. New York: Oak Tree Press,1969. 123 pp.

1700. Seldes, George. *The Great Quotations*. Lyle Stuart, New York: Caesar-Stuart, 1960. 893 pp.

1701. Seldes, George. *The Great Thoughts*. New York: Ballantine Books, 1985. 490 pp.

1702. Shafritz, Jay M. *Words on War: Military Quotations from Ancient Times to the Present*. New York: Prentice Hall, 1990. 559 pp.

1703. Shapiro, Fred R. *The Oxford Dictionary of American Legal Quotations*. New York: Oxford University Press, 1993. 582 pp.

1704. Shapiro, Fred R. *The Yale Book of Quotations*. New Haven, Connecticut: Yale University Press, 2006. 1068 pp.

1705. Shepard, Priscilla (ed.). *Fields of Gold: A Classical Collection of Inspirational Quotations from Ancient and Modern Times*. Norwalk, Connecticut: C.R. Gibson, 1975. 161 pp. With illustrations.

1706. Sherrin, Ned. *The Oxford Dictionary of Humorous Quotations*. Oxford: Oxford University Press, 1995. 543 pp.

1707. Sherry, Kevin. *I'm the Biggest Thing in the Ocean ["Big Fish Eat Little Fish"]*. New York: Scholastic, 2008. 32 pp. (children's book).

1708. Simpson, James B. *Contemporary Quotations*. New York: Galahad Books, 1964. 500 pp. Revised ed. as *Simpson's Contemporary Quotations*. Boston: Houghton Mifflin, 1988. 495 pp.

1709. Simpson, John A. *The Concise Oxford Dictionary of Proverbs*. Oxford: Oxford University Press, 1982. 256 pp.

1710. Simpson, John A. *The Concise Oxford Dictionary of Proverbs*. With the Assistance of Jennifer Speake. 2nd ed. Oxford: Oxford University Press, 1992. 316 pp.

1711. Simpson, John A., and Jennifer Speake. *The Concise Oxford Dictionary of Proverbs*. 3rd ed. Oxford: Oxford University Press, 1998. 333 pp.

1712. Skeat, Walter W. *The Proverbs of Alfred. Re-edited from the Manuscript*. Oxford: Clarendon Press, 1907; rpt. Darnby, Pennsylvania: Folcroft Library Editions, 1974. 94 pp.

1713. Skeat, Walter W. *Early English Proverbs. Chiefly of the Thirteenth and Fourteenth Centuries with Illustrative Quotations*. Oxford: Clarendon Press, 1910; rpt. Darby, Pennsylvania: Folcroft Library Editions, 1974. 147 pp.

1714. Smith, Charles G. *Shakespeare's Proverb Lore. His Use of the Sententiae of Leonard Culman and Publilius Syrus*. Cambridge, Massachusetts: Harvard University Press, 1963 (2nd ed., 1968). 181 pp.

1715. Smith, Charles G. *Spenser's Proverb Lore. With Special Reference to His Use of the Sententiae of Leonard Culman and Publilius Syrus*. Cambridge, Massachusetts: Harvard University Press, 1970. 365 pp.

1716. Smith, Cornelia Marshall. *Browning's Proverb Lore*. Waco, Texas: Baylor University, 1989. 124 pp.

1717. Smith, John B. "Dorset and Somerset Dialects. Unrecorded Words and Sayings." *Notes & Queries for Somerset and Dorset*, 30, part 309 (1979), 395-397.

1718. Smith, John B. "Whim-Whams for a Goose's Bridle: A List of Put-Offs and Related Forms in English and German." *Lore and Language*, 3, no. 3 (1980), 32-49.

1719. Smith, John B. "Proverbs from the SW Midlands." *FLS News. The Newsletter of the [British] Folklore Society,* no volume given, no. 51 (2007), 9.

1720. Smith, John R. (ill.). *Bookish Quotations*. Blewbury, Oxfordshire: The Rocket Press, 1985. 16 pp.

1721. Smith, Lloyd E. *A Book of Familiar Quotations*. Girard, Kansas: Haldeman-Julius Company, 1925. 61 pp.

1722. Smith, Logan Pearsall. *Words and Idioms. Studies in the English Language*. Boston: Houghton Mifflin, 1925. 300 pp. (English idioms, pp. 167-278; somatic idioms, pp. 279-292).

1723. Smith, William George. *The Oxford Dictionary of English Proverbs*. With an introduction and index by Janet E. Heseltine. Oxford: Clarendon Pess, 1935. 644 pp. 2nd ed. revised by Sir Paul Harvey. Oxford: Clarendon Press, 1948. 740 pp. 3rd ed. revised by F.P. Wilson. Oxford: Clarendon Press, 1970. 930 pp.

1724. Smyth, Alice Mary (ed.). *The Oxford Dictionary of Quotations*. London: Oxford University Press, 1941. 879 pp. (2nd ed. 1953), 1003 pp.; (3rd ed. 1979), 907 pp.; (4th ed. 1992), 1061 pp.; (5th ed. 1999), 1136 pp.

1725. Snow, Richard F. (ed.). *Thoughts on Wisdom. Thoughts and Reflections from History's Great Thinkers*. New York: American Heritage, 1997. 152 pp.

1726. Snow, Richard F. (ed.). *Thoughts on Success. Thoughts and Reflections from History's Great Thinkers*. New York: American Heritage, 2000. 150 pp.

1727. Sobieski, Janet, and Wolfgang Mieder (eds.). *"So Many Heads, So Many Wits". An Anthology of English Proverb Poetry*. Burlington, Vermont: The University of Vermont, 2005. 274 pp.

1728. Sommer, Elyse, and Mike Sommer (eds.). *Similes Dictionary. A Collection of More Than 16,000 Comparison Phrases from Ancient Times to the Present*. Detroit: Gale Research Company, 1988. 950 pp.

1729. Sommer, Elyse, and Dorrie Weiss. *Metaphors Dictionary*. Detroit: Gale Research Company, 1995. 833 pp.

1730. Sørensen, Knud. "Neologisms; Archaisms." In K. Sørensen. *Charles Dickens: Linguistic Innovator*. Aarhus: Arkona, 1985. 115-169 and 170-171.

1731. Speake, Jennifer (ed.). *The Oxford Dictionary of Proverbs*. 4th ed. Oxford: Oxford University Press, 2003. 375 pp. (5th ed. 2008). 388 pp. (the designation of "Concise Dictionary" of the first three editions by John A. Simpson and Jennifer Speake was dropped).

1732. Spears, Richard A. *Slang and Euphemism. A Dictionary of Oaths, Curses, Insults, Sexual Slang and Metaphor, Racial Slurs,*

Drug Talk, Homosexual Lingo, and Related Matters. Middle Village, New York: Jonathan David, 1981. 448 pp.

1733. Spector, David A. *The Book of Nicknames*. Burlington, Vermont: Verve Editions, 2006. 191 pp.

1734. Sperling, Susan K. *Tenderfeet and Ladyfingers. A Visceral Approach to Words and Their Origins*. Illustrations by Michael C. Witte. New York: Viking Press, 1981. 150 pp.

1735. Spink, Kathryn (ed.). *The Wisdom of Mother Teresa*. Illustrations by David Axtell. Oxford, England: Lion Publishing, 1998; rpt. Louisville, Kentucky: Westminster John Knox Press, 2000. 38 pp.

1736. Sporschil, Johann. *Kraft und Geist der englischen Sprache in Sprichwörtern, Kernsprüchen und eigenthümlichen Redensarten des englischen Volkes*. Leipzig: Friedrich Volckmar, 1837. 103 pp.

1737. Spurgeon, Charles Haddon. *The Salt Cellars. Being a Collection of Proverbs*. New York: A.C. Armstrong, 1889. 334 pp. Rpt. as *Spurgeon's Proverbs and Sayings with Notes*. Grand Rapids, Michigan: Baker Book House, 1975. 334 pp.

1738. Spurgeon, Charles Haddon. *The Wit and Wisdom of Rev. Charles H. Spurgeon [1834-1892], Containing Selections from His Writings, and a Sketch of His Life and Work*. Ed. Richard B. Cook. New York: Lenox Publishing, 1892. 536 pp. ("Salt-Cellars", proverbs on pp. 436-472).

1739. Stefanovich, G.A., L.I. Shvydkaia, L.I. Mustaeva, and O.E. Tereshchenko. *Angliiskii iazyk v poslovitsakh i pogovorkakh. English through Proverbs*. Moskva: Prosveshchenie, 1987. 95 pp.

1740. Steindl-Rast, David. *Words of Common Sense for Mind, Body, and Soul*. Philadelphia: Templeton Foundation Press, 2002. 91 pp.

1741. Stern, Henry R., and Richey Novak. *A Handbook of English-German Idioms and Useful Expressions*. New York: Harcourt, Brace, Jovanovich, 1973. 248 pp.

1742. Steuck, Udo. *One Thousand and More Animal Proverbs*. London: Minerva Press, 1997. 135 pp. With illustrations.

1743. Stevens, James S. *Quotations and References in Charles Dickens*. Boston: The Christopher Publishing House, 1929. 102 pp.

1744. Stevenson, Burton Egbert. *The Home Book of Quotations, Classical and Modern*. New York: Dodd, Mead & Co., 1934. 2605 pp. (5th ed. 1947). 2812 pp.

1745. Stevenson, Burton Egbert. *The Home Book of Proverbs, Maxims and Familiar Phrases*. New York: Macmillan, 1948. Seventh printing as *The Macmillan Book of Proverbs, Maxims, and Familiar Phrases*. New York: Macmillan, 1968. 2957 pp.

1746. Stewart, Roy L. *Quotations with an Attitude. A Wickedly Funny Source Book*. New York: Sterling Publishing, 1995. 160 pp.

1747. Stibbs, Anne. *Like a Fish Needs a Bicycle ... and Over 3000 Quotations by and about Women*. London: Bloomsbury, 1992. 307 pp.

1748. Strauss, Maurcie B. (ed.). *Familiar Medical Quotations*. Boston: Little, Brown and Company, 1968. 968 pp.

1749. Stul'nikova, S.V. *555 angliiskikh poslovits i pogovorok*. Moskva: "Os'-89", 1999. 31 pp.

1750. Sugar, Bert Randolph. *The Book of Sports Quotes*. New York: Quick Fox, 1979. 149 pp.

1751. Sumrall, Amber Coverdale. *Write to the Heart: Wit & Wisdom of Women Writers*. Freedom, California: The Crossing Press, 1992. 200 pp.

1752. Swainson, Charles. *A Handbook of Weather Folk-Lore Being a Collection of Proverbial Sayings in Various Languages Relating to the Weather, with Explanatory and Illustrative Notes*. Edinburgh: William Blackwood, 1873; rpt. Detroit: Gale Research Company, 1974. 275 pp.

1753. Taggart, Caroline. *An Apple a Day: Old Fashioned Proverbs and Why They Still Work*. London: Michael O'Mara, 2009. 182 pp.

1754. Taylor, Jefferys. *Old English Sayings Newly Expounded in Prose and Verse*. London: Wightman and Cramp, 1827. 147 pp.

1755. Taylor, Joseph. *Antiquitates Curiosae: The Etymology of Many Remarkable Old Sayings, Proverbs, and Singular Customs*. London: T. and J. Allman, 1818. 152 pp.

1756. Taylor, Archer. "Proverbia Britannica [out of Johannes Gruterus' *Florilegium Ethicopoliticum* (1611), II, 172-188]." *Washington University Studies, Humanities Series*, 11, no. 2 (1924), 409-423.

1757. Taylor, Archer. "Proverbial Comparisons in the Plays of [Francis] Beaumont and [John] Fletcher." *Journal of American Folklore*, 70 (1957), 25-36.

1758. Taylor, Archer. "Proverbial Phrases in the Plays of [Francis] Beaumont and [John] Fletcher." *Bulletin of the Tennessee Folklore Society*, 23 (1957), 39-59.

1759. Taylor, Archer. "Proverbs in the Plays of [Francis] Beaumont and [John] Fletcher." *Southern Folklore Quarterly*, 24 (1960), 77-100.

1760. Templeton, John Marks. *Golden Nuggets*. Radnor, Pennsylvania: Templeton Foundation Press, 1997. 86 pp.

1761. Templeton, John Marks. *Worldwide Laws of Life. 200 Eternal Spiritual Principles*. Philadelphia: Templeton Foundation Press, 1997. 502 pp.

1762. Terban, Marvin. *In a Pickle. And Other Funny Idioms*. Illustrations by Giulio Maestro. New York: Clarion Books, 1983; rpt. New York: Clarion Books, 2007. 64 pp.

1763. Terban, Marvin. *Mad as a Wet Hen! And Other Funny Idioms*. Illustrations by Giulio Maestro. New York: Clarion Books, 1987; rpt. New York: Clarion Books, 2007. 64 pp.

1764. Terban, Marvin. *Punching the Clock. Funny Action Idioms*. Illustrations by Tom Huffman. New York: Clarion Books, 1990. 64 pp.

1765. Terban, Marvin. *Scholastic Dictionary of Idioms. More than 600 Phrases, Sayings & Expressions*. New York: Scholastic, 1996. 245 pp.

1766. Thiselton-Dyer, T. F. *Folk-Lore of Shakespeare*. New York: Harper & Brothers, 1884. 559 pp. (proverbs, pp. 444-474).

1767. Thomsett, Michael C. *A Treasury of Business Quotations*. New York: Ballantine Books, 1990. 211 pp.

1768. Tilley, Morris Palmer. *Elizabethan Proverb Lore in Lyly's "Euphues" and in Pettie's "Petite Pallace" with Parallels from Shakespeare*. New York: Macmillan, 1926. 461 pp.

1769. Tilley, Morris Palmer. *A Dictionary of the Proverbs in England in the Sixteenth and Seventeenth Centuries*. Ann Arbor, Michigan: University of Michigan Press, 1950. 854 pp.

1770. Tilley, Morris Palmer, and James K. Ray. "Proverbs and Proverbial Allusions in [Christopher] Marlowe." *Modern Language Notes*, 50 (1935), 347-355.

1771. Titcomb, Timothy. *Gold-Foil, Hammered from Popular Proverbs*. New York: Charles Scribner, 1872. 340 pp.

1772. Titelman, Gregory Y. *Random House Dictionary of Popular Proverbs and Sayings: Over 1,500 Proverbs and Sayings with 10,000 Illustrative Citations*. New York: Random House, 1996. 468 pp. (2nd ed. 2000). 480 pp. Rpt. as *Popular Proverbs and Sayings: An A-Z Dictionary of over 1,500 Proverbs and Sayings, with 10,000 Ilustrative Examples*. New York: Gramercy Books, 1997. 468 pp.

1773. Tóthné Litovkina, Anna. *A Proverb a Day Keeps Boredom Away*. Szekszárd: IPF-Könyvek, 2000. 386 pp. With illustrations.

1774. Treffry, Elford Eveleigh. *Stokes' Encyclopedia of Familiar Quotations. Containing Five Thousand Selections from Six Hundred Authors*. New York: Frederick A. Stokes, 1906. 763 pp.

1775. Trent, D.C. *Best Wit of the English People. Proverbs of England*. Girard, Kansas: E. Haldeman-Julius Publications, 1927. 32 pp.

1776. Tripp, Rhoda Thomas. *The International Thesaurus of Quotations*. New York: Harper & Row, 1970; rpt. New York: Harper & Row, 1987. 1088 pp.

1777. Trusler, John Rev. *Proverbs Exemplified, and Illustrated by Pictures from Real Life*. Illustrations by John Bewick. London: Literary Press, 1790; rpt. New York: Johnson Reprint Corporation, 1970. 196 pp.

1778. Tuleja, Tad. *The Cat's Pajamas. A Fabulous Fictionary of Familiar Phrases*. New York: Fawcett Columbine, 1987. 226 pp.

1779. Tuleja, Tad. *Marvelous Monikers: The People Behind More than 400 Words and Expressions*. New York: Harmony Books, 1990. 206 pp.

1780. Tuleja, Tad. *Quirky Quotations. More than 500 Fascinating, Quotable Comments and the Stories Behind Them*. New York: Harmony Books, 1992. 192 pp.

1781. Tulloch, Tom. "Sayings from North Yell [Shetland]." *Tocher*, no vol., no. 47 (Winter 1993-1994), 298-309.

1782. Tupper, Martin Farquhar. *Proverbial Philosophy: A Book of Thoughts and Arguments, Originally Treated*. Boston: Philips,

Sampson and Company, 1850. 282 pp. Rpt. as *Proverbial Philosophy: A Book of Thoughts and Arguments, Originally Treated. With an Essay on "The Philosophy of Proverbs"*. Philadelphia: E.H. Butler, 1852. 276 pp. (essay, pp. IX-XXXVI).

1783. Urdang, Laurence. *"The Whole Ball of Wax" and other Colloquial Phrases. What They Mean and How They Started*. New York: Perigee Books, 1988. 157 pp.

1784. Urdang, Laurence. *The Facts on File Dictionary of Numerical Allusions*. New York: Facts on File Publications, 1986. Rpt. as *Three-Toed Sloths and Seven-League Boots: A Dictionary of Numerical Expressions*. New York: Barnes & Noble, 1992. 324 pp.

1785. Urdang, Laurence, and Frank R. Abate. *Idioms and Phrases Index. An Unrivaled Collection of Idioms, Phrases, Expressions, and Collocutions of Two or More Words which Are Part of the English Lexicon and for which the Meaning of the Whole is not Transparent from the Sum of the Meanings of the Constituent Parts*. 3 vols. Detroit, Michigan: Gale Research Company, 1983. 1691 pp.

1786. Urdang, Laurence, Walter W. Hunsinger, and Nancy LaRoche. *Picturesque Expressions: A Thematic Dictionary*. Detroit, Michigan: Gale Research Company, 1985. 770 pp.

1787. Urdang, Laurence, and Nancy LaRoche. *Picturesque Expressions: A Thematic Dictionary*. Detroit, Michigan: Gale Research Company, 1980. 405 pp. (1st ed. of previous entry).

1788. Urdang, Laurence, and Ceila Dame Robbins (eds.). *Slogans. A Collection of More Than 6,000 Slogans, Rallying Cries, and Other Exhortations Used in Advertising, Political Campaigns, Popular Causes and Movements*. Detroit, Michigan: Gale Research Company, 1984. 556 pp.

1789. Urdang, Laurence, Ceila Dame Robbins, and Frank R. Abate. *Mottoes. A Compilation of More Than 9,000 Mottoes from Around the World and Through-out History, with Foreign Examples Identified and Translated into English, etc*. Detroit, Michigan: Gale Research Company, 1986. 1162 pp.

1790. Urdang, Laurence, and Frederick G. Ruffner (eds.). *Allusions – Cultural, Literary, Biblical, and Historical. A Thematic Dictionary*. Detroit, Michigan: Gale Research Company, 1986. 634 pp.

1791. Ustinov, Peter. *Quotable Ustinov*. Illustrations by Peter Ustinov. Amherst, New York: Prometheus Books, 1995. 201 pp.

1792. Uthe-Spencker, Angela. *English Proverbs. Englische Sprichwörter*. Illustrations by Frieda Wiegand. München: Deutscher Taschenbuch Verlag, 1977. 84 pp.

1793. Vanoni, Marvin. *Great Expressions. How Our Favorite Words and Phrases Have Come to Mean What They Mean*. Illustrations by Chris Demarest. New York: William Morrow, 1989. Rpt. as *I've Got Goose Pimples. Our Great Expressions and How They Came to Be*. New York: William Morrow, 1989. 221 pp.

1794. Vizetelly, Frank H., and Leander J. de Bekker. *A Desk-Book of Idioms and Idiomatic Phrases in English Speech and Literature*. New York: Grosset & Dunlap, 1923. 498 pp.

1795. Voss, Karl. *Redensarten der englischen Sprache*. Frankfurt am Main: Ullstein, 1967 (2nd ed. 1975). 172 pp.

1796. Wallace, A. *Popular Sayings Dissected*. London: T. Fisher Unwin, 1894. 160 pp.

1797. Walley, Dean (ed.). *Little Book of Proverbs*. Illustrations by Pat Paris. Kansas City, Missouri: Hallmark Editions, 1968. 40 pp.

1798. Walsh, William. *The International Encyclopedia of Prose and Poetical Quotations from the Literature of the World*. Philadelphia: John C. Winston, 1908. 1029 pp.

1799. Walter, Elizabeth et al. *Cambridge International Dictionary of Idioms*. Cambridge: Cambridge University Press, 1998. 587 pp.

1800. Wanamaker, John. *Maxims of Life and Business*. New York: Harper & Brothers, 1923. 129 pp.

1801. Ward, Anna L. *A Dictionary of Quotations in Prose from American and Foreign Authors, including Translations from Ancient Sources*. New York: Thomas Y. Crowell, 1889. 701 pp.

1802. Ward, Anna L. *A Dictionary of Quotations from English and American Poets*. New York: Thomas Y. Crowell, 1883 (2nd ed. 1911). 761 pp.

1803. Watkins, Dana. *The Idiom Advantage: Fluency in Speaking and Listening*. New York: Addison-Wesley, 1995. 241 pp. With illustrations.

1804. Watts, Karen (ed.). *21st Century Dictionary of Slang*. New York: The Philip Lief Group, 1994. 339 pp.

1805. Webber, Elizabeth, and Mike Feinsilber. *Merriam-Webster's Dictionary of Allusions.* Springfield, Massachusetts: Merriam-Webster, 1999. 597 pp.

1806. White, Rolf B. (ed.). *The Great Business Quotations.* Secaucus, New Jersey: Lyle Stuart, 1986. 271 pp.

1807. Whiting, Bartlett Jere. "Proverbs in Certain Middle English Romances in Relation to Their French Sources." *Harvard Studies and Notes in Philology and Literature,* 15 (1933), 75-126.

1808. Whiting, Bartlett Jere. *Chaucer's Use of Proverbs.* Cambridge, Massachusetts: Harvard University Press, 1934; rpt. New York: AMS Press, 1973. 297 pp. (proverb index, pp. 155-194).

1809. Whiting, Bartlett Jere. "Proverbial Material in the Popular Ballad." *Journal of American Folklore,* 47 (1934), 22-44.

1810. Whiting, Bartlett Jere. "Proverbs in the *Ancren Riwle* and the *Recluse.*" *Modern Language Review,* 30 (1935), 502-505.

1811. Whiting, Bartlett Jere. "A Handful of Recent Wellerisms." *Archiv für das Studium der neueren Sprachen und Literaturen,* 169 (1936), 71-75.

1812. Whiting, Bartlett Jere. *Proverbs in the Earlier English Drama with Illustrations from Contemporary French Plays.* Cambridge, Massachusetts: Harvard University Press, 1938; rpt. New York: Octagon Books, 1969. 505 pp.

1813. Whiting, Bartlett Jere. "The Devil and Hell in Current English Literary Idiom." *Harvard Studies and Notes in Philology and Literature,* 20 (1938), 207-247.

1814. Whiting, Bartlett Jere. "The English Proverbs of Stéphane Mallarmé." *Romanic Review,* 36 (1945), 134-141.

1815. Whiting, Bartlett Jere. "Sir Richard Baker's *Cato Variegatus* (1636)." *Humaniora. Essays in Literature, Folklore, Bibliography. Honoring Archer Taylor on His Seventieth Birthday.* Eds. Wayland D. Hand and Gustav Arlt. Locust Valley, New York: J.J. Augustin, 1960. 8-16.

1816. Whiting, Bartlett Jere. "A Collection of Proverbs in B[ritish] M[useum] Additional MS. 37075." *Franciplegius: Medieval and Linguistic Studies in Honor of Francis Peabody Magoun.* Eds. Jess B. Bessinger and Robert P. Creed. New York: New York University Press, 1965. 274-289.

1817. Whiting, Bartlett Jere. *Proverbs, Sentences, and Proverbial Phrases from English Writings Mainly Before 1500*. Cambridge, Massachusetts: Harvard University Press, 1968. 733 pp.

1818. Widdowson, John D.A. "Proverbs and Sayings from Filey." *Patterns in the Folk Speech of the British Isles*. Ed. Martyn F. Wakelin. London: The Athlone Press of the University of London, 1972. 50-72.

1819. Widdowson, John D.A. "A Checklist of Newfoundland Expressions." *Lore and Language*, 2, no. 10 (1979), 33-40.

1820. Wilcox, Frederick B. (ed.). *A Little Book of Aphorisms*. New York: Charles Scribner's Sons, 1947. 257 pp.

1821. Wilkinson, P.R. *Thesaurus of Traditional English Metaphors*. London: George Routledge, 1993. 777 pp.

1822. Wilson, F.P. *The Oxford Dictionary of English Proverbs*. 3rd ed. Oxford: Clarendon Press, 1970. 930 pp. 1st ed. William George Smith. With an introduction and index by Janet E. Heseltine. Oxford: Clarendon Pess, 1935. 644 pp. 2nd ed. revised by Sir Paul Harvey. Oxford: Clarendon Press, 1948. 740 pp.

1823. Wilstach, Frank J. *A Dictionary of Similes*. Boston: Little, Brown & Company, 1916. 488 pp.

1824. Winters, Jonathan. *Mouse Breath, Conformity and Other Social Ills*. Indianapolis, Indiana: Bobbs-Merrill Company, 1965. 66 pp. With illustrations. (insults).

1825. Wood, Frederick T. *English Verbal Idioms*. New York: St. Martin's, 1964. 325 pp. Revised ed. New York: Washington Square Press, 1967. 359 pp.

1826. Wood, James. *The Nuttall Dictionary of Quotations. From Ancient and Modern, English and Foreign Sources*. London: Frederick Warne, 1930. 659 pp. and 28 pp. (supplement and index).

1827. Wood, Katharine B. *Quotations for Occasions*. New York: The Century Company, 1896 (2nd ed. 1903). 220 pp.

1828. Woodburn, Roland Ripley. *Proverbs in Health Books of the English Renaissance*. Diss. Texas Tech University, 1975. 94 pp. (proverb index, pp. 61-94).

1829. Wooléver, Adam. *Encyclopedia of Quotations. A Treasury of Wisdom, Wit and Humor, Odd Comparisons and Proverbs*. Philadelphia: David McKay, 1876 (6th ed. 1898). 527 pp. (proverbs, pp. 493-516).

1830. Wright, Elizabeth Mary. "Popular Phrases and Sayings." In E.M. Wright. *Rustic Speech and Folk-Lore.* Oxford: Oxford University Press, 1913; rpt. Detroit: Gale Research Company, 1968. 158-190.

1831. Wright, Larry. *Happy as a Clam and 9,999 Other Similes.* New York: Prentice Hall, 1994. 248 pp.

1832. Wykeham, Reginald. *1000 idiomatische Redensarten Englisch. Mit Erklärungen und Beispielen.* Berlin: Langenscheidt, 1936. 214 pp. Revised ed. Wolfgang Schmidt-Hidding and H. Robert Dodd. Berlin: Langenscheidt, 1959 (13th ed. 1975). 246 pp.

1833. Yeoman, James. *Shields Sayings: A Manner of Speech. Proverbial Phrases and Idioms.* South Shields, Northcumberland: J. Greenwood, 1960. 30 pp.

1834. Yurtbaşi, Metin. *How to Learn English through Proverbs.* Istanbul: Türkiye Iş Bankasi Beylikdüzü, 1999. 60 pp. With illustrations.

1835. Zupitza, Julius. "The Prouerbis of Wysdom." *Archiv für das Studium der neueren Sprachen und Literaturen,* 90 (1893), 241-268.

Esperanto

1836. Fiedler, Sabine. *Plamsprache und Phraseologie. Empirische Untersuchungen zu reproduziertem Sprachmaterial im Esperanto.* Frankfurt am Main: Peter Lang, 1999. 444 pp. (phraseologism index, pp. 419-430).

1837. Fiedler, Sabine, and Pavel Rak. *Ilustrita [Esperanto] frazeologio.* Dobřichovice (Prago): Kava-Pech, 2004. 136 pp.

1838. Golden, Bernard. "Kiel rilati al la diablo per proverboj." *Israela Esperantisto,* no. 110 (February 1992), 8-10.

1839. Golden, Bernard. "Proverboj pri veturado sur reloj." *Israela Esperantisto,* no. 112 (October 1992), 6-8.

1840. Zamenhof, Lazaro Ludoviko. *Proverbaro Esperanta. Lau la verko frazeologhio rusa-pola-franca-germana de M.F. Zamenhof.* Paris: Esperantista Centra Librejo, 1925. 82 pp.

Estonian

1841. Hussar, A., Arvo Krikmann, and Ingrid Sarv. *Vanasõna-raamat*. Tallinn: Kirjastus "Eesti Raamat", 1984. 624 pp.

1842. Krikmann, Arvo (ed.). *Meri andab. meri ottab. Valimik lahemaa vanasõnu*. Tallinn: Valgus, 1981. 116 pp.

1843. Krikmann, Arvo, and Ingrid Sarv. *Eesti vanasõnad. 1-5000*. Tallinn: "Eesti Raamat", 1980. I, 910 pp.

1844. Krikmann, Arvo, and Ingrid Sarv. *Eesti vanasõnad. 5001-10000*. Tallinn: "Eesti Raamat", 1983. II, 866 pp.

1845. Krikmann, Arvo, and Ingrid Sarv. *Eesti vanasõnad. 10001-15140*. Tallinn: "Eesti Raamat", 1985. III, 911 pp.

1846. Krikmann, Arvo, and Ingrid Sarv. *Eesti vanasonad. Lisad*. Tallinn: "Eesti Raamat", 1988. IV, 530 pp.

1847. Krikmann, Arvo, and Ingrid Sarv. *Estonskie poslovitsy. 1-15140*. Tallinn: "Eesti Raamat", 1986. V,1, 400 pp.

1848. Krikmann, Arvo, and Ingrid Sarv. *Estnische Sprichwörter. 1-15140*. Tallinn: "Eesti Raamat", 1987. V,2, 438 pp.

Ethiopian

1849. Cotter, George. *Salt for Stew: Proverbs and Sayings of the Oromo People with English Translations*. Debre Zeit, Ethiopia: Maryknoll Fathers, 1990. 580 pp.

1850. Cotter, George. *Gurra Miti Qalbi Male: Wangela Goftaa Ye-sus Kiristosif Mamaaksa Oromo / The Ears are not Important, It's the Mind that Counts: The Gospel of Our Lord Jesus Christ and the Proverbs of the Oromo*. Addis Ababa, Ethiopia: United Printers, 1991. 554 pp.

1851. Cotter, George. *Ethiopian Wisdom: Proverbs and Sayings of the Oromo People*. Pretoria: University of South Africa Press, 1997. 248 pp.

1852. Leslau, Wolf. *Gurage Folklore: Ethiopian Folktales, Proverbs, Beliefs, and Riddles*. Wiesbaden: Steiner, 1982. 327 pp.

1853. Richter, Renate, and Eshetu Kebbede. *Sprichwörter aus Äthiopien*. Köln: Rüdiger Köppe, 1994. 136 pp.

157

1854. Sumner, Claude. *Oromo Wisdom Literature: Proverbs - Collection and Analysis.* Addis Ababa, Ethiopia: Gudina Tumsa Foundation, 1995. 482 pp.

Finnish

1855. Florinus, Henrik. *Wanhain Suomalaisten Tawaliset ja Suloiset Sananlascut.* Turku: Johan Winterilda, 1702. Rpt. ed. Matti Kuusi. Helsinki: Suomalaisen Kirjallisuuden Seura, 1987. 77 pp.

1856. Idström, Anna, and Hans Morottaja. *Inarinsaamen idiomisanakirja.* Inari, Finland: Saamelaiskäräjät, 2007. 108 pp.

1857. Korhonen, Jarmo. *Alles im Griff – Homma hanskassa. Saksa-suomi-idiomisanakirja – Idiomwörterbuch Deutsch-Finnisch.* Helsinki: Werner Söderström, 2001. 683 pp.

1858. Kuusi, Matti. *Vanhan kansan sananlaskuviisaus.* Illustrations by Helga Sjöstedt. Helsinki: Werner Söderström, 1953 (3rd ed. 1990). 539 pp.

1859. Kuusi, Matti. *Suomen kansan vertauksia.* Illustrations by Kimmo Kaivanto.Vaasa: Suomalaisen Kirjallisuuden Seura, 1960, (2nd ed. 1979, 3rd ed. 1982). 552 pp.

1860. Kuusi, Matti. *Rapatessa roiskuu. Nykysuomen sananparsikirja.* Illustrations by Hannu Lukkarinen. Helsinki: Suomalaisen Kirjallisuuden Seura, 1988. 437 pp.

1861. Kuusi, Matti, and Outi Lauhakangas. *Maailman sananlaskuviisaus.* Helsinki: Werner Söderström, 1993. 403 pp.

1862. Laukkanen, Kari, and Pekka Hakamies. *Sananlaskut. 15904 sananlaskua kansanrunousarkistosta.* Vaasa: Suomalaisen Kirjallisuuden Seura, 1978 (2nd ed. 1984). 598 pp.

1863. Lönnrot, Elias. *Suomalaisia Sananlaskuja.* Porvoossa: Werner Söderström, 1892; rpt. Porvoo: Werner Söderström, 2002. 42 pp.

1864. Schellbach-Kopra, Ingrid. *Finnisch-Deutsches Sprichwörterbuch. Suomalais-saksalainen sananlaskukirja.* Helsinki: Suomalaisen Kirjallisuuden Seurta, 1980. 138 pp.

1865. Schellbach-Kopra, Ingrid. *Suomi-saksa fraasi-sanakirja. Finnisch-deutsche Idiomatik.* Helsinki: Werner Söderström, 1985. 304 pp.

1866. Schellbach-Kopra, Ingrid. *Zwei Finnen brauchen keinen Dolmetscher. Finnische Sprichwörter*. Berlin: Frank & Timme, 2011. 285 pp.

1867. Tanttu, Erkki (ill.). *Sata sananparttasata kuvaa. Suomen kansan sananparsia*. Helsingissä: Kustannusosakeyhtiö Otava, 1945. 100 pp.

1868. Tanttu, Erkki (ill.). *Kirpusta keisariin. Kuvitettuja sananparsia*. Helsingissä: Kustannusosakeyhtiö Otava, 1962. 81 pp.

1869. Tanttu, Erkki (ill.). *Repliikit reiraan. Kuvitettuja sananparsia*. Helsingissä: Kustannusosakeyhtiö Otava, 1964. 81 pp.

1870. Tanttu, Erkki (ill.). *Mutkat suoraks. Kuvitettuja sananparsia*. Helsingissä: Kustannusosakeyhtiö Otava, 1966. 85 pp.

1871. Tanttu, Erkki (ill.). *Sattuuhan sitä. Suomalaisia sananparsia kuvin*. Helsingissä: Kustannusosakeyhtiö Otava, 1968. 73 pp.

1872. Tanttu, Erkki (ill.). *Viisastellast vähä. Suomalaisia sananparsia kuvin*. Helsingissä: Kustannusosakeyhtiö Otava, 1976. 101 pp.

1873. Väänänen-Jensen, Inkeri. *Finnish Proverbs*. Illustrations by Esther Feske. Iowa City, Iowa: Penfield Press, 1990. 51 pp.

1874. Virkkunen, Sakari. *Suomalainen fraasisanakirja*. Keuruu: Otava, 1983. 420 pp.

French

1875. Alibert, Louis. *Proverbes de l'Aude, classés et mis en orthographe occitane*. Andouque, France: Vent Terral, 1998. 250 pp.

1876. Anonymous. *French Wit and Wisdom*. Illustrations by Fritz Kredel. Mount Vernon, New York: Peter Pauper Press, 1956. 61 pp.

1877. Baralt, Rafael María. *Diccionario de galicismos, ó sea de la voces, locuciones y frases de la lengua francesa que se han introducido en el habla castellana moderna*. Madrid: Impretna Nacional, 1855. 709 pp. 2nd ed. Madrid: Leocadio Lopez, 1874. 627 pp.

1878. Bárdosi, Vilmos, Stefan Ettinger, and Cécile Stölting. *Redewendungen Französisch/Deutsch. Thematisches Wörter- und Übungsbuch*. Tübingen: Francke, 1992. 259 pp.

1879. Blum, Geneviève. *Les Idiomatics français-anglais*. Illustrations by Nestor Salas. Paris: Virgule, 1989. 95 pp.

1880. Brezin-Rossignol, Monique. *Dictionnaire des proverbes français/anglais. Dictionary of Proverbs English/French.* Paris: La Maison du Dictionnaire, 1997. New York: Hippocrene Books, 1997. 479 pp.

1881. Cahier, Le P.Ch. *Quelque six mille proverbes et aphorismes usuels.* Paris: Julien et Lanier, 1856. 579 pp.

1882. Caillot, A. *Nouveau dictionnaire proverbial, satirique et burlesque.* Paris: Dauvin, 1826. 538 pp.

1883. Calvez, Daniel Jean. *Le langage proverbial de Voltaire dans sa correspondance du 29 décembre 1704 au 31 décembre 1769.* Diss. University of Georgia, 1980. 343 pp. Also as *Le langage proverbial de Voltaire dans sa correspondance (1704-1769).* New York: Peter Lang, 1989. 312 pp.

1884. Cantera Ortiz de Urbina, Jesús, and Julia Sevilla Muñoz. *El calendario en el refranero francés.* Madrid: Guillermo Blázquez, 2001. 129 pp. (weather proverbs).

1885. Combet, Louis, and Julia Sevilla Muñoz. "Proverbes, expressions proverbiales, sentences et lieux communs sentencieux de la langue française d'aujourd'hui avec leur correspondance en espagnol." *Paremia,* 4 (1995), 7-95.

1886. Di Stefano, Giuseppe. *Dictionnaire des locutions en moyen français.* Montréal: Editions CERES, 1991. 930 pp.

1887. Diaféria, Michèle G. *Les Proverbes au conte de Bretaigne: A Critical Edition and Study.* Diss. Florida State University, 1988. 80 pp. Also as *Li Proverbes au conte de Bretaigne. Critical Edition and Study.* New York: Peter Lang, 1990. 166 pp.

1888. Dournon, Jean-Yves. *Le dictionnaire des proverbes et dictons de France.* Paris: Hachette, 1986. 351 pp.

1889. Duneton, Claude. *La puce à l'oreille. Anthologie des expressions populaires avec leur origine.* Paris: Stock, 1978; rpt. Paris: Balland, 1985 (2nd ed. 1991). 501 pp.

1890. Ehrlich, Eugene. *Les Bons Mots. How to Amaze "Tout le Monde" with Everyday French.* New York: Henry Holt, 1997. 312 pp.

1891. Éluard, Paul, and Benjamin Péret. "Sprichwörter." *Surrealismus in Paris 1919-1939. Ein Lesebuch.* Ed. Karlheinz Barck. Leipzig: Reclam, 1990. 213-215.

1892. Éluard, Paul, and Benjamin Péret. *152 Sprichwörter auf den neuesten Stand gebracht.* Ed. and trans. Unda Hörner and Wolfram Kiepe. Gießen: Anabas Verlag, 1995. 168 pp. French original: *152 proverbes mis au goût du jour.* Paris: Bureau de recherches surréalistes, 1925.

1893. Éluard, Paul, and Benjamin Péret. "152 Proverbs Brought up to Date [English and French]." *Chicago Review*, 50, nos. 2-4 (2004-2005), 173-184.

1894. Finod, J. de. *A Thousand Flashes of French Wit, Wisdom, and Wickedness.* New York: D. Appleton, 1880. 251 pp.

1895. Flonta, Teodor. *A Dictionary of English and French Equivalent Proverbs.* Hobart, Tasmania: De Proverbio.com, 2001. 255 pp.

1896. Frank, Grace. "Proverbes en Rimes (B)." *Romanic Review*, 31 (1940), 209-238.

1897. Frank, Grace, and Dorothy Miner (eds.). *Proverbes en Rimes. Text and Illustrations of the Fifteenth Century from a French Manuscript in the Walters Art Gallery, Baltimore.* Baltimore, Maryland: The Johns Hopkins Press, 1937. 303 pp. With 186 illustrations.

1898. Gennep, Arnold van. "Wellérismes français." *Mercure de France*, 248 (15. December, 1933), 700-704. Also in *Le Folklore Brabançon*, 13 (1933-1934), 331-333.

1899. Gennep, Arnold van. "Wellérismes français." *Mercure de France*, 253 (1. July, 1934), 209-215.

1900. Gennep, Arnold van. "Wellérismes français et flamands." *Mercure de France*, 270 (15. September, 1936), 645-648. Also in *Le Folklore Brabançon*, 16 (1936-1937), 291-294.

1901. Gottschalk, Walter. *Die sprichwörtlichen Redensarten der französischen Sprache. Ein Beitrag zur französischen Stilistik, Kultur- und Wesenskunde.* 2 vols. Heidelberg: Carl Winter, 1930. I, 281 pp.; II, 265 pp.

1902. Grandville (pseud. Jean Ignace Isidore Gérard) (ill.).. *Cent proverbes.* Paris: H. Fourmier, 1845. 400 pp. Rpt. ed. M. Quitard. Paris: Garnier, 1887. 551 pp. (one of my personal treasures given to me by my friend Alan Dundes – W.M.).

1903. Guerlac, Othon. *Les citations françaises.* Paris: Librairie Armand Colin, 1961. 459 pp.

1904. Hassell, James Woodrow. *Middle French Proverbs, Sentences, and Proverbial Phrases*. Toronto: Pontifical Institute of Mediaeval Studies, 1982. 275 pp.

1905. Kadler, Alfred. *Sprichwörter und Sentenzen der altfranzösischen Artus- und Abenteuerromane*. Marburg: N.G. Elwert, 1886. 104 pp. Proverb index, pp. 43-100)

1906. Kastner, Georges. *Parémiologie musicale de la langue française ou explication des proverbes, locutions proverbiales, mots figurés qui tirent leur origine de la musique*. Paris: Brandus et Dufour, 1895. 682 pp.

1907. Klein, Hans Wilhelm. *1000 idiomatische Redensarten Französisch. Mit Erklärungen und Beispielen*. Berlin: Langenscheidt, 1937 (21st ed. 1976). 220 pp.

1908. Kösters-Roth, Ursula (ed.). *Locutions: Lexikon der französischen Redewendungen. Französisch-Deutsch*. Eltville am Rhein: Bechtermünz, 1990. 510 pp.

1909. La Mesangère, Pierre de. *Dictionnaire des proverbes français*. Paris: Treuttel et Würtz, 1821. 591 pp.

1910. Lafleur, Bruno. *Dictionnaire des locutions idiomatiques françaises*. Bern: Peter Lang, 1979. 669 pp.

1911. Larsen, Judith Clark. *Proverbial Material in the "Roman de la Rose"*. Diss. University of Georgia, 1978. 140 pp.

1912. L'Aulnaye, M. de. "Rabelaesiana: Recueil de sentences, adages, proverbes, façons de parler proverbiales, jeux de mots, paronomasies, jurons, imprécations." *Ouevres de F. Rabelais*. 3 vols. Paris: Louis Janet, 1823. III, 499-672.

1913. Le Roux de Lincy, Adrien Jean Victor. *Le livre des proverbes français*. 2 vols. Paris: Paulin, 1842. I, CXX, 259 pp.; II, 422 pp. 2nd ed. Paris: Adolphe Delahays, 1859. 2 vols. I, CXV, 409 pp.; II, 619 pp.; rpt. Genève: Slatkine, 1968. I, CXV, 409 pp.; II, 619 pp.

1914. Le Roux de Lincy, Adrien Jean Victor. *Le livre des proverbes français*. 2 vols. Paris: Paulin, 1842. I, CXX, 259 pp.; II, 422 pp. Rpt. in one volume. Paris: Hachette Livre, 1996. XI, 985 pp.

1915. Lewis, Edward (ed.). *The French on Life and Love*. Illustrations by John Trotta. Kansas City, Missouri: Hallmark Cards, 1967. 60 pp.

1916. Loubens, Didier. *Les proverbes et locutions de la langue française, leurs origines et leur concordance avec les proverbes et locutions des autres nations.* Paris: Weil & Nicolas, 1889. 313 pp.

1917. Loux, Françoise, and Philippe Richard. *Sagesses du corps. La santé et la maladie dans les proverbes français.* Paris: G.-P. Maisonneuve et Larose, 1978. 353 pp.

1918. Maloux, Maurice. *Dictionnaire des proverbes, sentences et maximes.* Paris: Librairie Larousse, 1960. 628 pp.

1919. Martin, Johannes. *Les Proverbes au Conte de Bretaigne.* Diss. Universität Erlangen, 1892. Erlangen: Friedrich Junge, 1892. 34 pp.

1920. Massebeuf, Albert. "Expressions, dictons et proverbes de Brioude et du Brivadois." *Bizà Neirà*, no volume given, no. 109 (2001), 3-7; and no. 112 (2001), 2-7.

1921. McNeal, Doris Schuckler. *The Proverbs in the French Works of Henri Estienne.* Diss. University of Georgia, 1972. 424 pp.

1922. Mertvago, Peter. *Dictionary of 1000 French Proverbs.* New York: Hippocrene Books, 1996. 135 pp.

1923. Montreynaud, Florence, Agnès Pierron, and François Suzzoni (eds.). *Dictionnaire de proverbes et dictons.* Paris: Dictionnaires Le Robert, 1989. 756 pp.

1924. Montreynaud, Florence, Agnès Pierron, and François Suzzoni (eds.). *Dictionnaire de proverbes et dictons.* Paris: Dictionnaires Le Robert, 1993. 491 pp.

1925. Olivier, René, and Hans-Manfred Militz. *Französische idiomatische Redewendungen. Locutions françaises.* Leipzig: VEB Verlag Enzyklopädie, 1969 (3rd ed. 1984). 391 pp.

1926. Peretz, Bernhard. *Altprovenzalische Sprichwörter mit einem kurzen Hinblick auf den mittelhochdeutschen Freidank.* Erlangen: Andreas Deichert, 1887. 43 pp. Also in *Romanische Forschungen*, 3 (1887), 415-457.

1927. Pfeffer, Wendy. *Proverbs in Medieval Occitan Literature.* Gainesville, Florida: University Press of Florida, 1997. 155 pp. (proverb index, pp. 115-128).

1928. Pignolo, Marie-Thérèse, and Hans-Georg Heuber. *Ne mâche pas tes mots. Nimm kein Blatt vor den Mund! Französische Re-*

dewendungen und ihre deutschen Pendants. Illustrations by Birgit Rieger. Reinbek: Rowohlt, 1982. 119 pp.

1929. Quitard, Pierre-Marie. *Dictionnaire étymologique, historique, et anecdotique des proverbes et locutions proverbiales de la langue française.* Paris: P. Bertrand, 1842; rpt. Genève: Slatkine Reprints, 1968. 701 pp.

1930. Quitard, Pierre-Marie. *Études historiques, littéraires et morales sur les proverbes français et le langage proverbial contenant l'explication et l'origine d'un grand nombre de proverbes remarquables oubliés dans tous les recueils.* Paris: Techener, 1860. 460 pp.

1931. Rassart-Eeckhout, Emmanuelle, and Tania Van Hemelryck (eds.). *Les proverbes illustrés [du moyen âge].* Montréal: Éditions CERES, 2001. 100 pp. With illustrations.

1932. Rat, Maurice. *Dictionnaire des locutions françaises.* Paris: Librairie Larousse, 1957. 430 pp. Revised ed. Paris: Librairie Larousse, 1982. 448 pp.

1933. Rey, Alain, and Sophie Chantreau (eds.). *Dictionnaire des expressions et locutions.* Paris: Dictionnaires Le Robert, 1979. 946 pp. Revised ed. Paris: Dictionnaires Le Robert, 1988. 1036 pp. (2nd ed. 1993). 888 pp.

1934. Sainéan, L. "Proverbes et dictons." In L. Sainéan. *La langue de Rabelais.* Paris: E. de Boccard, 1922. I, 343-448.

1935. Schemann, Hans, and Alain Raymond. *Idiomatik Deutsch-Französisch. Dictionnaire Idiomatique Allemand-Français.* Stuttgart: Ernst Klett, 1994. 1235 pp.

1936. Schmarje, Susanne. *Das sprichwörtliche Material in den Essais von Montaigne.* Diss. Universität Hamburg, 1970. 2 vols. Berlin: Walter de Gruyter, 1973. I, 242 pp.; II, 161 pp. (collection).

1937. Schulze-Busacker, Elisabeth. *Proverbes et expressions proverbiales dans la littérature narrative du moyen âge français. Recueil et analyse.* Paris: Librairie Honoré Champion, 1985. 356 pp. (proverb index, pp. 167-323).

1938. Segalen, Martine. "Le mariage, l'amour et les femmes dans les proverbes populaires français." *Ethnologie française,* 5 (1975), 119-160 and 6 (1976), 33-88.

1939. Sellner, Alfred. *Französisch im Alltag. Alphabetisch geordnetes Nachschlagewerk von französischen Sentenzen, Sprichwör-*

tern, Phrasen. Floskeln, Redewendungen, Zitaten und Formeln.
Wiesbaden: VMA-Verlag, 1986. 125 pp.

1940. Sevilla Muñoz, Julia, and Jesús Cantera Ortiz de Urbina (eds.). *Diccionario temático de locuciones francesas con su correspondencia española*. Madrid: Gredos, 2004. 782 pp.

1941. Tobler, Adolf (ed.). *Li Proverbe au Vilain. Die Sprichwörter des gemeinen Mannes. Altfranzösische Dichtung, nach den bisher bekannten Handschriften herausgegeben*. Leipzig: S. Hirzel, 1895. 188 pp.

1942. Troxler, H.J. *Proverbes d'Alsace. Elsässische Sprichwörter*. Greisbach: Bastberg, 1977. 231 pp.

1943. Vartier, Jean. *Le blason populaire de France: Sobriquets, dictons, facéties*. Paris: Maisonneuve et Larose, 1992. 449 pp.

1944. Voss, Karl. *Redensarten der französischen Sprache*. Frankfurt am Main: Ullstein, 1966 (3rd ed.1975). 214 pp.

1945. Wandelt, Oswin. *Sprichwörter und Sentenzen des altfranzösischen Dramas (1100-1400)*. Diss. Universität Marburg, 1887. Marburg: Fr. Sömmering, 1887. 75 pp.

1946. Wathelet, Jean-Marc. *Dictons des bêtes, des plantes et des saisons*. Illustrations by Christian Quennehen. Paris: Eugène Belin, 1985. 303 pp.

1947. Whiting, Bartlett Jere. "Proverbial Material in the Old-French Poems on Reynard the Fox." *Harvard Studies and Notes in Philology and Literature*, 17 (1935), 235-270.

1948. Whiting, Bartlett Jere. "Proverbs in the Writings of Jean Froissart." *Speculum*, 10 (1935), 291-321.

1949. Whiting, Bartlett Jere. "Proverbial Material in the Poems of Baudouin and Jean de Condé." *Romanic Review*, 27 (1936), 204-223.

1950. Widmer, Walter. *Volkstümliche Vergleiche im Französischen nach dem Typus "Rouge comme un coq"*. Diss. Universität Basel 1929. Basel: Zbinden & Hügin, 1929. 135 pp.

Frisian

1951. Kuip, Frederik Johan van der. *De Burmania-sprekwurden. Santjinde-ieuske Fryske sprekwurden ferklearre en yn har tiid besjoen*. Leeuwarden/Ljouwert: Fryske Akademy, 2003. 765 pp.

1952. Kuip, Frederik Johan van der. *Register op De Burmania-sprekwurden. Santjinde-ieuske Fryske sprekwurden ferklearre en yn har tiid besjoen.* Leeuwarden/Ljouwert: Fryske Akademy, 2004. 146 pp.

1953. Wilts, Ommo. *Friesisches Sprichwörterlexikon. Friesisch-Deutsch.* vol. 1: *Sprichwörter und Redensarten der Bökingharde.* Illustrations by Gisela Backmann. Neumünster: Karl Wachholtz, 1992. 264 pp.

Georgian

1954. Fähnrich, Heinz. *Ein Wort zur rechten Zeit. Georgische Sprichwörter.* Aachen: Verlag Shaker, 1994. 90 pp.

1955. Shurgaia, Tea (ed.). *Hezar va yek zarbolmathal-e Gorji [One Thousand and One Georgian Proverbs].* Tehran: Publishing Center of the Ministry of Foreign Affairs of Iran, 2002. 214 pp.

German

1956. Ade, Walter Frank Charles. *Das Sprichwort in den deutschen Werken des Andreas Gryphius (1616-1664).* Diss. Northwestern University, 1949. 662 pp.

1957. Adolphi, Otto. *Das große Buch der Fliegenden Worte, Zitate, Sprüche und Redensarten. Eine umfangreiche, praktische und zuverlässige Sammlung von mehr als zehntausend geflügelten Worten und volkstümlichen Redensarten, Zitaten aus Klassikern und bekannten neueren Dichtern, Sprichwörtern sowie lateinischen, französischen und englischen Sentenzen.* Berlin: W. Herlet, 1890. 616 pp.

1958. Agricola, Erhard. *Wörter und Wendungen. Wörterbuch zum deutschen Sprachgebrauch.* Leipzig: VEB Verlag Enzyklopädie, 1962; rpt. München: Max Hueber, 1970. 792 pp.

1959. Agricola, Johannes. *Sybenhundert und fünfftzig Teütscher Sprichwörter verneüwert und gebessert.* Hagenaw: no publisher given, 1534; rpt. ed. Mathilde Hain. Hildesheim: Georg Olms, 1970. 426 leaves.

1960. Agricola, Johannes. *Die Sprichwörtersammlungen [Sybenhundert und fünfftzig Teütscher Sprichwörter verneüwert und gebessert (1534) – Fünfhundert Gemainer Newer Teütscher Sprüchwörter (1548)].* Ed. Sander L. Gilman. 2 vols. Berlin: Walter de Gruyter, 1971. I, 555 pp.; II, 534 pp.

1961. Akdoğan, Memiş. *Almanca-Türkçe Deyimler Sözlüğü / Deutsch-Türkische Idiome.* Istanbul: Öğretim Yayinevi, 1965. 165 pp.

1962. Alsleben, Brigitte. *Flotte Sprüche & geflügelte Worte: Geschichten und Anekdoten rund um Zitate, Sprichwörter und Redensarten.* Mannheim: Dudenverlag, 1998. 256 pp.

1963. Alsleben, Brigitte, Carolin Mülverstedt, and Werner Scholze-Stubenrecht (eds.). *Duden. Das große Buch der Zitate und Redewendungen.* Mannheim: Dudenverlag, 2002. 837 pp. With illustrations.

1964. Amels, Peter. *Weisheiten und Bosheiten. Zitate und Sprüche.* Frankfurt am Main: Fouqué Literaturverlag, 2002. 65 pp.

1965. Anderson, Beatrix, and Maurcie North. *Cassell's Colloquial German. A Handbook of Idiomatic Usage.* London: Cassell, 1980. 176 pp.

1966. Anonymous. *Erklärung der vornehmsten Teutschen Sprichwörter nach ihrem Ursprung und wahren Verstande.* Leipzig: Friedrich Lanckischens Erben, 1748. 120 pp.

1967. Anonymous. *Sprichwörter, deutsche, eine Auswahl vorzüglich alter Denk- und Weisheitssprüche zur Veredlung des Geistes und Herzens. Ein Bilderbuch für die Jugend.* Nürnberg: Renner, 1836. Partial reprint ed. Bruno Mariacher as *Das Glück ist kugelrund. Eine Auswahl erprobter Denk- und Weisheits-Sprüche zur Veredlung des Geistes und Herzens. In bildlichen Darstellungen gegeben, mit Versen erläutert.* Zürich: Artemis, 1972. 46 pp. With illustrations.

1968. Anonymous. *Deutsche Sprüchwörter und Spruchreden in Bildern und Gedichten.* Düsseldorf: Arnz & Comp., 1852. 60 pp. With 20 illustrations.

1969. Anonymous. *Allotria. Ungeflügelte Worte aus dem jocosen Citaten-Schatz des Gymnasial-Directors.* Berlin: Denicke, 1875. 154 pp.

1970. Anonymous. *Deutsche Sprichwörter als Materialien zu Aufsatz- und Diktando-Übungen und Hausaufgaben für die Oberklassen der deutschen Volksschule.* Bearbeitet von einem unterfränkischen Lehrer. Würzburg: J. Staudinger, 1875. 58 pp.

1971. Anonymous. "Sprüchwörter mit Nachsatz." *Fliegende Blätter*, 71 (1879), 7. (anti-proverbs).

1972. Anonymous. "Verschiedene Todesarten [in Redensarten]." *Aus alten deutschen Volkskalendern.* Ed. Hannes Paesler. Berlin: Eckart, 1935. 93-95.

1973. Anonymous. *Wer lacht mit? Lustiges Sprichwörterbuch.* Elmshorn, Holstein: Holsteinische Margarinewerke Wagner, ca. 1952. 49 pp. With illustrations. (my very first proverb collection [I was eight years old] of proverb pictures handed out with the purchase of Wagner Margarine and then glued into this book with spaces for them and printed texts explainng the proverbs for us children – W.M.).

1974. Anonymous. *Gestickte Sprüche für Haus und Küche.* Frankfurt am Main: Historisches Museum, 1979. (7 postcards).

1975. Anonymous. *Kölsche Sprichwörter. Ein Kalender für 1980.* Illustrations by "Odysseus". Köln: J.P. Bachem, 1979. (52 postcards).

1976. Anonymous. *Zitatenschatz von A-Z.* München: Delphin, 1983. 512 pp.

1977. Anonymous. *Lieber mehr Glück als Verstand. Mini-Graffiti.* München: Wihlem Heyne, 1985 (6th ed. 1987). 121 pp. (miniature book).

1978. Anonymous. *Ich glaub', mein Hamster bohnert.* Rastatt: Arthur Moewig, 1986. 156 pp. With illustrations. (graffiti and antiproverbs).

1979. Anonymous. *Lob des Brotes. Sprichwörter, Spruchweisheiten und Redensarten.* Ulm: Deutsches Brotmuseum, 1990. 48 pp.

1980. Anonymous. *Kölsche Sprichwörter. Ein Kalender für 1992.* Illustrations by "Odysseus". Köln: J.P. Bachem, 1991. (52 postcards).

1981. Anonymous. *Sächsische Wein- und Trinksprüche.* Illustrations by Christian Schöpfler. Meißen: Brück, 1998. 32 pp.

1982. Anonymous. *Das große Buch der Bauernregeln & Sprichwörter.* Köln: Anaconda Verlag, 2009. 592 pp.

1983. Anze, Eva M. (ed.). *Dumme Sprüche für Frauen.* Augsburg: Weltbild, 2010. 160 pp.

1984. Appel, Andrea. *Die Katze im Sack kommt mir spanisch vor. Redensarten auf den Grund gegangen.* Illustrations by Frauke Trojahn. Berlin: Arani, 1987. 171 pp.

1985. Arzberger, S., T. Heyse, A. Klepsch, and A. Mang. *"Mer sachd ja nix, mer redd ja bloß". Redensarten aus Mittelfranken.* Illustrations by Gerd Bauer. Cadolzburg: ars vivendi, 2004. 208 pp.

1986. Assion, Peter (ed.). *"Entweder et ränt - oder de Schranke sin zo": Bönnsche/Kölsche Redensarten.* Illustrations by Markus Hockenbrink and Walter J. Divossen. Bonn: Divossen, 1997. 149 pp.

1987. Bahlmann, P. "Die Sprichwörter aus des Johannes Murmellius *Pappa puerorum* [1513]." *Germania,* 35 (1890), 400-402.

1988. Bajewsky, Manfred (ed.). *Der Sprücheklopfer.* Illustrations by Gerhard Dörner. Berlin: Semikolon, 2004. 55 pp. (anti-proverbs).

1989. Baller, Kurt. *Abendrot – Gutwetterbot. 1000 Bauern- und Wetterregeln.* München: W. Ludwig, 1992. 103 pp.

1990. Balzer, Berit, Consuelo Moreno, Rosa Piñel, Margit Raders, and María Luisa Schilling. *Kein Blatt vor den Mund nehmen / No tener pelos en la lengua. Phraseologisches Wörterbuch Deutsch-Spanisch / Diccionario fraseológico alemán-español.* Madrid: Editorial Idiomas – Hueber Verlag, 2010. 460 pp.

1991. Balzer, Hans. *Wilhelm Buschs Spruchweisheit.* Rudolstadt: Greifenverlag, 1955; rpt. Wiesbaden: Modernes Antiquariat, 1981. 263 pp.

1992. Barth, Ludwig (ed.). *Scheidemünze. Aus dem Deutschen Sprichwörter-Lexikon des Karl Friedrich Wilhelm Wander.* Illustrations by Horst Hussel. Berlin: Volk und Wissen Verlag, 1979. 103 pp.

1993. Barth, Ludwig (ed.). *Neue Scheidemünze. Aus dem Deutschen Sprichwörter-Lexikon des Karl Friedrich Wilhelm Wander.* Illustrations by Horst Hussel. Berlin: Volk und Wissen Verlag, 1985 (4th ed. 1988). 111 pp.

1994. Bartoszewicz, Iwona. *Deutsch-polnisches Sprichwörterlexikon: Eine repräsentative Auswahl.* Heidelberg: Julius Groos, 1998. 159 pp.

1995. Baumgartner, Ueli. *Wenn der Hahn kräht auf dem Mist ... Wetterregeln für 100% sichere Prognosen.* Bern: Sinwel, 1986. 52 pp. (weather proverbs).

1996. Bebel, Heinrich. *Proverbia Germanica collecta atque in Latinum traducta.* Argentine: Johannes Grüninger, 1508. Ed. Willem H.D. Suringar. Leiden: E.J. Brill, 1879; rpt. Hildesheim: Georg Olms, 1969. 615 pp.

1997. Beck, Harald (ed.). *Graffiti*. Stuttgart: Philipp Reclam, 2004. 87 pp. With illustrations.

1998. Beer, Ulrich (ed.). *Manchmal ernsthaft, manchmal närrisch. Lebensweisheiten bei Wilhelm Busch*. Düsseldorf: Benziger, 2001. 96 pp.

1999. Behaghel, Otto. "Die neuhochdeutschen Zwillingswörter." *Germania*, 23 (1878), 257-292.

2000. Beier, Brigitte, Matthias Herkt, Bernhard Pollmann, and Barbara Pietsch. *Harenberg Lexikon der Sprichwörter & Zitate*. Dortmund: Harenberg, 1997. 1600 pp.

2001. Bekh, Wolfgang Johannes. *Nur da Not koan Schwung lassn. Bairische Spruchweisheit für jede Gelegenheit*. Pfaffenhofen: W. Ludwig, 1987. 238 pp. With illustrations.

2002. Bender, Andreas. *Gelegenheit macht Liebe. Sprichwörter, Redensarten und Zitate verdreht und auf die seichte [sic] Schulter genommen*. Illustrations by "Ralph". Frankfurt am Main: Eichborn, 1986. 70 pp. (anti-proverbs).

2003. Bender, Andreas. *Kleine Socken jucken auch. Sprichwörter, Redensarten und Zitate – verdreht*. Illustrations by "Ralph". Frankfurt am Main: Eichborn, 1987. 70 pp. (anti-proverbs).

2004. Beran, Margret. *"Hitting the Nail on the Head": 3000 Redensarten Deutsch-Englisch*. München: Max Hueber, 1995. 348 pp. Revised ed. Köln: Anaconda Verlag, 2007. 314 pp.

2005. Berger, Franz Severin, and Elisabeth Tschachler-Roth. *"Das Blaue von Himmel". Alltägliche Redensarten und ihre Herkunft*. München: Herbig, 2003. 272 pp. With illustrations.

2006. Berger, Franz Severin, and Elisabeth Tschachler-Roth. *Heiliger Bimbam & Teufels Küche. Alltägliche Redensarten und ihre Herkunft*. Erfstadt: Area-Verlag, 2006. 317 pp. With illustrations.

2007. Bergmann, Gunter. "'Geh nich zu dein' Ferscht, wenn de nich gerufen werscht!' [Sächsische Sprichwörter und Redensarten]." In G. Bergmann. *Polyglott-Sprachführer: Sächsisch*. München: Polyglott-Verlag, 1992. 28-34.

2008. Bergmann, Gunter (ed.). *"Wie's kommt, werd's gefressen": Sächsische Sprichwörter und Redensarten*. Leipzig: Lehmstedt, 2006. 141 pp.

2009. Bergmann, Karl. *Deutsche Ahnenweisheit. Ein verpflichtendes Erbe*. Stuttgart: Verlag für nationale Literatur Gebr. Rath, 1939. 455 pp. (anti-Semitic collection).

2010. Berteloot, Amand. "Köln in Redensarten aus den Niederlanden und Flandern." *Alt-Köln: Mitteilungen des Heimatvereins*, no. 92 (1994), 16-19.

2011. Beyer, Horst, and Annelies Beyer. *Sprichwörterlexikon. Sprichwörter und sprichwörtliche Ausdrücke aus deutschen Sammlungen vom 16. Jahrhundert bis zur Gegenwart*. Leipzig: VEB Bibliographisches Institut, 1984. München: C.H. Beck, 1985. 712 pp. With illustrations.

2012. Beyer, Horst, and Annelies Beyer. *Sprichwörterlexikon. Nemetskie poslovitsy i pogovorki*. Leipzig: VEB Bibliographisches Institut, 1989. Moskva: Vysshaia shkola, 1989. 392 pp.

2013. Bien, Fritz. *Lieben Sie Floskeln? Eine vergnügliche Sammlung abgeschliffener Formulierungen, nützlicher Leerformeln, intellektueller Gemeinplätze des täglichen Gebrauchs*. Thun: Ott Verlag, 1993. 88 pp.

2014. Billier, Pascal et al. (ed.). *Dem Volk aufs Maul geschaut. Echte "Sprich"-Wörter*. Saarbrücken: Universität des Saarlandes, Französische Abteilung, 1986. 67 pp.

2015. Birlinger, Anton. *So sprechen die Schwaben. Sprichwörter, Redensarten. Reime*. Berlin: Dümmler, 1868; rpt. Stuttgart: Lithos, 1982. 136 pp.

2016. Biscioni, Renato (ed.). *"... außer Rolf, der klebt am Golf". Kindersprüche – rotzfrech*. München: Wilhelm Goldmann, 1987. 141 pp. (anti-proverbs).

2017. Bittrich, Dietmar. *Böse Bauernsprüche für jeden Tag*. Illustrations by Thomas August Günther. München: Deutscher Taschenbuch Verlag, 2005. 126 pp. (weather proverbs).

2018. Blaschzok, Iris (ed.). *Ächt Ätzend! Gesprühte Sprüche mit Esprit*. Münster: F. Coppenrath, 1983. 94 pp. With illustrations. (graffiti).

2019. Blaschzok, Iris (ed.). *Die zehnte Muse heißt Pampel. Geistesblitze unter der Bank*. Münster: F. Coppenrath, 1984. 78 pp. With illustrations. (graffiti).

2020. Blay, Elisabeth (ed.). *Nicht alles, was zwei Backen hat, ist ein Gesicht. Klosprüche*. Illustrations by Erik Liebermann. München: Wilhelm Heyne, 1987 (24th ed. 1998). 119 pp. (miniature book).

2021. Blay, Elisabeth (ed.). *Steter Tropfen leert das Hirn. Neue Schüler-Sprüche*. Illustrations by Herbert Horn. München: Wilhelm Heyne, 1988. 117 pp. (miniature book).

2022. Blay, Elisabeth (ed.). *Die zweite Spülung. Neue Klosprüche*. Illustrations by Erik Liebermann. München: Wilhelm Heyne, 1993 (9th ed. 1999). 125 pp. (miniature book).

2023. Blay, Elisabeth (ed.). *Die letzte Spülung. Neue Klosprüche*. Illustrations by Peter Butschkow. München: Wilhelm Heyne, 1996 (5th ed. 1998). 120 pp. (miniature book).

2024. Blechinger, Nicolai. *Kölner Sprüche*. Ed. Ertay Hayit. Illustrations by Klaus Rosenbaum. Köln: J.P. Bachem, 2003 (3rd ed. 2004). 61 pp.

2025. Blechinger, Nicolai. *Kölner Sprüche. Teil 2*. Köln: J.P. Bachem, 2003. 61 pp.

2026. Bluhm, Lothar, and Heinz Rölleke. *"Redensarten des Volks, auf die ich immer horche": Märchen – Sprichwort – Redensart. Zur volkspoetischen Ausgestaltung der "Kinder- und Hausmärchen" durch die Brüder Grimm*. Stuttgart: S. Hirzel, 1997. 192 pp. (proverb keyword index, pp. 181-192).

2027. Blum, Joachim Christian. *Deutsches Sprichwörterbuch. 2* vols in one. Leipzig: Weygand, 1780 and 1782; rpt. ed. Wolfgang Mieder. Hildesheim: Georg Olms, 1990. I, 223 pp; II, 248 pp. (introduction I, pp. 1*-32*).

2028. Bolte, Johannes. "Der Spiegel der Weisheit. Eine Kölner Spruchsammlung des 16. Jahrhunderts (um 1540, gereimt)." *Niederdeutsches Jahrbuch*, 34 (1908), 103-109.

2029. Borchardt, Wilhelm. *Die sprichwörtlichen Redensarten im deutschen Volksmunde nach Sinn und Ursprung erläutert*. Ed. Gustav Wustmann. 5th ed. (1st ed. 1888). Leipzig: F.A. Brockhaus, 1895. 534 pp.

2030. Borchardt, Wilhelm. *Die sprichwörtlichen Redensarten im deutschen Volksmund nach Sinn und Ursprung erläutert*. Ed. Georg Schoppe. 6th ed. Leipzig: F.A. Brockhaus, 1925. 518 pp. With 35 illustrations.

2031. Borchardt, Wilhelm. *Die sprichwörtlichen Redensarten im deutschen Volksmund nach Sinn und Ursprung erläutert*. Ed. Alfred

Schirmer. 7th ed. Leipzig: F.A. Brockhaus, 1954. 539 pp. With 21 illustrations.

2032. Borneman, Ernest. *Unsere Kinder im Spiegel ihrer Lieder, Reime, Verse und Rätsel.* Olten: Walter, 1973. 413 pp.

2033. Borneman, Ernest. *Wir machen keinen langen Mist ... 614 Kinderverse, gesammelt in Deutschland, Österreich und der Schweiz in den zwei Jahrzehnten 1960-1980.* Frankfurt am Main: Fischer, 1981. 143 pp.

2034. Borovski, Conrad. *Active German Idioms. German-English / English-German.* München: Max Hueber, 1974 (2nd ed. 1985). 64 pp.

2035. Borowsky, Lothar. *Hunde, die bellen, beißen nicht. Sprichwörter aus aller Welt.* Welsermühl, Österreich: Lothar Borowsky, 1978. 396 pp. (basically a reprint of the 4th ed. of Karl Simrock's *Die deutschen Sprichwörter* [1881] with illustrations taken from Grandville's *Cent Proverbes* [1845]).

2036. Bosch, Martha Maria, and Julius Haidle. *Schwäbische Sprichwörter und Redensarten.* Reutlingen: Karl Knödler, 1965 (2nd ed. 1977). 63 pp.

2037. Bote, Hermann. *Der Köker. Niederdeutsches Lehrgedicht aus dem Anfang des 16. Jahrhunderts.* Ed. Gerhard Cordes. Tübingen: Max Niemeyer, 1963. 95 pp.

2038. Böttcher, Kurt, Karl Heinz Berger, Kurt Krolop, and Christa Zimmermann. *Geflügelte Worte. Zitate, Sentenzen und Begriffe in ihrem geschichtlichen Zusammenhang.* Leipzig: VEB Bibliographisches Institut, 1981. 780 pp.

2039. Bozarth, George S. "Johannes Brahms's Collection of *Deutsche Sprichworte* (German Proverbs)." *Brahms Studies.* Ed. David Brodbeck. Lincoln, Nebraska: University of Nebraska Press, 1994. I, 1-29.

2040. Braun, Hermann. *Neks vöi Sprüch: 1313 Sprichwörter und sprichwörtliche Redensarten dem Spruchbeutel der Sachsämter, Stift- und Egerländer entnommen.* Markredwitz: Volksschule der Stadt, 1982. 160 pp.

2041. Brecht, F. Albert. *Großer Zitatenschatz für den Redner und Vortragenden.* Berlin: R. Halbeck, 1921. 279 pp.

2042. Bremen, Friedrich. *Sprüche (ab)klopfen. Redensarten und ihre Bedeutung.* Illustrations by Heinz Langer. Wiesbaden: Englisch, 1986. 112 pp.

2043. Brings, Rolly, and Christa Bhatt. *Lück sin och Minsche. Enzyklopädie der Kölner Redensarten.* Köln: Greven Verlag, 2008. 320 pp.

2044. Brink, Karl-Erich. *Hals- und Beinbruch og 2017 andre tyske udtryk og talemåder.* København: Høst, 1993. 190 pp.

2045. Brisolla, Thyrso (ill.). *Das Ei des Kolumbus und andere deutsche Redensarten.* Buch am Ammersee: Dussa Verlag, 1983. 56 pp.

2046. Broma, Adolph. *Erzählungen nach Sprichwörtern, zur belehrenden und bildenden Unterhaltung der Jugend.* Neustadt an der Orla: Joh. Karl Gottfried Wagner, 1830. 172 pp.

2047. Brückl, Reinhold (ed.). *E Vertel waam Achtel geschnitte am Stick. Frankfurter Sprüch' und Redensarten.* Illustrations by Edwin Grazioli. Frankfurt am Main: Haag + Herchen, 1980. 149 pp.

2048. Brugger, Hans Peter. *Der treffende Vergleich. Eine Sammlung treffsicherer Vergleiche und bildhafter Formulierungen.* Thun: Ott Verlag, 1993. 261 pp.

2049. Brüllmann, Richard. *Lexikon der treffenden Martin-Luther-Zitate.* Thun: Otto, 1983. 248 pp.

2050. Büchmann, Georg. *Geflügelte Worte. Der Citatenschatz des deutschen Volkes.* Berlin: Haude & Spener, 1864. 220 pp.

2051. Büchmann, Georg. *Geflügelte Worte. Der Citatenschatz des deutschen Volkes.* 5th ed. Berlin: Haude & Spener, 1868. 278 pp.

2052. Büchmann, Georg. *Geflügelte Worte. Der Citatenschatz des deutschen Volkes.* 8th ed. Berlin: Haude & Spener, 1874. 318 pp.

2053. Büchmann, Georg. *Geflügelte Worte. Der Citatenschatz des deutschen Volkes.* 9th ed. Berlin: Haude & Spener, 1876. 349 pp.

2054. Büchmann, Georg. *Geflügelte Worte. Der Citatenschatz des deutschen Volkes.* Ed. Walter Robert-tornow. 15th ed. Berlin: Haude & Spener, 1887. 523 pp.

2055. Büchmann, Georg. *Geflügelte Worte. Der Citatenschatz des deutschen Volkes.* Ed. Walter Robert-tornow. 16th ed. Berlin: Haude & Spener, 1889. 592 pp.

2056. Büchmann, Georg. *Geflügelte Worte. Der Citatenschatz des deutschen Volkes*. Ed. Walter Robert-tornow. 18th ed. Berlin: Haude & Spener, 1895. 699 pp.

2057. Büchmann, Georg. *Geflügelte Worte. Der Zitatenschatz des deutschen Volkes*. Ed. Bogdan Krieger. 24th ed. Berlin: Haude & Spener, 1910. 739 pp.

2058. Büchmann, Georg. *Geflügelte Worte. Der Zitatenschatz des deutschen Volkes*. Ed. Bogdan Krieger. 25th ed. Berlin: Haude & Spener, 1912. 688 pp.

2059. Büchmann, Georg. *Geflügelte Worte. Der Zitatenschatz des deutschen Volkes*. Volks-Ausgabe. Ed. Bogdan Krieger. Berlin: Haude & Spener, 1914. 490 pp.

2060. Büchmann, Georg. *Geflügelte Worte. Der Zitatenschatz des deutschen Volkes*. Ed. Adolf Langen. Berlin: Schreiter, 1915. 375 pp.

2061. Büchmann, Georg. *Geflügelte Worte. Der Zitatenschatz des deutschen Volkes*. Ed. Walter Heichen. Berlin: Paul Franke, 1915. 698 pp.

2062. Büchmann, Georg. *Geflügelte Worte. Der Zitatenschatz des deutschen Volkes*. Ed. Bogdan Krieger. 26th ed. Berlin: Haude & Spener, 1920. 722 pp.

2063. Büchmann, Georg. *Geflügelte Worte. Der Zitatenschatz des deutschen Volkes*. Volks-Ausgabe. Ed. Bogdan Krieger. Berlin: Haude & Spener, 1920. 508 pp.

2064. Büchmann, Georg. *Geflügelte Worte. Der Zitatenschatz des deutschen Volkes*. Volks-Ausgabe. Ed. Bogdan Krieger. Berlin: Haude & Spener, 1926. 543 pp.

2065. Büchmann, Georg. *Geflügelte Worte. Der Zitatenschatz des deutschen Volkes*. Ed. L. Heinemann. Berlin: Th. Knaur, 1928. 378 pp.

2066. Büchmann, Georg. *Geflügelte Worte*. Ed. Valerian Tornius. Leipzig: Philipp Reclam, 1935. 315 pp.

2067. Büchmann, Georg. *Geflügelte Worte. Der Zitatenschatz des deutschen Volkes*. Eds. Gunther Haupt and Werner Rust. 28th ed. Berlin: Haude & Spener, 1937. 788 pp.

2068. Büchmann, Georg. *Geflügelte Worte. Der Zitatenschatz des deutschen Volkes*. Volksausgabe. Ed. Gunther Haupt. Berlin: Haude & Spener, 1937. 557 pp.

2069. Büchmann, Georg. *Geflügelte Worte. Der Zitatenschatz des deutschen Volkes*. Eds. Gunther Haupt and Werner Rust. 29th ed. Berlin: Haude & Spener, 1942. 788 pp. (nazified edition).

2070. Büchmann, Georg. *Geflügelte Worte. Der Zitatenschatz des deutschen Volkes*. Volksausgabe. Ed. Werner Rust. Berlin: Haude & Spener, 1943. 558 pp.

2071. Büchmann, Georg. *Geflügelte Worte und Zitatenschatz*. Ed. Fritz Martini. Zürich: Werner Classen, 1950. Stuttgart: Johannes Asmus, 1950. 427 pp.

2072. Büchmann, Georg. *Geflügelte Worte. Die klassische Zitatensammlung*. Eds. Josef Falkenberg and Roger Diener. Berlin: Verlag Praktisches Wissen, 1956. 438 pp.

2073. Büchmann, Georg. *Geflügelte Worte*. Ed. Paul Dorpert. Frankfurt am Main: Fischer Bücherei, 1957. 351 pp.

2074. Büchmann, Georg. *Geflügelte Worte*. Neue Ausgabe. No editor given. München: Knaur, 1959. 320 pp.

2075. Büchmann, Georg. *Geflügelte Worte*. 2nd ed. (1st ed. 1956). Ed. Hanns Martin Elster. Stuttgart: Philipp Reclam, 1964. 639 pp.

2076. Büchmann, Georg. *Geflügelte Worte. Der Zitatenschatz des deutschen Volkes*. Ed. Alfred Grunow. 31st ed. Berlin: Haude & Spener, 1964. Zürich: Buchclub Ex Libris, 1964. 990 pp.

2077. Büchmann, Georg. *Geflügelte Worte. Der Zitatenschatz des deutsches Volkes*. Ed. Alfred Grunow. 3 vols. München: Deutscher Taschenbuch Verlag, 1967. I, 383; II, 380 pp., III, 152 pp. (based on the 31st ed. of 1964).

2078. Büchmann, Georg. *Geflügelte Worte. Der Zitatenschatz des deutschen Volkes*. Eds. Gunther Haupt and Winfried Hofmann. 32nd ed. Berlin: Haude & Spener, 1972. 1039 pp.

2079. Büchmann, Georg. *Geflügelte Worte. Der Zitatenschatz des deutschen Volkes*. Ed. Winfried Hofmann. 33rd ed. Frankfurt am Main: Ullstein, 1986. 543 pp.

2080. Büchmann, Georg. *Der neue Büchmann. Geflügelte Worte*. Ed. Eberhard Urban. Niedernhausen/Ts.: Bassermann, 1994. 695 pp.

2081. Büchmann, Georg. *Geflügelte Worte. Der klassische Zitatenschatz*. Ed. Winfried Hofmann. 40th ed. Berlin: Ullstein, 1995. 614 pp.

2082. Bücken, Hajo. *Redensarten und ihre Bedeutung*. Reichelsheim: Edition XXL, 2003. 195 pp.

2083. Bücking, Johann Jacob Heinrich. *Versuch einer medicinischen und physikalischen Erklärung deutscher Sprichwörter und sprichwörtlicher Redensarten*. Stendal: Franzen und Grosse, 1797; rpt. Leipzig: Zentralantiquariat der DDR, 1976. 578 pp.

2084. Budde, Nadia, and Thomas Richter Eigenhufe. *Illustrierte Literaturrätsel*. Berlin: Seitenstraßen Verlag, 2005. 64 pp. With illustrations.

2085. Büld, Heinrich. *Niederdeutsche Schwanksprüche zwischen Ems und Issel*. Münster: Aschendorff, 1981. 152 pp. (wellerisms).

2086. Büld, Heinrich. *Niederdeutsche Sprichwörter zwischen Ems und Issel. Eine Lebens- und Sittenlehre aus dem Volksmund*. Münster: Aschendorff, 1983. 306 pp.

2087. Bülow, Ralf (ed.). *Neues an deutschen Wänden. Graffiti 2*. München: Wilhelm Heyne, 1984. 123 pp. With illustrations.

2088. Bülow, Ralf (ed.). *Phantasie an deutschen Wänden. Graffiti 3*. München: Wilhelm Heyne, 1985. 123 pp. With illustrations.

2089. Bülow, Ralf (ed.). *Der Geist sprüht, wo er will. Graffiti. Neue Folge*. Gütersloh: Bertelsmann, 1986. Combined rpt. of *Graffiti 2* (1984) and *Graffiti 3* (1985). 240 pp. With illustrations.

2090. Bülow, Ralf (ed.). *Lieber nett im Bett als cool auf dem Stuhl. Graffiti 4*. München: Wilhelm Heyne, 1986. 123 pp. With illustrations.

2091. Bungert, Gerhard. *Alles geschwätzt. Saarländische Redewendungen und Sprichwörter*. Illustrations by Charly Lehnert. Saarbrücken: Queißer, 1983. 72 pp.

2092. Bünting, Karl-Dieter. *Lexikon der Zitate und Redensarten*. Königswinter: Tandem, 2005. 320 pp.

2093. Busch, Moritz. "Komische Redensarten und Sprichwörter, Appositionen und Priameln." In M. Busch. *Deutscher Volkshumor*. Leipzig: Friedrich Wilhelm Grunow, 1877. 133-148.

2094. Caliebe, Dieter. *Caliebe's Handbook of Headlines*. Hamburg: Gruner & Jahr, 1994. 295 pp. (German advertising headlines).

2095. Capelle, Torsten (ed.). *Rettet dem Dativ! Noch mehr Hörsaalbänke – zweckentfremdet*. Münster: F. Coppenrath, 1982 (6th ed. 1983). 108 pp. With illustrations. (graffiti)

2096. Cartwright, Thea. *Humorvolle deutsche und englische Redensarten.* Frankfurt am Main: Edition Fischer, 2006. 35 pp. With illustrations.

2097. Christen, Jürgen (ed.). *Frauenfeindliche Sprüche. Vergiß die Peitsche nicht.* Illustrations by Udo Linke. Frankfurt am Main: Eichborn, 1991. 71 pp. (quotations).

2098. Christoffel, Karl. *Wein-Weisheiten. Ein Jahr-Gang in Sprüchen und Bildern.* Mannheim: Südwestdeutsche Verlagsanstalt, 1972 (2nd ed. 1974). 63 pp. With illustrations.

2099. Clemen, Otto (ed.). "Sprichwörter." In O. Clemen (ed.). *Luther im Kreise der Seinen. Briefe, Gedichte, Fabeln, Sprichwörter und Tischreden.* Frankfurt am Main: Insel Verlag, 1917 (5th ed. 1983). 70-79.

2100. Cooper, Barbara, and Thomas C. Cooper. *Teen Speak: A Collection of German and American Slang.* Vermillion, South Dakota: Verlag Schatzkammer, 2001. 163 pp.

2101. Cooper, Thomas C., and Lieselotte Kuntz. "Jugendjargon im Vergleich: Amerika und Deutschland." *Schatzkammer der deutschen Sprache, Dichtung und Geschichte,* 13 (1987), 88-110; rpt. in *Schatzkammer,* 15 (1989), 39-59.

2102. Cornette, James C. *Proverbs and Proverbial Expressions in the German Works of Martin Luther.* Diss. University of North Carolina at Chapel Hill, 1942. 225 pp. Posthumously edited and published by Wolfgang Mieder and Dorothee Racette. Bern: Peter Lang, 1997. 236 pp.

2103. Coulon, Bettina. *Deutsche und französische idiomatische Redewendungen.* Leipzig: VEB Verlag Enzyklopädie, 1983. 152 pp.

2104. Cowie, Murray Aiken. *Proverbs and Proverbial Phrases in the German Works of Albrecht von Eyb.* Diss. University of Chicago, 1942. 106 pp.

2105. Cramer-Klett, Elisabeth von. *Alte Bauernregeln.* München: Wilhelm Heyne, 1982. 150 pp. (weather proverbs).

2106. Crummenerl, Rainer, and Franz Persch (eds.). *"Alles ist Samenkorn": Aphorismen, Weisheiten und Gedanken um und über unser tägliches Brot.* Illustrations by Roland Beier. Neustadt: VEB Kombinat Fortschritt Landmaschinen, 1979. 71 pp.

2107. Cyriacks, Hartmut, and Peter Nissen. *Sprichwörter Plattdüütsch und ihre Bedeutungen.* Hamburg: Quickborn, 1999. 105 pp.

2108. Dahms, Emmy. *Der Spielmüller und andere Sprichwort-Märchen.* Berlin: Frieling, 2007. 62 pp. With illustrations.

2109. Dalbiac, Lilian. *A Dictionary of Quotations (German).* New York: Frederick Ungar, 1958. 485 pp.

2110. Dannenberg, Hans-Dieter. *Schwein haben: Historisches und Histörchen vom Schwein.* Jena: Gustav Fischer, 1990. 243 pp. (proverbs, pp. 197-205). With illustrations.

2111. Dick, Jo. *Öcher Spröchwöed. Au Öcher Spröch, jesöömelt än opjeschreäve.* Illustrations by Otto Mennicken. Aachen: Mainz, 2008. 288 pp.

2112. Dicks, Karl, and Peter Völker. *"Häs'e al gehüert": Redensarten und Weisheiten in Vogteier Mundart.* Illustrations by Doris Greven. Schwalmtal: Phil-Creativ, 2005. 166 pp.

2113. Dirksen, Carl. *Ostfriesische Sprichwörter und sprichwörtliche Redensarten mit historischen und sprachlichen Anmerkungen.* 2 vols. Ruhrort: Andreae, 1889-1891; rpt. in one volume. Walluf bei Wiesbaden: Martin Sändig, 1973. I, 109 pp.; II, 95 pp.

2114. Dirx, Ruth (ed.). *Sprichwörter und Lebensweisheiten: Wortschätze.* Kevelaer: Butzon & Bercker, 1992. 92 pp. (miniature book).

2115. Dittrich, Hans. *Redensarten auf der Goldwaage. Herkunft und Bedeutung in einem munteren ABC erklärt.* Bonn: Ferdinand Dümmler, 1970. 286 pp. With illustrations.

2116. Dobel, Richard (ed.). *Lexikon der Goethe-Zitate.* Zürich: Artemis, 1968. Also as *Dtv-Lexikon der Goethe-Zitate.* 2 vols. München: Deutscher Taschenbuch Verlag, 1972. 1307 cols.

2117. Domzalski, Oliver Thomas (ed.). *"Ich geh' kaputt – gehst Du mit?" Das goldene Album der Sponti-Sprüche.* Frankfurt am Main: Eichborn, 2006. Combined rpt. of Willi Hau (ed.), *Ich geh kaputt, gehst Du mit?* (1981); Willi Hau (ed.), *Es wird Zeit, daß wir lieben* (1982); Eduard Moriz (ed.), *Nimm's leicht, nimm mich!* (1983); Eduard Moriz (ed.), *Ohne Dings kein Bums* (1984); Eduard Moriz (ed.), *Lieber intim als in petto* (1984); Eduard Moriz (ed.), *Lieber sauweich als eberhard* (1986). 311 pp. With illustrations. (anti-proverbs).

2118. Dove, N.R. (pseud. Karl Friedrich Wilhelm Wander). *Politisches Sprichwörterbrevier. Tagebuch eines Patrioten der fünfziger Jahre, zur Charakteristik jener Zeit.* Leipzig: Otto Wigand, 1872. 296 pp. Rpt. ed. Wolfgang Mieder. Bern: Peter Lang, 1990. 333 pp. (proverbial aphorisms and anti-proverbs).

2119. Dröscher, Vitus B. *Mit den Wölfen heulen*. *"Fabelhafte" Spruchweisheiten aus dem Tierreich*. Illustrations by Wilhelm Eigener. Düsseldorf: Econ, 1978. 141 pp. Rpt. as *Mit den Wölfen heulen*. *Spruchweisheiten aus dem Tierreich und was dahintersteckt*. Reinbek: Rowohlt, 1981. 124 pp.

2120. Dröscher, Vitus B. *Mich laust der Affe*. *"Fabelhafte" Redensarten aus der Welt der Tiere*. Illustrations by Wilhelm Eigener. Düsseldorf: Econ, 1981. 143 pp.

2121. Dröscher, Vitus B. *"Sie turteln wie die Tauben"*. Illustrations by Wolf-Rüdiger Marunde. Hamburg: Rasch und Röhring, 1988. Revised combined edition of *Mit den Wölfen heulen* (1978) and *Mich laust der Affe* (1981). 373 pp.

2122. Drosdowski, Günther, and Werner Scholze-Stubenrecht (eds.). *Duden: Redewendungen und sprichwörtliche Redensarten. Wörterbuch der deutschen Idiomatik*. Mannheim: Dudenverlag, 1992. 864 pp.

2123. Dürr, H.R. *Humoristische Uhrensprüche und Cartoons, Aphorismen, Zitate, Weisheiten und Sprichwörter über die Uhr und die Zeitmessung*. Thun: Vetter Druck, 2001. 35 pp. With illustrations.

2124. Eberth, Hans Heinrich. *Die Sprichwörter in Sebastian Brants "Narrenschiff"*. *Ein Beitrag zur deutschen Sprichwortgeschichte*. Greifswald: L. Bamberg, 1933. 111 pp.

2125. Eckart, Rudolf. *Niederdeutsche Sprichwörter und volkstümliche Redensarten*. Braunschweig: Appelhans & Pfenningstorff, 1893; rpt. Hildesheim: Georg Olms, 1975. 586 columns.

2126. Egenolff, Christian. *Sibenthalbhundert Sprichwörter, Wie und wo sie in Teutscher Spraach, von Zier und Abkürtzung wegen der Rede, gebraucht werdenn*. Frankfurt am Main: Christian Egenolph, 1532. 55 leaves. Rpt. as *Sebastian Franck's erste namenlose Sprichwörtersammlung vom Jahre 1532 in getreuem Abdruck mit Erläuterungen und cultur- und literargeschichtlichen Beilagen*. Ed. Friedrich Latendorf. Poesneck: Carl Latendorf, 1876; rpt. Hildesheim: Georg Olms, 1970. 368 pp. (the collection is not by Sebastian Franck but rather Christian Egenolff's shortened version of Johannes Agricola's two-part collection of 1529 that was published as one volume in 1534).

2127. Egenolff, Christian. *Sprichwörter / Schöne, Weise Klugreden. Darinnen Teutscher vnnd anderer Spraachenn Höflicheit / Zier / Höhste Vernunfft vnd Klugheit* . Frankfurt am Main: Christian Egenolff, 1548; rpt. Darmstadt: Wissenschafltiche Buchgesellschaft, 1972. 182 leaves in columns.

2128. Egenolff, Christian. *Sprichwörter / Schöne / Weise Klugredenn. Darinnen Teutscher vnd anderer Spraachen Höflicheit / Zier / Höhste Vernunfft vnd Klugheit*. Frankfurt am Main: Christian Egenolff, 1552. Ed. Hans Henning. München-Pullach: Verlag Dukumentation, 1968. 390 leaves.

2129. Ehnert-Aubret, Françoise, and Rolf Ehnert. "Sprichwörtlich übersetzt [Texte von Hans Hunfeld]." *"I Beg to Differ": Beiträge zum sperrigen interkulturellen Nachdenken über eine Welt in Frieden. Festschrift für Hans Hunfeld*. Eds. Hans-Eberhard Piepho and Angelika Kubanek-German. München: Iudicium, 1998. 302-305.

2130. Eichelberger, Ursula. *Zitatenlexikon*. Leipzig: VEB Bibliographisches Institut, 1981. Wiesbaden: VMA-Verlag, 1981. 920 pp.

2131. Eichelberger, Ursula. *Über Krieg und Frieden. Sentenzen aus zweieinhalb Jahrtausenden*. Berlin: Militärverlag der DDR, 1986. 291 pp. (miniature book).

2132. Eikelmann, Manfred, and Tomas Tomasek (eds.). *Handbuch der Sentenzen und Sprichwörter im höfischen Roman des 12. und 13. Jahrhunderts*. Vol. 2: *Artusromane nach 1230, Gralromane, Tristanromane*. Eds. Tomas Tomasek, Hanno Rüther, and Heike Bismark. Berlin: Walter de Gruyter, 2009. II, 695 pp.

2133. Eiselein, Josua. *Die Sprichwörter und Sinnreden des deutschen Volkes in alter und neuer Zeit*. Freiburg: Friedrich Wagner, 1840; rpt. Leipzig: Zentralantiquariat der DDR, 1980. 675 pp.

2134. Eiselein, Josua. *Die reimhaften, anklingenden und ablautartigen Formeln der hochdeutschen Sprache in alter und neuer Zeit*. Leipzig: F. Fleischer, 1841. 68 pp.

2135. Eiselt, Marianne, and Franz Eppert. *Den Nagel auf den Kopf treffen! Redewendungen verstehen und anwenden*. Illustrations by Thomas Dankoff. Frankfurt am Main: Moritz Diesterweg, 1997. 82 pp.

2136. Emrich, Agnes. *Heiteres Zitaten-Lexikon*. Heidelberg: Kemper, 1963. 127 pp.

2137. Engelien, August, and Wilhelm Lahn. *Der Volksmund in der Mark Brandenburg. Sagen, Märchen, Spiele, Sprichwörter und Gebräuche.* Berlin: Wilhelm Schultze, 1868; rpt. Hildesheim: Georg Olms, 1976. 285 pp. ("Sprichwörter und sprichwörtliche Redensarten", pp. 213-224).

2138. Englisch, Paul. "Skatologische Sprichwörter." In P. Englisch. *Das skatologische Element in Literatur, Kunst und Volksleben.* Stuttgart: Julius Püttmann, 1928. 129-137.

2139. Eppert, Franz. *Sprichwörter und Zitate.* München: Verlag Klett Edition Deutsch, 1990. 80 pp.

2140. Essig, Rolf-Bernhard. *Wie die Kuh aufs Eis kam. Wundersames aus der Welt der Worte.* Berlin: Aufbau Verlagsgruppe, 2007. 162 pp.

2141. Essig, Rolf-Bernhard. *Da wird doch der Hund in der Pfanne verrückt. Die lustigen Geschichten hinter unseren Redensarten.* Illustrations by Marei Schweitzer. München: Carl Hanser, 2009. 144 pp.

2142. Essig, Rolf-Bernhard. *Warum die Schweine pfeifen. Wundersames aus der Welt der Worte.* Berlin: Kiepenheuer, 2009. 158 pp.

2143. Essig, Rolf-Bernhard. *Butter bei die Fische. Wie das Meer in unsere Sprache floss. Sprichwörter und Redewendungen gesammelt und erklärt.* Illustrations by Papan. Hamburg: Mareverlag, 2010. 191 pp.

2144. Eyering, Eucharius. *Proverbiorum Copia: Etlich viel Hundert / Lateinischer vnd Teutscher schöner vnd lieblicher Sprichwörter.* 3 vols. Eisleben: Henning Groß, 1601-1603. Rpt. ed. Wolfgang Mieder. Hildesheim: Georg Olms, 1999. I, 817 pp.; II, 721 pp.; III, 615 pp. (introduction I, pp. 1*-26*).

2145. Färver, Jupp. *Kölner Schimpfwörter.* Ed. Ertay Hayit. Illustrations by Harm Bengen. Köln: J.P. Bachem, 2003. 61 pp.

2146. Faust, Johann Heinrich. *"Das, was wir lieben," im Rahmen des Sprüchwortes. Humor, Witz und Satire über die Töchter Eva's.* Rohrersberg-Coblenz: A. von Busse, 1883. 102 pp.

2147. Fechner, Marco. *Nerv-Deutsch, Deutsch-Nerv. Blöde Sprüche, dumme Floskeln – alles, was wir nicht mehr hören wollen.* Leipzig: Neuer Europa Verlag, 2006. 224 pp.

2148. Feldmann, Christa et al. *Riemels. Plattdüütsch.* Kiel: Landesinstitut Schleswig-Holstein, 1987. 17 pp.

2149. Feldmann, Christa et al. *Sammelsuus,. Plattdüütsch*. Kiel. Landesinstitut Schleswig-Holstein, 1990. 17 pp.

2150. Fendl, Josef. *Nix wie lauter Sprüch*. Pfaffenhofen: W. Ludwig, 1975 (6th ed. 1982). 104 pp. With illustrations.

2151. Fendl, Josef. *Sprüch über die Handwerker*. Pfaffenhofen: W. Ludwig, 1989. 48 pp.

2152. Fendl, Josef. *Sprüch über die Pfarrer*. Pfaffenhofen: W. Ludwig, 1989. 48 pp.

2153. Fendl, Josef. *Sprüch übers Bier*. Pfaffenhofen: W. Ludwig, 1989. 47 pp. (wellerisms).

2154. Fieguth, Gerhard (ed.). *Deutsche Aphorismen*. Stuttgart: Philipp Reclam, 1978. 395 pp.

2155. Fink-Henseler, Roland W. *Hausbuch deutscher Sprichwörter. 5000 Redensarten und Sprichwörter für alle Lebenszeiten*. Bayreuth: Gondrom, 1983. Rpt. as *5005 Redensarten und Sprichwörter*. Bindlach: Gondrom Verlag, 1996. 640 pp. With illustrations.

2156. Flechsig, Werner. *Ostfälische Sprichwörter. Volksweisheit und Volkshumor aus fünf Jahrhunderten*. Braunschweig: Waisenhaus-Buchdruckerei, 1974. 227 pp.

2157. Fleckenstein, Sister Mary Thecla. *Das Sprichwort, sprichwörtliche und eigenartige Redensarten und Wortspiele in den Predigten "Auf, auf ihr Christen" von Abraham a Sancta [sic] Clara*. Diss. University of Pittsburgh, 1942. 86 pp.

2158. Forck, Ludwig. *Deutsche Inschriften an Haus und Geräth. Zur epigrammatischen Volkspoesie*. Berlin: Wilhelm Hertz, 1865. 82 pp. (2nd ed. 1875). 147 pp.

2159. Forck, Ludwig (ed.). *Altdeutscher Witz und Verstand. Reime und Sprüche aus dem sechszehnten und siebenzehnten Jahrhunderte*. Bielefeld: Velhagen & Blasing, 1888. 218 pp.

2160. Fraenger, Wilhelm. *Der Bauern-Bruegel und das deutsche Sprichwort*. Erlenbach-Züruch: Eugen Rentsch, 1923. 159 pp. With 49 illustrations. Shortened ed. as *Das Bild der "Niederländischen Sprichwörter": Pieter Bruegels Verkehrte Welt*. Ed. Michael Philipp. Amsterdam: Castrum Peregrini Presse, 1999. 84 pp. With 5 illustrations.

2161. Franck, Sebastian. *Sprichwörter / Schöne / Weise / Herrliche Clugreden / vnnd Hoffsprüch.* 2 parts. Franckenfurt am Meyn: Christian Egenolff, 1541. Rpt. ed. Wolfgang Mieder. Hildesheim: Georg Olms, 1987. I, 163 leaves; II, 211 leaves (introduction, pp. 5*-13*).

2162. Franck, Sebastian. *Sprichwörter / Schöne / Weise / Herrliche Clugreden / vnnd Hoffsprüch.* 2 parts. Franckenfurt am Meyn: Christian Egenolff, 1541. I, 163 leaves; II, 211 leaves. Rpt. ed. Peter Klaus Knauer. Bern: Peter Lang, 1993. 496 pp. (= Sebastian Franck, *Sämtliche Werke*, vol. 11).

2163. Franck, Sebastian. *Sprüchwörter / Gemeiner Tüetscher nation / erstlich durch Sebastian Francken gesammlet / nüwlich aber in kommliche ordnung gestellt vnd gebessert.* 2 parts. Zürich: Eustachin Froschouer, 1545. I, 257 leaves; II, 182 leaves (an anonymous modified version of the 1541 collection by Sebastian Franck – my most valuable personal treasure, W.M.).

2164. Franck, Sebastian. *Sprichwörter / das ist / Schöne / weise vnd kluge Reden (1541).* Ed. Alfred Böswald. Donauwörth: Pädagogische Stiftung Cassianeum, 2000. 252 pp. (partial reprint with introduction, pp. 7-102.).

2165. Frank, Ernst. *Lebensweisheiten des Alltags. Redewendungen und Aussprüche. Sag Trin – Sagte Katharina. In Niederrheinischer Mundart und Hochdeutsch.* Duisburg: Walter Braun, 1983. 129 pp.

2166. Franz, Angelika (ed.). *Das endgültige Buch der Sprüche & Graffiti.* München: Wilhelm Heyne, 1987. 456 pp. With illustrations.

2167. Franz, Angelika (ed.). *Es gibt viel zu tun – nix wie weg. Neue Bürosprüche.* München: Wilhelm Heyne, 1990. 121 pp. With illustrations. (miniature book). (anti-proverbs).

2168. Fredrickson, Scott E. *For Better or Wurst: A Collection of German Proverbs with Accompanying Worksheets, Activities, and Games for the Lively German Classroom.* Illustrated by Oliver Wilder. Jacksonville, Florida: Concordia Programs, 1996. 52 pp.

2169. Fredrickson, Scott E. *The Wurst is Yet to Come: A Collection of German Proverbs with Accompanying Posters, Worksheets and Activities for the Elementary German Classroom.* Illustrated by Oliver Wilder. Jacksonville, Florida: Concordia Programs, 1996. 74 pp.

2170. Freund, Leonhard. *Aus der Spruchweisheit des Auslandes. Parömiologische Skizzen.* Hannover: Carl Meyer, 1893. 44 pp.

2171. Frey, Christa, Annelies Herzog, Arthur Michel, and Ruth Schütze. *Deutsche Sprichwörter für Ausländer*. *Eine Auswahl mit Beispielen*. Leipzig: Brockhaus, 1970; rpt. Leipzig: VEB Verlag Enzyklopädie, 1974. 119 pp.

2172. Freytag, Ernst Richard. *Sachsens Geschichtlich-geographische Sprichwörter und Geflügelte Worte*. Leipzig: Ernst Wunderlich, 1898. 84 pp.

2173. Friebertshäuser, Hans. *Sprichwörter aus Hessen*. Husum: Husum Druck-und Verlagsgesellschaft, 1989. 67 pp.

2174. Friebertshäuser, Hans. *Redensarten aus Hessen*. Husum: Husum Druck- und Verlagsgesellschaft, 1990. 90 pp.

2175. Fried, Alfred Hermann. *Lexikon deutscher Citate*. Leipzig: Philipp Reclam, 1888. 310 pp.

2176. Fried, Alfred Hermann. *Lexikon fremdsprachlicher Citate*. Leipzig: Philipp Reclam, 1889. 288 pp.

2177. Friedenthal, Richard. *Goethe-Weisheiten im ernsten und heiteren Ton*. Stuttgart: Deutscher Bücherbund, 1971. 94 pp.

2178. Friederich, Wolf. *Moderne deutsche Idiomatik*. *Systematisches Wörterbuch mit Definitionen und Beispielen*. München: Max Hueber, 1966. 824 pp.

2179. Friederich, Wolf. *Moderne deutsche Idiomatik*. *Alphabetisches Wörterbuch mit Definitionen und Beispielen*. München: Max Hueber, 1976. 565 pp.

2180. Friedrich, Paul. *Deutscher Zitatenschatz*. Berlin: Kurt Wolff, 1934. 268 pp.

2181. Frischbier, Hermann. *Preußische Sprichwörter und volksthümliche Redensarten*. Berlin: Th.Chr.Fr. Enslin, 1864. 103 pp. (2nd enlarged ed. 1865); rpt. Hannover-Döhren: Harro von Hirschheydt, 1971. 311 pp.

2182. Frischbier, Hermann. *Preußische Sprichwörter und volksthümliche Redensarten*. 2. Sammlung. Berlin: Th.Chr.Fr. Enslin, 1876. 264 pp.

2183. Fritz, Karl August (ed.). *Das große illustrierte Buch der Sprichwörter und Spruchweisheiten*. Würzburg: Stürtz, 1997; rpt. Köln: Parkland Verlag, 2003. 312 pp. With illustrations from Pieter Bruegel's "Netherlandish Proverbs" (1559).

2184. Fritz, Klaus (ed.). *Nimm dir Zeit. Zitate, Aphorismen und Gedichte über die Zeit.* Illustrations by Rolf Krämer. Frankfurt am Main: Verlag Klaus Fritz, 1990. 127 pp.

2185. Gabrielli, Michael (ed.). *Fliegende Worte. Zitate, Aphorismen und Gedichte über das Fliegen.* Illustrations by Adino B. Kamarudin. Frankfurt am Main: Verlag Klaus Fritz, 1990. 109 pp.

2186. Gabrielli, Michael (ed.). *Geld in Worten. Zitate, Aphorismen und Gedichte über das Geld.* Photographs by Markus Nikot. Frankfurt am Main: Verlag Klaus Fritz, 1990. 111 pp.

2187. Gamber, Hans (ed.). *Graffiti. Was an deutschen Wänden steht. Szene-Sprüche.* München: Wilhelm Heyne, 1983 (4th ed. 1984). 122 pp. With illustrations.

2188. Gamber, Hans (ed.). *Freche Sprüche für jeden Tag.* Rastatt: Arthur Moewig, 1987. 128 pp. With illustrations. (anti-proverbs).

2189. Gamber, Hans, and Claudia Glismann (eds.). *Alle wollen zurück zur Natur – aber keiner zu Fuß. Graffiti-Sprüche aus der Szene.* Gütersloh: Bertelsmann, 1986. Combined rpt. of Hans Gamber (ed.), *Graffiti. Was an deutschen Wänden steht. Szene-Sprüche* (1983); Claudia Glismann (ed.), *Edel sei der Mensch, Zwieback und gut. Szene-Sprüche* (1984). 239 pp. With illustrations. (graffiti and anti-proverbs).

2190. Garmann, Bernhard, and Hans Taubken. *Plattdeutsche Sprichwörter, Redensarten und Bauernregeln aus dem Emsland.* Lingen: Schnell, 1978. 272 pp.

2191. Gaugler, Almut (ed). *Sprichwörter und Volksweisheiten.* Stuttgart: VS Verlagshaus, 1994; rpt. Rheda-Wiedenbrück: Bertelsmann-Club, 1998. 320 pp. With illustrations.

2192. Geiger, Karola. *Deutsche Verse. Gedichte, Reime und Sprüche als Wege zum gesprochenen Deutsch.* Bensheim: Verlag Bensheimer Stadtblatt, 1952. 105 pp.

2193. Gerke-Siefert, Hilde. *Sprichwörter und Redensarten bei Johann Fischart. Ein Betrag zur deutschen Sprichwortgeschichte.* Diss. Universität München, 1953. 319 pp.

2194. Gerr, Elke. *4000 Sprichwörter und Zitate.* München: Humboldt, 1995. 319 pp.

2195. Gierlichs, Eleonore. *Meenzer Sprüch: En Beidel voll Sprüch un Gebabbel fer angehende un fortgeschrittene Sprüchbeidel.*

Mainz: Verlagsgruppe Rhein Main, 1999 (2nd ed. 2000). 96 pp.
With illustrations.

2196. Glismann, Claudia (ed.). *Edel sei der Mensch, Zwieback und gut. Szene-Sprüche*. München: Wilhelm Heyne, 1984. 121 pp. With illustrations. (anti-proverbs).

2197. Glismann, Claudia (ed.). *Ich denke, also spinn ich. Schüler-Sprüche*. München: Wilhelm Heyne, 1984 (2nd ed 1985). 121 pp. With illustrations. (anti-proverbs).

2198. Glismann, Claudia (ed.). *Lieber ein Schäferstündchen als zwei Überstunden. Sprüche, Witze und Graffiti vom Arbeitsplatz*. München: Wilhelm Heyne, 1988. 123 pp. With illustrations. (graffiti and anti-proverbs).

2199. Glock, Johann Philipp. *Breisgauer Volksspiegel, eine Sammlung volkstümlicher Sprichwörter, Redensarten, Schwänke, Lieder und Bräuche in oberalemannischer Mundart*. Lahr: M. Schauenburg, 1909; rpt. Freiburg: R. Gaggstatter, 1988. 182 pp. (proverbs and proverbial expressions, pp. 6-60).

2200. Goethe, Johann Wolfgang von. *Goethes Sprüche in Reimen. Zahme Xenien und Invektiven*. Ed. Max Hecker. Leipzig: Insel-Verlag, 1908. 264 pp.

2201. Goethe, Johann Wolfgang von. *Maximen und Reflexionen*. Ed. Christoph Michel. Frankfurt am Main: Insel Verlag, 1976. 370 pp.

2202. Goethe, Johann Wolfgang von. *Sprüche in Prosa. Sämtliche Maximen und Reflexionen*. Ed. Harald Fricke. Frankfurt am Main: Insel Verlag, 2005. 486 pp.

2203. Goethe, Johann Wolfgang von. *Maximen und Reflexionen*. Ed. Helmut Koopmann. München: C.H Beck, Deutscher Taschenbuch Verlag, 2006. 256 pp.

2204. Göhring, Ludwig. *Volkstümliche Redensarten und Ausdrücke. Deutung noch unerklärter, unvollständig oder gar unrichtig erklärter volkstümlicher Redensarten und Ausdrücke*. München: Neuer Filser-Verlag, 1937. 309 pp.

2205. Gööck, Alexandra. *Das sagt man so ... Kleines Lexikon der Redensarten*. Illustrations by Jochen Bartsch. Gütersloh: Heinz Peter, 1974. 128 pp.

2206. Göock, Roland (ed.). *Gäben alle Küsse Flecken, wären alle Mädchen Schlecken. Weisheiten aus dem Volksmund.* München: Wilhelm Heyne, 1986. 141 pp. With illustrations.

2207. Gorbracht, Wernher. *Wer Glück hat, dem fohlt sogar der Wallach. Sprichwörter und Redensarten vom Pferd.* Bad Homburg: Limpert, 1978. 233 pp.

2208. Goris, Eva, and Claus-Peter Hutter. *Warum haben Gänse Füßchen? Vom Ursprung unserer Wörter und Redensarten.* München: Knaur Taschenbuch Verlag, 2008. 218 pp.

2209. Görner, Herbert. *Redensarten. Kleine Idiomatik der deutschen Sprache.* Leipzig: VEB Bibliographisches Institut, 1979. 262 pp.

2210. Gossel, J. *Buch der Wortspiele.* Köln: Hoursch & Bechstedt, 1923. 95 pp.

2211. Gossler, Erika. *Besser Arm dran als Bein ab. Anti-Sprichwörter und ihresgleichen.* Wien: Edition Praesens, 2005. 135 pp.

2212. Göttert, Karl-Heinz. *"Eile mit Weile". Herkunft und Bedeutung der Sprichwörter.* Stuttgart: Philipp Reclam, 2005. 245 pp. With illustrations.

2213. Gottschalk, Klaus, and Waldemar Cierpinski. *Sprichwörtlich Sport. Sprichwörtliches und Nachdenkliches zu Gesundheit und Sport von der Antike bis zur Gegenwart.* Halle (Saale): Projekte-Verlag, 2006. 215 pp.

2214. Gottsched, Johann Christoph. "Von den Kern- und Gleich-nißreden, inngleichen den Sprüchwörtern der deutschen Sprache." In J.Ch. Gottsched. *Vollständigere und Neuerläuterte Deutsche Sprachkunst. Nach den Mustern der besten Schriftsteller des vorigen und itzigen Jahrhunderts.* Leipzig: Bernh. Christ. Breitkopf, 1762; rpt. Hildesheim: Georg Olms, 1970. 538-558.

2215. Graf, Adolf Eduard. *6000 deutsche und russische Sprichwörter.* Halle: VEB Max Niemeyer, 1956 (3rd ed. 1960). 294 pp.

2216. Graf, Adolf Eduard. *Russische und deutsche idiomatische Redewendungen.* Leipzig: VEB Verlag Enzyklopädie, 1965; rpt. München: Max Hueber, 1976. 224 pp.

2217. Graf, Eduard, and Mathias Dietherr. *Deutsche Rechtssprich-wörter*. Nördlingen: C.H. Beck, 1869; rpt. Aalen: Scientia Verlag, 1975. 603 pp.

2218. Griesbach, Heinz, and Dora Schulz. *1000 idiomatische Re-densarten Deutsch. Mit Erklärungen und Beispielen*. Berlin: Lan-genscheidt, 1961. 253 pp. Revised edition as *1000 deutsche Re-densarten. Mit Erklärungen und Anwendungsbeispielen*. Illustra-tions by Theo Scherling. Berlin: Langenscheidt, 2000. 248 pp.

2219. Griesbach, Heinz, and Gudrun Uhlig. *Mit anderen Worten: Deutsche Idiomatik; Redensarten und Redeweisen*. München: Iudici-um, 1993. 123 pp.

2220. Gröbe, Volker. *"Spetze Zung – fründlije Wööt": Kölsche Spröch – vun hückzodaach*. Köln: J.P. Bachem, 1988. 140 pp. With illustrations.

2221. Gröbe, Volker. *Et kütt wie et kütt. Die originellen kölschen Sprichwörter*. München: Compact/Minipräsent Verlag, 2002. 255 pp. (miniature book).

2222. Gröbe, Volker. *Kölner Sprüche*. Part 2. Ed. Ertay Hayit. Illus-trations by Michaela Müller. Köln: J.P. Bachem, 2004. 61 pp.

2223. Grober-Glück, Gerda. *Motive und Motivationen in Redens-arten und Meinungen*. 2 vols. (text and maps). Marburg: N.G. El-wert, 1974 (= Atlas der deutschen Volkskunde, Beiheft 3). I, 561 pp.; II, 49 maps.

2224. Grosshans, Rainald. *Pieter Bruegel d. Ä., Die niederlän-dischen Sprichwörter (1559)*. Berlin: Staatliche Museen, Preussi-scher Kulturbesitz Berlin, 1973 (= Pamphlet no. 710). 5 pp. With 3 illustrations.

2225. Grosshans, Rainald. *Pieter Bruegel d. Ä. "Die nieder-ländischen Sprichwörter"*. Berlin: Gemäldegalerie, Staatliche Mu-seen zu Berlin, 2003. 161 pp. With 130 illustrations.

2226. Gruhle, Uwe, and Dö Van Volxem. *Das andere Sprichwör-ter-Lexikon: derb – aufmüpfig – unverblümt*. Frankfurt am Main: Eichborn, 1983. 124 pp. With illustrations.

2227. Gruhle, Uwe, and Dö Van Volxem. *Freche Sprichwörter für alle Lebenslagen. Jetzt mit den hundert zündendsten Spruch-Neuschöpfungen des ausgehenden Jahrtausends*. Frankfurt am Main: Eichborn, 1990. 128 pp. With illustrations.

2228. Grundmann, Günter, Michael Strich and Werner Richey. *Rechtssprichwörter*. Leipzig: VEB Bibliographisches Institut, 1980. 164 pp.

2229. Grüterich, Tobias, Alexander Eilers, and Eva Annabella Blume (eds.). *Neue deutsche Aphorismen. Eine Anthologie*. Dresden: Edition Azur, 2010. 287 pp.

2230. Gudkova, Olga. *Handbuch deutscher Sprachsymbole. Hundert Sprachporträts typischer Frauen und Männer in der deutschen Gesellschaft mit kulturell-historischen Kommentaren und russischen Äquivalenten*. Ed. Harry Walter. Illustrations by Juliane Block. Greifswald: Ernst-Moritz-Arndt-Universität, Institut für Fremdsprachliche Philologien – Slawistik, 2010. 134 pp.

2231. Gulbransson, Olaf (ill.) *Sprüche und Wahrheiten*. München: Albert Langen – Georg Müller, 1969; rpt. München: Deutscher Taschenbuch Verlag, 1974. 166 pp.

2232. Gundlach, Jürgen. *Von Aant bis Zäg'. Anderthalb Hundert plattdeutscher Wörter in 83 Abschnitten dargestellt*. Leipzig: Zentralhaus-Publikation, 1982. 72 pp.

2233. Guntermann, Paul (ed.). *Hörzu – das fängt ja gut an! Das Lustigste von Seite 3 aus Hörzu*. Hamburg: Springer, 1976. 129 pp. With illustrations. (quotations and anti-proverbs).

2234. Guntermann, Paul (ed.). *Hörzu – Das Beste von Seite 3. Das Lustigste von Seite 3 aus Hörzu*. Hamburg: Springer, 1978. 129 pp. With illustrations. (quotations and anti-proverbs).

2235. Günther, Erika, and Waldtraut Förster. *Wörterbuch verbaler Wendungen. Deutsch-Russisch. Eine Sammlung verbal-nominaler Fügungen*. Leipzig: VEB Verlag Enzyklopädie, 1987. 223 pp.

2236. Günther, Friedrich Joachim. *Entwürfe zu Vorträgen und Aufsätzen über 100 Sprichwörter und 100 Schillersche Sprüche für die oberen Klassen höherer Lehranstalten*. Eisleben: Reichardt, 1861. 2nd ed. ed. Carl August Peschel. Leipzig: George Reichardt, 1882. 460 pp.

2237. Gutekunst, Dieter. *Durch Weisheit wird ein Haus gebaut ... Weisheiten und Sprüche rund um Wohnungsbau und Wohnen*. Illustrations by Gunter Maurer. Heidelberg: Umschau-Braus, 1998. 164 pp.

2238. Gutknecht, Christoph. *Lauter böhmische Dörfer. Wie die Wörter zu ihrer Bedeutung kamen.* München: C.H. Beck, 1995. 212 pp.

2239. Gutknecht, Christoph. *Lauter spitze Zungen. Geflügelte Worte und ihre Geschichte.* Illustrations by Grandville. München: C.H. Beck, 1996. 292 pp.

2240. Gutknecht, Christoph (ed.). *Lauter Worte über Worte. Runde und spitze Gedanken über Sprache und Literatur.* München: C.H. Beck, 1999. 391 pp.

2241. Gutknecht, Christoph. *Lauter blühender Unsinn. Erstaunliche Wortgeschichten von Aberwitz bis Wischiwaschi.* München: C.H. Beck, 2001. 228 pp. With illustrations.

2242. Gutknecht, Christoph. *Pustekuchen! Lauter kulinarische Wortgeschichten.* München: C.H. Beck, 2002. 288 pp. With illustrations.

2243. Gutknecht, Christoph. *"Ich mach's dir mexikanisch". Lauter erotische Wortgeschichten.* München: C.H. Beck, 2004. 245 pp. With illustrations.

2244. Gutknecht, Christoph. *Von Treppenwitz bis Sauregurkenzeit. Die verrücktesten Wörter im Deutschen.* München: C.H. Beck, 2008. 237 pp. With illustrations.

2245. Habeck, Reinhard (ed.). *Saublöd ... Witzige Sprüche für alle Fälle. Sprüche, Verse und Reime.* Wien: Tosa-Verlag, 2004. 153 pp. With illustrations. (anti-proverbs).

2246. Habeck, Reinhard (ed.). *Saublöd ... Witzige Sprüche für Männer. Sprüche, Verse und Reime.* Wien: Tosa-Verlag, 2004. 154 pp. With illustrations. (anti-proverbs).

2247. Habeck, Reinhard (ed.). *Saublöde Sprüche für Frauen. Sprüche, Verse und Reime.* Wien: Tosa-Verlag, 2004. 153 pp. With illustrations. (anti-proverbs).

2248. Hacke, Axel, and Michael Sowa. *Der weiße Neger Wumbaba. Kleines Handbuch des Verhörens.* München: Antje Kunstmann, 2004. 63 pp.

2249. Hackmann, Bärbel. *Diätetik und Physiologie im Spiegel des Sprichwortes.* Diss. Universität Münster, 1964. 129 pp.

2250. (, Georg. *Wenn die Schwalben niedrig fliegen ... Bauern-regeln.* Niedernhausen/Taunus: Falken-Verlag, 1984. 77 pp. (weather proverbs).

2251. Haddenbach, Georg. *Wetter und Wind ändern sich geschwind. Beliebte Bauernregeln.* Niedernhausen/Ts.: Falken-Verlag, 1992. 88 pp. (weather proverbs).

2252. Haek, D. *Deutscher Zitatenschatz. Eine Sammlung deutscher Zitate, Redensarten, Schlagwörter und dgl.* Halle: Otto Hendel, 1903. 229 pp. (2nd ed. 1910). 278 pp. (same as #2261)

2253. Hagen, Edmund von. *Deutsche Sprachweisheit. Etymologische Aphorismen.* Hannover: Carl Schüßler, 1880. 60 pp.

2254. Hahnemann, Helga. *Die schärfsten Sprüche.* Ed. Angela Gentzmer. Berlin: Eulenspiegel Verlag, 2000 (2nd ed. 2001). 127 pp. With illustrations. (anti-proverbs).

2255. Hallstein, Reinhard. *Sprechen Sie Platt? Für Norddeutsche und solche, die es noch werden wollen.* Illustrations by Judith Kroboth. Wien: Tosa, 2006. 128 pp.

2256. Hamacher, Gustav. *Kölsche Redensarten und Sprichwörter.* Illustrations by Heinz Kroh. Köln: J.P. Bachern, 1986. 72 pp.

2257. Hars, Wolfgang. *Lexikon der Werbesprüche. 500 bekannte deutsche Werbeslogans und ihre Geschichte.* Frankfurt am Main: Eichborn, 1999. 406 pp. With illustrations.

2258. Hau, Willi (ed.). *Ich geh kaputt – gehst Du mit? Sponti-Sprüche.* Frankfurt am Main: Eichborn, 1981 (5th ed. 1982). 68 pp. With illustrations. (anti-proverbs).

2259. Hau, Willi (ed.). *Es wird Zeit, daß wir lieben. Sponti-Sprüche No. 2.* Frankfurt am Main: Eichborn, 1982. 67 pp. With illustrations. (anti-proverbs).

2260. Hauschka, Ernst R. *Handbuch moderner Literatur im Zitat. Sentenzen des 20. Jahrhunderts.* Regensburg: Friedrich Pustet, 1968. 558 pp.

2261. Helbing, Franz. *Deutscher Zitatenschatz. Eine Sammlung deutscher Zitate, Redensarten, Schlagwörter und dgl.* Halle: Otto Hendel, 1903. 229 pp. (2nd ed. 1910). 278 pp. (same as #2252)

2262. Heller, Karin (ed.). *Spruchweisheiten aus der deutschen Sprachinsel "Sette comuni vicentini". Gesammelt von Giulio Vesco-*

vi. Vienna: Verlag Verband der wissenschaftlichen Gesellschaften Österreichs, 1993. 89 pp.

2263. Hellwig, Gerhard. *Zitate und Sprichwörter von A-Z*. Gütersloh: Bertelsmann Lexikon, 1974. Rpt. as *Das Buch der Zitate. 15000 geflügelte Worte von A-Z*. München: Mosaik, 1981. 544 pp.

2264. Henisch. Georg. *Teütsche Sprach vnd Weißheit. Thesavrvs lingvae et sapientiae Germanicae*. Augsburg: David Franc, 1616; rpt. Hildesheim: Georg Olms, 1973. 1875 cols.

2265. Henschelsberg, Wolf von (ed.). *Tipp-Ex für den Direx. Schüler-Sprüche No. 4*. Illustrations by Holger Aue. Frankfurt am Main: Eichborn, 1993. 61 pp. (anti-proverbs).

2266. Hermann, Leonard. *Das Bier im Volksmund. Alte Sprichwörter und Redensarten*. Berlin: Reimar Hobbing, 1933. 208 pp.

2267. Herrmann-Winter, Renate. *Sprachbilder im Plattdeutschen. Redewendungen und Sprichwörter*. Rostock: Hinstorff, 2002. 397 pp.

2268. Hertslet, William Lewis. *Der Treppenwitz der Weltgeschichte. Geschichtliche Irrtümer, Entstellungen und Erfindungen*. Berlin: Haude & Spener, 1882. 251 pp. Revised 6th ed. Hans F. Helmolt. Berlin: Haude & Spener, 1905. 509 pp.

2269. Herzog, Heinrich. *Deutsche Sprichwörter. Gesammelt für Jung und Alt*. Aarau: H.R. Sauerländer, 1882. 171 pp.

2270. Herzog, Annelies, Arthur Michel, and Herbert Riedel. *Deutsche idiomatische Wendungen für Ausländer. Eine Auswahl mit Beispielen*. Leipzig: VEB Verlag Enzyklopädie, 1972 (4th ed. 1980). 175 pp.

2271. Herzog, Annelies, Arthur Michel, and Herbert Riedel. *Idiomatische Redewendungen von A - Z. Ein Übungsbuch für Anfänger und Fortgeschrittene*. Leipzig: Langenscheidt – Verlag Enzyklopädie, 1993. 156 pp.

2272. Hesse, Günter. *Die Wände im Knast ... Und sie reden doch. Graffiti aus deutschen Gefängnissen*. 2 vols. Bremen: Skarabäus Verlag, 1984. 248 pp. With illustrations.

2273. Hesse, Margret, and Heinz Hesse. *Arm wie eine Kirchenmaus: Sprichwörter, Redensarten, Albumverse*. Viersen: Volkshochschule Stadt Viersen, 1996. 106 pp.

2274. Hessky, Regina. *Deutsch-Ungarische phraseologische Sammlung.* Budapest: Tankönyvkiadó, 1982 (4th ed. 1991). 283 pp.

2275. Hessky, Regina. *Durch die Blume: Arbeitsbuch zur deutschen Phraseologie für Fortgeschrittene.* Budapest: Nemzeti Tankönyvkiadó, 1995. 214 pp.

2276. Hessky, Regina, and Stefan Ettinger. *Deutsche Redewendungen: Ein Wörter- und Übungsbuch für Fortgeschrittene.* Tübingen: Gunter Narr, 1997. 327 pp.

2277. Hetzel, S. *Wie der Deutsche spricht. Phraseologie der volkstümlichen Sprache. Ausdrücke, Redensarten, Sprichwörter und Citate aus dem Volksmunde und den Werken der Volksschriftsteller.* Leipzig: Fr. Wilh. Grunow, 1896. 355 pp.

2278. Heuseler, J.A. *Luthers Sprichwörter aus seinen Schriften gesammelt.* Leipzig: Johann Ambrosius Barth, 1824; rpt. Walluf bei Wiesbaden: Martin Sändig, 1973. 160 pp.

2279. Heyd, Werner P. *Bauernweistümer.* Vol. 1: *Wetterregeln und Lostagsprüche.* Vol. 2: *Wetterpropheten in der Natur.* Memmingen: Maximilian Dietrich, 1973. I, 207 pp.; II, 198 pp. (weather proverbs).

2280. Heyen, Asmus Geerds (ed.). *Ein Gedanke kann nicht erwachen, ohne andere zu wecken. Illustrierte Sinnsprüche.* Illustrations by Rüdiger Luckow. Lahr/Schwarzwald: SKV-Edition, 1985. 72 pp. (quotations).

2281. Hilgers, Heribert A. "Köln in Redensarten des Bergischen Landes." *Alt-Köln: Mitteilungen des Heimatvereins Alt-Köln,* no volume given, no. 90 (October 1993), pp. 10-13.

2282. Hilgers, Heribert A. "Köln im 'Volksmund' an der unteren Sieg." *Krune un Flamme: Mitteilungen des Heimatvereins Alt-Köln,* no vol. given, no. 4 (1997), 27-33.

2283. Hindermann, Federico, and Bernhard Heinser (ed.). *Deutsche Aphorismen aus drei Jahrhunderten.* Zürich: Manesse Verlag, 1987 (4th ed. 1992). 464 pp.

2284. Hirson, Christina. *Sprichwörter und Redewendungen für jeden Anlass. Mit hilfreichen Erklärungen.* München: Gräfe und Unzer, 2006. 96 pp.

2285. Hiss, Albert. "Volksweisheit in den Sprichwörtern und Redensarten des *Simplicissimus* von Johann Jakob Christoph von

Grimmelshausen." *Um Renchen und Grimmelshausen* (= *Grimmelshausen Archiv*), 1 (1976), 1-89.

2286. Hoefer, Edmund. *Wie das Volk spricht. Sprichwörtliche Redensarten.* Stuttgart: Adolph Krabbe, 1855. 48 pp. 7th ed. Stuttgart: A. Kröner, 1873. 220 pp. Rpt. as *Wie das Volk spricht. 2008 Sprichwörter und Redensarten. Samt den 193 Varianten und den Worterklärungen der Auflage von 1873.* Zürich: Oesch, 1997. 230 pp. (wellerisms).

2287. Hoefer, Edmund. *Wie das Volk spricht. Sprichwörtliche Redensarten.* Stuttgart: Adolph Krabbe, 1855. 48 pp. 9th ed. Stuttgart: Gebrüder Kröner, 1885. Rpt. as *Wie das Volk spricht. Deutsche Sagwörter.* Ed. Wolfgang Mieder. Hildesheim: Georg Olms, 1995. 227 pp. (introduction, pp. V-XLII). (wellerisms).

2288. Hoffmann, Detlef (ed.). *Das Kölner Kartenspiel des Johann Bussemacher [1591] / The Cologne Card Play by Johann Bussemacher.* München: Heimeran, 1980. 90 pp. and 52 playing cards.

2289. Hoffmann von Fallersleben, August Heinrich. "Die ältesten deutschen Sprichwörtersammlungen [*Proverbia seriosa*, Antonius Tunnicius, Johannes Fabri]." *Weimarisches Jahrbuch für deutsche Sprache, Literatur und Kunst*, 2 (1855), 173-186.

2290. Hoffmann von Fallersleben, August Heinrich. "Volkswörter. Aus der deutschen Scherz-, Spott und Gleichnis-Sprache." *Archiv für die Geschichte deutscher Sprache*, 1 (1874), 241-290. Rpt. as *Volkswörter. Aus der deutschen Scherz-, Spott und Gleichnis-Sprache.* Amsterdam: Rodopi, 1968. 50 pp.

2291. Hofmann, Winfried. *Das rheinische Sagwort. Ein Beitrag zur Sprichwörterkunde.* Siegburg: F. Schmitt, 1959. 194 pp. (wellerisms).

2292. Holm, Hans Henning. *Da bist Du platt! Unterhaltsames Sammelsurium niederdeutscher Wörter und Redensarten.* Illustrations by Anneli Reichert. Neumünster: Karl Wachholtz, 1972 (2nd ed. 1980). 92 pp.

2293. Hönes, Winfried (ed.). *Seit Äskulaps Zeiten. Aphorismen für Mediziner.* Wiesbaden: Drei Lilien Verlag, 1988. 100 pp. With illustrations.

2294. Hönes, Winfried (ed.). *Alles über die Dummheit. Eine intelligente Aphorismensammlung über die Stupidologie.* Illustrations by René Fehr. Rorschach: Nebelspalter-Verlag, 1993. 127 pp.

2295. Hopf, Angela, and Andreas Hopf (eds.). *Das große Buch der Weisheiten und Aphorismen*. München: Wilhelm Heyne, 1983. 239 pp.

2296. Horstmann, Rudolf. *Wat so seggt ward. Niederdeutsche Sprichwörter und Redensarten aus Schleswig-Holstein*. Illustrations by Ilse Zielke. Neumünster: Karl Wachholz, 1980. 138 pp.

2297. Hruschka, Rudolf. "Die bildhafte Sprache des Volkes." *Sudetendeutsche Zeitschrift für Volkskunde*, 5 (1932), 156-164.

2298. Hucke, Helene (ed.). *Was ein Häkchen werden will ... Die bekanntesten Sprichwörter*. Zürich: Buch-Vertriebs-GmbH, 1983 (2nd ed. 1984). 128 pp.

2299. Hucke, Helene (ed.). *Bauernweisheiten, Bauernregeln rund ums Jahr*. Köln: Buch und Zeit Verlagsgesellschaft, 1986. 128 pp. (weather proverbs).

2300. Hucke, Helene (ed.). *Wer früh' aufsteht, wird reich. Lebensweisheiten,*. Köln: Buch und Zeit Verlagsgesellschaft, 1987. 128 pp. (quotations).

2301. Hügen, Ludwig. *"Watt Hänske neet liert..." (Was Hänschen nicht lernt....). Sprichwörter in niederrheinischer Mundart*. Illustrations by Joachim Klinger. Krefeld: Joh. van Acken, 1993. 80 pp.

2302. Hülsemann, Kurt. *Die niederdeutschen Sprichwörter in den Werken von Nicolaus Gryse*. Diss. Universität Hamburg, 1930. 125 pp.

2303. Hunfeld, Hans. *Sprich-wörtlich. Wenn ein Wort erst sprichwörtlich ist, spricht es dann noch wörtlich?* Illustrations by Christian Gröbel. München: Klett Edition Deutsch, 1989. 160 pp. (anti-proverbs).

2304. Huth, Mari [*sic*] Luise. *Das Sprichwort bei [Johann Michael] Moscherosch*. Diss. University of North Carolina, 1940. 121 pp. (proverb index, pp. 63-112).

2305. Ibele, Gisela, and Therese Nolte. *Mehr Himmel wagen: Nichtalltägliche Exerzitien [Sprichwörter und Redensarten]*. Freiburg: Herder, 2006. 128 pp. With illustrations.

2306. Ilgenstein, Erhard. *Das überschäumende Sprüchefäßchen. 532 Sprüche über das Bier*. Jena: VEB Gustav Fischer, 1987. 128 pp.

2307. Jannen, Reinhard. "Sprüchwörter in der Amrumschen Mundart aufgezeichnet von Lorenz Friedrich Marstrand Mechlenburg (1799-1875)." *Nordfriesisches Jahrbuch*, 35 (1999), 177-206.

2308. Jeep, John M. *Alliterating Word-Pairs in Old High German*. Bochum: Norbert Brockmeyer, 1995. 236 pp. (word-pair index, pp. 231-236).

2309. Jeep, John M. *Alliterating Word-pairs in Early Middle High German*. Baltmannsweiler: Schneider Verlag Hohengehren, 2006. 139 pp. (word-pair index, pp. 99-139).

2310. Jeromin, Rolf. *Zitatenschatz der Werbung. Slogans erobern Märkte*. Gütersloh: Heinz Peter, 1969. 192 pp.

2311. Jeromin, Rolf (ed.). *Einsichten und Aussichten. Erfolgsmaximen in 1000 Sprichwörtern und Lebensweisheiten*. Gütersloh: Heinz Peter, 1987. 128 pp.

2312. Jetter, Monika (ed.). *Von Abs bis Zadek. Sprüche für das ganze Leben. Lebensansichten prominenter Persönlichkeiten*. Hamburg: Hanseatische Edition, 1985. 86 pp. With illustrations.

2313. Jockel, Gabriele (ed.). *"Jemandem etwas durch die Blume sagen": Die schönsten Redewendungen*. Leonberg: Garant Verlag, 2007. 192 pp.

2314. Jogschies, Rainer. *Das neue Lexikon der Vorurteile*. Illustrations by Honoré Daumier. Frankfurt am Main: Eichborn, 1987. 126 pp.

2315. John, Johannes. *Reclams Zitaten-Lexikon*. Stuttgart: Philipp Reclam, 1992. 574 pp.

2316. Jührs, Carola (ed.). *Ächt too matsch. Das allerletzte Sprüchebuch*. Illustrations by Barbara Klöss. Münster: F. Coppenrath, 1985. 78 pp. (anti-proverbs).

2317. Kainis, Dr. *Die Derbheiten im Reden des Volkes*. Leipzig: Literatur-Bureau, 1872. 156 pp.

2318. Kaiser, Dietlind, and Stephan Kaiser. "Redensarten unter der Lupe." *Gut gesagt und formuliert. Ein unterhaltsamer Ratgeber für die deutsche Sprache*. Eds. Ingrid Weng-Goeckel et al. Stuttgart: Verlag Das Beste, 1988. 81-168.

2319. Keil, Reinhold. "Sprichwörter und Redensarten aus wolgadeutschen Siedlungen." *Jahrbuch für Ostdeutsche Volkskunde*, 22 (1979), 217-226.

2320. Keim, Anton Maria. *"Aufs Maul geschaut". Betrachtungen zu Redensarten vom Mittelrhein.* Illustrations by Hannes Gaab. Mainz: Hanns Krach, 1975. 61 pp.

2321. Kellermann, Dieter (ed.). *Trinksprüche, Richtersprüche, Gästebuchverse.* Illustrations by Marianne von Euw. Niederhausen/Ts.: Falken-Verlag, 1969 (2nd ed. 1982). 8 pp.

2322. Kelley, Edmond Morgan. *[Johann] Fischart's Use of the Proverb as a Stylistic Device in His "Geschichtsklitterung".* Diss. Michigan State University, 1968. 230 pp. (proverb index, pp. 123-227).

2323. Kerler, Christine, and Richard Kerler. *Gipfelsprüch. Eintragungen in Gipfelbüchern und Marterlsprüch.* Illustrations by Ortrud Proebst-Bergmann. Pfaffenhofen/Ilm: W. Ludwig, 1977 (3rd ed. 1982). 74 pp.

2324. Kerler, Christine, and Richard Kerler. *Warum? Ursprünge von Redensarten und Gewohnheiten.* Illustrations by Rudolf Angerer. München: Universitas Verlag, 1993. 213 pp.

2325. Kern, Heike, and Christine Kern (eds.). *Kuhfrauen haben den Busen unten. Die besten Kindersprüche.* München: Knaur Taschenbuch Verlag, 2007. 169 pp.

2326. Kiess, Arthur (ed.). *Adam, Eva und der Apfel. Mann und Frau in Zitaten und Sentenzen.* Illustrations by Inge Jastram. Leipzig: Bibliographisches Institut, 1990. 124 pp.

2327. Kiess, Arthur (ed.). *Liebe kennt kein Maß. Liebe und Ehe in Zitaten und Sentenzen.* Illustrations by Inge Jastram. Leipzig: Bibliographisches Institut, 1990. 136 pp.

2328. Kirchberger, Joe H. *Das große Krüger Zitatenbuch. 15.000 Zitate von der Antike bis zur Gegenwart.* Frankfurt am Main: Wolfgang Krüger, 1977 (2nd ed. 1981). 619 pp.

2329. Kirchberger, Joe H. *Sprichwörter von A-Z: Das große Sprichwörterbuch. Rund 20.000 Sprichwörter aus über 90 Sprachen und Kulturräumen.* München: Lexikographisches Institut, 1986; rpt. München: Orbis Verlag, 1993. 536 pp.

2330. Klapper, Joseph. *Die Sprichwörter der Freidankpredigten. Proverbia Fridanci. Ein Beitrag zur Geschichte des ostmitteldeutschen Sprichworts und seiner lateinischen Quellen.* Breslau: M.&H. Marcus, 1927. 112 pp.

2331. Knape, Rose-Marie, and Gunter Müller (eds.). *"Wir mussen die spruchwörter erretten": Sprichwörter und volkstümliche Redewendungen von Johannes Agricola und Martin Luther.* Illustrations by Elke Ligus. Halle: Janos Stekovics, 1996. 80 pp.

2332. Knoop, Ulrich. "Die Dialekte in Sprichwörtern und Redewendungen." In U. Knoop. *Wörterbuch deutscher Dialekte: Eine Sammlung von Mundartwörtern aus zehn Dialektgebieten im Einzelvergleich, in Sprichwörtern und Redewendungen.* Gütersloh: Bertelsmann Lexikon Verlag, 1997. 239-378.

2333. Knorr, Stefan, and Rainer Witt (eds.). *Das Lexikon der Vorurteile.* Frankfurt am Main: Eichborn, 1983. 128 pp. With illustrations.

2334. Koch, Mary. "Volga German Proverbs and Proverbial Expressions from the Colony of Dreispitz [Russia]." *Journal of the American Historical Society of Germans from Russia*, 2 (1979), 32-37.

2335. Köhler, Claus, Annelies Herzog, and Waltraud Kursitza. *Deutsche verbale Wendungen für Ausländer. Eine Auswahl mit Beispielen und Übungen.* Leipzig: VEB Verlag Enzyklopädie, 1984. 184 pp. (4th revised ed. 1989). 177 pp.

2336. Kopp, Thomas. "Wolgadeutsche Sprichwörter." *Muttersprache*, 69 (1959), 1-5.

2337. Körte, Wilhelm. *Die Sprichwörter und sprichwörtlichen Redensarten der Deutschen.* Leipzig: F.A. Brockhaus, 1837; rpt. Hildesheim: Georg Olms, 1974. 567 pp.

2338. Kossmann, L.S. *Deutsche Phraseologie. Übungsbuch (deutsch-russisch).* Moskva: Mezhdunarodnye Otnosheniia, 1964. 254 pp.

2339. Koster, Monika. *Großes Handbuch der Zitate, Sprichwörter und Redensarten.* Köln: Naumann & Göbel, 1983. 447 pp.

2340. Köster, Rudolf. *Duden, Redensarten: Herkunft und Bedeutung.* Illustrations by Barbara Theis. Mannheim: Dudenverlag, 1999. 256 pp.

2341. Krack, Karl Erich. *1000 Redensarten unter die Lupe genommen.* Stuttgart Friedrich Bassermann, 1965. 216 pp.; rpt. Frankfurt am Main: Fischer, 1969. 222 pp.

2342. Krämer, Julius. *Sprichwort – Wohrwort. Ausgewählte Sprichwörter und sprichwörtliche Redensarten der Pfälzer im Ausland*. Kaiserslautern: Heimatstelle Pfalz, 1961. 63 pp.

2343. Krämer, Walter, and Wolfgang Sauer. *Lexikon der populären Sprachirrtümer. Mißverständnisse, Denkfehler und Vorurteile von Altbier bis Zyniker*. Frankfurt am Main: Eichborn, 2001; rpt. München: Piper, 2003. 224 pp. With illustrations.

2344. Krebs, Gotthold. *Militärische Redensarten und Kunst-Ausdrücke*. Wien: L.W. Seidel, 1892. 183 pp.

2345. Krebs, Gotthold. *Militärische Sprichwörter und Redensarten*. Wien: L.W. Seidel, 1895. 213 pp.

2346. Kremer, Edmund Philipp. *German Proverbs and Proverbial Phrases with Their English Counterparts*. Stanford, California: Stanford University Press, 1955. 116 pp.

2347. Kreuzer, Peter. *Das Graffiti-Lexikon. Wandkunst von A-Z*. München: Wilhelm Heyne, 1986. 494 pp.

2348. Krienke, Eberhard. *Weisheit und Witz der Uckermärker [Brandenburg]. Sprichwörter und sprichwörtliche Redensarten. Plattdeutsch-Hochdeutsch*. Illustrations by Ines Noé. Milow: Schibri-Verlag, 2001. 67 pp.

2349. Kroker, E. "Sprichwörter." In E. Kroker (ed.). *D. Martin Luthers Werke. Kritische Gesamtausgabe. Tischreden*. Weimar: Hermann Böhlau, 1921. VI, 666-677.

2350. Krone, Sabine, and Helmut Walther. *Wörter, die Geschichte machten. Schlüsselbegriffe des 20. Jahrhunderts*. Gütersloh: Bertelsmann Lexikon Verlag, 2001. 224 pp.

2351. Krüger-Lorenzen, Kurt. *Das geht auf keine Kuhhaut. Deutsche Redensarten – und was dahinter steckt*. Illustrations by Franziska Bilek. Düsseldorf: Econ, 1960. 306 pp.

2352. Krüger-Lorenzen, Kurt. *Aus der Pistole geschossen. Deutsche Redensarten – und was dahinter steckt*. Illustrations by Franziska Bilek. Düsseldorf: Econ, 1966. 304 pp.

2353. Krüger-Lorenzen, Kurt. *Der lachende Dritte. Deutsche Redensarten – und was dahinter steckt*. Illustrations by Franziska Bilek. Düsseldorf: Econ, 1973. 283 pp.

2354. Krüger-Lorenzen, Kurt. *Deutsche Redensarten – und was dahinter steckt.* Illustrations by Franziska Bilek. München: Wilhelm Heyne, 1983. 860 pp. (the three previous books in one volume).

2355. Krumbholz, Eckart (ed.). *Martin Luther. "Euch stoßen, daß es krachen soll." Sprüche. Aussprüche, Anekdoten.* Berlin: Buchverlag der Morgen, 1983. 255 pp.

2356. Kuchmann, Dieter (ed.). *Rauh sind des Soldaten Wege. Zitate, Sprichwörter und Aphorismen aus Memoiren über den Großen Vaterländischen Krieg.* Berlin: Militärverlag der Deutschen Demokratischen Republik, 1987. 314 pp.

2357. Kuckertz, Beate (ed.). *Das große Buch der Büro-Sprüche.* Illustrations by Ernst Hürlimann. München: Wilhelm Heyne, 1992. 300 pp. (anti-proverbs).

2358. Küffner, Georg M. *Die Deutschen im Sprichwort. Ein Beitrag zur Kulturgeschichte.* Heidelberg: Carl Winter, 1899. 93 pp.

2359. Kunze, Horst. *Irren ist menschlich, sagte der Igel ... Alte und neue Beispielsprichwörter.* Berlin: Eulenspiegel Verlag, 1974 (2nd ed. 1976). 142 pp. With illustrations. (wellerisms).

2360. Küpper, Heinz. *Wörterbuch der deutschen Umgangssprache.* 6 vols. Hamburg: Claassen, 1963-1970. I, 533 pp.; II, 326 pp.; III, 270 pp.; IV, 291 pp.; V, 377 pp.; VI, 438 pp.

2361. Küpper, Heinz. *Illustriertes Lexikon der deutschen Umgangssprache.* 8 vols. Stuttgart: Klett, 1982-1984. 3216 pp. With illustrations.

2362. Küpper, Heinz. *Deutsch zum Anfassen. Moderne Redewendungen von "Abseilen" bis "Zoff".* Wiesbaden: VMA-Verlag, 1987. 128 pp.

2363. Kurzer, Michael (ed.). *Alte Handwerksweisheiten.* Mit Miniaturen aus dem Codex des Balthazar Behaim. Würzburg: Stürtz, 1998. 62 pp. With illustrations.

2364. Kurzer, Michael (ed.). *Das kleine Sprichwörterbuch.* Illustriert mit vielen Detailabbildungen des Gemäldes "Die Niederländischen Sprichwörter" von Pieter Bruegel d. Ä. Würzburg: Stürtz, 1998. 62 pp.

2365. Küttner, W.P. *Die Stoßstange ist aller Laster Anfang. Die frechsten Liebes-, Lust- und Lästersprüche.* Illustrations by W.P. Küttner. Frankfurt am Main: Eichborn, 1988. 61 pp. (anti-proverbs).

2366. Laber, Harry G. (ed.). *Dumme Sprüche für alle Fälle*. Augsburg: Weltbild, 2003. 160 pp. (anti-proverbs).

2367. Lang, Ewald (ed.). *Wendehals und Stasi-Laus. Demo-Sprüche aus der DDR*. München: Wilhelm Heyne, 1990. 171 pp. With illustrations.

2368. Latendorf, Friedrich. *Hundert Sprüche Luthers zum alten Testament in hochdeutscher, niederdeutscher und niederländischer Fassung*. Rostock: Carl Hinstorff, 1883. 26 pp.

2369. Latsch, Günter (ed.). *Das Handwerk in Holzschnitten, Versen, Signets und Sprichwörtern*. Leipzig: Hermann Duncker, 1987. 32 pp. With illustrations.

2370. Lauchert, Friedrich. "Sprichwörter und sprichwörtliche Redensarten bei P. Abraham a S. Clara." *Alemannia*, 20 (1892), 213-254

2371. Lautenbach, Ernst. *Goethe: Zitate, Redensarten, Sprichwörter* Hanau: Werner Dausien, 1986. 243 pp.

2372. Lautenbach, Ernst. *Lexikon Schiller-Zitate. Aus Werk und Leben*. München: Iudicium, 2003. 941 pp.

2373. Lautenbach, Ernst. *Lexikon Goethe-Zitate. Auslese für das 21. Jahrhundert. Aus Werk und Leben*. München: Iudicium, 2004. 1246 pp.

2374. Lebe, Reinhard. *War Karl der Kahle wirklich kahl? Über historische Beinamen und was dahinter steckt*. Wiesbaden: VMA-Verlag, 1980. 211 pp.

2375. Lechleitner, Franz (ed.). *Wartburg-Sprüche*. Ausgewählt und angebracht von Joseph Victor von Scheffel und Bernhard von Arnswald. Weimar: Hermann Böhlau, 1892. 207 pp.

2376. Leffts, Joseph. "Volkstümliche Spruchweisheit." In J. Leffts. *Die volkstümlichen Stilelemente in [Thomas] Murners Satiren*. Straßburg: Karl J. Trübner, 1915. 116-171.

2377. Legler, Erich. *Wie menschlich sind doch Tiere. Sprichworte [sic] und Redensarten für Menschen- und Tierfreunde*. Ulm: Süddeutsche Verlagsgesellschaft, 1979. 24 pp.

2378. Lehmann, Christoph. *Florilegium Politicum. Politischer Blumengarten, darin auserlesene politische Sentenz, Lehren, Reguln und Sprüchwörter aus Theologis, Juriconsultis, Politicis, Historicis, Philosophis, Poeten und eigener Erfahrung unter 286 Titeln [...] in locos* *communes zusammen getragen.* Lübeck: Johan Junge, 1639. 953 pp. Rpt. ed. Wolfgang Mieder. Bern: Peter Lang, 1986. 953 pp. (introduction, pp. 5*-*85*).

2379. Lehnert, Charly. *Hundert saarländische Weisheiten ohne die Geplotzte.* Saarbrücken-Bübingen: Lehnert, 2009. 36 pp. (miniature book).

2380. Leineweber, Heinrich. *Die Weisheit auf der Gasse. Zusammenstellung und Erklärung von Sprichwörtern und sprichwörtlichen Redensarten.* Paderborn: Ferdinand Schöningh, 1897. 232 pp. (3rd ed. 1922). 255 pp.

2381. Lemke, Luise. *Lieber'n bißken mehr, aber dafür wat Jutet. Berliner Sprüche.* Illustrations by Frauke Trojahn. Berlin: Arani-Verlag, 1981. 88 pp.

2382. Lemke, Luise. *Besser jut jelebt und det noch recht lange. Noch mehr Berliner Sprichwörter.* Illustrations by Frauke Trojahn. Berlin: Arani-Verlag, 1984. 109 pp.

2383. Lemp, Eleonore. *Schillers Welt- und Lebensanschauung in Aussprüchen aus seinen Werken und Briefen.* Frankfurt am Main: Moritz Diesterweg, 1905. 300 pp.

2384. Lenschau, Martha. *[Hans Jakob Christoffel von] Grimmelshausens Sprichwörter und Redensarten.* Frankfurt: Moritz Diesterweg, 1924; rpt. Hildesheim: Gerstenberg, 1973. 155 pp.

2385. Leon, Bernd (ed.). *Mit schönen Worten kocht man keinen Brei. Reichlich 600 kulinarische Sprüche.* Illustrations by Erika Baarmann. Berlin: Eulenspiegel Verlag 1989; Rosenheim: Rosenheimer Verlagshaus, 1989. 163 pp.

2386. Leon, Bernd (ed.). *Geiz hat für Venus keinen Reiz. Knapp 700 Sprüche um Geld und Gut.* Illustrations by Erika Baarmann. Berlin: Eulenspiegel Verlag, 1991. 158 pp.

2387. Leuthner, Roman. *Passende Sprichwörter für jede Gelegenheit.* Stuttgart: Urania, 2006. 96 pp.

2388. Lewinsky, Tamar. *Geflügelte Namen: Das Lexikon unbekannter Bekannter von Achilles bis Graf Zeppelin.* Zürich: Oesch, 1998. 325 pp.

2389. Limpach, Hannelene, and Alexander F. Hoffmann. *Fuchsteufelswild und lammfromm. Tierisch gute Redensarten von A bis Z.* Illustrations by F.W. Bernstein. Frankfurt am Main: Fischer Taschenbuch Verlag, 1993. 230 pp.

2390. Lincoln, Gisela H. *Andere Länder, andere Sitten. 100 Redewendungen im Gespräch.* Rowley, Massachusetts: Newbury House Publishers, 1982. 155 pp.

2391. Lindberg, Lola (ed.). *Super cool! Die frechsten Sprüche für jede Gelegenheit.* München: Knaur Taschenbuch Verlag, 2000. 93 pp. (anti-proverbs).

2392. Linden, Benedikt (ed.). *Kölsche Sprichwörter. Wie die Kölner meinen, was sie sagen.* Illustrations by "Odysseus". Köln: J.P. Bachem, 1984. 158 pp.

2393. Linde-Walther, H.E., and Elias Erasmus. "'Hummel, Hummel!': Niederdeutsche Sprichwörter [Sagwörter]." *Humor um uns! Ein lachendes Hausbuch.* Ed. Emil Escher. Berlin: Paul Franke, 1931. 235-237. With illustrations. (wellerisms).

2394. Lindow, Wolfgang. *Volkstümliches Sprachgut in der neuniederdeutschen Dialektdichtung.* 2 vols. Diss. Universität Kiel, 1960. I, 268 pp.; II, 171 pp. (proverb index).

2395. Lipp, Wolfgang. *Das Glück ist eine dumme Kuh. Fröhliche Spruchweisheit.* Illustrations by Maria Beck. Freiburg: Herder, 1979. 128 pp.

2396. Lipperheide, Franz Freiherr von. *Spruchwörterbuch. Sammlung deutscher und fremder Sinnsprüche, Wahlsprüche, Inschriften an Haus und Gerät, Grabsprüche, Sprichwörter, Aphorismen, Epigramme, von Bibelstellen, Liederanfängen, von Zitaten aus älteren und neueren Klassikern, sowie aus den Werken moderner Schriftsteller, von Schnaderhüpfln, Wetter- und Bauernregeln, Redensarten usw.* Berlin: Haude & Spener, 1907; rpt. Berlin: Haude & Spener, 1969. 1069 pp.

2397. Lippl, Alois Johannes. *Ein Sprichwort im Mund wiegt 100 Pfund. Weisheit des gemeinen Mannes in Sprüchen und Reimen.* Illustrations by Paul Ernst Rattelmüller. München: Süddeutscher Verlag, 1958. 111 pp. Rpt. München: W. Ludwig, 1989. 96 pp.

2398. Lobe, Adolf. *Neue Deutsche Rechtssprichwörter für jedermann aus dem Volke.* Leipzig: Dieterich, 1902. 148 pp.

2399. Loewe, Heinrich. *Deutsch-Englische Phraseologie in systematischer Ordnung.* Berlin: Langenscheidt, 1877. 222 pp. 13th ed. ca. 1910. 196 pp.

2400. Lohrengel, W. *Altes Gold. Deutsche Sprichwörter und Redensarten.* Clausthal: Grosse, 1860. 83 pp.

2401. Lüpkes, Wiard. *Seemannssprüche. Sprichwörter und sprichwörtliche Redensarten über Seewesen, Schiffer- und Fischerleben in den germanischen und romanischen Sprachen.* Berlin: Ernst Siegfried Mittler, 1900; rpt. Leipzig: Zentralantiquariat der DDR, 1987. 192 pp.

2402. Lupson, J.P. *Guide to German Idioms. Sprachführer zu deutschen Idiomen.* Lincolnwood, Illinois: Passport Books, 1984. 118 pp.

2403. Luther, Martin. *Luthers Sprichwörtersammlung. Nach seiner Handschrift zum ersten Male herausgegeben und mit Anmerkungen versehen.* Ed. Ernst Thiele. Weimar: Hermann Böhlau, 1900; rpt. Leipzig: Reprint-Verlag, 1996. 448 pp.

2404. Luther, Martin. *Luthers Sprichwörtersammlung.* Mit zwei Nachbildungen aus der Oxforder Handschrift von Luthers Sprichwörtersammlung. Eds. Ernst Thiele and O. Brenner. *D. Martin Luthers Werke. Kritische Gesamtausgabe.* Weimar: Hermann Böhlau, 1914; rpt. Graz: Akademische Druck- und Verlagsanstalt, 1967. LI, 634-731.

2405. Luther, Martin. *Martin Luthers Sprichwörtersammlung [ca. 1530].* Ed. R. Große. Leipzig: Insel-Bücherei, 1983. 100 pp.

2406. Luther, Martin. *Fabeln und Sprichwörter.* Ed. Reinhard Dithmar. Frankfurt am Main: Insel Verlag, 1989. 248 pp. (Luther's proverb collection on pp. 177-194 and pp. 231-233).

2407. Lux, Günter. *Die Axt im Hause wird selten fett. Ein Smalcalda-Sprich-wort-Bastelbuch.* Illustrations by Ulrich Forchner. Leipzig: Messedruck, 1981. 206 pp. (anti-proverbs).

2408. Lux, Günter. *Morgenstund ist aller Laster Anfang. Sprichwörter zum Selbstbasteln.* Illustrations by Bernd A. Chmura. Berlin: Eulenspiegel Verlag, 1987. Köln: Bund-Verlag, 1987. 256 pp. (anti-proverbs).

2409. Maas, Herbert. *Wou di Hasn Hosn un di Hosn Husn haßn. Ein Nürnberger Wörterbuch.* Illustrations by Toni Burghart. Nürnberg: Verlag Nürnberger Presse, 1962. 111 pp.

2410. Maaß, Winfried (ed.). *Worte der Woche. Die stärksten Sprüche bekannter Zeitgenossen.* Hamburg: Stern-Buch, 1988. 223 pp. With illustrations.

2411. Mackensen, Lutz. *Zitate, Redensarten, Sprichwörter.* Stuttgart: Fackelverlag, 1973. 887 pp.

2412. Madaus, Christian. *Sprichwörter und Redensarten aus Mecklenburg.* Husum: Husum Druck- und Verlagsgesellschaft, 1984. 51 pp.

2413. Maess, Thomas. *Dem Luther aufs Maul geschaut. Kostproben seiner sprachlichen Kunst.* Leipzig: Koehler & Amelang, 1982; rpt. Wiesbaden: Drei Lilien Verlag, 1983. 105 pp. (proverbs, pp. 96-100).

2414. Magg, Wotan Wolfgang. *Augschburg-Moskau: Moskauer-Russische Sprichwörter in Augschburger City-Schwäbisch.* Illustrations by Shitt von Teplitz. Augsburg: Wolfgang Magg, 1991. 72 pp.

2415. Magg, Wotan Wolfgang. *M. Luther jagt Augschburger Sprichwörter. Sentenzen zweisprachig in Lutherdeutsch von 1518 und Augschburger City-Schwäbisch.* Augsburg: Nana Yaa Press, 1998. 93 pp.

2416. Mai, Manfred (ed.). *Dein Glück ist heute gut gelaunt. Schiller-Aphorismen.* Mit humoristischen Zeichnungen von Friedrich Schiller. München: Sanssouci, 2008. 80 pp. With 10 illustrations.

2417. Malberg, Horst. *Bauernregeln: Ihre Deutung aus meteorologischer Sicht.* Berlin: Springer, 1989. 141 pp. With illustrations and maps. (weather proverbs).

2418. Manruhf, Heinrich (ed.). *Mänatschment zum Schmunzeln.* Illustrations by Reinhard Habeck. Wien: Tosa Verlag, 2005. 157 pp. (quotations and anti-proverbs).

2419. Marbach, Gotthard Oswald. *Sprichwörter und Spruchreden der Deutschen.* Illustrations by Ludwig Richter. Leipzig: Otto Wigand, 1847; rpt. Wiesbaden: Ralph Suchier, 1977. 250 pp.

2420. Matzek, Robert. *Schwäbisches à la carte. Sprichwörter, Reime und Texte über Essen und Trinken.* Illustrations by Rudolf Hungreder. Stuttgart: Idee Verlag, 1979. 101 pp. 3rd ed. Stuttgart: Idee Verlag, 1982 109 pp.

2421. Matzek, Robert. *Trink und iß, die Liebe nicht vergiß! Sprichwörter und Reime über Essen und Trinken.* Stuttgart: Idee Verlag, 1982. 109 pp. With illustrations.

2422. Matzinger-Pfister, Regula. *Paarformeln, Synonymik und zweisprachiges Wortpaar. Zur mehrgliedrigen Ausdrucksweise der mittelalterlichen Urkundensprache.* Zürich: Juris Verlag, 1972. 231 pp. (word-pair index, pp. 126-185).

2423. Mauritz, Christina (ed.). *Freche Frauensprüche*. München: Ars Edition, 1999. 108 pp. (miniature book).

2424. McDonald, Julie Jensen, Lynn Hattery-Beyer, Joan Liffring-Zug, and John Zug. *German Proverbs*. Iowa City, Iowa: Penfield Press, 1988. 71 pp. With illustrations.

2425. McKillroy, John (ed.). *Von deutschen Bedürfnissen. Inschriften und Graffiti deutscher Bedürfnisanstalten*. Gräfeling bei München: Wissenschaftliche Verlagsanstalt zur Pflege deutschen Sinngutes, 1969. 76 pp.

2426. Mehring, Margit (ed.). *Zitate und Sprichwörter von A bis Z*. Niedernhausen/Ts.: Bassermann, 1993. 300 pp.

2427. Meier-Pfaller, Hans-Josef. *Das große Buch der Sprichwörter*. Esslingen: Bechtle, 1970. 253 pp. (2nd ed. 1979). 304 pp.

2428. Meisinger, Othmar. *Hinz und Kunz. Deutsche Vornamen in erweiterter Bedeutung*. Dortmund: F. Wilh. Ruhfus, 1924. 97 pp.

2429. Meitsch, Rudolf. *Lorbas, nimm noch e Schlubberche. Sprichwörter, Redensarten und Schwänke aus Ostpreußen*. Illustrations by Hannelore Uhse. Leer: Gerhard Rautenberg, 1989. 157 pp. (proverbs and proverbial expressions, pp. 7-99).

2430. Meitsch, Rudolf. *Ostpreußische Redensarten, Sprichwörter, Schwänke*. Illustrations by Hannelore Uhse. Würzburg: Rautenberg, 2003. 157 pp.

2431. Mejsner, Ernst. *Ein Hundert Drey-undreyßig Gotteslästerliche / gottlose / schändliche und schädliche / auch unanständige / und theils falsche teutsche Sprüch-Wörter*. Eisenberg: Jakob Peter Kückelhahnen, 1705; rpt. Leipzig: Zentralantiquariat der DDR, 1976. 143 pp.

2432. Mellado Blanco, Carmen . *Phraseologismos somáticos del alemán. Un studio léxico-semántico*. Frankfurt am Main: Peter Lang, 2004. 267 pp. (phraseologism index, pp. 207-246).

2433. Menzel, Hans (ed.). *Illustrierte Spruch-Auslese. Leitsprüche, Sprichwörter, Zitate und Aphorismen zu 31 Themen*. Illustrations by Heinrich Kühn. 2 vols. Hinterbrühl bei Wien: Bellaprint-Verlag, 1984. I, 256 pp.; II, 256 pp.

2434. Mertvago, Peter. *Dictionary of 1000 German Proverbs*. New York: Hippocrene Books, 1997. 142 pp.

2435. Meyer, Hans Georg. *Der richtige Berliner in Wörtern und Redensarten*. Berlin: H.S. Hermann, 1878. 46 pp. Rev. edition ed. Walther Kiaulehn. München: Biederstein, 1965. 270 pp.

2436. Michael, Roland (ed.). *Treffend bemerkt. Das Buch der 1000 Aphorismen*. Illustrations by Georg Hornberger. Gütersloh: Heinz Peter, 1983. 126 pp.

2437. Michael, Roland (ed.). *Schönes Wetter heute? Kalendersprüche und Bauernregeln aus fünf Jahrhunderten*. Gütersloh: Heinz Peter, 1987. 127 pp. (weather proverbs).

2438. Mieder, Wolfgang. *Das Sprichwort in der deutschen Prosaliteratur des neunzehnten Jahrhunderts*. München: Wilhelm Fink, 1976. 197 pp. (proverb indices, pp. 28-34, 41-47, 56-67, 80-92, 101-106, 116-128, 141-151, 163-167, 180-187).

2439. Mieder, Wolfgang. *Antisprichwörter*. 3 vols. Wiesbaden: Verlag für deutsche Sprache, 1982 (2nd ed. 1983) and 1985. Wiesbaden: Quelle & Meyer, 1989. I, 235 pp.; II, 222 pp.; III, 215 pp. With illustrations.

2440. Mieder, Wolfgang. *Honig klebt am längsten. Das Anti-Sprichwörter-Buch*. München: Wilhelm Heyne, 1985 (rpt. of W. Mieder's first volume of *Antisprichwörter*. Wiesbaden: Verlag für deutsche Sprache, 1982). 251 pp. With illustrations.

2441. Mieder, Wolfgang. *"Findet, so werdet ihr suchen!" Die Brüder Grimm und das Sprichwort*. Bern: Peter Lang, 1986. 181 pp. (keyword proverb index, pp. 177-181).

2442. Mieder, Wolfgang (ed.). *"Kommt Zeit - kommt Rat!?" Moderne Sprichwortgedichte von Erich Fried bis Ulla Hahn*. Frankfurt am Main: Rita G. Fischer, 1990. 139 pp.

2443. Mieder, Wolfgang (ed.). *"Deutsch reden". Moderne Redensartengedichte von Rose Ausländer bis Yaak Karsunke*. Frankfurt am Main: Rita G. Fischer, 1992. 190 pp.

2444. Mieder, Wolfgang (ed.). *"Hasen im Pfeffer". Sprichwörtliche Kurzprosatexte von Marie Luise Kaschnitz bis Martin Walser*. Frankfurt am Main: Rita G. Fischer Verlag, 1995. 151 pp.

2445. Mieder, Wolfgang. *Ver-kehrte Worte: Antizitate aus Literatur und Medien*. Wiesbaden: Quelle & Meyer, 1997. 356 pp. With illustrations.

2446. Mieder, Wolfgang. *"Der Mensch denkt: Gott lenkt - keine Red davon!" Sprichwörtliche Verfremdungen im Werk Bertolt*

Brechts. Bern: Peter Lang, 1998. 195 pp. (keyword proverb index, pp. 189-195) (anti-proverbs).

2447. Mieder, Wolfgang. *Verdrehte Weisheiten: Antisprichwörter aus Literatur und Medien*. Wiesbaden: Quelle & Meyer, 1998. 407 pp. With illustrations.

2448. Mieder, Wolfgang. *Phrasen verdreschen: Antiredensarten aus Literatur und Medien*. Wiesbaden: Quelle & Meyer, 1999. 407 pp. With illustrations.

2449. Mieder, Wolfgang. *Sprichwörtliche Aphorismen: Von Georg Christoph Lichtenberg bis Elazar Benyoëtz*. Wien: Edition Praesens, 1999. 326 pp. (keyword proverb index, pp. 319-326). (proverbial aphorisms and anti-proverbs).

2450. Mieder, Wolfgang (ed.).*"Geht einmal euren Phrasen nach"*. *Sprachkritische Lyrik und Kurzprosa zur deutschen Vergangenheit*. Burlington, Vermont: The University of Vermont, 2001. 219 pp.

2451. Mieder, Wolfgang (ed.). *"In der Kürze liegt die Würze"*. *Sprichwörtliches und Spruchhaftes als Basis für Aphoristisches*. Burlington, Vermont: The University of Vermont, 2002. 159 pp.

2452. Mieder, Wolfgang (ed.). "200 Sprichwörter von Karl Simrock zum 200. Geburtstag desselben." *Karl Simrock 1802-1876. Einblicke in Leben und Werk*. Ed. Gerhard Reifferscheid et al. Bonn: Karl-Simrock-Forschung, 2002. 84-89.

2453. Mieder, Wolfgang (ed.). *"Der Klügere gibt nicht nach"*: *Sprichwörtliche Aphorismen von Gerhard Uhlenbruck*. Köln: Ralf Reglin, 2003. 212 pp. (aphorisms and anti-proverbs).

2454. Mieder, Wolfgang, (ed.). *"Liebe macht blind"*. *Sprichwörtliche Lyrik und Kurzprosa zum Thema der Liebe*. Burlington, Vermont: The University of Vermont, 2004. 251 pp.

2455. Mieder, Wolfgang (ed.). *"Kein Blatt vor den Mund nehmen"*: *Redensartliche Aphorismen von Gerhard Uhlenbruck*. Köln: Ralf Reglin, 2005. 194 pp. (aphorisms and anti-proverbs).

2456. Mieder, Wolfgang (ed.). *"Auf Herz und Nieren prüfen"*: *Phraseologische Aphorismen von Gerhard Uhlenbruck*. Köln: Ralf Reglin, 2007. 215 pp. (aphorisms and anti-proverbs).

2457. Mieder, Wolfgang. *"Geben Sie Zitatenfreiheit!" Friedrich Schillers gestutzte Worte in Literatur, Medien und Karikaturen*. Wien: Praesens Verlag, 2009. 356 pp. With illustrations. (anti-quotations).

2458. Mieder, Wolfgang. *Wie anders wirkt dies Zitat auf mich ein!" Johann Wolfgang von Goethes entflügelte Worte in Literatur, Medien und Karikaturen.* Wien: Praesens Verlag, 2011. 422 pp. With illustrations. (anti-quotations).

2459. Mieder, Wolfgang, and Andreas Nolte. *"Ich habe den Kopf so voll": Wilhelm Heinse als sprichwortreicher Literat im 18. Jahrhundert.* Bern: Peter Lang, 2006. 333 pp. (proverb index, pp. 95-333).

2460. Miller, Arthur Maximilian. *Schwäbische Sinnsprüche. Volksweisheit für zweiundfünfzig Wochen.* Illustrations by Heinz Schubert. Kempten: Allgäuer Zeitungsverlag, 1973 (2nd ed. 1985). 60 pp.

2461. Molnár, Judit (ed.). *Witzig und gescheit. Aphorismen, Anekdoten und Sprichwörter.* Budapest: Holnap Kiadó, 2003. 119 pp.

2462. Morgen, Christian (ed.). *Zitate und Sprichwörter von A bis Z.* Menden: Detlev Vehling, 1986. 367 pp.

2463. Moriz, Eduard (ed.). *Nimm's leicht, nimm mich! Sponti-Sprüche No. 3.* Frankfurt am Main: Eichborn, 1983. 70 pp. With illustrations. (anti-proverbs).

2464. Moriz, Eduard (ed.). *Ohne Dings kein Bums. Sponti-Sprüche No. 4.* Illustrations by Erich Rauschenbach. Frankfurt am Main: Eichborn, 1984. 68 pp. (anti-proverbs).

2465. Moriz, Eduard (ed.). *Lieber intim als in petto. Sponti-Sprüche No. 5.* Illustrations by Rolf Kutschera. Frankfurt am Main: Eichborn, 1984. 68 pp. (anti-proverbs).

2466. Moriz, Eduard (ed.). *Lieber "Bums" als "Fallera". Sprüche aus der Beziehungskiste.* Illustrations by Erich Rauschenbach. Frankfurt am Main: Eichborn, 1985. 70 pp. (anti-proverbs).

2467. Moriz, Eduard (ed.). *Lieber sauweich als eberhard. Sponti-Sprüche No. 6.* Frankfurt am Main: Eichborn, 1986. 70 pp. With illustrations. (anti-proverbs).

2468. Müller, Klaus (ed.). *Lexikon der Redensarten. 4000 deutsche Redensarten. Ihre Bedeutung und Herkunft.* Gütersloh: Bertelsmann Lexikon Verlag, 1994. 781 pp.

2469. Müller-Hegemann, and Luise Otto. *Das kleine Sprichwörterbuch.* Leipzig: VEB Bibliographisches Institut, 1965. 152 pp. (12th ed. 1983). 164 pp.

2470. Müller-Thurau, Claus Peter. *Laß uns mal 'ne Schnecke angraben. Sprache und Sprüche der Jugendszene.* Düsseldorf: Econ, 1983. 176 pp. (words and phrases, pp. 98-172).

2471. Müller-Thurau, Claus Peter. *Lexikon der Jugendsprache.* Illustrations by Marie Marcks. Düsseldorf,: Econ, 1985. 198 pp.

2472. Nagel, Ulrich. *Bauen ist eine Lust. Sprüche, Gedichte, Lieder und Bräuche vom Bauen.* Illustrations by Klaus-Dieter Steinberg. Berlin: Verlag für Bauwesen, 1987 (2nd ed. 1988). 176 pp.

2473. Neander, Michael. *Ethice vetus et sapiens vetervm latinorvm sapientvm. Tertia Pars: Vetervm sapientvm Germanorum sapientia.* Leipzig: M. Lantzenberger, 1590. 321-351. Rpt. as *Michael Neanders deutsche Sprichwörter.* Ed. Friedrich Latendorf. Schwerin: Bärensprung, 1864. 58 pp.

2474. Nehry, Hans. *Citatenschatz. Geflügelte Worte und andere denkwürdige Aussprüche aus Geschichte und Literatur.* Leipzig: Fr. Wilh. Grunow, 1895. 623 pp.

2475. Nelson, Timothy C. *"O du armer Luther ..." Sprichwörtliches in der antilutherischen Polemik des Johannes Nas (1534-1590).* Diss. Uppsala Universitet, 1990. 305 pp. Bern: Peter Lang, 1992. 334 pp. With illustrations. (proverb index, pp. 206-326).

2476. Neumann, Gisela, and Siegfried Neumann. *Geduld, Vernunft un Hawergrütt. Volksweisheit im Sprichwort.* Illustrations by Werner Schinko. Rostock: Hinstorff, 1971 (3rd ed. 1985). 107 pp.

2477. Neumann, Renate. *Das wilde Schreiben. Graffiti, Sprüche und Zeichen am Rand der Straßen.* Essen: Verlag Die Blaue Eule, 1986. 341 pp. With illustrations. (graffiti and anti-proverbs, pp. 272-333).

2478. Neumann, Siegfried. *Sprichwörtliches aus Mecklenburg: Anekdotensprüche, Antisprichwörter, apologische Sprichwörter, Beispielsprichwörter, erzählende Sprichwörter, Sagte-Sprichwörter, Sagwörter, Schwanksprüche, Wellerismen, Zitatensprichwörter.* Göttingen: Otto Schwartz, 1996. Rpt. as *Mecklenburgs Sprichwortschatz. Beispielsprichwörter, Sagte-Sprichwörter, Schwanksprüche.* Rostock: Ingo Koch, 2005. 469 pp.

2479. Neumann, Siegfried. *Vergnügliches aus Mecklenburg. Spaßige Sprichwörter [Sagwörter].* Illustrations by Armin Münch. Rostock: Ingo Koch, 2006. 72 pp. With illustrations.

2480. Neumann, Siegfried. *Vergnügliches aus Mecklenburg über unsere Tiere*. Aus der Sammlung Richard Wossidlos und aus eigenen Aufzeichnungen. Rostock: Ingo Koch, 2009. 83 pp. (especially wellerisms).

2481. Nieter, Christoph Georg Heinrich. *Erklärung und Berichtigung einiger Sprichwörter*. Halberstadt: J.G. Groß, 1798. 191 pp.

2482. Nissen, Moritz Momme. *Eiderstedter Sprichwörter und Erzählungen aus der Chronik von Eiderstedt*. Ed. Wolfgang Londow. Sankt Peter-Ording: H. Lühr & Dircks, 1976. 78 pp.

2483. Nitsch, Thomas. *Mach nur geene Mährde. Die originellsten sächsischen Sprichwörter*. München: Compact Verlag, 1994. 255 pp. (miniature book).

2484. Nitsche, Franz. *Sammlung erklärter Sprichwörter und sprichwörtlicher Redensarten als Materialien zu Aufsatzübungen und Hausaufgaben*. Leipzig: Dürr, 1879 (2nd ed. 1906). 40 pp.

2485. Nolte, Andreas. *"Mir ist zuweilen so als ob das Herz in mir zerbrach". Leben und Werk Mascha Kalékos im Spiegel ihrer sprichwörtlichen Dichtung*. M.A. Thesis University of Vermont, 2003. 286 pp. Bern: Peter Lang, 2003. 327 pp. (keyword proverb index, pp. 321-327).

2486. Nolte, Andreas. *"Ich bin krank wie ein Hund, arbeite wie ein Pferd, und bin arm wie eine Kirchenmaus". Heinrich Heines sprichwörtliche Sprache. Mit einem vollständigen Register der sprichwörtlichen und redensartlichen Belege im Werk des Autors*. Hildesheim: Georg Olms, 2006. 364 pp. (proverb index, pp. 125-364).

2487. Olschansky, Heike. *Täuschende Wörter. Kleines Lexikon der Volksetymologien*. Stuttgart: Philipp Reclam, 1999. 253 pp.

2488. Osten, Alexander (ed.). *Das große Buch der Redewendungen*. Wien: Tosa, 1997. 424 pp.

2489. Otto, Manfred, and Bernd Bock. *Wenn ich den Appetit verliere, verliere ich den Verstand. 333 Sprichwörter, Aphorismen und Zitate*. Berlin: Verlag Die Wirtschaft, 1988. Frankfurt am Main: Deutscher Fachverlag, 1988. 128 pp.

2490. Pastor, Eilert. *Deutsche Volksweisheit in Wetterregeln und Bauernsprüchen*. Berlin: Deutsche Landbuchhandlung, 1934. 454 pp. (weather proverbs).

2491. Pechau, Jochem. *Sprichwörter. Vierundzwanzig Holz-schnitte.* Köln: Henry Deckner, 1969. No pp. With 24 woodcuts.

2492. Peltzer, Karl. *Das treffende Zitat. Gedankengut aus drei Jahrtausenden und fünf Kontinenten.* Thun: Ott, 1957. 740 pp. (4th ed. 1968). 864 pp.

2493. Petlevannyi, G.P. *400 nemetskikh rifmovannykh poslovits i pogovorok.* Moskva: Vysshaia shkola, 1990. 48 pp.

2494. Petri (Peters), Friedrich. *Der Teutschen Weissheit / Das ist: Außerlesen kurtze / sinnreiche / lehrhaffte vnd sittige Sprüche vnd Sprichwörter in schönen Reimen oder schlecht ohn Reim.* Hamburg: Philipp von Ohr, 1604-1605. Rpt. ed. Wolfgang Mieder. Bern Peter Lang, 1983. 1052 pp. (introduction, pp. 5*-74*).

2495. Petschel, Günter. *Plattdeutsche Sprichwörter aus Nieder-sachsen.* Husum: Husum Druck- und Verlagsgesellschaft, 1986. 80 pp.

2496. Pfauntsch, Michael. "Oberpfälzer Redensarten." *Die Ober-pfalz,* 68 (1980), 174-175 and 210-214.

2497. Pfeffer, J. Alan. *The Proverb in Goethe.* Diss. Columbia University, 1948. New York: Columbia University Press, 1948. 200 pp.

2498. Pfeiffer, Herbert. *Das große Schimpfwörterbuch: Über 10.000 Schimpf-, Spott- und Neckwörter zur Bezeichnung von Per-sonen.* Frankfurt am Main: Eichborn, 1996. 557 pp.

2499. Philippi, Jule (ed.). *Wir müssen den Kindern mehr Deutsch lernen. Weise Worte aus Politik und Gesellschaft.* Reinbek: Rowohlt, 2005. 122 pp. With illustrations. (quotations).

2500. Piirainen, Elisabeth. *Phraseologie der westmünsterländi-schen Mundart.* 2 vols. Vol. 1: *Semantische, kulturelle und pragma-tische Aspekte dialektaler Phraseologismen.* Vol. 2: *Lexikon der westmünsterländischen Redensarten.* Illustrations by Oleg Dobro-vol'skij. Baltmannsweiler: Schneider Verlag Hohengehren, 2000. I, 535 pp.; II, 464 pp. (collection).

2501. Plaut, M. *Deutsches Land und Volk im Volksmund. Eine Sammlung von Sprichwörtern, Sprüchen und Redensarten als Bei-trag zur Kunde des deutschen Landes und Volkes.* Breslau: Ferdi-nand Hirt, 1897. 120 pp.

2502. Pohlke, Annette, and Reinhard Pohlke. *"Alle Wege führen nach Rom": Deutsche Redewendungen aus dem Lateinischen.* Illustrations by Margarete Moos. Düsseldorf: Artemis und Winkler, 2001. 180 pp.

2503. Pohlke, Reinhard. *Das wissen nur die Götter. Deutsche Redensarten aus dem Griechischen.* Illustrations by Honoré Daumier. Düsseldorf: Artemis und Winkler, 2000; rpt. Düsseldorf: Albatros, 2008. 240 pp.

2504. Polt-Heinzl, Evelyne (ed.). *Weisheit für alle Tage.* Stuttgart: Philipp Reclam, 1997. 151 pp.

2505. Polt-Heinzl, Evelyne (ed.). *Gedanken für alle Tage.* Stuttgart: Philipp Reclam, 1999. 133 pp.

2506. Polt-Heinzl, Evelyne (ed.). *Gute Gedanken für alle Tage.* Stuttgart: Philipp Reclam, 2000. 276 pp.

2507. Porter, Mary Gray. *Proverbs and Proverbial Expressions in the German Works of Andreas Gryphius.* M.A. Thesis University of North Carolina at Chapel Hill, 1955. 210 pp. (proverb index, pp. 23-204).

2508. Prahl, August. *Sprichwörter und Redensarten bei Johann Fischart.* M.A. Thesis Washington University at St. Louis, 1928. 90 pp. (proverb index, pp. 10-87).

2509. Prenzel, Eberhard (ed.). *Wetter und Wind ändern sich geschwind. Wettersprüche aus alter Zeit.* Leipzig: VEB Bibliographisches Institut, 1988. 124 pp. (weather proverbs).

2510. Prinz, Friedrich (ed.). *Der Weisheit eine Gasse. Klassische Aphorismen.* München: Deutscher Taschenbuch Verlag, 1989. 169 pp.

2511. Pritchard, Ilka Maria. *"Des Volkes Stimme ist auch eine Stimme". Zur Sprichwörtlichkeit in Carl Zuckmayers Dramen "Der Fröhliche Weinberg", "Der Hauptmann von Köpenick" und "Des Teufels General".* M.A. Thesis University of Vermont, 2001. 156 pp. Burlington, Vermont: The University of Vermont, 2001. 171 pp. (proverb index, pp. 113-157).

2512. Probst, Alfred. *Amideutsch. Ein kritisch-polemisches Wörterbuch der anglodeutschen Sprache.* Frankfurt am Main: Fischer Taschenbuch Verlag, 1989. 176 pp.

2513. Prossliner, Johann. *Das Lexikon der Nietzsche-Zitate.* München: Deutscher Taschenbuch Verlag, 2001. 415 pp.

2514. Prossliner, Johann. *Kleines Lexikon der Schiller-Zitate.* München: Deutscher Taschenbuch Verlag, 2004. 255 pp.

2515. Pruys, Karl Hugo. *Die deutsche Phrasenparade: 99 Allgemeinplätze.* Bonn: Bouvier, 1998. 150 pp.

2516. Puchner, Günter. *Ein Flitterfinkchen mit sieben Zinkchen. Ein Buch mit sieben Siegeln.* München: Heimeran, 1974. 47 pp.

2517. Puchner, Günter. *Sprechen Sie Rotwelsch. 2448 Wörter und Redewendungen der deutschen Gaunersprache.* München: Heimeran, 1975. 62 pp.

2518. Puetzfeld, Carl. *Jetzt schlägt's dreizehn. Tausend Redensarten und ihre Bedeutung.* Berlin: Alfred Metzner, 1937. 142 pp.

2519. Puntsch, Eberhard. *Zitatenhandbuch.* München: Moderne Verlags Gmbh, 1965. 1015 pp. Revised 5th ed. 1971. 1056 pp.

2520. Quadbeck-Seeger, Hans-Jürgen (ed.). *"Der Wechsel allein ist das Beständige". Zitate und Gedanken für innovative Führungskräfte.* Weinheim: Wiley-VCH, 2002. 431 pp. With illustrations.

2521. Quadbeck-Seeger, Hans-Jürgen (ed.). *Ein Wörterbuch paradoxer Weisheiten.* Leipzig: Philipp Reclam, 2004. 177 pp.

2522. Raab, Heinrich. *Deutsche Redewendungen. Von Abblitzen bis Zügel schießen lassen.* Wien: Hippolyt Verlag, 1952. 176 pp. Rpt. Wien: Wancura Verlag, 1964. 160 pp.

2523. Ramage, Craufurd Tait. *Familar Quotations from German and Spanish.* London: George Routledge, 1868. 559 pp.

2524. Raub, Julius. *Plattdeutsche Sprichwörter und Redensarten zwischen Ruhr und Lippe.* Münster: Aschendorff, 1976. 332 pp.

2525. Rauchberger, Karl Heinz (ed.). *"Club-Sprüche". Eingesandt von Hörern der NDR-Jugendsendung "Der Club".* Illustrations by Ulf Harten. 2 vols. Hamburg: Verlag Hanseatische Edition, 1983-1984. I, 86 pp.; II, 84 pp. (anti-proverbs).

2526. Rehbein, Detlev. *Viel Geschrei und wenig Wolle ... Deutsche Sagwörter.* Illustrations by Wolfgang Würfel. Berlin: Eulenspiegel Verlag, 1991. 238 pp. (wellerisms).

2527. Reidel, Marlene (ill.). *Sprichwörter.* Eching bei München: Sellier, 1984. 20 pp. (children's book).

2528. Reiners, Ludwig. *Wer hat das nur gesagt? Zitatenlexikon.* München: Pual List, 1956. 186 pp.

2529. Reiser, Karl. *Sagen, Gebräuche und Sprichwörter des All-gäus.* 2 vols. Kempten: Jos. Kösel, 1895 and 1902. Rpt. Hildesheim: Georg Olms, 1993. I, 567 pp.; II, 764 pp. (proverbs and proverbial expressions, II, 556-682).

2530. Reller, Gisela (ed.). *666 und sex mal Liebe. Auserlesenes.* Illustrations by Egbert Herfurth. Halle: Mitteldeutscher Verlag, 1987. 198 pp. (quotations).

2531. Richey, Werner. *Seefahren ist kein Zuckerlecken. Sprichwör-ter und Redensarten über Seefahrt, Seemann, Schiff und Meer.* Rostock: Hinstorff, 1990. 219 pp.

2532. Richey, Werner, and Michael Strich. *Der Honig ist nicht weit vom Stachel. Sprichwörter. Redensarten, Wetterregeln und Rätsel aus dem Bauernleben.* Leipzig: Koehler & Amelang, 1984. Wiesbaden: VMA-Verlag, 1985. 157 pp. With illustrations.

2533. Richter, Albert. *Deutsche Redensarten. Sprachlich und kul-turgeschichtlich erläutert.* Leipzig: Richard Richter, 1889. 168 pp. 2nd ed. Leipzig: Friedrich Brandstetter, 1893. 190 pp.

2534. Riege Rudolf (ill.). *Plattdeutsche Sprichwörter in Holz-schnitten.* Wolffenbüttel: Georg Kallmeyer, 1942. 46 pp.

2535. Riffl, Karoline. *Gestickte Sprüche aus alter Zeit. Duftig zart und blütenweiß.* Graz: Stocker, 2004. 142 pp. With illustrations.

2536. Risse, Anna. "Sprichwörter und Redensarten bei Thomas Murner." *Zeitschrift für deutschen Unterricht,* 31 (1917), 215-227, 289-303, 359-369 and 450-458.

2537. Rittendorf, Michael, Jochen Schäfer, and Heipe Weiss. *An-gesagt: Scene-Deutsch. Ein Wörterbuch.* Illustrations by Chlodwig Poth. Frankfurt am Main: Extrabuch-Verlag, 1983. 69 pp.

2538. Roche, Reinhard. "Demosprüche und Wandgesprühtes." *Muttersprache,* 93 (1983), 181-196 (graffiti and anti-proverbs).

2539. Roderich, Albert (ed.). *Gedankensplitter. Gesammelt aus den "Fliegenden Blättern".* München: Braun & Schneider, ca. 1885. 296 pp. ("Glossierte Sprichwörter", pp. 281-26).

2540. Röhl, Klaus Rainer. *Deutsches Phrasenlexikon. Lehrbuch der politischen Korrektheit für Anfänger und Fortgeschrittene.* Frank-furt am Main: Ullstein, 1995. 232 pp. Rpt. as *Deutsches Phrasenle-xikon: Politisch korrekt von A-Z.* München: Universitas Verlag, 2000. 238 pp.

2541. Röhrich, Lutz. *Gebärde – Metapher – Parodie. Studien zur Sprache und Volksdichtung.* Düsseldorf: Pädagogischer Verlag Schwann, 1967. 238 pp. Rpt. ed. Wolfgang Mieder. Burlington, Vermont: The University of Vermont, 2006. 246 pp. With illustrations. (proverbs, anti-proverbs, and quotations, pp. 173-214).

2542. Röhrich, Lutz. *Lexikon der sprichwörtlichen Redensarten.* 2 vols. Freiburg: Herder, 1973 (5th ed. 1978). Also published in four paperbacks, Freiburg: Herder, 1977 (3rd ed. 1982). 1256 pp. With 600 illustrations.

2543. Röhrich, Lutz. *Das große Lexikon der sprichwörtlichen Redensarten.* 3 vols. Freiburg: Herder, 1991-1992; rpt. Darmstadt: Wissenschaftliche Buchgesellschaft, 2001. Also published in five paperbacks, Freiburg: Herder, 1994. As CD-ROM: München: Rossipaul, 1996; later also in the "Digitale Bibliothek", vol. 42. Berlin: Directmedia, 2001. 1910 pp. With 1044 illustrations.

2544. Rölleke, Heinz, and Lothar Bluhm (eds.). *"Redensarten des Volks, auf die ich immer horche". Das Sprichwort in den "Kinder- und Hausmärchen" der Brüder Grimm.* Bern: Peter Lang, 1988. 227 pp. (proverb keyword index, pp. 215-227).

2545. Roman, Christian (ed.). *Lieber 'ne Sechs, als überhaupt keine persönliche Note. Schüler-Sprüche No. 1.* Illustrations by Johannes Hickel. Frankfurt am Main: Eichborn, 1984. 70 pp. (anti-proverbs).

2546. Roman, Christian (ed.). *Reden ist Silber, Schweigen ist fünf. Schüler-Sprüche No. 2.* Frankfurt am Main: Eichborn, 1985. 70 pp. With illustrations. (anti-proverbs).

2547. Roman, Christian (ed.). *Big Mäc is Watching You! Schüler-Sprüche No. 3.* Illustrations by Erich Rauschenbach. Frankfurt am Main: Eichborn, 1986. 70 pp. (anti-proverbs).

2548. Ronner, Markus M. *Der treffende Geistesblitz. 10.000 Aphorismen, Pointen und Bonmots des 20. Jahrhunderts.* Thun: Ott Verlag, 1990. 359 pp.

2549. Ronner, Markus M. *Zitate zu Lesen und Schreiben. Pointen von Zeitgenossen.* Illustrations by Ivan Steiger. Bern: Zytglogge, 1990. 95 pp.

2550. Rosen, Heinrich. *Die sprichwörtlichen Redensarten in den Werken von Hans Sachs, nach Entstehung, Bildung, Bedeutung, Vorkommen untersucht und sachlich geordnet.* Diss. Universität Bonn, 1922. 105 pp.

2551. Rosié, Paul. *Geprügelte Worte*. Berlin: Eulenspiegel Verlag, 1958. 107 pp. With illustrations. (anti-quotations).

2552. Rössing, Roger. *Russisches Roulette und schwedische Gardinen: Neue unbekannte Geschichten zu bekannten Begriffen*. Illustrations by Lothar Otto. Frechen: Komet, 2001. 208 pp.

2553. Rother, Karl. *Die schlesischen Sprichwörter und Redensarten*. Breslau: Ostdeutsche Verlagsanstalt, 1928; rpt. Darmstadt: Bläschke & Brentano, 1969; rpt. Osnabrück: Reinhard Kuballe, 1984. 476 pp.

2554. Rottgardt, Hans-Heinrich. *Läver'n Dickkopp as'n Dööskopp. Niederdeutsche Redewendungen aufgeschlüsselt*. Illustrations by Gert Köppe. Neumünster: Karl Wachholtz, 1976. 104 pp.

2555. Rottmann, Johannes. *Plattdeutsche Sprichwörter und Redensarten aus Kirchhellen*. Gelsenkirchen-Buer: Heisterkamp, 1978. 91 pp.

2556. Ruelius, Hermann. *Auf der Palme. Bilder in der Sprache*. Illustrations by Fritz Fischer. Frankfurt am Main: Linotype, 1961. 42 pp.

2557. Rühmkorf, Peter. *Über das Volksvermögen. Exkurse in den literarischen Untergrund*. Reinbek: Rowohlt, 1967. 189 pp.

2558. Sailer, Johann Michael. *Die Weisheit auf der Gasse oder Sinn und Geist deutscher Sprichwörter*. Augsburg: Martin Veith und Michael Rieger, 1810. 404 pp.; rpt. Nördlingen: Franz Greno, 1987. 336 pp.; rpt. Frankfurt am Main: Eichborn Verlag, 1996. 357 pp.

2559. Sailer, Johann Michael. *Die Weisheit auf der Gasse. Deutsche Sprichwörter*. Ed. Dieter Narr. Wiesbaden: Insel, 1959. 54 pp. (selection).

2560. Sanders, Daniel. *Citatenlexikon. Sammlung von Citaten, Sprichwörtern, sprichwörtlichen Redensarten und Sentenzen*. Leipzig: J.J. Weber, 1899. 712 pp.

2561. Sandtner, Hilda. *Schwäbische Sprüch'*. Illustrations by Hilda Sandtner. Rosenheim: Alfred Förg, 1981. 287 pp.

2562. Sandvoss, Franz. *Sp spricht das Volk. Volksthümliche Redensarten und Sprichwörter*. Berlin: E. Schotte, 1860 (2nd ed. 1861). 70 pp.

2563. Sandvoss, Franz. *Sprichwörterlese aus Burkhard Waldis mit einem Anhange*. Friedland: Th. A. Richter, 1866. 160 pp.

2564. Sandvoss, Franz. *Gute alte deutsche Sprüche. Ausglesen und erläutert für Schule und Haus*. Berlin: Georg Stilke, 1897. 156 pp.

2565. Sattler, Johann Rudolph. *Teutsche Orthographey und Phraseologey*. Basel: Ludwig Könige, 1617; rpt. Hildesheim: Georg Olms, 1975. 583 pp.

2566. Schaeffler, Julius. *Der lachende Volksmund. Scherz und Humor in unseren Sprichwörtern, Wörtern und Redensarten*. Berlin: Ferd. Dümmlers Verlag, 1931. 166 pp.

2567. Schaible, Karl Heinrich. *Deutsche Stich- und Hieb-Worte. Eine Abhandlung über deutsche Schelt-, Spott- und Schimpfwörter, altdeutsche Verfluchungen und Flüche*. Strassburg: Karl J. Trübner, 1879 (2nd ed., 1885). 91 pp.

2568. Schambach, Georg. *Die plattdeutschen Sprichwörter der Fürstentümer Göttingen und Grubenhagen*. Göttingen: Vandenhoeck & Ruprecht, 1851; rpt. Hannover-Döhren: Harro von Hirschheydt, 1974. 91 pp.

2569. Schattenhofer, Monika (ed.). *Dieser dicke Strich erinnert Dich an mich. Sprüche aus dem Poesiealbum*. München: Knaur Taschenbuch Verlag, 1986. 122 pp. With illustrations.

2570. Schaufelbüel, Adolf. *Treffende Redensarten, viersprachig. 2000 Redewendungen und 500 Sprichwörter nach deutschen Stichwörtern alphabetisch geordnet; mit ihren Entsprechungen im Französischen, Italienischen und Englischen*. Thun: Ott Verlag, 1986 (2nd ed. 1987). 301 pp.

2571. Scheffel, Fritz. *Der gepfefferte Spruchbeutel. Alte deutsche Spruchweisheit*. Illustrations by Paul Neu. Erfurt: Richters, 1941; rpt. München: Alexander Duncker, 1951. 160 pp.

2572. Scheffler, Heinrich. *Wörter auf Wanderschaft. Schicksale von Wörtern und Redensarten*. Pfullingen: Günther Neske, 1986 (2nd 1987). 350 pp.

2573. Schellhorn, Andreas. *Teutsche Sprichwörter, sprichwörtliche Redensarten und Denksprüche gesammelt, in Ordnung gebracht, und mit den nöthigsten Erklärungen begleitet. Nebst einem Anhange von Sprichwörtern und Denksprüchen in lateinischen Versen für Studierte und Studierende*. Nürnberg: Steinische Buchhandlung, 1797. Rpt. ed. Wolfgang Mieder. Hildesheim: Georg Olms, 2008. 160 pp. and 56 pp. (introduction, pp. 5*-36*).

2574. Schemann, Hans. *Synonymwörterbuch der deutschen Redensarten.* Straelen: Straelener Manuskripte Verlag, 1989. 428 pp.

2575. Schemann, Hans. *Deutsche Idiomatik. Die deutschen Redewendungen im Kontext.* Stuttgart: Ernst Klett, 1993. 1037 pp.

2576. Schemann, Hans. *Deutsche Redensarten.* Stuttgart: Ernst Klett, 2000. 311 pp.

2577. Schemann, Hans, and Paul Knight. *Idiomatik Deutsch-Englisch. German-English Dictionary of Idioms.* Stuttgart: Ernst Klett, 1995. 1253 pp.

2578. Schemann, Hans, and Paul Knight. *Ergänzungsband Englisch-Deutsch zur Idiomatik Deutsch-Englisch.* Stuttgart: Ernst Klett, 1997. 555 pp.

2579. Scherer, Burkhard, Udo P. Schewietzek, and Helmut Schmid (eds.). *Ein guter Spruch zur rechten Zeit. Demosprüche von den Sechzigern bis heute.* Gießen: Focus-Verlag, 1981. 128 pp. With illustrations. (anti-proverbs).

2580. Schindler, Eva. *Großmutters Weisheiten.* München: Ars-Edition, 2008. 232 pp. With illustrations.

2581. Schlesinger, Saskia (ed.). *Mach dir einen schönen Lenz und schwänz. Schülersprüche – Schülerwitze.* München: Wilhelm Heyne, 1987. 123 pp. With illustrations.

2582. Schlie, Tania, Hubertus Rabe, and Johannes Thiele (eds.). *Die allerschönsten Geistesblitze. Die witzigsten Zitate und Sprüche der Welt.* Berlin: Ullstein, 2005. 720 pp.

2583. Schlüter, Christiane. *"Da liegt der Hase im Pfeffer". Redewendungen und ihre Herkunft.* Bindlach: Gondrom, 2005. 160 pp.

2584. Schmid, Angela (ed.). *"Der kluge Mann baut vor". Die bekanntesten Schiller-Zitate.* München: Compact-Verlag, 2005. 255 pp. (miniature book).

2585. Schmidkunz, Walter. *Nahrhafte Sprüche.* München: Münchener Buchverlag, 1942. 15 pp.

2586. Schmidkunz, Walter. *Waschechte Weisheiten. Bairisch-bäurische Sprichwörter und Redensarten – 700 Stück.* Illustrations by Paul Neu. Rosenheim: Alfred Förg, 1977. 143 pp.

2587. Schmidt, Lothar. *Aphorismen von A-Z. Das große Handbuch geflügelter Definitionen.* München: Moderne Verlags GmbH, 1971. 6th ed. Wiesbaden: Drei-Lilien-Verlag, 1985. 620 pp.

2588. Schmidt, Lothar. *Das treffende Zitat zu Politik, Recht und Wirtschaft*. Thun: Ott Verlag, 1984. 385 pp.

2589. Schmidt, Lothar, and Peter Feistel (eds.). *Gewinn. Zitate und Aphorismen*. Königstein/Ts. Königsteiner Wirtschaftsverlag, 1992. 79 pp.

2590. Schmidt, Lothar, and Peter Feistel (eds.). *Kommunikation. Zitate und Aphorismen*. Königstein/Ts.: Königsteiner Wirtschaftsverlag, 1992. 79 pp.

2591. Schmidt, Lothar, and Peter Feistel (eds.). *Geld. Zitate und Aphorismen*. Königstein/Ts. Königsteiner Wirtschaftsverlag, 1993. 79 pp.

2592. Schmidt, Lothar, and Peter Feistel (eds.). *Sekretärin. Zitate und Aphorismen*. Illustrations by Fritz Wolf. Königstein/Ts.: Königsteiner Wirtschaftsverlag, 1993. 79 pp.

2593. Schmidt, Lothar, and Peter Feistel (eds.). *Zeit und Management. Zitate und Aphorismen*. Königstein/Ts.: Königsteiner Wirtschaftsverlag, 1993. 79 pp.

2594. Schmidt, Rudolf. *Tierisches in unserer Muttersprache*. Illustrations by Maria Reiner-Richter. Gerabronn-Crailsheim: Hohenloher Druck- und Verlagshaus, 1972. 135 pp.

2595. Schmidt, Rudolf. *Der Mensch im Spiegel der deutschen Sprache*. Illustrations by Maria Reiner-Richter. Gerabronn-Crailsheim: Hohenloher Druck- und Verlagshaus, 1974. 236 pp.

2596. Schmidt-Wiegand, Ruth, and Ulrike Schowe (eds.). *Deutsche Rechtsregeln und Rechtssprichwörter. Ein Lexikon*. München: C.H. Beck, 1996. 402 pp.

2597. Schmitt, Christa. *Die Katze in Sprichwort und Redensart*. Photographs by Gertrud Glasow. Aarau, Schweiz: AT Verlag, 1988. 96 pp.

2598. Schmitt, Richard. *Deutsche Redensarten. Quiz- und Übungsbuch*. Stuttgart: Ernst Klett, 1975. 97 pp.

2599. Schmitt, Walter (ed.). *Aphorismen, Sentenzen und anderes – nicht nur für Mediziner*. Leipzig: J.A. Barth, 1980 (3rd ed. 1985). 139 pp.

2600. Schmitt-Menzel, Isolde. *Viele Mäuse sind der Katze Not*. München: Wilhelm Heyne, 1991. 121 pp. (miniature book). (antiproverbs).

2601. Schmitz, Franz. "Redensarten und Sprichwörter." In F. Schmitz, *Wie mir schwätze. Das Neuwieder Mundart-Wörterbuch.* Neuwied: Peter Kehrein, 1993. 18-39.

2602. Schmude, Albert A. (ed.). *Freiheit für Grönland / weg mit dem Packeis! 200 Sprüche von den Wänden der Frankfurter Universität.* Frankfurt am Main: Rita G. Fischer, 1982. 70 pp. With illustrations. (graffiti).

2603. Schneider, Elke (ed.). *Verse und Sprichwörter für Poesiealbum und Gästebuch.* Köln: Buch und Zeit Verlagsgesellschaft, 1987. 191 pp. With illustrations.

2604. Schoeps, Hans-Joachim. *Ungeflügelte Worte. Was nicht im Büchmann stehen kann.* Berlin: Haude & Spener, 1971. 277 pp. Revised ed. Julius H. Schoeps. Sachsenheim: Burg Verlag, 1990; rpt. Hildesheim: Georg Olms, 2005. 335 pp.

2605. Scholze-Stubenrecht, Werner (ed.). *Duden: Zitate und Aussprüche. Herkunft und aktueller Gebrauch.* Mannheim: Dudenverlag, 1993. 827 pp.

2606. Schomburg, Eberhard. *176 gebräuchliche Redensarten und ihre Bedeutung (Zuordnungsrätsel).* Kassel: Verlag Schule und Elternhaus, 1979. 24 pp.

2607. Schön, Marion. *Deutsch: Sprichwörter und Redewendungen.* München: Compact Verlag, 1995. 446 pp.

2608. Schönwerth, Franz Xaver von. *Sprichwörter des Volkes der Oberpfalz in der Mundart.* Stadtamhof: Joseph Mayr, 1873. 136 pp.

2609. Schottelius, Justus Georg. "Von den Teutschen Sprichwörteren Und anderen Teutschen Sprichwortlichen Redarten." In J.G. Schottelius. *Ausführliche Arbeit Von der Teutschen HaubtSprache.* Braunschweig: Chrstoff Friedrich Zilligern, 1663. Rpt. ed. Wolfgang Hecht. Tübingen: Max Niemeyer, 1967. 1099-1147.

2610. Schrader, Herman. *Der Bilderschmuck der deutschen Sprache in Tausenden volkstümlicher Redensarten. Nach Ursprung und Bedeutung erklärt.* Berlin: H. Dolfuβ, 1886. 379 pp. 7th ed. Berlin: Emil Felber, 1912. Rpt. ed. Wolfgang Mieder. Hildesheim: Georg Olms, 2005. 543 pp. (introduction, pp. I*-XXVI*).

2611. Schrader, Herman. *Das Trinken in mehr als fünfhundert Gleichnissen und Redensarten. Eine sprachwissenschaftliche Untersuchung aus der Methyologie.* Berlin: Hans Lüstenöder, 1890. 111 pp.

2612. Schrader, Herman. *Aus dem Wundergarten der deutschen Sprache*. Weimar: Emil Felber, 1896. 288 pp.

2613. Schrader, Herman. *Scherz und Ernst in der Sprache*. Weimar: Emil Felber, 1897. 162 pp.

2614. Schranka, Eduard Maria. *Ein Buch vom Bier. Cerevisiologische Studien und Skizzen*. Frankfurt an der Oder: B. Waldmann, 1886. 591 pp. (proverbs on pp. 347-359).

2615. Schulte-Kemminghausen, Karl. "Über eine ungedruckte westfälische Sprichwörtersammlung aus dem vorigen Jahrhundert (A.F.C. Honcamp)." *Zeitschrift des Vereins für rheinische und westfälische Volkskunde*, 25 (1928), 190-192; and 26 (1929), 67-71.

2616. Schulte-Mattenklotz, Hildegard (ed.). *Wat me seo seggt. Sprichwörter*. Illustrations by Ernst Höning. Störmede: Traditionsverein Störmede, 2006. 56 pp.

2617. Schulz, Marianne. *Der frühe Vogel fängt den Wurm oder Pfade des Sinnens. Redewendungen mit Erklärungen, Begriffe verschiedener Arten, Sprüche und mehr*. Leipzig: Engelsdorfer Verlag, 2007. 80 pp.

2618. Schulze, Carl. "Die sprichwörtlichen Formeln der deutschen Sprache." *Archiv für das Studium der neueren Sprachen und Literaturen*, 48 (1871), 435-450; 49 (1872), 139-162; 50 (1873) 83-122; 51 (1874), 195-212; 52 (1874), 61-80 and 375-392; 54 (1875), 55-74 and 303-316.

2619. Schulze, Carl. "Deutsche Spruchweisheit auf Münzen, Medaillen und Marken." *Archiv für das Studium der neueren Sprachen und Literaturen*, 56 (1876), 59-90; 57 (1877), 17-40; and 58 (1877-1878), 321-344.

2620. Schulze, Carl. "Spruchbuch der jungen Pfalzgräfin Anna Sophia, nachherigen Aebtissin von Quedlinburg, vom Jahre 1630." *Archiv für das Studium der neueren Sprachen und Literaturen*, 59 (1878), 318-338.

2621. Schulze, Günter. *Pfeffernüsse aus den Werken von Doktor Martin Luther*. Berlin: Volk und Wissen Verlag, 1982. 110 pp. (proverbs pp. 85-96).

2622. Schuster, Friedrich Wilhelm. "Siebenbürgisch-sächsische Sprichwörter, Rätsel und Kinderreime." In F.W. Schuster. *Aus meinem Leben. Erinnerungen, Gedichte, Übersetzungen. Aus der*

Volksdichtung der Siebenbürger Sachsen. Ed. Horst S. Anger. Bukarest: Kriterion Verlag, 1981. 225-239 (p. 298 notes).

2623. Schuster, Theo. *In Aurich ist es schaurig ... Ortsneckereien und Verwandtes aus Ostfriesland und umto.* Illustrations by Holger Fischer. Leer: Schuster, 2004. 152 pp.

2624. Schuster, Theo. *Anscheten, Herr Pastor! Sprichwörtliches [Sagwörter] zwischen Ems und Weser.*Illustrations by Holger Fischer. Leer: Schuster, 2005. 165 pp. (wellerisms).

2625. Schuster, Theo. *Ostfriesische Vornamen nebst Redensarten, Neckreimen und Schimpfnamen zwischen Ems und Weser.* Illustrations by Holger Fischer. Leer: Schuster, 2006. 123 pp.

2626. Schütze, Johann Friedrich. "Apologische Sprüchwörter der niedersächisch-holsteinischen Volkssprache." *Neuer Teutscher Merkur*, 3 (Oktober 1800), 112-115. (wellerisms).

2627. Schwab, Julius. *Rassenpflege im Sprichwort. Eine volkstümliche Sammlung.* Leipzig: Alwin Fröhlich, 1937. 64 pp. (anti-Semitic collection).

2628. Schweitzer, Charles. "Sprichwörter und sprichwörtliche Redensarten bei Hans Sachs." *Hans Sachs Forschungen. Festschrift.* Ed. Arthur Ludwig Stiefel. Nürnberg: Rau, 1894. 353-381.

2629. Schweizer, Blanche-Marie. *Sprachspiel mit Idiomen. Eine Untersuchung am Prosawerk von Günter Grass.* Diss. Universität Zürich, 1978. Zürich: Juris, 1978. 141 pp. (list of idioms, pp. 125-134).

2630. Seibig, Adolf. *Gellhäuser Deutsch. Eine Sammlung mundartlicher Ausdrücke, Beispielsätze, Redewendungen, Ausrufe und Sprichwörter.* Gelnhausen: Jakob Kurle, 1977. 540 pp.

2631. Seidensticker, Bernd, and Antje Wessels (eds.). *Mythos Sisyphos. Texte von Homer bis Günter Kunert.* Leipzig: Reclam Verlag, 2001. 286 pp.

2632. Seidl, Helmut A. *Medizinische Sprichwörter im Englischen und Deutschen. Eine diachrone Untersuchung zur vergleichenden Parömiologie.* Frankfurt am Main: Peter Lang, 1982. 406 pp.

2633. Seidl, Helmut A. *Medizinische Sprichwörter. Das große Lexikon deutscher Gesundheitsregeln.* Norderstedt: Books on Demand, 2008; rpt. Darmstadt: Wissenschaftliche Buchgesellschaft, 2010. 518 pp.

2634. Selk, Paul. *Sprichwörter und Redensarten aus Schleswig-Holstein*. Husum: Husum Druck- und Verlagsgesellschaft, 1980. 111 pp.

2635. Sick, Bastian. *"Zu wahr, um schön zu sein": Verdrehte Sprichwörter. 16 Postkarten*. Köln: Kiepenheuer & Witsch, 2008. (16 postcards with anti-proverbs).

2636. Siebenkees, Johann Christian. *Deutsche Sprichwörter mit Erläuterungen*. Nürnberg: Bauer und Mann, 1790. Rpt. ed. Wolfgang Mieder. Hildesheim: Georg Olms, 2011. 135 pp. (introduction, pp. 5*– 69*).

2637. Sillner, Leo. *Gewußt woher. Ursprungshandbuch deutschsprachiger Wörter und Redensarten*. Frankfurt am Main: Societäts-Verlag, 1973. 371 pp.

2638. Simon, Irmgard (ed.). *Sagwörter. Plattdeutsche Sprichwörter aus Westfalen*. Münster: Aschendorff, 1988. 240 pp. (wellerisms).

2639. Simrock, Karl. *Die deutschen Sprichwörter*. Frankfurt am Main: H.L. Brönner, 1846. 591 pp. Rpt. ed. Hermann Bausinger. Dortumnd: Die bibliophilen Taschenbücher, 1978 (postscript, pp. 1-10).

2640. Simrock, Karl. *Die deutschen Sprichwörter*. Frankfurt am Main: H.L. Brönner, 1846. 591 pp. Rpt. ed. Wolfgang Mieder. Stuttgart: Philipp Reclam, 1988; rpt. Düsseldorf: Albatros, 2003. 631 pp. (introduction pp. 7-19).

2641. Simrock, Karl. *Die deutschen Sprichwörter*. Basel: Benno Schwabe, 1892; rpt. Hildesheim: Georg Olms, 1974. 677 pp.

2642. Simrock, Karl. *Deutsche Sprichwörter mit mehr als 100 Illustrationen*. Anonyme Neuauflage. Eltville am Rhein: Bechtermünz, 1988. 403 pp. With illustrations.

2643. Skupy, Hans-Horst (ed.). *Das große Handbuch der Zitate. 25.000 treffende Aussprüche und Sprichwörter von A-Z*. Gütersloh: Bertelsmann Lexikon Verlag, 1993. 1136 pp.

2644. Sochatzy, Klaus (ed.). *Mehr Anarchie, weniger Chaos. Sprüche aus dem Frankfurter Uni-Turm. Graffiti als Ausdruck studentischen Bewußtseins*. Frankfurt am Main: Rita G. Fischer, 1982. 92 pp.

2645. Sochatzy, Klaus (ed.). *Auf die Dauer hilft nur Power. Sprüche aus dem Frankfurter Uni-Turm. Graffiti als Ausdruck studen-*

tischen Bewußtseins. Frankfurt am Main: Rita G. Fischer, 1983. 95 pp. With illustrations.

2646. Söhns, Franz. "Erweiterungen und Ergänzungen zu [Borchardts und] Wustmanns *Sprichwörtlichen Redensarten* [1895]." *Zeitschrift für den deutschen Unterricht*, 21 (1907), 483-499, 564-574, 635-649, and 692-700.

2647. Soler i Marcet, Maria-Lourdes. *Locuciones idiomáticas en [Thomas Mann's] "Buddenbrooks"*. Diss. Universidad de Barcelona, 1969. XXXVIII pp. and 632 pp. (phrase index, pp. 50-613).

2648. Spalding, Keith. *Bunte Bilderwelt: Phraseologische Streifzüge durch die deutsche Sprache*. Tübingen: Gunter Narr, 1996. 119 pp.

2649. Spalding, Keith, and Kenneth Brooke. *An Historical Dictionary of German Figurative Usage*. 6 vols. (60 fasc.). Oxford: Blackwell, 1952-2000. 2862 pp.

2650. Spicker, Friedemann (ed.). *Es lebt der Mensch, solang er irrt. Deutsche Aphorismen*. Stuttgart: Philipp Reclam, 2010. 331 pp.

2651. Spörl, Gerhard (ed.). *Nagel' mal 'nen Pudding an die Wand. Eine Auswahl aus den "Worten der Woche" aus der Wochenzeitung "Die Zeit"*. Frankfurt am Main: Rita G. Fischer, 1983. 110 pp. (quotations).

2652. Stambaugh, Ria. *Proverbs and Proverbial Phrases in the Jestbooks of [Michael] Lindener, [Martin] Montanus and [Valentin] Schumann*. Diss. University of North Carolina, 1963. 381 pp. (proverb index, pp. 43-367).

2653. Stauffer, Charles. *"... wie eim de Schnawel gewachse isch". Sprichwörter und Redensarten aus dem Elsass*. Illustrations by E.H. Cordier. Schirmeck: Salde, 1986. 114 pp.

2654. Stechow, Walter. *Sprichwörter, Redensarten und moralische Betrachtungen in den Werken Konrads von Würzburg*. Diss. Universität Greifswald, 1921. 117 pp. (proverb index, pp. 17-105).

2655. Steiger, Karl. *Pretiosen deutscher Sprichwörter mit Variationen*. St. Gallen: Scheitlin und Zollikofer, 1843. 490 pp.

2656. Stein, Ingo. *Das kleine Buch für große Sprücheklopfer*. Illustrations by Klaus Oliv. Oldenburg: Lappan, 2007. 55 pp. (anti-proverbs).

2657. Steinmeyer, Beate (ed.). *Wer seine Hände in den Schoß legt, muß deshalb nicht untätig sein. Die neuesten Bürosprüche.* Illustrations by Ernst Hürlimann. München: Wilhelm Heyne, 1989. 120 pp. (anti-proverbs).

2658. Stöber, August. "Sprichwörter und sprichwörtliche Redensarten aus Johann Michael Moscherosch's Schriften." *Alsatia*, no volume given (1868-1872), 319-338.

2659. Stöber, August. "Sprichwörter und sprichwörtliche Redensarten aus Johann Pauli's *Schimpf und Ernst.*" *Alsatia*, no volume given (1873-1874), 83-96.

2660. Stoltze, Friedrich. *Frankfurt in seinen Sprichwörtern und Redensarten.* Frankfurt am Main: August Hase, 1939; rpt. Frankfurt am Main: Wolfgang Weidlich, 1980. 101 pp.

2661. Straubinger, Otto Paul. *Given Names in German Proverbs.* Diss. University of California at Los Angeles, 1946. 360 pp.

2662. Strich, Christian (ed.). *Das große Diogenes Lebenshilfe-Buch. 333 handfeste alte Tips.* Zürich: Diogenes, 1979. 179 pp. (miniature book).

2663. Strich, Michael, and Werner Richey. *Berufe im Sprichwort.* Illustrations by Jost Amman. Leipzig: VEB Bibliographisches Institut, 1983. 134 pp.

2664. Strutz, Henry. *2001 German and English Idioms / 2001 Deutsche und englische Redewendungen.* Hauppauge, New York: Barron's Educational Series, 1995. 519 pp.

2665. Strutz, Henry. *German Idioms.* Hauppauge, New York: Barron's Educational Series, 1996. 326 pp.

2666. Susan, S. *Sammlung Wörter, Sprichwörter und Redensarten. Mit besonderer Rücksicht auf die ähnlichen Wortlaute, die Rection und die Eigenheiten der deutschen und niederländischen Sprache.* Groningen: Noordhoff & Smit, 1879. 90 pp.

2667. Tange, Ernst Günter (ed.). *Wörterbuch für Querdenker. Boshafte Definitionen.* Frankfurt am Main: Eichborn, 1987. 124 pp. With illustrations. (quotations).

2668. Tange, Ernst Günter (ed.). *Sag's mit Biß. Das Wörterbuch der boshaften Definitionen.* Illustrations by Peter Gaymann. Frankfurt am Main: Eichborn, 1985. 128 pp. (quotations).

2669. Tange, Ernst Günter (ed.). *Funk-Sprüche. Geistesblitze zum Thema Fernsehen.* Illustrations by Jürgen von Tomei. Frankfurt am Main: Eichborn, 1988. 119 pp. (quotations).

2670. Tange, Günter Ernst (ed.). *Die Klugheit ist weiblich. Zitatenschatz von Frauen für Frauen.* Illustrations by Wenzel Kofron. Frankfurt am Main: Eichborn, 1993. 64 pp.

2671. Tange, Ernst Günter. *Lexikon der boshaften Zitate. Bissige Definitionen, treffende Bonmots und charmante Gemeinheiten.* Frankfurt am Main: Eichborn, 1997. 588 pp.

2672. Tange, Ernst Günter. *Zitatenschatz für Lebenskünstler.* Frankfurt am Main: Eichborn, 2000. 95 pp.

2673. Tard, Françoise. *Expressions et locutions allemandes. Exemples, emplois, traductions.* Paris: Bordas, 1994. 128 pp.

2674. Taylor, Ronald, and Walter Gottschalk. *A German-English Dictionary of Idioms. Idiomatic and Figurative German Expressions with English Translations.* München: Max Hueber, 1960 (4th ed. 1973). 598 pp.

2675. Teichmann, Jo. *Was hat das Schwein mit Glück zu tun? Tierische Redewendungen von aalglatt bis wieselflink.* Illustrations by Oliver Sebel. Frankfurt am Main: Eichborn, 1994. 95 pp.

2676. Tenzler, Gisela (ed.). *Katzen-, Hund- und Pferde-Sprüch.* Illustrations by Albrecht von Bodecker. Berlin: Buchverlag Der Morgen, 1987 (2nd ed. 1988). 122 pp.

2677. Tenzler, Wolfgang (ed.). *Liebes-, Lust- und Leibs-, Manns- und Weibs-Sprüch.* Berlin: Buchverlag Der Morgen, 1983. 111 pp. With illustrations.

2678. Tenzler, Wolfgang (ed.). *Eß- und Trink-, Rauch- und Medizin-Sprüch.* Berlin: Buchverlag Der Morgen, 1987. Köln: Bund-Verlag, 1987. 122 pp. With illustrations.

2679. Thomsen, Bernd (ed.). *Haste was, pisste was. Klo-Sprüche.* Illustrations by Erik Liebermann. München: Wilhelm Heyne, 1985. 120 pp. (graffiti and anti-proverbs).

2680. Thomsen, Bernd (ed.). *Ihr geht mit der Welt um als hättet ihr eine zweite im Keller! Polit-Graffiti & Demo-Sprüche.* München: Wilhelm Heyne, 1986. 123 pp. With illustrations. (graffiti and anti-proverbs).

2681. Thomsen, Bernd (ed.). *Lieber die dunkelste Kneipe als den hellsten Arbeitsplatz. Neue Büro-Sprüche.* Illustrations by Ernst Hürlimann. München: Wilhelm Heyne, 1986. 123 pp. (anti-proverbs).

2682. Thomsen, Bernd (ed.). *Pissen ist Macht. Neue Klo-Sprüche.* Illustrations by Erik Liebermann. München: Wilhelm Heyne, 1986. 121 pp. (graffiti and anti-proverbs).

2683. Thomsen, Bernd (ed.). *Wer im Bett lacht, lacht am besten. Horizontale Graffiti, Witze, Bilder und Sprüche.* Illustrations by Michael Ffolkes [*sic*]. München: Wilhelm Heyne, 1986. 154 pp. (graffiti and anti-proverbs).

2684. Tilles, Sally Simon. *Der Jude im Citat und im Sprichwort. Ein Bädeker für Anti- und Philo-Semiten.* Berlin: Paul Heichen, 1892. 64 pp. (anti-Semitic collection).

2685. Trenkle, Bernhard (ed.). *Das Aha!-Handbuch der Aphorismen und Sprüche für Therapie, Beratung und Hängematte.* Heidelberg: Carl-Auer-Systeme Verlag, 2004. 204 pp. (quotations).

2686. Trenkler, Robert. *6275 deutsche Sprüchwörter [sic] und Redensarten.* München: Albert Medler, 1884. 211 pp.

2687. Treskow, Irene von (ill.). *Mit fremden Federn ... Suchbilder und Texte zu Sprichwörtern und Redensarten.* Berlin: Benteli, 1983. 79 pp.

2688. Tschinkel, Wilhelm. "Sprichwörter und sprichwörtliche Redensarten." In W. Tschinkel. *Gottscheer Volkstum in Sitte, Brauch, Märchen, Sagen, Legenden und anderen volkstümlichen Überlieferungen.* Ljubljana: Založba, 2004. 468-481.

2689. Tunnicius, Antonius. *Antonii Tunicii Monasterienisis in Germanorum paroemias studiosae iuventuti perutiles Monosticha.* Colonie: Martinum, 1514. 32 leaves. Rpt. as *Tunnicius. Die älteste niederdeutsche Sprichwörtersammlung, von Antonius Tunnicius gesammelt und in lateinische Verse übersetzt. Mit hochdeutscher Übersetzung, Anmerkungen und Wörterbuch.* Ed. August Heinrich Hoffmann von Fallersleben. Berlin: Robert Oppenheim, 1870; rpt. Amsterdam: Rodopi, 1967. 224 pp.

2690. Tüshaus, Friedrich. *Deutsche Sprichwörter nach Federzeichnungen von Fritz Tüshaus, in Holzschnitten von B. Brend'amour.* Leipzig: J.A. Barth, 1872. 13 pp. With illustrations.

2691. Uhlenbruck, Gerhard (ed.). *Ein gebildeter Kranker. Trost- und Trutz-Sprüche für und gegen Ärzte von Gerhard Uhlenbruck, Hans-Horst Skupy, and Hanns-Hermann Kersten.* Illustrations by Heinz Langer. Stuttgart: Gustav Fischer, 1981. 105 pp. (3rd ed. 1990). 144 pp. (aphorisms).

2692. Uhlenbruck, Gerhard, and Hans-Horst Skupy (eds.). *Treffende Zitate zum Thema "Der Mensch und sein Arzt". 3000 Aphorismen, Zitate, Meinungen, Aussprüche, Definitionen, Fragen und Antworten.* Illustrations by Miroslav Barták. Thun: Ott Verlag, 1980. 248 pp.

2693. Ulrich, Karl-Heinz. *Das goldene Buch der Zitate. Eine Sammlung von Aussprüchen, Sprichwörtern, Sinnsprüchen, Aphorismen, volkstümlichen Lebenseregeln, sprichwörtlichen Redensarten und Bauernregeln.* Berlin: F.W. Peters, 1968. 384 pp.

2694. Umurova, Gulnas. *Was der Volksmund im Sprichwort verpackt. Moderne Aspekte des Sprichwortgebrauchs – anhand von Beispielen aus dem Internet.* Diss. Universität Basel, 2004. 371 pp. Also as *Was der Volksmund in einem Sprichwort verpackt … Moderne Aspekte des Sprichwortgebrauchs anhand von Beispielen aus dem Internet.* Bern: Peter Lang, 2005. 362 pp. (corpus, pp. 193-362).

2695. Ungar, Frederick. *Practical Wisdom. A Treasury of Aphorisms and Reflections from the German.* New York: Frederick Ungar Publishing, 1977. 152 pp.

2696. Unterweger, Wolf-Dietmar, and Ursula Unterweger. *Aus Großmutters Schatztruhe. Gestickte Spruchweisheiten mit immerwährender Gültigkeit.* Würzburg: Stürtz, 1994. 112 pp. With illustrations.

2697. Unterweger, Wolf-Dietmar, and Ursula Unterweger. *Das kleine Buch der Bauernweisheiten.* Würzburg: Stürtz Verlag, 1995. 64 pp. (weather proverbs).

2698. Vollmann, Herbert. *Wahrheiten und Weisheiten in Sprichwörtern und Redensarten.* Stuttgart: Verlag der Stiftung Gralsbotschaft, 1984. 44 pp.

2699. Wachler, Ludwig. "Auszug aus Seb. Franck's Sprichwörtern [1541]." *Philomathie von Freunden der Wissenschaft und Kunst,* 1 (1818), 239-247.

2700. Wächter, Oskar Eberhard Siegfried von. *Sprichwörter und Sinnsprüche der Deutschen in neuer Auswahl.* Gütersloh: C. Bertelsmann, 1888. 392 pp.

2701. Waeger, Gerhart. *Die Katze hat neun Leben. Katzennärrische Ausdrücke, Redewendungen und Sprichwörter.* Bern: Benteli, 1976. 144 pp. With illustrations.

2702. Wagener, Samuel Christoph. *Sprichwörter-Lexikon mit kurzen Erläuterungen. Ein Hausbuch fürs gemeine Leben auch zum Gebrauch in Volksschulen.* Quedlinburg: Gottfried Basse, 1813. Rpt. ed. Wolfgang Mieder. Hildesheim: Georg Olms, 2005. 212 pp. (introduction, pp. 1*-23*).

2703. Wagenfeld, Karl. *Ick will di maol wat seggen. Sprichwörter und Redensarten, Kinderreime und Lieder, Glauben und Aberglauben, Namen und Begriffe, der "Allerwerteste" im Volksmund des Münsterlandes.* Ed. Hannes Demming. Münster: Aschendorff, 1983. 295 pp.

2704. Wager, Wulf. *Schwäbischer Spruchbeutel.* Illustrations by Björn Locke. Tübingen: Silberburg-Verlag, 2005. 95 pp.

2705. Walter, Harry. *Wörterbuch deutscher sprichwörtlicher und phraseologischer Vergleiche.* Teil 1. Hamburg: Kovač, 2008. 332 pp.

2706. Walter, Harry, and Valerii M. Mokienko. *(K)Ein Buch mit sieben Siegeln. Historisch-etymologische Skizzen zur deutschen Phraseologie. Nemetsko-russkii fraseologicheskii slovar' s istoriko-etimologicheskii kommentariiami.* Greifswald: Ernst-Moritz-Arndt-Universität, 2011. 460 pp. (German title and phrases, everything else in Russian).

2707. Wander, Karl Friedrich Wilhelm. *Scheidemünze, ein Taschenbuch für Jedermann. Oder: 5000 neue deutsche Sprichwörter. Erste Gabe.* Hirschberg: E. Nesener, 1831. Neiße: Hennings, 1831. (2nd ed. 1835). 251 pp.

2708. Wander, Karl Friedrich Wilhelm. *Scheidemünze, oder neue deutsche Sprichwörter biblischen, naturgeschichtlichen, fabellehrigen und vermischten Inhalts. Mit beinah 500 erklärenden Winken und Bemerkungen. Zweite und letzte Gabe.* Neiße: Hennings, 1832; rpt. Hirschberg: E.F. Zimmer, 1836. 264 pp.

2709. Wander, Karl Friedrich Wilhelm. *Das Sprichwort, angewandt zu Unterredungen über die Sonn- und Festtagsevangelien. Besonders für Lehrer in Volksschulen, aber auch für Prediger brauchbar.* Berlin: Carl Heymann, 1836. 203 pp.

2710. Wander, Karl Friedrich Wilhelm. *Abrahamisches Parömiakon. Oder: Die Sprichwörter, sprichwörtlichen Redensarten und schönen* *sinnreichen Gleichnisse des P. Abraham a St. Clara, nebst den dazu gehörigen, erklärenden und anwendenden Stellen.* Breslau: Ignaz Kohn, 1838. 412 pp.

2711. Wander, Karl Friedrich Wilhelm. *Der Sprichwörtergarten. Oder: Kurze und faßliche Erklärung von 500 Sprichwörtern, ein Lesebuch für die Jugend, ein Handbuch für Lehrer, welche die Sprichwörter als moralisches Bildungsmittel und als Stoff zu Denkübungen benützen wollen.* Breslau: Ignaz Kohn, 1838. 300 pp.

2712. Wander, Karl Friedrich Wilhelm. "Sammlung schlesischer Sprichwörter." *Schlesische Provinzialblätter*, new series, 1 (1862), 287-291 and 680-685.

2713. Wander, Karl Friedrich Wilhelm. *Deutsches Sprichwörter-Lexikon. Ein Hausschatz für das deutsche Volk.* 5 vols. Leipzig: F.A. Brockhaus, 1867-1880; rpt. Darmstadt: Wissenschafltiche Buchgesellschaft, 1964; rpt. Stuttgart: Akademie Verlagsgesellschaft Athenaion, 1987. Also as CD-ROM in the "Digitale Bibliothek", vol. 62. Berlin: Directmedia Publishing, 2001. I, A – Gothen, 1802 cols.; II, Gott – Lehren, 1884 cols.; III, Lehrer – Satte (der), 1870 cols.; IV, Sattel – Wei, 1874 cols.; V, Weib – Zweig (Zusätze und Ergänzungen), 1824 cols.

2714. Wegener, Hans. *Alte deutsche Bauernweisheit.* Leipzig: J.J. Weber, 1935. 64 pp. (weather proverbs.)

2715. Weidinger, Birgit (ed.). *Warum freut sich der Schneekönig und wie kommt die Leiche in den Keller? Sprichwörter, Redensarten – und was dahinter steckt.* München: Süddeutsche Zeitung Edition, 2008. 203 pp.

2716. Weise, Oskar. "Die volkstümlichen Vergleiche in den deutschen Mundarten." *Zeitschrift für deutsche Mundarten*, 16 (1921), 169-179.

2717. Weise, Wilhelm. *Die Sentenz bei Hartmann von Aue.* Diss. Universität Marburg, 1910. Bielefeld: A. von der Mühlen, 1910. 104 pp. (sententious remarks index, pp. 49-101).

2718. Weiss, Carl Theodor. "Sprichwort und Lebensklugheit aus dem XVIII. Jahrhundert." *Alemannia*, 27 (1890), 124-152.

2719. Weitnauer, Alfred. *Allgäuer Sprüch, das ist Samblung [sic] etlicher fürnehmer Sprüch und Gesätzlein.* Illustrations by Johann Miller. Lindau: Johannes Thomas Stettner, 1935. 47 pp.

2720. Weitnauer, Alfred. *Allgäuer Sprüche*. Illustrations by Siegfried Sambs. Altusried: Franz Brack, 1980. 125 pp.

2721. Werkner, Turi. *Idiomatik. Mit Wortliste deutsch/englisch*. Innsbruck: Innsbruck University Press, 2008. 272 pp.

2722. Werner, Elyane. *Bayerische Sprichwörter*. Illustrations by Andreas Reiner. München: W. Ludwig, 1991. 42 pp. (miniature book).

2723. Wertheimer, Hans Stefan. *Spruch and Widerspruch: Zitate und "Gegenzitate" thematisch geordnet*. Thun: Ott Verlag, 1994. 166 pp.

2724. Wertheimer, Hans Stefan. *Lexikon der heiteren Weisheiten*. Thun: Ott Verlag, 1996 (2nd ed. 1997). 361 pp.

2725. Wettig, Knut-Hannes (ed.). *Vorm Wind ist gut segeln. Seemannssprüche. Aus der Sammlung Wiard Lüpkes' [1900] ausgewählt*. Illustrations by Matthias Gubig. Berlin: Union Verlag, 1985. 94 pp.

2726. Wiese, Joachim. *Berliner Wörter & Wendungen*. Illustrations by Hartmut Lindemann. Berlin: Akademie Verlag, 1987. 160 pp.

2727. Wigand, Paul. *Der menschliche Körper im Munde des deutschen Volkes. Eine Sammlung und Betrachtung der dem menschlichen Körper entlehnten sprichwörtlichen Ausdrücke und Redensarten*. Frankfurt am Main: Alt, 1899; rpt. Münster: Lit-Verlag, 1981. 119 pp.

2728. Wigand, Paul. *Der menschliche Körper im Munde des deutschen Volkes*. Frankfurt am Main: Alt, 1899. 119 pp. Rpt. ed. by Henning Eichberg. Münster: Lit Verlag, 1987. 130 pp.

2729. Wilcke, Karin, and Lothar Bluhm. "Wilhelm Grimms Sammlung mittelhochdeutscher Sprichwörter." *Brüder Grimm Gedenken*. Ed. Ludwig Denecke. Marburg: N.G. Elwert, 1988. VIII, 81-122.

2730. Willnat, Wolfgang (ed.). *Sprüche, Sprayer, Spontis. Spaß mit Graffiti*. Wiesbaden: Englisch, 1985. 120 pp. With illustrations. (graffiti and anti-proverbs).

2731. Wilson, April. *German Quickly. A Grammar for Reading German*. New York: Peter Lang, 1989. 356 pp.; revised edition New York: Peter Lang, 2004. 432 pp. (based to a large degree on proverbs).

2732. Winkler, Leonhard. *Deutsches Recht im Spiegel deutscher Sprichwörter.* Leipzig: Quelle und Meyer, 1927; rpt. Leipzig: Zentralantiquariat der Deutschen Demokratischen Republik, 1977. 272 pp. (proverb index, pp. 230-265).

2733. Winter, Fritz, and Klaus Winter. *"Wein, Weib und Gesang, liebt jeder Pfälzer sein Leben lang!" Pfälzer Weisheiten rund um den Wein.* Landau, Pfalz: Verlag Pfälzer Kunst Blinn, 2005. 154 pp. With illustrations.

2734. Winter, Georg. *Unbeflügelte Worte, zugleich Ergänzungen zu Büchmann, von Loeper, Strehlke etc.* Augsburg: Adelbert Votsch, 1888. 186 pp.

2735. Wittstock, Albert. *Die Erziehung im Sprichwort oder Die deutsche Volks-Pädagogik.* Leipzig: C.G. Naumann, 1889. 281 pp.

2736. Woeste, Friedrich. "Apologische Sprichwörter in Mundarten des märkischen Süderlandes." *Die deutschen Mundarten,* 3 (1856), 253-264 (wellerisms).

2737. Wolf, Judith. *Morgenstund ist aller Laster Anfang und andere Heitweisspruchen [sic].* Illustrations by Lina Wolf. Callenberg: Mühle-1-Verlag, 2009. 20 pp. With 10 illustrations. (anti-proverbs).

2738. Wolle, Helmut. *Von der Weisheit der Sprüche. Aphorismen, Zitate, Sprichwörter.* Berlin: Verlag Neues Leben, 1981 (2nd ed. 1984). 275 pp.

2739. Wortig, Kurt. *Zitate mit Pfiff und Schliff.* Vol. 1: *Aus Geschichte, Gesellschaft, Medizin, Politik und Wirtschaft.* Vol. 2: *Aus Kunst, Literatur, Natur, Philosophie, privater Sphäre, Wissenschaft.* München: Wilhelm Goldmann, 1979. I, 219 pp.; II. 202 pp.

2740. Wotjak, Barbara. "Rede-Wendungen in Wende-Reden." *Das Wort: Germanistisches Jahrbuch,* no volume given (1991), 38-41.

2741. Wotjak, Barbara, and Manfred Richter. *Deutsche Phraseologismen. Ein Übungsbuch für Ausländer.* Illustrations by Gabriele Richter. Leipzig: VEB Verlag Enzyklopädie, 1988. 152 pp.

2742. Wotjak, Barbara, and Manfred Richter. *Sage und schreibe. Deutsche Phraseologismen in Theorie und Praxis.* Illustrations by Christoph Kirsch. Leipzig: Langenscheidt – Verlag Enzyklopädie, 1993. 150 pp.

2743. Wunderlich, Gottlob. *Deutsche Sprichwörter volkstümlich erklärt und gruppiert.* Langensalza: F. Greßler, 1878. 72 pp. (8th ed. 1904). 88 pp.

2744. Wunderlich, Gottlob. *Sprichwörtliche und bildliche Redens-arten. Zur Pflege vaterländischer Sprachkenntnis in der Volks-schule*. Langensalza: F. Greßler, 1882. 155 pp.

2745. Wurzbach, Constant von. *Historische Wörter, Sprichwörter und Redensarten*. Prag: J.L. Klober, 1863. 367 pp.; 2nd ed. Leipzig: Jean Paul Friedrich Eugen Richter, 1866. 428 pp.

2746. Zahn, Benedict Wilhelm. *Bäiderla af alli Subbm: Die Sprichwörtersammlung des Benedict Wilhelm Zahn [1738-1819]*. Ed. Herbert Maas. Nürnberg: Selbstverlag des Stadtrats zu Nürnberg, 1997. 237 pp. With illustrations.

2747. Zarnack, August. *Deutsche Sprichwörter zu Verstandes-übungen für die Schulen bearbeitet, nebst einer Anweisung, auf welchen Wegen ein Schatz der lehrreichsten Sprichwörter unter die Volksjugend gebracht werden könne, worin zugleich eine aus-erwählte Sammlung von mehr als elfhundert der passendsten Kern-sprüche Deutscher Weisheit zum Gebrauch der Schulen enthalten ist. Ein Handbuch für Lehrer und Erzieher*. Berlin: Maurer, 1820. 380 pp.

2748. Zarncke, Friedrich. *Der deutsche Cato. Geschichte der deutschen Übersetzungen der im Mittelalter unter dem Namen Cato bekannten Distichen bis zur Verdrängung derselben durch die Übersetzung Seb. Brants am Ende des 15. Jahrh*. Leipzig: Georg Wigand, 1852. 198 pp.

2749. Zerlett-Olfenius, Walter. *Aus dem Stegreif. Plaudereien über Redensarten*. Illustrations by Erwin Bindewald. Berlin: Aufwärts-Verlag Maxim Klieber, 1943. 144 pp.

2750. Zincgref, Julius Wilhelm. *Teutsche Apophthegmata das ist Der Teutschen Scharfsinnige kluge Sprüche*. 2 vols. Amsterdam: Ludwig Elzevier, 1653. Rpt. ed. Wolfgang Mieder. Hildesheim: Weidmann, 2006. I, 456 pp.; II. 480 pp. (introduction, pp. V-XXXIX).

2751. Zincgref, Julius Wilhelm. *Julius Wilhelm Zinkgref's scharfsin-nige Sprüche der Teutschen, Apophthegmata genannt. Auswahl*. Ed. B.F. Guttenstein. Mannheim: Heinrich Hoff, 1835. 396 pp.

2752. Zincgref, Julius Wilhelm. *Julius Wilhelm Zincgref. Der Teutschen Scharfsinnige Kluge Sprüch [Frankfurt1683]*. Ed. Karl-Heinz Klingenberg. Leipzig: Philipp Reclam, 1982. 192 pp. (selec-tions).

2753. Zingerle, Ignaz V. "Farbenvergleiche im Mittelalter." *Germania*, 9 (1864), 385-402.

2754. Zingerle, Ignaz V. *Die deutschen Sprichwörter im Mittelalter*. Wien: Wilhelm Braumüller, 1864; rpt. Walluf bei Wiesbaden: Martin Sändig, 1972. 199 pp.

2755. Zinnecker, Jürgen. "Wandsprüche." *Jugend '81. Lebensentwürfe, Alltagskulturen, Zukunftsbilder*. Ed. Arthur Fischer. Hamburg: Jugendwerk der Deutschen Shell, 1981. 2nd ed. Opladen: Leske und Budrich, 1982. I, 430-476. (graffiti and anti-proverbs).

2756. Zitelmann, Arnulf (ed.). *Ich, Martin Luther. Starke Sprüche über Weiber, Fürsten, Pfaffen undsoweiter*. Frankfurt am Main: Eichborn, 1982. 67 pp.

2757. Zoozmann, Richard. *Zitaten- und Sentenzenschatz der Weltliteratur. Eine Sammlung von Zitaten, Sentenzen, geflügelten Worten, Aphorismen, Epigrammen, Sprichwörtern und Redensarten, Inschriften an Haus und Gerät, Kinderreimen, Gesundheits-, Wetter- und Bauernregeln, Totentanzversen, Marterln, Grabschriften usw. nach Schlagworten geordnet*. Leipzig: Hesse und Becker, 1910. 1384 cols. (2nd ed. 1911) 1712 cols. (4th ed. 1919). 1520 cols. (6th ed. 1928). 1520 cols.

2758. Zoozmann, Richard. *Unsere Klassiker im Volksmund. Ein kleiner Zitatenschatz*. Leipzig: Hesse & Becker, 1911. 186 pp.

2759. Zoozmann, Richard. *Unartige Musenkinder. Ein buntes Sträußchen lustiger Pflanzen, aus Treibhausbeeten alter und neuer Zeit*. Leipzig: Hesse & Becker, 1915. 568 pp.

2760. Zoozmann, Richard. *Zitatenschatz der Weltliteratur. Eine Sammlung von Zitaten, Sentenzen, Aphorismen, Epigrammen, Sprichwörtern, Redensarten und Aussprüchen nach Schlagwörtern geordnet*. Ed. Otto A. Kielmeyer. Berlin: Verlag Praktisches Wissen F.W. Peters, 1970; rpt. Königstein/Ts.: Athenäum, 1980. Rpt. as *Rororo Zitatenschatz der Weltliteratur*. Reinbek: Rowohlt, 1984. 548 pp. (in columns).

2761. Zwanzger, Hans. *Sonderbare Sprachfrüchte. Streifzüge durch unsere Umgangssprache*. Wien: Verlag für Jugend und Volk. 1949. 186 pp.

Greek

2762. Barakles, Charalampos. *Gnomika kai paroimies: Gnomika kai apospasmata ton archaion Hellenon (archaio keimeno, meta-*

236

phrase), paroimies, paroimiakes phraseis, demotika disticha. Athena: Hestias, 1977 (8th ed. 1998). 280 pp.

2763. Böhm, Richard. *Die Weisheit der Völker. IV. Sprüche der Griechen*. Wiesbaden: Wiesbadener Graphische Betriebe, 1963. No pp.

2764. Bühler, Winfried (ed.). *Zenobii Athoi proverbia*. Volumen quartum, libri secundi proverbia 1-40 complexum. Göttingen: Vandenhoeck & Ruprecht, 1982. 349 pp.

2765. Bühler, Winfried (ed.). *Zenobii Athoi proverbia*. Volumen primum, prolegomena complexum, in quibus codices describuntur. Göttingen: Vandenhoeck & Ruprecht, 1987. 434 pp.

2766. Bühler, Winfried (ed.). *Zenobii Athoi proverbia*. Volumen quintum, libri secundi proverbia 41-108 complexum. Göttingen: Vandenhoeck & Ruprecht, 1999. 734 pp

2767. Dibbley, Dale Corey. *From Achilles Heel to Zeus's Shield. A Lively, Informative Guide to More Than 300 Words and Phrases Born of Mythology*. New York: Fawcett Columbine, 1993. 230 pp.

2768. Georgis, Takiss. *Modern Greek Proverbs*. Girard, Kansas: Haldeman-Julius Company, 1925. 22 pp.

2769. Giebel, Marion (ed.). *Antike Weisheit*. Stuttgart: Philipp Reclam, 1995. 255 pp.

2770. Karagiorgos, Panos. *Greek and English Proverbs*. Corfu, Greece: Ionian University, 1999. 213 pp.

2771. Köhler, Carl Sylvio. *Das Tierleben im Sprichwort der Griechen und Römer. Nach Quellen und Stellen in Parallele mit dem deutschen Sprichwort herausgegeben*. Leipzig: Fernau, 1881; rpt. Hildesheim: Georg Olms, 1967. 221 pp.

2772. Lelli, Emanuele. *I proverbi greci. Le racolte di Zenobio e Diogeniano*. Soveria Mannelli: Rubbettino, 2006. 565 pp.

2773. Leutsch, Ernst Ludwig, and Friedrich Wilhelm Schneidewin (eds.). *Corpus Paroemigraphorum Graecorum*. 2 vols. Göttingen: Vandenhoeck & Ruprecht, 1839 and 1851; rpt. Hildesheim: Georg Olms, 1965. I, 541 pp.; II, 867 pp.

2774. Leutsch, Ernst Ludwig, and Friedrich Wilhelm Schneidewin (eds.). *Corpus Paroemigraphorum Graecorum. Supplementum*. No editor given. Contains studies by Leopold Cohn, Otto Crusius, and Heinrich Jungblut. Hildesheim: Georg Olms, 1961. 672 pp.

2775. Liapis, Vayos. *Menandrou: Gnomai monostichoi. Eisagoge, metaphrase, scholia.* Athena: Stigme, 2002. 529 pp.

2776. Loukatos, Démétrios. *Neoellenikoi Paroimiomythoi.* Athena: Ekdotike Ermes, 1972. 183 pp. (2nd ed. 1978). 201 pp.

2777. Loukatos, Démétrios. "Soixante dictons populaires de Crète: In memoriam de deux anciennes folkloristes: M. Lioudaki et Ph. Saréyanni." *Laographia*, 36 (1990-1992), 207-213 (in Greek).

2778. Macrone, Michael. *It's Greek to Me! Brush up Your Classics.* Illustrations by Tom Lulevitch. New York: HarperCollins, 1991. 238 pp.

2779. Marketos, B.J. (ed.). *A Proverb For It: 1510 Greek Sayings.* New York: New World Publishers, 1945. 191 pp.

2780. Papadopoullos, Theodore. "Kypriakai paroimiai." *Meletai kai Ypomnimata*, 2 (1991), i-xxiv and 1-221 (Cypriot proverbs).

2781. Paschales, Demetrios P. *Paroimiai kai paroimiodeis phraseis tou laou tes Androu.* With additions from new publications by Anna G. Palaiokrassa. Andros, Greece: Kaireios Bibliotheke, 1996. 255 pp.

2782. Rohlfs, Gerhard. *Italogriechische Sprichwörter in linguistischer Konfrontation mit neugriechischen Dialekten.* München: Verlag der Bayerischen Akademie der Wissenschaften, 1971. 186 pp.

2783. Schuhmann, Elisabeth. *Lebensweisheiten der Griechen und Römer.* Illustrations by Karl-Georg Hirsch. Leipzig: Teubner, 1895. 194 pp.

2784. Sellner, Alfred. *Altgriechisch im Alltag. Alphabetisch geordnetes Nachschlagewerk von altgriechischen Sentenzen, Sprichwörtern, Phrasen, Floskeln, Redewendungen, Zitaten und Formeln.* Wiesbaden: VMA-Verlag, 1998. 135 pp.

2785. Soyter, G. "Die neugriechischen Sprichwörter in der Volksliedersammlung Werner von Haxthausens." *Byzantinisch-neugriechische Jahrbücher*, 16 (1940), 171-189.

2786. Strömberg, Reinhold. *Greek Proverbs. A Collection of Proverbs and Proverbial Phrases which Are not Listed by the Ancient and Byzantine Paremiographers.* Göteborg: Wettergren & Kerbers Förlag, 1954. 145 pp.

2787. Strömberg, Reinhold. *Griechische Sprichwörter. Eine neue Sammlung.* Göteborg: Akademiförlaget-Gumperts, 1961. 48 pp..

2788. Walther, Richard. *Altgriechische Lebensweisheit. Denksprüche und Sprichwörter.* München-Lochhausen: Schild-Verlag, 1964. 135 pp.

2789. Werner, Jürgen. *Altgriechische Sprichwörter nach Sachgruppen geordnet.* Diss. Universität Leipzig, 1957. 133 pp.

Guatemalan

2790. Rodas Estrada, Haroldo. "El refranero guatemalteco." *Tradiciones de Guatemala*, 39 (1993), 7-81.

Guyanese

2791. Speirs, James. *The Proverbs of British Guiana with an Index of Principal Words, and Index of Subjects, and a Glossary.* Demerara: The Argosy Company, 1902. 88 pp.

Gypsy (Roma, Sinti)

2792. Ariste, Paul. "Einige Sprichwörter der Čuchny-Zigeuner." *Proverbium*, 18 (1972), 692-693.

2793. Morwood, Vernon S. "Popular Gipsy Proverbs." In V.S. Morwood. *Our Gipsies in City, Tent, and Van. Containing an Account of Their Origin and Strange Life.* London: Sampson Low, Marston, Searle, & Rivington, 1885. 69.

2794. Sampson, John. "A Hundred Shelta Sayings." *Journal of the Gypsy Lore Society*, 1 (1907-1908), 272-277.

2795. Ventzel, T.V. "[Gypsy] Proverbs." In T.V. Ventzel. *The Gypsy Language.* Moscow: "Nauka" Publishing House, 1983. 93-98.

Haitian

2796. Préval, Guerdy. *Proverbes haïtiens illustrés.* Ottawa, Canada: National Museums of Canada. 1985. 215 pp. With illustrations.

Hawaiian

2797. Corum, Ann Kondo (ill.). *Folk Wisdom from Hawaii or Don't Take Bananas on a Boat.* Honolulu, Hawaii: The Bess Press, 1985. 114pp.

2798. Judd, Henry P. *Hawaiian Proverbs and Riddles*. Honolulu, Hawaii: Bernice P. Bishop Museum, 1930; rpt Millwood, New York: Kraus Reprint, 1978. 91 pp.

2799. Provenzano, Renata. *A Little Book of Aloha*. *Hawaiian Proverbs & Inspirational Wisdom*. Honolulu, Hawaii: Mutual Publishing, 2001. 80 pp. With illustrations.

2800. Pukui, Mary Kawena. *'Ōlelo No'eau*. *Hawaiian Proverbs and Poetical Sayings*. Illustrations by Dietrich Varez. Honolulu, Hawaii: Bishop Museum, 1983. 351 pp.

Hebrew

2801. Anonymous. *Sayings of the Sages of the Mishnah*. *Sprüche der Weisen der Mischnah*. *Préceptes des sages de la Michnah*. Jerusalem: Korén Publishers, 1997. 50 pp.

2802. Böhm, Richard. *Die Weisheit der Völker*. *II*. *Sprüche der Hebräer*. Wiesbaden: Wiesbadener Graphische Betriebe, 1961. 29 pp.

2803. Cohen, A. *Wisdom of the East*. *Ancient Jewish Proverbs*. London: John Murray, 1911; rpt. Darby, Pennsylvania: Folcroft Library Editions, 1980. 127 pp.

2804. Cowan, Lore, and Maurice Cowan. *The Wit of the Jews*. London: Leslie Frewin Publishers, 1970; Nashville, Tennessee: Aurora Publishers, 1970. 152 pp.

2805. Gross, David C. *Dictionary of 1000 Jewish Proverbs*. New York: Hippocrene Books, 1997. 125 pp.

2806. Kolatch, Alfred J. *Great Jewish Quotations*. Middle Village, New York: Jonathan David Publishers, 1996. 612 pp.

2807. Nulman, Macy. *The Encyclopedia of the Sayings of the Jewish People*. Northvale, New Jersey: Jason Aronson, 1997. 358 pp.

Hungarian

2808. Bárdosi, Vilmos (ed.). *Magyar szólástár. Szólások, helyzetmondatok, közmondások értelmező és fogalomköri szótára*. Budapest: Tinta Könyvkiadó, 2003. 954 pp.

2809. Bárdosi, Vilmos (ed.). *Magyar szólások, közmondások értelmező és fogolomköri szótára* [A Dictionary – According to Meaning and Logical Categories – of Hungarian Sayings and Proverbs.].

Budapest: Tinta Könyvkiadó, 2009. 990 pp. (revised ed. of previous entry).

2810. Bárdosi, Vilmos, Stefan Ettinger, Cécile Stölting, and Ekaterina Boutina. *Frazeologizmy frantsuzskogo iazyka. Slovar '– praktikum.* Ekaterinburg: Ural'skoe Izdatel'stvo, 2002. 247 pp.

2811. Bárdosi, Vilmos, and Gábor Kiss. *Közmondások. 3000 magyar közmondás és szójárás betűrendes értelmező dióhéjszótára.* Budapest: Tinta Könyvkiadó, 2005. 173 pp.

2812. Bárdosi, Vilmos, and Gábor Kiss. *Szólások. 5000 magyar állandósult szókapcsolat betűrendes értelmező dióhéjszótára.* Budapest: Tinta Könyvkiadó, 2005. 231 pp.

2813. Bura, László. *Szatmári szólások és közmondások.* Budapest: ELTE Magyar Nyelvtörténeti és Nyelvjárási Tanszéke, 1987. 147 pp.

2814. Decsi, Janos Baronyai (= Decius, Baronius Ioannes). *Adagiorvm Graecolatinovngaricorvm Chiliades quinque. Ex Des. Erasmo. Hadriano Iunio Ionne Alexandro, Cognato Gilberto excerptac ac Vngaricis prouerbiis ...* Bartphae: Iacubvs Klöβ, 1598; rpt. Budapest: Eötvös Lórand Tudományegyetem, 1978. 424 pp.

2815. Forgács, Tamás. *Magyar szólások és közmondások szótára. Mai nyelvünk állandósult szókapcsolatai példákkal szemléltetve.* Budapest: Tinta Könyvkiadó, 2003. 822 pp.

2816. Jósa, Iván. *Okos, mint a kecskeméti szélmalom. 1000 kecskeméti és Kecskemét környéki szólás [Wise as the Windmill of Kecskemét. 1000 Hungarian Proverbs from Kecskemét and Its Neighborhood].* Kecskemét: Kecskemét Monográfia Szerk, 2001. 103 pp.

2817. Keszeg, Vilmos. "Proverbiumok (Aranyosszéken) [Hungarian Proverbs in Aranyosszék, Transylvania]." In V. Keszeg. *Aranyosszék népköltészete.* 2 vols. Marosvásárhely: Mentor Kiadó, 2004. I, 345-361.

2818. Lábadi. Károly. *Ahogy rakod tüzed. Drávaszögi magyar proverbiumok.* Eszék: Horvátországi Magyarok Szövetsége, 1986. 350 pp.

2819. Litovkina, Anna T. *Magyar közmondástár. Közmondások értelmező szótára példákkal szemléltetve.* Budapest: Tinta Könyvkiadó, 2005. 818 pp.

2820. Litovkina, Anna T., and Katalin Vargha. *"Éhes diák pakkal álmodik". Egyetemisták közmondás-elváltoztatásai.* Illustrations by

Ágnes Vörös and Anita Kékesi. Budapest: Walég, 2005. 94 pp. (anti-proverbs).

2821. Litovkina, Anna T., and Katalin Vargha. *"Viccében él a nemzet"*. *Magyar közmondás-paródiák*. Budapest: Walég, 2005. 102 pp. With illustrations. (anti-proverbs).

2822. Litovkina, Anna T., and Katalin Vargha. *"Viccében él a nemzet"*. *Válogatott közmondás-paródiák*. Illustrations by Gáspár Baksa. Budapest: Nyitott Könyvműhely, 2006. 169 pp. (anti-proverbs).

2823. Margalits, Ede. *Magyar közmondások és közmondásszerü szólások*. Budapest: Lajos Kókai, 1896; rpt. Budapest: Akadémiai Kiadó, 1990. 770 pp.

2824. Nagy, Gábor O. *"Mi fán terem?"* *Magyar szólásmondások eredete*. Budapest: Gondolat Kiadó, 1957. 386 pp. (revised 3rd ed. 1979); rpt. Budapest: Gondolat Kiadó, 1988. 520 pp.

2825. Nagy, Gábor O. *Magyar szólások és közmondások*. Budapest: Gondolat Kiadó, 1966 (2nd ed. 1976). 860 pp.

2826. Nagy, Géza. *Karcsai szólások és közmondások*. Budapest: ELTE Magyar Nyelvtörténeti és Nyelvjárási Tanszéke, 1987. 69 pp.

2827. Paczolay, Gyula. *Magyar közmondások és szólások*. *[Hungarian Proverbs]*. Veszprém: Pannon Nyomda, 1989. 115 pp.

2828. Paczolay, Gyula. *Magyar közmondások és szólások*. *700 ungarische Sprichwörter und Redewendungen*. Veszprém: Pannon Nyomda, 1990. 127 pp. (miniature book).

2829. Paczolay, Gyula. *750 Magyar közmondás és szólás*. *750 Hungarian Proverbs*. Veszprém: Veszprémi Nyomda, 1991. 127 pp.

2830. Paczolay, Gyula. *750 Magyar közmondás és szólás*. *750 ungarische Sprichwörter und Redensarten*. Veszprém: Veszprémi Nyomda, 1991. 136 pp. (miniature book).

2831. Paczolay, Gyula. *Magyar-japán közmondások és szólások / Corresponding Hungarian and Japanese Proverbs*. *With English Translations*. Ercsi: Polgármesteri Hivatal, 1994. 119 pp.

2832. Paczolay, Gyula. *Ezer magyar közmondás és szólas – angol, észt, finn és német fordítással*. *1000 Hungarian Proverbs*. *1000 ungari vanasõna ja kõnekäändu*. *1000 unkarilaista sananlaskua ja sanontaa*. *1000 ungarische Sprichwörter und Redensarten*. Budapest: Bárczi Géza Ertékőrző Kiejtési Alapítvány, 2000. 154 pp.

2833. Pusko, Gábor. "'Megadja a módját, mint kálosiak az óbégatásnak!' Proverbiumok egy munkaközösség tagjainak szókészletében a gömöri Tornalján [Hungarian Proverbs in a Workplace Community in Tornalja, Gömör County, Slovakia]." *Acta Ethnologica Danubiana*, 4 (2002), 83-112.

2834. Schanda, Eva. *Hungarian-English, English-Hungarian Mini Dictionary of Sayings. Magyar-angol, angol-magyar mini szólás szótár*. Budapest: János Schanda, 2000. 206 pp.

2835. Szemerkényi, Ágnes. *Szólások és közmondások*. Budapest: Osiris Kiadó, 2009. 1461 pp.

2836. Vasvári, Lajos. *20,000 English-Hungarian Proverbs – Sayings from All Over the World. 20,000 Angol-Magyar közmondások – Mondások az egész világból*. 2 vols. Budapest: Első kiadás, 1993. I, 605 pp.; II, 670 pp.

2837. Vöö, Gabriella. *Igaz ember igazat szól. Közmondások a romániai magyar folklórból*. Bucuresti: Kriterion Könyvkiadó, 1989. 315 pp.

2838. Wildner, Ödön. *Leleküditő azaz szellemi kincsestár gondolatok és elmés idézetek gyüjteménye*. Budapest: Göncöl Kiadó, 1989. 182 pp.

Icelandic

2839. Halldórsson, Halldór. *Islenzk Ordtök. Drög ad rannsóknum á myndhverfun ordtökum í islenzku*. Reykjavik: Isafoldarprentsmidja, 1954. 416 pp.

2840. Halldórsson, Halldór. *Örlög Ordanna*. Akureyi: Bókaforlag Odds Björnssonar, 1958. 201 pp.

Indian Languages

2841. Achappa, H.S. *Granthastha Gadegalu – Proverbs and Quotations from Kannada Classics*. Mysore, India: H.S. Achappa, 1969. 648 pp.

2842. Barman, Mrinal Deb. "Some Kok-Borok (Tripuri) Proverbs with Illustrations." *Folklore* (Calcutta), 19, no. 2 (1978), 52-56.

2843. Bhati, Gulab (ed.). *Deutsch-Hindi Sprichwörterbuch*. New Delhi: German Vidhyapith Publication, 1991. 433 pp.

2844. Bhatt, M. Marippa, N. Venkata Rao, R.P. Sethu Pillai, and S.K. Nayar. *Nalnudi-Namudi. Kannada, Telugu, Tamil, Malayala*

Bhashegallalina Samana Gadegalu - Kannada Version of Comparative Proverbs in Dravidan Languages. Mysore: Talukina Vankannayyanavara Smaraka Granthamale - T.S. Venkanniah Memorial Publications, 1962. 125 pp.

2845. Borua, Shri P.C. *Assamese Proverbs.* Calcutta: Nabajiban Press, 1962. 290 pp.

2846. Carr, Mark William. *A Collection of Telugu Proverbs. Translated, Illustrated and Explained. Together with Some Sanskrit Proverbs.* Madras: C.K.S., 1868. London: Trübner, 1868; rpt. New Delhi: Asian Educational Services, 1993. 635 pp. (including a supplement).

2847. Carr, Mark William. *A Selection of Telugu Proverbs.* Madras: Ramaswamy Sastrula, 1922; rpt. New Delhi: Asian Educational Services, 1993. 123 pp.

2848. Chavan, V.P. *The Konkani Proverbs.* Bombay: T.S. Talmaki, 1923; rpt. New Delhi: Asian Educational Services, 1995. 87 pp.

2849. Fallon, S.W. *A Dictionary of Hindustani Proverbs, including many Marwari, Punjabi, Maggah, Bhojpuri and Tirhuti Proverbs, Sayings, Emblems, Aphorisms, Maxims, and Similes.* Benares: Lazarus, 1886. London: Trübner, 1886; rpt. New Delhi: Asian Educational Services, 1996. 324 pp.

2850. Gowda, S. "Kannada Proverbs." *Folklore* (Calcutta), 19 (1978), 81-85.

2851. Hockings, Paul. *Counsel from the Ancients. A Study of Badaga [India] Proverbs, Prayers, Omens and Curses. With an Outline of the Badaga Language by Christiane Pilot-Raichoor.* Amsterdam: Mouton de Gruyter, 1988. 796 pp.

2852. Jensen, Herman. *A Classified Collection of Tamil Proverbs.* Madras: Methodist Episcopal Publishing House, 1897. London: Trübner, 1897; rpt. New Delhi: Asian Educational Services, 1993. 499 pp. (preface and index, pp. iii-xxiv).

2853. Knowles, James Hinton. *A Dictionary of Kashmiri Proverbs and Sayings.* Bombay: Education Society's Press, 1885; rpt. New Delhi: Asian Educational Services, 1985. 263 pp.

2854. Lazarus, John. *A Dictionary of Tamil Proverbs. With an Introduction and Hints in English on Their Meaning and Application.*

Madras: Albinion Press, 1894; rpt. New Delhi: Asian Educational Services, 1991. 662 pp.

2855. Manwaring, Alfred. *Marathi Proverbs*. Oxford: Clarendon Press, 1899; rpt. New Delhi: Asian Educational Services, 1991. 284 pp.

2856. Percival, Peter. *Tamil Proverbs with Their English Translations, Containing Upwards of Six Thousand Proverbs*. Madras: Dinavartamini Press, 1874; rpt. New Delhi: Asian Educational Services, 1996. 573 pp.

2857. Petrov, P. *Tamil'skie narodnye poslovitsy i pogovorki*. Moskva: Izdatel'stvo Inostrannoi literatury, 1962. 67 pp. With illustrations.

2858. Ponette, Pierre. "The Proverbs of the Mundas (Bihar)." *Anthropos*, 72 (1977), 522-528.

2859. Primrose, Arthur John. *A Manipuri Grammar, Vocabulary and Phrase Book to which are Added Manipuri Proverbs*. Shillong: Assam Secretariat Press, 1888; rpt. New Delhi: Asian Educational Services, 1995. 100 pp.

2860. Rao, Narasinga. *A Handbook of Kannada Proverbs*. Madras: S.P.C.K. Press, 1906; rpt. New Delhi: Asian Educational Services, 1994. 84 pp.

2861. Schmidt, Wolfgang J. *Indische Sprichwörter*. *Lebens- und Todesweisheiten der Hindus*. Frankfurt am Main: Qumran Verlag, 1981. 20 pp. (introduction and loose cards).

2862. Sethi, Narendra K. *Hindu Proverbs and Wisdom*. Illustrations by Jeff Hill. Mount Vernon, New York: Peter Pauper Press, 1962. 61 pp.

2863. Trivedi, Devkumar. "Proverbs of India." *ETC: A Review of General Semantics*, 65, no. 1 (2008), 62-63.

Indonesian

2864. Pusposaputro, Sarwono. *Kamus Peribahasa*. Jakarta: Penerbit PT Gramedia Pustaka Utama, 2001. 379 pp.

2865. Summerfield, Anne, John Summerfield, and Taufik Abdullah. "Peribahasa (Minangkabau Proverbs and Sayings)." A. and J. Summerfield and T. Abdullah. *Walk in Splendor*. *Ceremonial Dress and the Minangkabau*. Los Angeles, California: Fowler Museum of Cultural History, 1999. 330-333.

Irish (Gaelic)

2866. An Seabhac (pseud. P. Ó Siochfhradha). *Seanfhocail na Muimhneach*. Dublin: The Educational Company of Ireland, 1926. 261 pp. Rpt. as *Seanfhocail na Mumhan*. Ed. Pádraig Ua Maoileoin Dublin: An Gúm, 1984. 214 pp.

2867. Bailey, Karen. *Irish Proverbs*. Belfast: Appletree Press, 1985. 60 pp. With illustrations.

2868. Bailey, Karen. *The Pick of Irish Proverbs*. Belfast: Appletree Press, 1996. 48 pp.

2869. Bannister, Garry. *Proverbs in Gaelic / Seanfhocail in Gaeilge*. Dublin: ForSai Publications, 2005. 300 pp.

2870. Bryan, George B., and Wolfgang Mieder. *The Proverbial Bernard Shaw: An Index to Proverbs in the Works of George Bernard Shaw*. Westport, Connecticut: Greenwood Press, 1994. 286 pp.

2871. Carson (Williams), Fionnuala. *The County Monaghan Proverbs in the Department of Irish Folklore's Schools' Collection*. M.A.Thesis University College, Dublin, 1973. 708 pp.

2872. Dent, Robert William. *Colloquial Language in "Ulysses" [James Joyce]. A Reference Tool*. Newark, Delaware: University of Delaware Press, 1994. 294 pp.

2873. Dhomhnaill, Cáit Ni. "Seanráite na Ceathrú Rua." *Bealoideas: The Journal of the Folklore of Ireland*, 48-49 (1980-1981), 74-85.

2874. Flanagan, Laurence. *Irish Proverbs*. Illustrations by Fiona Fewer. Dublin: Gill & Macmillan, 1995. 115 pp.

2875. Gaffney, Sean, and Seamus Cashman (eds.). *Proverbs & Sayings of Ireland*. Portmarnock/Dublin: Wolfhound Press, 1974 (2nd ed. 1978). 124 pp.

2876. Guiterman, Arthur. *A Poet's Proverbs. Being Mirthful, Sober, and Fanciful Epigrams on the Universe, with Certain Old Irish Proverbs, All in Rhymed Couplets*. New York: E.P. Dutton, 1924. 124 pp.

2877. Hart, Clive. "An Index of Motifs [and Proverbs] in *Finnegan's Wake* [James Joyce]." In C. Hart, *Structure and Motif in "Finnegan's Wake"*. Evanston, Illinois: Northwestern University Press, 1962. 211-247.

2878. Hewetson, Cecil (ed.). *Wit and Wisdom of Oscar Wilde*. New York: Philosophical Society, 1967. 56 pp. With illustrations.

2879. Hore, Herbert F. "Rustic Proverbs Current in Ulster." *The Ulster Journal of Archaeology*, 2 (1854), 126-129.

2880. Hughes, Arthur John. *Robert Shipboy MacAdam (1808-95): His Life and Gaelic Proverb Collection*. Belfast: The Institute of Irish Studies, The Queen's University of Belfast, 1998. 226 pp. (proverbs, pp. 73-170).

2881. Kelly, Fergus. *The Three Best Things: An Illustrated Selection of Irish Triads*. Illustrations by Aislinn Adams. Belfast: The Appletree Press, 1993. 59 pp.

2882. Kelly, Joan Larson. *Irish Wit and Wisdom*. Illustrated by Pat Stewart. Mount Vernon, New York: Peter Pauper Press, 1976. 62 pp.

2883. Lover, Samuel. *Legends and Stories of Ireland to Which is Added "Illustrations of National Proverbs" (= The Collected Writings of Samuel Lover)*. Boston: Little, Brown and Company, 1903. 277 pp. (proverbs, pp. 191-277).

2884. Mac Con lomaire, Liam. *Ireland of the Proverb*. Photographs by Bill Doyle. Dublin: Town House, 1988. Grand Rapids, Michigan: Masters Press, 1988. 232 pp.

2885. MacDonald, Flora. "[Gaelic] Proverbs from North Uist." *Tocher*, no volume given, no. 47 (Winter 1993-1994), 290-297.

2886. McCann, Sean (ed.). *The Wit of Oscar Wilde*. New York: Barnes & Noble Books, 1969. 128 pp.

2887. Murphy, Colin, and Donal O'Dea. *The Feckin' Book of Irish Sayings for When You Go on the Batter with a Shower of Savages*. Dublin: The O'Brien Press, 2005. 64 pp. With illustrations.

2888. Nicolson, Alexander. *A Collection of Gaelic Proverbs and Familiar Phrases Based on Donald Macintosh's Collection*. Edinburgh: Maclachlan and Stewart, 1881. 421 pp.

2889. Ó Corráin, Ailbhe. *A Concordance of Idiomatic Expressions in the Writings of Séamus Ó Grianna*. Belfast: Institute of Irish Studies, The Queen's University, 1989. 419 pp.

2890. Ó Muirithe, Diarmaid. *The Words We Use*. Dublin: Four Courts Press, 1996. 134 pp.

2891. O'Donnell, James. *Classic Irish Proverbs in English and Irish*. Illustrations by Brian Fitzgerald. Belfast: Appletree Press, 1997; rpt. San Francisco: Chronicle Books, 1998. 80 pp.

2892. O'Donoghue, D.J. "Selected Irish Proverbs, etc." In D.J. O'Donoghue. *The Humor of Ireland*. London: Walter Scott, 1894. 414-420.

2893. O'Donoghue, Jo. *Favourite Irish Proverbs*. Photographs by Lily Lenihan. Dublin: Currach Press, 2008. 93 pp.

2894. O'Farrell, Padraic. *Irish Proverbs and Sayings. Gems of Irish Wisdom*. Dublin: Mercier Press, 1980. 91 pp.

2895. O'Griofa, Mairtin. *Irish Folk Wisdom*. Illustrations by Daniel Maclise. New York: Sterling Publishing, 1993. 128 pp.

2896. O'Rahilly, Thomas F. *A Miscellany of Irish Proverbs*. Dublin: The Talbot Press, 1922; rpt. Darby, Pennsylvania: Folcroft Library Editions, 1976. 174 pp.

2897. Partridge, Angela. *A Hundred Irish Proverbs and Sayings*. Dublin: Folens Publishers, 1978. 36 pp.

2898. Quin, E. G. "A Book of Irish Proverbs." *Éigse: A Journal of Irish Studies*, 10, no. 2 (1962), 127-143 (transcription of an unpublished manuscript).

2899. Reynolds, Joe. *Irish Proverbs*. Illustrations by Niamh O'Donnell. Bray, County Wicklow, Ireland: Real Ireland Design Ltd., 1989. 32 pp. (miniature book).

2900. Rosenstock, Gabriel. *The Wasp in the Mug: Unforgettable Irish Proverbs*. Illustrations by Pieter Sluis. Dublin: Mercier Press, 1993. 112 pp.

2901. Rosenstock, Gabriel. *Irish Proverbs in Irish and English*. Dublin: Mercier Press, 1999. 79 pp.

2902. Ross, W.A., and H.R. Ross (eds.). *Gaelic Proverbs. Gaelic and English*. Illustrations by Brian Fitzgerald. Belfast: Appletree Press, 1996. 60 pp.

2903. Seoighe, Mainchín (ed.). *The Irish Quotation Book. A Literary Companion*. New York: Barnes & Noble, 1993. 96 pp. With illustrations.

2904. Ua Cnáimhsi, Pádraig. "An Béal Beo (ar leanas)." *An tUltach*, 70, no. 1 (1993), 26 (Gaelic proverbs).

2905. Ua Donnchadha, Tadhg. *Sean-fhocail na Munhan*. Baile Atha Cliath, Ireland: Conradh na Gaedhilge, 1902. 16 pp. (proverbs of Munster).

2906. Uí Bhraonáin, Donla. *500 Seanfhocal [sic], Proverbs, Refranes, Przysłów*. With illustrations by Fintan Taite. Baile Atha Cliath, Ireland: Cois Life, 2007. 202 pp.

2907. Watson, Seosamh. "Proverbs and Traditional Sayings from Easter Ross." *Northern Lights: Following Folklore in North-Western Europe. Essays in Honour of Bo Almqvist*. Ed. Séamas Ó Catháin. Dublin: University College Dublin Press, 2001. 342-361.

2908. William, Tony Catherine Antoine. *Seanfhocail as Acaill*. Indreabhán, Conamara (Ireland): Cló Iar-Chonnachta, 1995. 58 pp.

2909. Williams, Fionnuala Carson. "Triads and Other Enumerative Proverbs from South Ulster." *Ulster Folklife*, 34 (1988), 60-67.

2910. Williams, Fionnuala Carson. *Irish Proverbs*. Swords, County Dublin: Poolbeg, 1992. 141 pp.

2911. Williams, Fionnuala Carson. "Irish Proverbs and *Európai Közmondások*." *Acta Ethnographica Hungarica*, 45, nos. 3-4 (2000), 421-437. Also in *"Igniculi sapientiae". János-Baranyai-Decsi-Festschrift*. Eds. Gábor Barna, Ágnes Stemler, and Vilmos Voigt. Budapest: Osiris Kiadó, 2004. 227-251.

2912. Williams, Fionnuala Carson. *Irish Proverbs: Traditional Wit & Wisdom*. Illustrations by Marlene Ekman. New York: Sterling Publishing, 2000. 128 pp.

2913. Williams, Fionnuala Carson. *Wellerisms in Ireland. Towards a Corpus from Oral and Literary Sources*. Burlington, Vermont: The University of Vermont, 2003. 321 pp.

Italian

2914. Antoni, Anna Maria, and Carlo Lapucci. *I proverbi dei mesi*. Bologna: Cappelli, 1975. 293 pp. (weather proverbs).

2915. Basile, Paola (ed.). *A buon itenditor ... poche parole. Proverbi, modi di dire e giochi di parole in figurina*. Modena: Museo della Figurina, 2010. 120. With illustrations.

2916. Besso, Marco. *Roma e il Papa nei proverbi e nei modi di dire*. Roma: Fondazione M. Besso, 1971. 427 pp.

2917. Boggione, Valter, and Lorenzo Massobrio. *Dizionario dei proverbi. I proverbi italiani organizzati per temi. 30.000 detti raccolti nelle regioni italiane e tramandati dalle fonti letterarie.* Torino: UTET, 2004. 922 pp.

2918. Cervini, Claudia. "Proverbi italiani relativi a bovini (dal materiale dell' *Atlante Paremiologico Italiano*)." *Paremia*, 3 (1994), 139-142.

2919. Cibotto, Giovanni Antonio. *Proverbi del Veneto.* Firenze: A. Martello-Giunti, 1977; rpt. Firenze: Giunti Gruppo Editoriale. 1995. 121 pp.

2920. Corso, Raffaele. "Wellerismi italiani." *Folklore* (Napoli), 2, nos. 3-4 (1947-1948), 3-26.

2921. Donato, Elena, and Gianni Palitta. *Il grande libro dei proverbi.* Roma: Newton & Compton, 1998. 394 pp.

2922. Flonta, Teodor. *A Dictionary of English and Italian Equivalent Proverbs.* Hobart, Tasmania: De Proverbio.com, 2001. 265 pp.

2923. Fort, Francesco. *Proverbi friulani commentati.* Bologna: Mida, 1990. 138 pp.

2924. Franceschi, Temistocle. "Proverbi e detti alabro-lucani." *Bollettino dell'Atlante Linguistico Italiano*, 11-12 (1965), 17-38.

2925. Franceschi, Temistocle, and Claudia Cervini. *Atlante Paremiologico Italiano: Questionario ventimila detti proverbiali raccolti in ogni regione d'Italia.* Alessandria: Edizioni dell'Orso, 2000. 672 pp.

2926. Franceschi, Temistocle, A.M. Mancini, Maria Valeria. Miniati, and L.B. Porto. *Atlante paremiologico italiano: Questionario.* Urbino: Presso l'universita degli studi di Urbino, 1984. (= *Studi Urbinati di storia filosofia e letteratura, supplemento linguistico*, 3 [1981-1984], 410 pp.). 410 pp.

2927. Frenzel, Herbert. *1000 idiomatische Redensarten Italienisch. Mit Erklärungen und Beispielen.* Berlin: Langenscheidt, 1939. 204 pp. Revised ed. Hermann Willers. Berlin: Langenscheidt, 1974 (5th ed. 1978). 214 pp.

2928. Guazotti, Paola, and Maria Frederica Oddera. *Il grande dizionario dei proverbi italiani.* Bologna: Zanichelli, 2006. 991 pp.

2929. Guazotti, Paola, and Maria Federica Oddera. *Il mini dizionario dei proverbi.* Bologna: Zanichelli, 2008. 672 pp.

2930. Kradolfer, J. "Das italienische Sprichwort und seine Beziehungen zum deutschen." *Zeitschrift für Völkerpsychologie*, 9 (1877), 185-271.

2931. Lapucci, Carlo. *Dizionario dei proverbi italiani. 25.000 detti memorabili*. Milano: Arnoldo Mondadori, 2007. 1854 pp.

2932. Lauri, Achille. "Wellerismi della media Valle del Liri." *Folklore* (Napoli), 3, nos. 3-4 (1948-1949), 107-113; 4, nos. 1-2 (1949), 109-118; and 6, nos. 1-2 (1951), 58-67.

2933. Luciani, Vincent. *Italian Idioms with Proverbs*. New York: S.F. Vanni, 1964 (2nd ed. 1981). 101 pp.

2934. Marangoni, Giovanni. *Proverbi di casa nostra [18th century]*. Venezia: Filippi Editore, 1970. 79 pp.

2935. Massa, Gaetano. *Italian Idioms and Proverbs*. New York: Las Americas Publishing, 1940. 137 pp.

2936. Melo, Verissimo de. "Wellerism." *Tradicion: Revista Peruana de Cultura*. 2, no. 3 (1951), 31-37.

2937. Merbury, Charles. *Proverbi vulgari, raccolti in diversi luoghi d'Italia*. London: Vautrollier, 1581. 31 pp. Rpt. as *Charles Merbury "Proverbi vulgari"*. Ed. Charles Speroni. *University of California Publications in Modern Philology*, 28, no. 3 (1946), 63-157.

2938. Mertvago, Peter. *Dictionary of 1000 Italian Proverbs*. New York: Hippocrene Books, 1997. 145 pp.

2939. Mitelli, Giuseppe Maria. *Proverbi Figurati di Giuseppe Maria Mitelli [1678]*. Eds Lorenzo Marinese and Alberto Manfredi. Milano: Casa Editrice Cerastico, 1963. 78 pp. With 48 illustrations.

2940. Mitelli, Giuseppe Maria. *Proverbi figvrati consecrati al Serenissimo Principe Francesco Maria di Toscana ... /1678/*. Rpt. ed. Alfredo Petrucci as *Proverbi Figurati di Giuseppe Maria Mitelli*. Roma: Banca Nazionale dell' Agricoltura, 1967. Rpt. ed. Alberto Milano. Milano: Edizione il Meneghello, 1985. 66 pp. With 48 illustrations.

2941. Möller, Ferdinand. *Proverbi italiani. ltalienische Sprichwörter*. München: Deutscher Taschenbuch Verlag, 1978. 84 pp.

2942. Möller, Ferdinand. *Proverbes français. Französische Sprichwörter*. Illustrations by Frieda Wiegand. München: Deutscher Taschenbuch Verlag, 1979. 95 pp. (misplaced—W.M.)

2943. Neumann, Manfred. *Italienische idiomatische Redewendungen und Sprichwörter*. Leipzig: VEB Verlag Enzyklopädie, 1977 (3rd 1986). 108 pp.

2944. Orsini, Stéphanie. *Pruverbii è altri detti ... Proverbes, adages et autres dits ...*. Illustrations by Alain Luciani. Ajaccio, Corsica: Albania, 2003. 103 pp.

2945. Petroselli, Francesco. *Blasoni Popolari della Provincia di Viterbo*. 2 vols. Viterbo: Quatrini A. & Figli, 1978 and 1986. I, 227 pp.; II, 279 pp.

2946. Pitrè, Giuseppe. *Proverbi Siciliani raccolti et confrontati con quelli degli altri dialetti d'Italia*. 4 vols. Palermo: Lauriel, 1880; rpt. Palermo: "Il Vespro", 1978. I, V-CCXXXIV (introduction) and 356 pp.; II, 452 pp.; III, 389 pp.; IV, 411 pp.

2947. Pitrè, Giuseppe. *Proverbi siciliani. Con traduzione in italiano*. Milano(?): Martin, ca. 1996. 191 pp.

2948. Ricapito, Joseph. "The Wisdom of Proverbs: Proverbs from Italy in Italian and in Dialect from Giovinazzo in Apulia." *Romance Languages Annual*, 11 (1999), 347-357.

2949. Rotondo, Antonio. *Proverbi Napoletani ovvero La filosofia di un popolo*. Illustrations by Carlo Lindström from 1836. Napoli: Il Libro in Piazza, 1992. 454 pp.

2950. Salvante, A. Raffaele. *Proverbi Calitrani*. Firenze: Edizioni "l Calitrano", 1986. 181 pp.

2951. Santi, Antonio. *The Book of Italian Wisdom*. New York: Citadel Press, 2003. 212 pp. With illustrations.

2952. Schwamenthal, Riccardo, and Michele L. Straniero. *Dizionario dei proverbi italiani. 6.000 voci e 10.000 varianti dialettali*. Milano: RCS Rizzoli Libri, 1991 (2nd printing 1993). 565 pp.

2953. Sciortino, Andrea. *La vita di oggi nei proverbi di ieri*. Palermo: Editrice de "Il Vespro", 1978. 110 pp. With illustrations.

2954. Sellner, Alfred. *Italienisch im Alltag. Alphabetisch geordnetes Nachschlagewerk von italienischen Sentenzen, Sprichwörtern, Phrasen, Floskeln, Redewendungen, Zitaten und Formeln*. Wiesbaden: VMA-Verlag, 1988. 131 pp.

2955. Speroni, Charles. *Folklore in [Alighieri Dante's] "The Divine Comedy"*. Diss. University of California at Berkeley, 1938. 339 pp. (proverbs, pp. 230-307).

2956. Speroni, Charles. "Proverbs and Proverbial Phrases in [Giambattista] Basile's *Pentameron*." *University of California Publications in Modern Philology*, 24, no. 2 (1941), 181-288.

2957. Speroni, Charles. *The Italian Wellerism to the End of the Seventeenth Century*. Berkeley, California: University of California Press, 1953. 71 pp.

2958. Tucci, Giovanni. "Inchiesta sui wellerismi della Campania." *Rivista di Etnografia*, 16 (1962), 3-51.

2959. Tucci, Giovanni. "Wellerismi della Campania." *Rivista di Etnografia*, 17 (1963), 3-50.

2960. Tucci, Giovanni. *Dicette Pulicenella ... Inchiesta di Antropologia culturale sulla Campania*. Milano: Silva Editore, 1966. 348 pp. With illustrations. (wellerisms, pp. 20-342).

2961. Varrini, Giulio, and Maler [Friedrich] Müller. *Proverbi / Sprichwörter [1668 und 1809]*. Eds. Ulrike Leuschner and Ingrid Sattel Bernardini. Heidelberg: Carl Winter, 2000. 78 pp. With illustrations.

2962. Voss, Karl, Domenico Longo, and Gisela Pasetti-Bombardella. *Redensarten der italienischen Sprache*. Frankfurt am Main: Ullstein, 1968. 206 pp.

2963. Zagari, Rosa. *Il proverbio come espediente tematico nelle opere di Giovanni Verga*. Diss. Rutgers University, 1998. 403 pp. (proverb index, pp. 337-392).

2964. Zavatti, Silvio. "Proverbi meteorologici raccolti nel maceratese." *Lares*, 36 (1970), 51-69.

Jamaican

2965. Anderson, Izett, and Frank Cundall. *Jamaica Negro Proverbs and Sayings*. Kingston, Jamaica: The Institute of Jamaica, 1910. 48 pp.

2966. Anderson, Izett, and Frank Cundall. *Jamaican Negro Proverbs and Sayings*. London: Institute of Jamaica, 1927; rpt. Shannon: Irish University Press, 1972. 128 pp.

2967. Bates, William C. "Creole Folk-Lore from Jamaica: Proverbs." *Journal of American Folklore*, 9 (1896), 38-42.

2968. Beckwith, Martha Warren. *Jamaica Proverbs*. Poughkeepsie, New York: Vassar Cooperative Book Shop, 1925; rpt. New York: Negro Universites Press, 1970. 137 pp.

2969. Burnett, Vivienne. *Mi Granny Seh – Fi Tell Yu Seh. The A to Z of Jamaicanisms*. Illustrations by Ray Jackson. Kingston, Jamaica: Jamrite Publications, 2001. 62 pp.

2970. Franck, Harry A. "Jamaica Proverbs." *Dialect Notes*, 5 (1918-1927), 98-108.

2971. Jackson, Pastor L.A. "Proverbs of Jamaica." *The Language of the Black Experience. Cultural Expression through Word and Sound in the Caribbean and Black Britain*. Eds. David Sutcliffe and Ansel Wong. Oxford: Basil Blackwell, 1986. 32-36.

2972. Morris-Brown, Vivien. *The Jamaica Handbook of Proverbs. With Standard English Translations and Explanations*. Illustrations by Paul Clayton. Mandeville, Jamaica: Island Heart Publishers, 1993. 197 pp.

2973. Watson, G. Llewellyn. *Jamaican Sayings. With Notes on Folklore, Aesthetics, and Social Control*. Tallahassee, Florida: Florida A&M University Press, 1991. 292 pp.

Japanese

2974. Akiyama, Aisaburo. *Japanese Proverbs and Proverbial Phrases*. Yokohama: Yoshikawa Book Store, 1940. 305 pp.

2975. Anada, Yoshiyuki. *Daigakusei no Kotowaza Zukuri*. (Proverb Compositions by College Students). Tokyo: Yugishya, 1996. 186 pp. (in Japanese).

2976. Anonymous. *Japanese Proverbs*. Illustrations by Jeff Hill. Mount Vernon, New York: Peter Pauper Press, 1962. 62 pp.

2977. Anonymous. *Kotawaza Jiten* [Proverb Dictionary]. Hiroshima: Daisou Sangyou, 2000. 208 pp. (in Japanese).

2978. Arai, Toshimitsu et al. *Kotowaza Dai-Jiten*. (The Dictionary of Proverbs). Tokyo: Shogakukan, 1992. 1998 pp. (in Japanese).

2979. Berndt, Jürgen (ed.). *Sprichwörter aus Japan*. Berlin: Verlag Volk und Welt, 1984. 70 pp.

2980. Berndt, Jürgen (ed.). *Gutes ist am besten gleich getan: 100 Sprichwörter aus Japan*. Illustrations by Suiko Simon. Berlin: edition q, 1992. 208 pp.

2981. Buchanan, Daniel Crump. *Japanese Proverbs and Sayings.* Norman, Oklahoma: University of Oklahoma Press, 1965 (2nd ed. 1979). 280 pp.

2982. Diener, Christian (ed.).. *Die Weisheit Japans.* München Wilhelm Heyne, 1979. 74 pp. With illustrations.

2983. Ehmann, P. *Die Sprichwörter und bildlichen Ausdrücke der japanischen Sprache.* Tokyo: Tokyo Tsukiji Type Foundry, 1897. 2nd ed. Tokyo: Verlag der Asia Major, 1927. 425 pp.

2984. Fink-Henseler, Roland W. *Brevier fernöstlicher Weisheit. Sprichwörter, Aphorismen und Gedichte aus Japan und China.* Bayreuth: Gondrom, 1984. 216 pp. With illustrations.

2985. Galef, David. *"Even Monkeys Fall far from Trees" and Other Japanese Proverbs.* Illustrations by Jun Hashimoto. Rutland, Vermont: Charles E. Tuttle, 1987. 226 pp.

2986. Galef, David. *Even a Stone Buddha Can Talk. The Wit and Wisdom of Japanese Proverbs.* Illustrations by Jun Hashimoto. Rutland, Vermont: Tuttle, 2000. 230 pp.

2987. Hettinger, Eugen (ed.). *Quellen japanischer Weisheit.* Illustrations by Josef Tannheimer. St. Gallen: Verlag Leobuchhandlung, 1988. 42 pp.

2988. Hisa, Michitaro. "Some Japanized Chinese Proverbs." *Journal of American Folklore,* 9 (1896), 132-138.

2989. Huzii, Otoo. *Japanese Proverbs.* Illustrations by Senpan Maekawa. Tokyo: Board of Tourist Industry, Japanese Government Railways, 1940. 111 pp.

2990. Ikeda, Yasaburo, Donald Keene, and Hokojiro Jona (eds.). *Nichiei Koji Kotowaza Jiten. [A Dictionary of English-Japanese Fables and Proverbs].* Tokyo: Asahi Evening News, 1982; rpt. Tokyo: Hokuseido-Shoten, 1994. 541 pp.

2991. Kawanabe, Kusumi (ill.). *Kyosai Hyakuzu [100 Proverb Pictures].* Texts translated into English by Yoshikatsu Kitamura. Warabi: Kawanabe Kyosai Memorial Museum, 1982. 55 pp. and 6 pp. (English translation). With illustrations. (in Japanese).

2992. Kitamura, Yoshikatsu. *Sekai no Kotowaza* (World Proverb Dictionary). Tokyo: Tokyodo, 1987. 420 pp. With illustrations (in Japanese).

2993. Kitamura, Yoshikatsu, and Katsuaki Takeda. *A Dictionary of Everyday English Proverbs*. Tokyo: Tokyo-do shuppan, 1997. 248 pp.

2994. Korpiola, Kyösti. *Japanilaisia ja suomalaisia sananlaskuja*. Julkaisu: Suomalais-Japanilainen Yhdistys, 1992. 123 pp. (in Japanese).

2995. Korpiola, Kyösti. *Japanin Viisaus*. Julkaisu: Suomalais-Japanilainen Yhdistys, 1995. 160 pp. (in Japanese)

2996. Mori, Yoko. *Bryugeru no Kotowaza no Sekai. [The Proverb World of Brueghel]*. Tokyo: Hakuoshya, 1992. 692 pp. With illustrations. (in Japanese).

2997. Muş, Ali Osman, and Mariko Erdoğan. *Japonca-türkçe atasözleri sözlüğü*. Istanbul: Birinsi Baski, 1996. 238 pp.

2998. Okutsu, Fumio. *Eigo no Kotowaza: Nihongo no Kotowaza tono Hikaku*. [English and Japanese Proverbs: A Comparative Study]. Tokyo: The Simul Press, 1988. 240 pp.

2999. Reinirkens, Hubert (ed.). *Sprichwörter und Redensarten. Deutsch-Japanisch*. Wiesbaden: Otto Harrossowitz, 1955. 111 pp.

3000. Saiga, Yohei. *Sports Kotowaza Sho-Jiten*. [The Dictionary of Sports' Proverbs]. Tokyo: Yugishya, 1992. 207 pp. With illustrations. (in Japanese).

3001. Steenackers, Francis, and Véda Tokunosuké. *Cent proverbes japonais*. Paris: Leroux, 1886. 214 pp. Rpt. in Japanese as: *Etoki Edo Shomin no Kotowaza (Edo Citizens' Proverbs Explained with Drawings)*. Illustrations by Gyosai Kawanabe. Tokyo: Tokyodo, 1991. 231 pp.

3002. Sudau, Günter. *Die religiöse Gedankenwelt der Japaner im Spiegel ihres Sprichworts*. Leipzig: Werkgemeinschaft, 1932. 95 pp.

3003. Suwarno, Peter. *Dictionary of Javanese Proverbs and Idiomatic Expressions*. Yogyakarta: Gadjah Mada University Press, 1999. 422 pp. (misplaced—W. M.)

3004. Suzuki, Tozo. *Shinpen Koji Kotowaza Jiten*. [The New Proverb Dictionary]. Tokyo: Sotakushya, 1992. 1638 pp. (in Japanese).

3005. Taylor, Archer. "Some Japanese Proverbial Comparisons." *Western Folklore*, 15 (1956), 59-60.

3006. Tokita, Masamizu. *Illustrated Dictionary of Proverbs*. Tokyo: Tokyo Shoseki Publishing Company, 2009. 847 pp. (2200 proverbs with 4300 illustrations; in Japanese).

3007. Vande Walle, Willy, and Bart Mesotten. *Geen mosselen op het veld. Japanese spreekwoorden en hoe ze klinken in het Nederlands*. Illustrations by Hoshu Nakano.Tielt: Lannoo, 1989. 128 pp.

3008. Yamaguchi, H.S.K. "Japanese Proverbs." In H.S.K. Yamaguchi and Alsuharu Sakai. *We Japanese. Being Descriptions of Many of the Customs, Manners, Ceremonies, Festivals, Arts and Crafts of the Japanese Besides Numerous Other Subjects*. Miyanoshita: Fujiya Hotel, 1950. 174-183. With 11 illustrations.

3009. Yamazaki, Naomi et al. *Seigo Dai-Jien: Koji Kotowaza Meigen Meiku*. [Big Dictionary: Famous Proverb Collection]. Tokyo: Shufu-to-Seikatsusha, 1995. 1468 pp. With illustrations. (in Japanese).

3010. Yoshioka, Masahiro. *Furansugo Kotowaza-shu / Proverbes français*. Tokyo: Surugadai Shuppansha, 1990. 168 pp. (in Japanese).

3011. Yoshioka, Masahiro. *Roshiago Kotowaza-shu / Russkie poslovitsy / Russian Proverbs / Proverbes russes*. Tokyo: Surugadai Shuppansha, 1992. 176 pp. (in Japanese).

3012. Zona, Guy A. *Even Withered Trees Give Prosperity to the Mountain and Other Proverbs of Japan*. New York: Touchstone, 1996. 127 pp.

Karachai

3013. Chagarov, O.A. *Poslovitsy i pogovorki na karachaevskom iazyke*. Cherkessk: Karachaevo-cherkesskoe knizhnoe izlatel'stvo, 1963. 482 pp.

3014. Ortabaeva, R. et al. *Poslovitsy i pogovorki narodov karachaevo-cherkesii*. Stavropol': Stavropol'skoe knizhnoe izdatel'stvo, 1990. 368 pp.

Kazakh

3015. Akkozin, Madat Akhilbaevich. *Kazakhskie poslovitsy ipogovorki*. Alma-Ata: Kazakhstan, 1986. 140 pp.

3016. Kirchner, Mark (ed.). *Sprichwörter der Kasachen*. Wiesbaden: Otto Harrassowitz, 1993. 196 pp.

Komi

3017. Plesovskii, Fedor Vasilevich. *Komi shus'ög"ias da kyviöz"ias. Komi poslovitsy i pogovorki.* Illustrations by A.V. Moshev. Syktyvkar: Komi knizhnoe izdatel'stvo. 1983. 208 pp.

3018. Sakharova, Marfa Aleksandrovna, and Nina Andreevna Kolegova. "Poslovitsy, pogovorki, frazeologicheskie sochetaniia i otdel'nye vyrazheniia." *Pechorskii dialekt komi iazyka.* Eds. M.A. Sakharova, N.N. Sel'kov, and N.A. Kolegova. Syktyvkar: Komi knizhnöi izdatel'stvo, 1976. 138-149. (Syryenian [Komi] langauge).

Korean

3019. Chung, Chong-wha. *Dictionary of Korean and English Proverbs.* Seoul: Korea University Press, 1991 (2nd ed. 1995). (in Korean). 389 pp.

3020. Ha, Tae Hung. *Maxims and Proverbs of Old Korea.* Seoul: Yonsei University Press, 1970. 315 pp.

3021. Holt, Daniel D. *Tigers, Frogs, and Rice Cakes. A Book of Korean Proverbs.* Illustrations by Soma Han Stickler. Auburn, California: Shen's Books, 1999. 32 pp.

3022. Kim, Yong-il. *Yongo ro paeunun Hanguk soktam [Korean Proverb Learning from English].* Seoul: Kyongjin Munhwasa, 2005. 180 pp. (in Korean).

3023. Kim-Werner, Samhwa. *Phraseologisches Wörterbuch. Deutsch-Koreanisch. Am Beispiel der somatischen Phraseologismen.* Seoul: Yulin-Madang Publishing, 1996. 202 pp. (dictionary, pp. 103-185).

3024. Luomala, Katharine. "Proverbs from Korean Visiting Students in Hawaii." *Proverbium,* no. 16 (1971), 602-606.

3025. Su, Lim. *Koreiskie narodnye izrecheniia na koreiskom i russkom iazykakh.* Moskva: Nauka, 1982. 359 pp.

Kurdish

3026. Amin, Abdul-Kader. *Kurdish Proverbs.* Photographs by Ismet Cherif Vanly. Brooklyn, New York: Kurdish Times, 1989. 76 pp.

3027. Dzhalil, Ordikhane, and Dzhalile Dzhalil. *Kurdskie poslovitsy i pogovorki.* Moskva: Glavnaia redaktsiia vostochnoi literatury, 1972. 456 pp.

Lamut (Even)

3028. Sotavalta, Arvo, and Harry Halén. "Sprichwörter, beratende Sprüche od. Beispielwörter der Lamuten." In A. Sotavalta and H. Halén. *Westlamutische Materialien.* Helsinki: Suomalais-Ugrilainen Seura, 1978. 31-34.

Latin

3029. Bartels, Klaus. *Veni, vidi, vici: Geflügelte Worte aus dem Griechischen und Lateinischen.* Mainz: Philipp von Zabern, 2008. 216 pp.

3030. Bartels, Klaus, and Ludwig Huber. *Veni, vidi. vici. Geflügelte Worte aus dem Griechischen und Lateinischen.* Zürich: Artemis, 1966 (3rd ed. 1976). 87 pp.

3031. Bartsch, Karl. "[Lateinische] Sprichwörter des XI. Jahrhunderets." *Germania*, 18 (1873), 310-353

3032. Bayer, Karl. *Nota bene! Das lateinische Zitatenlexikon.* München: Artemis und Winkler, 1994. 576 pp.

3033. Binder, Wilhelm. *Novus Thesaurus Adagiorum Latinorum. Lateinischer Sprichwörterschatz.* Stuttgart: Fischhaber, 1861; rpt. Niederwalluf bei Wiesbaden: Martin Sändig, 1971. 404 pp.

3034. Dale, Darley. "Medieval Latin Proverbs." *American Catholic Review*, 46 (1921), 336-342.

3035. Dalitz, Günter. *Lateinische Sprichwörter und sprichwörtliche Redensarten nach Sachgruppen geordnet.* Diss. Universität Leipzig, 1966. 479 pp.

3036. Ehrlich, Eugene. *Amo, Amas, Amat and More. How to Use Latin to Your Oen Advantage and to the Astonishment of Others.* New York: Harper & Row, 1985. 328 pp.

3037. Erasmus of Rotterdam, Desiderius. *Proverbes or Adagies.* Ed. Richard Tauerner. London: Whyte Harte, 1539; rpt. New York: Da Capo Press, 1969. 124 pp.

3038. Erasmus of Rotterdam, Desiderius. *Apothegmes.* London: Ricardi Grafton, 1542; rpt. New York: Da Capo Press, 1969. 359 leaves.

3039. Erasmus of Rotterdam, Desiderius. *Opera Omnia. Tomvs Secvndvs. Complectens Adagia.* Lvgdvni Batavorum: Petri Vander,

1703; rpt. Hildesheim: Georg Olms, 2001. 1212 cols. (plus 54 pp. index).

3040. Erasmus of Rotterdam, Desiderius. *Adages Ii1 to Iv100* (= *Collected Works of Erasmus*, vol. 31). Translated by Margaret Mann Phillips and annotated by R.A.B. Mynors. Toronto: University of Toronto Press, 1982. 493 pp.

3041. Erasmus of Rotterdam, Desiderius. *Adages Ivi1 to Ix100* (= *Collected Works of Erasmus*, vol. 32). Translated and annotated by R.A.B. Mynors. Toronto: University of Toronto Press, 1989. 412 pp.

3042. Erasmus of Rotterdam, Desiderius. *Adages IIi1 to IIvi100* (= *Collected Works of Erasmus*, vol. 33). Translated and annotated by R.A.B. Mynors. Toronto: University of Toronto Press, 1991. 479 pp.

3043. Erasmus of Rotterdam, Desiderius. *Adages IIvii1 to IIIiii100* (= *Collected Works of Erasmus*, vol. 34). Translated and annotated by R.A.B. Mynors. Toronto: University of Toronto Press, 1992. 458 pp.

3044. Erasmus of Rotterdam, Desiderius. *Adages IIIiv1 to IVii100* (= *Collected Works of Erasmus*, vol. 35). Translated and annotated by Denis L. Drysdall, edited by John N. Grant. Toronto: University of Toronto Press, 2005. 592 pp.

3045. Erasmus of Rotterdam, Desiderius. *Adages IViii1 to Vii51* (= *Collected Works of Erasmus*, vol. 36). Translated and annotated by John N. Grant and Betty I. Knott, edited by John N. Grant. Toronto: University of Toronto Press, 2006. 677 pp.

3046. Erasmus of Rotterdam, Desiderius. *Erasmus von Rotterdam. Adagia. Vom Sinn und vom Leben der Sprichwörter*. Ed. Theodor Knecht. Zürich: Manesse, 1984. 328 pp.

3047. Erasmus of Rotterdam, Desiderius. *The Adages of Erasmus*. Ed. William Barker. Toronto: University of Toronto Press, 2001. 405 pp.

3048. Erasmus von Rotterdam, Desiderius. *Dialogus cui titulus Ciceronianus. Adagiorum Chilades (Adagia Selecta)*. (= *Ausgewählte Schriften in 8 Bänden*. Ed. Werner Welzig. Bd. 7). Ed. Theresia Payr. Darmstadt: Wissenschaftliche Buchgesellschaft, 1972. 633 pp. (adagia pp. 357-633).

3049. Erasmus von Rotterdam, Desiderius. *Adagia. Lateinisch / Deutsch*. Ed. Anton Gail. Stuttgart: Philipp Reclam, 1983. 224 pp.

3050. Faselius, August. *Latium oder das alte Rom in seinen Sprüchwörtern*. Weimar: Bernhard Friedrich Voigt, 1859. Rpt. as

Latium: Sprichwörter des alten Rom. Leipzig: Reprint-Verlag, 1997. 276 pp.

3051. Fumagalli, Giuseppe. *L'ape latina. Dizionarietto di 2948 sentenze, proverbi, motti, divise frasi e locuzioni latine.* Milano: Hoepli, 1911; rpt. Milano: Hoepli, 1969; rpt. Milano: Hoepli, 1992. 361 pp.

3052. Häussler, Reinhard (ed.). *Nachträge zu A. Otto, Sprichwörter und sprichwörtliche Redensarten der Römer [1890].* Hildesheim: Georg Olms, 1968. 324 pp.

3053. Heimann, Gabi. *Quod licet Iovi ... Die bekanntesten lateinischen Sprichwörter und Redensarten.* München: Compact/Minipräsent Verlag, 2002. 255 pp. (miniature book).

3054. Heimeran, Ernst, and Michel Hofmann. *Antike Weisheit. Eine Sammlung lateinischer und griechischer Gedanken.* München: Ernst Heimeran, 1937. 143 pp.

3055. Helfer, Christian. *Crater Dictorum. Lateinische Sprich- und Schlagwörter, Wahlsprüche und Inschriften des 15.-20. Jahrhunderts.* Saarbrücken: Verlag der Societas Latina, 1993. 176 pp.

3056. Henderson, Alfred. *Latin Proverbs and Quotations with Translations and Parallel Passages.* London: Sampson Low, 1869. 505 pp.

3057. Hennes, William R. "Latin Mottoes and Proverbs." *Classical Bulletin*, 2 (1925-1926), 80.

3058. Hettinger, Eugen (ed.). *Quellen römischer Weisheit. Texte und Bilder der antiken Welt.* St. Gallen: Leobuchhandlung, 1965. 42 pp. With illustrations (miniature book).

3059. Kasper, Muriel. *Reclams Lateinisches Zitaten-Lexikon.* Stuttgart: Philipp Reclam, 1996. 432 pp.

3060. Kocher, Christian Friedrich. *Phraseologia Corneliana, Das ist Außzug der vornehmsten Redens-Arten, welche in dem Cornelio Nepote gefunden werden, samt einiger Analogia Phrasium, zum Nutzen der Schul-Jugend in das Teutsche übersetzt.* Ulm: Daniel Bartholomaeus, 1715. 312 pp. (one of my personal tresures – W.M.).

3061. Liebs, Detlef. *Lateinische Rechtsregeln und Rechtssprichwörter.* München: C.H. Beck, 1982. 277 pp.

261

3062. Macrone, Michael. *By Jove! Brush Up Your Mythology.* Illustrations by Tom Lulevitch. New York: HarperCollins, 1992. 237 pp.

3063. Mall, Iosephus. *Latinitate optima originali non magistrorum cum gaudio. Docebis disces linguam latinam: 5.500 formulis, verborum lusibus, sententiis, electis e poetis locis [Beispielhaftes Originallatein für fast alle Fragen der Grammatik].* Münster: Aschendorff, 1995. 272 pp.

3064. Massing, Jean Michel. *Erasmian Wit and Proverbial Wisdom: An Illustrated Moral Compendium for François I. Facsimile of a Dismembered Manuscript with Introduction and Description.* London: The Warburg Institute, University of London, 1995. 212 pp. With 45 folios and 47 illustrations.

3065. Meech, Sanford B. "A Collection of [medieval Latin-English] Proverbs in Rawlinson MS D 328." *Modern Philology*, 38 (1940), 113-132.

3066. Otto, August. "Die Götter und Halbgötter im Sprichworte." *Archiv für lateinische Lexikographie*, 3 (1886), 207-229 and 384-387.

3067. Otto, August. "Die historischen und geographischen Sprichwörter." *Archiv für lateinische Lexikographie*, 3 (1886), 355-384.

3068. Otto, August. "Das Pflanzenreich im Sprichwort." *Archiv für lateinische Lexikographie und Grammatik*, 4 (1887), 189-196.

3069. Otto, August. "Die Natur im Sprichwort." *Archiv für lateinische Lexikographie und Grammatik*, 4 (1887), 14-43.

3070. Otto, August. "Essen und Trinken im Sprichwort." *Archiv für lateinische Lexikographie und Grammatik*, 4 (1887), 345-357.

3071. Otto, August. "Der menschliche Körper und seine Teile im Sprichwort." *Archiv für lateinische Lexikographie und Grammatik*, 6 (1889), 309-340.

3072. Otto, August. "Geldverkehr und Besitz im Sprichwort." *Archiv für lateinische Lexikographie und Grammatik*, 6 (1889), 47-58.

3073. Otto, August. "Landwirtschaft, Jagd und Seeleben im Sprichwort." *Archiv für lateinische Lexikographie und Grammatik*, 6 (1889), 9-24.

3074. Otto, August. *Die Sprichwörter und sprichwörtlichen Redensarten der Römer.* Leipzig: Teubner, 1890; rpt. Hildesheim: Georg Olms, 1871. 436 pp.

3075. P. "Zu den lateinischen Sprichwörtern und sprichwörtlichen Redensarten." *Archiv für lateinische Lexikographie und Grammatik,* 3 (1886), 59-69.

3076. Reichert, Heinrich G. *Urban und human. Gedanken über lateinische Sprichwörter.* Hamburg: Marion von Schröder, 1957. 534 pp. Rpt. as *Urban und human. Unvergängliche lateinische Spruchweisheit.* Wiesbaden: Panorama Verlag, 1987. 376 pp.

3077. Seiler, Friedrich. "Deutsche Sprichwörter in mittelalterlicher lateinischer Fassung." *Zeitschrift für deutsche Philologie,* 45 (1913), 236-291.

3078. Seiler, Friedrich. "Mittellateinische Sprichwörter, die in deutscher Fassung nicht nachweisbar sind." Zeitschrift für Deutschkunde, 35 (1921), 299-308, 463-469, and 532-537.

3079. Sellner, Alfred. *Latein im Alltag. Alphabetisch geordnetes Nachschlagewerk von lateinischen Sentenzen, Sprichwörtern, Phrasen, Redewendungen, Zitaten und Formeln sowie deren Abkürzungen mit 800 Stichwörtern aus allen Lebensbereichen.* Wiesbaden: VMA-Verlag, 1980. 128 pp.

3080. Serz, Georg Thomas. *Teutsche Idiotismen, Provinzialismen, Volksausdrücke, sprichwörtliche und andere im täglichen Leben vorkommende Redensarten in entsprechendes Latein übertragen und nach dem Alphabet geordnet.* Nürnberg: Adam Gottlieb Schneider und Weigel, 1797. 185 pp.

3081. Sinapius-Horčička, Daniel. *Neo-forum Latino-Slavonicum.* Roku Páne, Slovakia: no publisher given, 1678. Rpt. ed. Josef Minárik. Bratislava: Tatran, 1988. 267 pp.

3082. Sommer, Robin Langley (ed.). *Nota bene: A Guide to Familiar Latin Quotes and Phrases.* Oxford, England: Past Times, 1995. 64 pp.

3083. Steiner, Arpad. "The Vernacular Proverb in Mediaeval Latin Prose." *American Journal of Philology,* 65 (1944), 37-68.

3084. Stone, Jon R. *Latin for the Illiterati: Exorcizing the Ghosts of a Dead Language.* New York: Routledge, 1996. 201 pp.

3085. Stone, Jon R. *Dictionary of Latin Quotations. The Illiterati's Guide to Latin Maxims, Mottoes, Proverbs, and Sayings.* New York: Routledge, 2005. 394 pp.

3086. Szelinski, Victor. *Nachträge und Ergänzungen zu "Otto, Die Sprichwörter und sprichwörtlichen Redensarten der Römer" [1890].* Diss. Universität Jena, 1892. 38 pp.

3087. Tosi, Renzo. *Dizionario delle sentenze latine e greche. 10.000 citazioni dall'antichità al rinascimento nell'originale e in traduzione con commento storico letterario e filologico.* Milano: Rizzoli, 1991. 891 pp.

3088. Walther, Hans. "Scherz und Ernst in der Völker- und Stämme-Charakteristik mittellateinischer Verse." *Archiv für Kulturgeschichte*, 41 (1959), 263-301.

3089. Walther, Hans. *Proverbia sententiaeque latinitatis medii aevi. Lateinische Sprichwörter und Sentenzen des Mittelalters in alphabetischer Anordnung.* 6 vols. Göttingen: Vandenhoeck & Ruprecht, 1963-1969. I, A-E, 1095 pp.; II, F-M, 1030 pp.; III, N-P, 1027 pp.; IV, Q-Sil, 1055 pp.; V, Sim-Z, 945 pp.; VI, 209 pp. (Name, subject, and word indices).

3090. Walther, Hans. *Proverbia sententiaeque latinitatis medii ac recentioris aevi. Lateinische Sprichwörter und Sentenzen des Mittelalters und der frühen Neuzeit in alphabetischer Anordnung.* Neue Reihe. Aus dem Nachlaß von Hans Walther. Ed. Paul Gerhard Schmidt. 3 vols. Göttingen: Vandenhoeck & Ruprecht, 1982-1986. VII, A-G, 941 pp.; VIII, H-O, 992 pp.; IX, P-Z, 831 pp.

3091. Werner, Jakob. *Lateinische Sprichwörter und Sinnsprüche des Mittelalters.* Heidelberg: Carl Winter, 1912. 112 pp. Revised 2nd ed. by Peter Flury. Heidelberg: Carl Winter, 1966. 140 pp.

3092. Williams, Rose (ed.). *Latin Quips at Your Fingertips. Witty Latin Sayings by Wise Romans.* New York: Barnes & Noble, 2001. 127 pp.

Latvian

3093. Kokare, Elza. *Latviešu un lietuviešu sakāmvārdu paralēles.* Riga: Zinatne, 1980. 397 pp.

3094. Kokare, Elza. *Latviešu un vācu sakāmvārdu paralēles. Lettische und deutsche Sprichwörterparallelen.* Riga: Zinatne, 1988. 309 pp.

Lithuanian

3095. Grigas, Kazys, Lilija Kudirkienė, Rasa Kašėtienė, Gedimi-nas Radvilas, and Dalia Zaikauskienė. *Lietuvių patarlés ir priežodžiai*. 5 vols. Vilnius: Lietuvių literatūros ir tautosakos insti-tutas, 2000. I, 928 pp.

3096. Grigas, Kazys, Giedrė Bufienė, Rasa Kašėtienė, Lilija Ku-dirkienė, and Dalia Zaikauskienė. *Lietuvių patarlés ir priežodžiai*. 5 vols. Vilnius: Lietuvių literaturos ir tautosakos institutas, 2008. II, 830 pp.

3097. Radvilas, Gediminas. *"Savam krašte ir tvoros žydi": Lietuvių patarlių ir priežodžiu rinktine*. Vilnius: Žinijos, 1991. 64 pp.

3098. Smoliakovas, Grigorijus. "Iš Lietuvos žydu mažosius tautosa-kos." *Tautosakos Darbai*, 2 (old series vol. 9) (1993), 212-228.

3099. Stundžiene, Brone. "Smulkioji tautosaka Kazimiero Šaulio veikale 'Juodžiunu tarme'." *Tautosakos Darbai*, 2 (old series vol. 9) (1993), 157-196.

Livonian

3100. Viitso, Tiit-Rein. "Liivi vanasõnu [Livonian Proverbs]." *Minor Uralic Languages: Grammar and Lexis*. Ed. Ago Künnap. Tartu / Groningen: University of Tartu / University of Groningen, 1995. 193-200.

Luxembourgish

3101. Borschette, Emile. *Dem Mulles sénger Schnoken an illus-tréiert Spréchwierder a Riedensaarten*. 2 vols. Lëtzebuerg: Sankt-Paulus-Dréckerei, 1983 and 1986. I, 96 pp.; II, 96 pp. With illustra-tions.

3102. Filatkina, Natalia. *Phraseologie des Lëtzebuergeschen. Em-pirische Untersuchungen zu strukturellen, semantisch-pragma-tischen und bildlichen Aspekten*. Heidelberg: Carl Winter, 2005. 468 pp.

Malay

3103. Fanany, Ismet, and Rebecca Fanany. *Wisdom of the Malay Proverbs*. Kuala Lumpur: Dewan Bahasa dan Pustaka, 2003. 446 pp.

3104. Hamilton, A.W. *Malay Proverbs. Bidal Mĕlayu.* Singapore: Printers Ltd., 1937. 85 pp.; rpt. Singapore: Eastern Universities Press, 1961. 111 pp.

3105. Winstedt, Richard Olof. *Malay Proverbs.* London: John Murray, 1950. 85 pp.

Maltese

3106. Aquilina, Joseph. *Maltese Meteorological and Agricultural Proverbs.* Malta: Malta University Press, 1961. 80 pp.

3107. Aquilina, Joseph. *A Comparative Dictionary of Maltese Proverbs.* Malta: The Royal University of Malta, 1972. 694 pp.

Manx

3108. Breatnach, R.A. "[Archibald] Cregeen's Manx Proverbs and Familiar Phrases." *Eigse: A Journal of Irish Studies*, 27 (1993), 1-34.

Maori

3109. Brougham, Aileen E., and Alexander W. Reed. *Māori Proverbs.* Wellington: A.H. and A.W. Reed, 1963. 135 pp. Rpt. as *The Reed Book of Māori Proverbs.* Ed. Timoti Karetu. Auckland: Reed Books, 1987. 187 pp.

3110. McDonnell, A.F. *Maori Songs and Proverbs (Ancient and Modern).* Auckland: A.F. McDonnell, 1923. 21 pp.

3111. Mead, Hirini Moko, and Neil Grove. *Ngā Pēpeha a ngā Tīpuna. The Sayings of the Maori Ancestors.* Wellington, New Zealand: Victoria University Press, 2001. 448 pp.

3112. Riley, Murdoch (ed.). *Māori Sayings and Proverbs.* Paraparaumu, New Zealand: Viking Sevenseas, 1990. 89 pp.

Mexican

3113. Altamirano, Ignacio Manuel. *Proverbios mexicanos.* Ed. Andrés Henestrosa. México, D.F., México: Miguel Angel Porrúa, 1997. 97 pp.

3114. Atri, Mauricio. *Refranero legal mexicano.* México, D.F.: Editorial Porrúa, 2005 (2nd ed. 2006). 185 pp.

3115. Ballesteros, Octavio A. *Mexican Proverbs: The Philosophy, Wisdom and Humor of a People.* Burret, Texas: Eakin Press, 1979. 66 pp.

3116. Gossen, Gary H. "Chamula Tzotzil Proverbs: Neither Fish Nor Fowl." *Meaning in Mayan Languages. Ethnolinguistic Studies.* Ed. Munro S. Edmondson. The Hague: Mouton, 1973. 205-233. Also in *Wise Words: Essays on the Proverb.* Ed. Wolfgang Mieder. New York: Garland Publishing, 1994. 351-392. (Tzotzil Indians).

3117. López Chiñas, Gabriel. *Xhtiidxa guendananna / Palabras de sabiduria [de los Zapotecas].* México, S.A.: Tálleres Graficos, 1969. 43 pp. (Zapotec Indians).

3118. Sánchez Bringas, Ángeles, and Pilar Vallés. *"La que de amarillo se viste ..." La mujer en el refranero mexicano.* México, D.F.: Universidad Autónoma Metropolitana, 2008. 255 pp.

3119. Sellers, Jeff M. *Proverbios y dichos Mexicanos / Folk Wisdom of Mexico.* Ilustrations by Annika Maria Nelson. San Francisco: Chronicle Books, 1994. 77 pp.

3120. Speck, Charles H. "Zapotec [Indians in Mexico] Proverbs." In C.H. Speck. *Zapotec Oral Literature. El Folklore de San Lorenzo Texmelucan.* Dallas, Texas: The Summer Institute of Linguistics, 1990. 199-212.

3121. Velasco Valdés, Miguel. *Refranero popular mexicano.* México. D.F.: B. Costa-Amic, 1961 (7th ed. 1978). 174 pp.

Mongolian

3122. Aalto, Pentti. "Some South-Mongolian Proverbs." *Suomalais-ugrilaisen Seuran Toimituksia*, 98 (1950), 1-12.

3123. Frye, Stanley N. "Two Hundred and Fifty Mongolian Proverbs." *Mongolian Folktales, Stories and Proverbs.* Ed. John R. Krueger. Bloomington, Indiana: The Mongolia Society, 1967. 61-83.

3124. Hangin, John Gombojab, John R. Krueger, R.G. Service, and William V. Rozycki. "Mongolian Folklore: A Representative Collection from the Oral Literary Tradition. Part One." *Mongolian Studies*, 9 (1985-1986), 13-78 (proverbs and sayings, pp. 13-60).

3125. Rashidonduk, Sh. "Words of Wisdom and Words of Mockery – Remembered by an Old Mongol." *Documenta Barbarorum. Festschrift für Walter Heissig.* Eds. Annemarie von Gabain and Wolfgang Veenker. Wiesbaden: Otto Harrassowitz, 1983. 282-285.

3126. Raymond, Janice. *Mongolian Proverbs. A Window into Their World.* San Diego, California: Alethinos Books, 2010. 374 pp.

3127. Whymant, Neville J. "Mongolian Proverbs: A Study in the Kalmuck Colloquial." *Journal of the Royal Asiatic Society of Great Britain and Ireland*, no volume given (April, 1926), 257-267.

Nepali

3128. Inchley, Valerie M. *Sitting in My House Dreaming of Nepal: Nepal Through the Eyes of Its Proverbs. Nepali Proverbs Analysed, Classified and Compared with English Proverbs and also A List of Common Nepali Proverbs*. Kathmandu, Nepal: Ekta Books, 2010. 521 pp.

3129. Lall, Kesar. "Proverbs." In K. Lall. *Nepalese Customs and Manners*. Kathmanda, Nepal: Ratna Pustak Bhandar, 1990. 62-72.

Norwegian

3130. Aasen, Ivar. *Norske ordsprog*. Christiana: Werner, 1856. 4th ed. as *Norske ordtak*. Eds. Johannes Gjerdåker and Gudmund Harildstad. Bergen: Vigmostad & Bjørke, 2003. 377 pp.

3131. Asala, Joanne (ed.). *Norwegian Proverbs*. Illustrations by J. & G. Nicholls. Iowa City, Iowa: Penfield Press, 1994. 63 pp.

3132. Asala, Joanne (ed.). *Proverbs from the North: Words of Wisdom from the Vikings*. Illustrations by Paul Chaillu. Iowa City, Iowa: Penfield Press, 1994. 64 pp.

3133. Erichsen, Gerda Moter. *400 uttrykh og vendinger på norsk, engelsk, tysk og fransk*. Bergen: Kunnskapsforlaget, 1982. 133 pp.

3134. Gering, Hugo. "Altnordische Sprichwörter und sprichwörtliche Redensarten." *Arkiv för Nordisk Filologi*, 32 (1916), 1-30.

3135. Hinrichsen, Helmut (ed.). *Hávamál. So sprachen die Wikinger*. Reykjavik: Gudrun, 2001. 93 pp.

3136. Jónasson, Björn (ed.). *Hávamál: The Sayings of the Vikings*. Reykjavik: Gudrun, 1992. 92 pp.

3137. Speight, E.E. "A Few Norwegian Proverbs [Collected by Einar Sagen]." *Folklore* (London), 22, no. 2 (1911), 213-218

Ossetic

3138. Dzagurova, G.A. *Osetinskie (Digorskie) narodnye izrecheniia*. Moskva: Nauka, 1980. 355 pp.

3139. Reller, Gisela (ed.). *Aus Tränen baut man keinen Turm. Ein kaukasischer Spruchbeutel. Weisheiten der Adygen, Dagestaner und Osseten.* Berlin: Eulenspiegel Verlag, 1983. 159 pp.

Pakistani

3140. Tiffou, Etienne. *Hunza Proverbs [from Pakistan].* Calgary, Alberta: University of Calgary Press, 1993. 252 pp.

Palauan

3141. McKnight, Robert K. "Proverbs of Palau [Islands]." *Journal of American Folklore*, 81 (1968), 3-33.

Panamanian

3142. Rueda de Taylor, Evelia (ed.). *Mil y más frases para disfrutar.* Panamá: Novo Art, 2000. 72 pp.

Paraguayan

3143. López Bréard, Miguel Raúl. *El 'ñe eñga: Refranes, adagios, máximas, sentencias y dichos célebres en el área guaranítica.* Asunción, Paraguay: Intercontinental Editora, 2001. 162 pp.

Pashto (Afghan)

3144. Benawa, A.R. *Pashto Proverbs.* Translated into English by A.M. Shinwari. Kabul: Government Printing Press, 1979. 460 pp.

3145. Tair, Mohammad Nawaz, and Thomas C. Edwards. *Rohi Mataluna. Pashto Proverbs.* Peshawar: Pashto Academy, University of Peshawar, 1982. 282 pp. Revised edition by Leonard N. Bartlotti and Wali Shah Khattak. Peshawar: InterLit Foundation and Pashto Academy, University of Peshawar, 2006. 385 pp.

Persian

3146. Abrishami, Ahmad. *A Dictionary of Persian-English Proverbs.* Tehran: Zivar Publications, 1997. 220 pp.

3147. Abrishami, Ahmad. *A Modern Dictionary of Selected Persian Proverbs.* Tehran: Zivar Publications, 1997. 404 pp. (in Persian).

3148. Abrishami, Ahmad. *A Modern Dictionary of Persian Proverbs Prevalent in Kerman (A Province of Iran).* Tehran: Zivar Publications, 1998. 316 pp. (in Persian).

3149. Bahar, Hadi. *Human Body in Persian Proverbs*. Illustrations by Mohammad Nasseripour. Rockville, Maryland: International Travelers' Clinic, 1991. 392 pp. (in Persian).

3150. Bahar, Hadi. *The Book of Heart: "Heart" in Persian Proverbs, Aphorisms, Epigrams and Colloquial Expressions*. Rockville, Maryland: International Travelers' Clinic, 1997. 444 pp. (in Persian).

3151. Elwell-Sutton, L.P. *Persian Proverbs*. London: John Murray, 1954. 103 pp.

3152. Maschke, George W. *Proverbial and Idiomatic Language in a Modern Persian Novel: A Contextual Analysis Based on Iraj Pezeshkzad's "Da'i Jan Napel'on"*. Diss. University of California at Los Angeles, 2006. 199 pp. (proverb index, pp. 59-189).

Peruvian

3153. Arora, Shirley L. *Proverbial Comparisons in Ricardo Palma's "Tradiciones Peruanas"*. Berkeley, California: University of California Press, 1966. 205 pp.

Philippine

3154. Eugenio, Damiana L. *Philippine Proverb Lore*. Quezon City: University of the Philippines, 1967. 191 pp. (= *The Philippine Social Sciences and Humanties Review*, 31, nos. 3-4 [1966], 231-421).

Polish

3155. Asala, Joanne (ed.). *Polish Proverbs*. Illustrations by Alice Wadowski-Bak. Iowa City, Iowa: Penfield Press, 1995. 64 pp.

3156. Bąba, Stanisław, and Jarosław Liberek. *Słownik frazeologiczny współczesnej polszczyzny*. Warszawa: Wydawnictwo Naukowe PWN, 2002. 1096 pp.

3157. Berner, Janusz. *Mądrej głowie dość ... przysłowie*. Illustrations by Edward Lutczyn. Lomza: "Stopka", 1992. 381 pp.

3158. Bieniok, Henryk. *Trzy razy pomyśl, raz zrob, czyli zasady organizacji i kierowania w polskich przysłowiach i powiedzeniach*. Illustrations by Mirosław Pokora. Warzawa: Młodziezowa Agencja Wydawnicza, 1985. 263 pp.

3159. Bieniok, Henryk. *Jaki gazda – taka jazda, czyli poradnik kierowcy z polskich przysłów i powiedzeń ludowych ułożony*. Warszawa: Wydawnictwa Komunikacji i Łacznosci, 1989. 32 pp. (miniature book).

3160. Bodek, Bernadeta, Monika Buława, and Renata Brozowska (eds.). *Praktyczny słownik frazeologiczny*. Kraków: Wydawnictwo Zielona Sowa, 2003. 320 pp.

3161. Bralczyk, Jerzy. *Porzekadła na każdy dzień*. Warszawa: Wydawnictwo Naukowe PWN, 2009. 412 pp.

3162. Dynak, Władysław. *Łowy, łowcy i zwierzyna w przysłowiach polskich*. Wrocław: Towarzystwo Przyjaciół Polonistyki Wrocławskiej, 1993. 358 pp. With illustrations.

3163. Ehegötz, Erika, Walter Duda, Maria Frenzel, Maria Gehrmann, and Stanisław Skorupka. *Phraseologisches Wörterbuch. Polnisch-Deutsch*. Leipzig: VEB Verlag Enzyklopädie, 1990. 299 pp.

3164. Głuch, Wojciech, and Alicja Nowakowska (eds.). *Słownik frazeologiczny*. Wrocław: Wydawnictwo Europa, 2003. 472 pp.

3165. Kośka, Lidia (ed.). *Glosy z Aszkenaz. Żydowskie przysłowia i powiedzenia ze zbioru Ignaza Bernsteina*. Kraków: Stowarzyszenie Pardes, 2007. 280 pp.

3166. Krzyżanowski, Julian. *Nowa księga przysłów i wyrażeń przysłowiowych polskich*. 4 vols. Warszawa: Państwowv Instytut Wydawniczy, 1969-1978. I, A-J, 881 pp.; II, K-P, 1165 pp.; III, R-Z, 996 pp.; IV, 631 pp. (bibliography and indices).

3167. Krzyżanowski, Julian. *Mądrej głowie dość dwie słowie. Pieć centuryj przysłów polskich i diabelski tuzin*. 3 vols. Warszawa: Państwowy Instytut Wydawniczy, 1975. I, 346 pp.; II, 342 pp.; III, 360 pp.

3168. Lewandowska, Anna. *Sprichwort-Gebrauch heute. Ein interkulturell-kontrastiver Vergleich von Sprichwörtern anhand polnischer und deutscher Printmedien*. Diss. Universität Halle-Wittenberg, 2005. 441 pp. Bern: Peter Lang, 2008. 366pp. (corpus, pp. 335-363).

3169. Lipiński, Erik (ill.). *Jak Kuba Bogu tag Bóg Kubie. Przysłowia polskie w rysunkach Erika Lipińskiego*. Lublin: Krajowa Agencja Wydawnicza, 1985. 110 pp.

3170. Lipinski, Miroslaw. *Dictionary of 1000 Polish Proverbs*. New York: Hippocrene Books, 1997. 129 pp.

3171. Małdzyjewa, Wiara, and Janina Wójtowiczowa. *Polskie i bułgarskie związki frazeologiczne. Polski i bułgarski frazeologizmi.* Warszawa: Wydawnictwa Uniwersytetu Warszawskiego, 1994. 346 pp.

3172. Masłowscy, Danuta, and Włodzimierz Masłowscy (eds.). *Księga przysłów polskich.* Kęty: Wydawnictwo Antyk, 2000. 601 pp.

3173. Masłowscy, Danuta, and Włodzimierz Masłowscy (eds.). *Przysłowia polskie.* Katowice: Videograf Edukacja, 2003. 364 pp.

3174. Mrozowski, Teresa. *Słownik frazeologiczny / Phraseologisches Wörterbuch. Polsko-Niemiecki / Polnisch-Deutsch.* Warszawa: Wydawnictwo C.H. Beck, 2007. 639 pp.

3175. Müldner-Nieckowski, Piotr. *Wielki słownik frazeologiczny języka polskiego.* Warszawa: Świat Książki, 2003. 1088 pp.

3176. Nitecki, Jan. *Słowniczek pryzysłów.* Warszawa: Wydawnictwa Szkolne i Pedagogiczne, 1993. 176 pp.

3177. Nyczaj, Stanisław. *Mała księga przysłów polskich.* Radom: Oficyna Wydawnicza Ston, 1994 (2nd printing 1996). 273 pp.

3178. Piątkowska, Renata. *Z przysłowiami za pan brat.* Illustrations by Marcin Piwowarski. Warszawa: "bis", 2005. 125 pp. (children stories with proverbs).

3179. Prędota, Stanisław. *Mały niderlandzko-polski słownik przysłów. Klein nederlands-pools spreekwoordenboek.* Wrocław: Wydawnictwo Uniwersytetu Wrocławskiego, 1986. 128 pp.

3180. Prędota, Stanisław. *Mały niemiecko-polski słownik przysłów. Kleines deutsch-polnisches Sprichwörterbuch.* Warszawa: Wydawnictwo Naukowe PWN, 1992 (2nd ed. 1993). 260 pp.

3181. Pyczewska-Pilarek, Jadwiga. *Przysłowie prawde, Ci powie. Przysłowia i cytaty antologia od A do Z.* Łódz: Wydawnictwo Akapit Press, 1993. 146 pp. With illustrations.

3182. Reichhart, Bogusław. *... i starca "odmłodzi". Przysłowia, aforyzmy, złote myśli, maksymy, sentencje, o pracy.* Illustrations by Jerzy Treutler. Warszawa: Instytut Wydawniczy Zwiazków Zawodowych, 1988. 224 pp.

3183. Sielicki, Franciszek. *Podania, legendy, anegdoty i przysłowia na Wilejszczyznie w okresie miedzywojennym.* Wrocław: Wydawnictwo Uniwersytetu Wrocławskiego, 1993. 215 pp. (proverbs and proverbial expressions, pp. 114-207).

3184. Skriabin, Agnieszka. *Podręczny słownik frazeologiczny*. Warszawa: Wydawnictwo Naukowe PWN, 2006. 414 pp.

3185. Sommerfeldt, Josef. "Die Juden in den polnischen Sprichwörtern und sprichwörtlichen Redensarten." *Die Burg. Vierteljahrsschrift des Instituts für deutsche Ostarbeit Krakau*, 3 (1942), 313-354 (anti-Semitic collection).

3186. Stypuła, Ryszard. *Słownik przysłów rosyjsko-polski i polskorosyjski*. Warszawa: Wiedza Powszechna, 1974. 557 pp.

3187. Swirko, Stanisław (ed.). *Na wszystko jest przysłowie*. Illustrations by Stanisław Rozwadowski. Poznań: Wydawnictwo Poznańskie, 1985. 319 pp.

3188. Szałas, Roman. *Przysłowia staropolskie / Old Polish Proverbs*. Wydawca: Prasowe Zaklady Graficzne, 1995. 34 pp. With illustrations.

3189. Szydłowska, Natalia (ed.). *Mądrość jako wartość w przysłowiach ludowych. Materiały z badań*. Białystok: Wojewódzki Ośrodek Animacji Kultury, 2008. 211 pp.

3190. Tokarczuk, Olga. *Mały angielsko-polski słownik przysłów*. Warszawa: UNUS, 1993. 180 pp.

3191. Warewicz, Barbara. *Ja jedyna. Aforyzmy powiedzonka i przysłowia o kobiecie*. Warszawa: Instytut Wydawniczy Związków Zawodowych, 1986. 165 pp.

3192. Wurzbach, Constant von. *Die Sprichwörter der Polen historisch erläutert*. Wien: Pfautsch & Voss, 1852; rpt. Osnabrück: Reinhard Kuballe, 1983; rpt. Leipzig: Zentralantiquariat der DDR, 1985. 355 pp.

Ponapean

3193. Riesenberg, Saul H., and J.L. Fischer. "Some Ponapean [Micronesian] Proverbs." *Journal of American Folklore*, 68 (1955), 9-18.

Portuguese

3194. Borges, Ana Eleonora. *Provérbios sobre Plantas*. Lisboa: Apenas Livros, 2005. 93 pp.

3195. Braga, Theophilo. "Adagiário português (Coligido das fontes escritas)." *Revista Lusitana*, first series, 18, nos. 3-4 (1914), 225-275; and 19, no. 1 (1915), 16-64.

3196. Brazão, José Ruivinho. *Os Provérbios Estão Vivos no Algarve: Pesquisa Paremiológica em Paderne*. Lisboa: Editorial Notícias, 1998. 367 pp.

3197. Brazão, José Ruivinho. *Os Provérbios Estão Vivos em Portugal*. Lisboa: Editorial Notícias, 2004. 367 pp.

3198. Camargo, Sidney, and Herbert Bornebusch. *Wörterbuch metaphorischer Redewendungen Deutsch-Portugiesisch mit thematischem Inhaltsverzeichnis / Dicionário de expressões idiomáticas metafóricas Alemão-Português com índice remissivo temático*. São Paulo: Editora Pedagógica e Universitária, 1996. 166 pp.

3199. Éme, Eza. *Provérbios repenteados*. Illustrations by Emílo Remelhe. Lisboa: Universidade Nova de Lisboa, Instituto Estudos de Literatura, 2005. 53 pp.

3200. Estanqueiro, António (ed.). *A sabedoria dos provérbios. As pessoas e as instituições nos provérbios portugueses*. Lisboa: Editorial Presença, 1996. 146 pp.

3201. Ettinger, Stefan, and Manuela Nunes. *Portugiesische Redewendungen. Ein Wörter- und Übungsbuch für Fortgeschrittene*. Hamburg: Helmut Buske, 2006. 153 pp.

3202. Flonta, Teodor. *A Dictionary of English and Portuguese Equivalent Proverbs*. Hobart, Tasmania: De Proverbio.com, 2001. 207 pp.

3203. Funk, Gabriela, and Matthias Funk. *Pérolas da Sabedoria Popular Portuguesa. Provérbios de S. Miguel*. Lisboa: Edições Salamandra, 2001. 181 pp.

3204. Funk, Gabriela, and Matthias Funk. *Pérolas da Sabedoria Popular Portuguesa. Os Provérbios Açorianos nos EUA*. Lisboa: Edições Salamandra, 2001. 228 pp.

3205. Funk, Gabriela, and Matthias Funk. *Pérolas da Sabedoria Popular Portuguesa. Provérbios das Ilhas do Grupo Central dos Açores (Faial, Graciosa, Pico, São Jorge e Terceira)*. Lisboa: Edições Salamandra, 2002. 192 pp.

3206. Funk, Gabriela, and Matthias Funk. *Dicionário Prático de Provérbios Portugueses*. Chamusca: Cosmos, 2008. 547 pp.

3207. Lopes da Costa, Elisa Maria (ed.). *Ditos e reditos. Provérbios da Lusofonia*. Prior Velho, Portugal: Paulinas, 2005. 154 pp. With illustrations.

3208. Lourenço, Tomás. *Provérbios pós-modernos*. Illustrations by Pedro Pousada. Lisboa: Âncora, 2000. 131 pp. (anti-proverbs).

3209. Machado, José Pedro. *O Grande Livro dos Provérbios*. Lisboa: Editorial Notícias, 1996 (2nd ed. 1998). 639 pp.

3210. Marques da Costa, José Ricardo. *O Livro dos Provérbios Portugueses*. Lisboa: Editorial Presença, 1999. 551 pp.

3211. Moreira, António. *Provérbios portugueses*. Lisboa: Editorial Notícias, 1996 (3rd ed. 1997). 407 pp.

3212. Schemann, Hans. *Idiomatik Deutsch-Portugiesisch. Dicionário Idiomático Alemão-Português*. Stuttgart: Ernst Klett, 2002. 1228 pp.

3213. Sereno, Maria Helena Sampaio. *As funções dos provérbios na narrativa de José Saramago*. Diss. Universitat de València, 2009. 511 pp. (proverb index, pp. 230-244).

3214. Soares, Rui J.B. *Do Ano ao Santo tudo é encanto. Ditos populares ao longo do ano*. Torres Novas: Almondina, 2002. 288 pp. (weather proverbs).

3215. Vasconcelos, Carolina Michaëlis de. "Mil provérbios portugueses." *Revista Lusitana*, new series, 7 (1986), 29-71.

3216. Viterbo, Sousa. "Materiaes para o estudo da paremiographia portuguesa." *Revista Lusitana*, first series, no volume given, no. 1 (1897), 161-166; no volume given, no. 1 (1902), 97-103.

Puerto Rican

3217. Diaz Rivera, María Elisa. *Refranes más usados en Puerto Rico*. San Juan, Puerto Rico: Universidad de Puerto Rico, 1984. 148 pp. (2nd ed. 1994). 174 pp.

3218. Fernández Valledor, Roberto. *Del refranero puertoriqueno en al contexto hispanico y antillano*. Madrid: Sociedad Estatal Quinto Centenario, 1991. 275 pp.

Romanian

3219. Albu, Iuliu M. *Picături de înțelepciune. Culegere de aforisme, cugetări, proverbe*. Timisoara: Editura Eurobit, 1997. 189 pp.

3220. Andrei, Al. *Proverbe, zicători, ghicitori*. Bucureşti: Regis, 1999. 141 pp.

3221. Beza, Marcu. *Rumanian Proverbs*. London: A.M. Philpot, 1921. 63 pp.

3222. Bratu, Ion. *Sfaturi bune pentru toţi sau cărticica cu proverbe*. Bucureşti: Editura TEOPA, 1996. 64 pp.

3223. Bratu, Ion. *Înţelepciunea dâmboviţeanâ: Dicţionar de proverbe, zicători, sfaturi întelepte şi expresii proverbiale din judeţul Dâmboviţa*. Târgoviste: Editura Bibliotheca, 1999. 270 pp.

3224. Cibotto, Giovanni Antonio, and Giovanni Del Drago. *Proverbi romaneschi*. Milano: Martello, 1975; rpt. Firenze: Giunti Gruppo Editoriale. 1996. 114 pp. With illustrations.

3225. Colfescu, Silvia. *Păcală – snoave, proverbe, ghicitori*. Bucureşti: Editura Vremea, 1999. 159 pp.

3226. Dumistrăcel, Stelian. *Pînă-n pînzele albe. Dicţionar de expresii româneşti*. Iaşi: Institutul European, 2001. 534 pp.

3227. Flonta, Teodor. *Dicţionar englez-român de proverbe echivalente. English-Romanian Dictionary of Equivalent Proverbs*. Bucureşti: Teopa, 1992. 172 pp.

3228. Flonta, Teodor. *A Dictionary of English and Romanian Equivalent Proverbs*. Hobart, Tasmania: De Proverbio.com, 2001. 169 pp.

3229. Golescu, Iordache. *Proverbe*. Craiova: Editura Hyperion, 1998. 178 pp.

3230. Hinţescu, I.C. *Proverbele Românilor*. Sibiu: Closius, 1877. 210 pp. Rpt. eds. Constantin Negreanu and Ion Bratu. Timişoara: Editura Facla, 1985. 311 pp.

3231. Muntean, George. *Proverbe româneşti*. Bucureşti: Editura Minerva, 1984. 414 pp.

3232. Robea, Mihail M. *Proverbe şi ghicitori*. Illustrations by Mariana Popescu. Bucureşti: Casa Editoriala Muntenia, 1998. 160 pp.

3233. Robea, Mihail M. *Proverbe, zicători, ghicitori şi strigături*. Illustrations by Mariana Popescu. Bucureşti: Casa Editoriala Muntenia, 1999. 160 pp.

3234. Stanciulescu-Bîrda (Bârda), Alexandru. *Proverbe şi expresii religioase (Proverbes et expressions religieuses)*. Bîrda: Editura "Cuget Românesc", 1991. 80 pp.

3235. Stanciulescu-Bîrda (Bârda), Alexandru. *Razboiul crucilor*. Bîrda: "Cuget Românesc", 1993. 32 pp.

3236. Stanciulescu-Bîrda (Bârda), Alexandru. *Cugetări şi reflecţii din cultura română de la origini până la 1848*. Bîrda: "Cuget Românesc", 2008. 286 pp.

3237. Zanne, Iuliu A. *Proverbele românilor din România, Basarabia, Bucovina, Ungaria, Istria şi Macedonia*. 10 vols. Bucureşti: Socecǔ, 1895-1912; rpt. ed. Mugur Vasiliu. Bucureşti: Asociatia Română pentru Cultură şi Ortodoxie, 2003. I, 781 pp.; II, 980 pp.; III, 763 pp.; IV, 779 pp.; V, 741 pp.; VI, 775 pp.; VII, 955 pp.; VIII, 771 pp.; IX, 744 pp.; X, 425 pp.

3238. Zanne, Iuliu A. *Proverbele romînilor. Proverbe, zigători, povăţuiri, cuvinte adevărate, asemănări, idiotisme şi cimilituri de Iuliu A. Zanne*. Ed. C. Ciuchindel. Bucureşti: Editura Tineretului, 1959. 631 pp.

Russian

3239. Altmann, Julius. "Die provinciellen Sprichwörter der Russen." *Jahrbücher für slawische Literatur, Kunst und Wissenschaft*, 1, nos. 6-7 (1853), 65-135.

3240. Anikin, V.P. *Starinnye russkie poslovitsy i pogovorki*. Illustrations by L. Ionova. Moskva: Detskaia literatura, 1983. 32 pp.

3241. Anikin, V.P. *Russkie poslovitsy i pogovorki*. Moskva: Khudozhestvennaia Literatura, 1988. 431 pp.

3242. Anonymous. *Russian Proverbs*. Illustrations by Aldren Watson. Mount Vernon, New York: Peter Pauper Press, 1960. 61 pp.

3243. Armalinskii, Mikhail. *Russkie besstyzhie poslovitsy i pogovorki*. Minneapolis, Minnesota: M.I.P. Company, 1992. 74 pp.

3244. Arsent'eva, E.F. *Russko-angliiskii frazeologicheskii slovar'*. Kazan': "Kheter", 1999. 318 pp.

3245. Berseneva, Katarina Gennadevna. *Russkie poslovitsi i pogovorki*. Moskva: ZAO Tsentrpoligraf, 2005. 384 pp.

3246. Berthelmann, Gundela, and Rainer Berthelmann. *Russische Sprichwörter und Redensarten. Russisch/Deutsch.* Stuttgart: Philipp Reclam, 2010. 198 pp.

3247. Birikh, Alexandr, Valerii M. Mokienko, and Liudmila Stepanova. *Slovar' frazeologicheskikh sinonimov russkogo iazyka.* Rostov-na-Donu: Feniks, 1997. 349 pp.

3248. Bodrova, Iu.V. *Russkie poslovitsy i pogovorki i ikh angliiskie analogi / Russian Proverbs and Sayings and Their English Equivalents.* Moskva: Ast, 2008. 159 pp.

3249. Budeus, Iris (ed.). *Das Leben ist kein Kinderspiel / Zhizn' prozhit' – ne pole pereiti. Russische Sprichwörter und Lebensweisheiten / Russkie poslovitsy i zhiteiskie nastavleniia.* Unna: Friedrichsborn-Verlag, 2002. 68 pp. With illustrations.

3250. Bukovskaia, M.V. et al. *Slovar' upotrebitel'nykh angliiskikh poslovits, 326 statei / A Dictionary of English Proverbs in Modem Use, 326 Entries.* Moskva: Russkii iazyk, 1985. 232 pp.

3251. Bulyko, A.N. *Frazeologicheskii slovar' russkogo iazyka.* Minsk: Kharvest, 2007. 445 pp.

3252. Chernelev, Vsevolod. *Russkie paremii – 7777: Sbornik starinnykh i novykh poslovits, pogovorok, zagadok, velerizmov i proch.* Kishinev: Paragon, 1998. 388 pp.

3253. Chernelev, Vsevolod. *Tri mudretsa. Sbornik krylatykh slov i vyrazhenii A.S. Pushkina, I.A. Krylova, A.S. Griboedova.* Kishinev: Nauchno-populiarnoe Izdanie, 1999. 252 pp.

3254. Chernelev, Vsevolod. *Armeiskie prikoly – 777: Sbornik shutok, pogovorok, aforizmov, perlov, khokhm, marazmov, okhrenizmov i prochikh paremii ofitserov i praporshchikov sovetsko-rossiiskoi armii.* Kishinev: "Registru", 2001. 104 pp.

3255. Chernelev, Vsevolod. *Velerizmy – 4444. Sbornik sovremennykh ustnopoeticheskikh i fol'klorizovannykh tekstov.* Kishinev: Copitec-Plus, 2005. 307 pp. (wellerisms).

3256. Chernelev, Vsevolod. *Armeiskie prikoly. Nostalgia: Sbornik shutok, pogovorok, aforizmov, perlov, khokhm, marazmov, okhrenizmov i prochikh paremii ofitserov i praporshchikov sovetskoi/rossiiskoi armii.* Kishinev: Copitec-Plus, 2006. 270 pp. With illustrations.

3257. Dal', Vladimir Ivanovich. *Poslovitsy russkago naroda.* Moskva: Universitetskaia Tipografiia, 1862; rpt. Leipzig: Zentralantiquariat der DDR, 1977. 1095 pp.

3258. Dal', Vladimir Ivanovich. *Poslovitsy russkago naroda*. 2 vols. Moskva: Khudozhestvennaia Literatura, 1984. I, 383 pp.; II, 399 pp.

3259. Dal', Vladimir Ivanovich. *Poslovitsy russkogo naroda*. *Sbornik v trekh tomakh*. 3 vols. Moskva: "Russkaia Kniga", 1993. I, 640 pp.; II, 704 pp.; III, 736 pp.

3260. Dal', Vladimir Ivanovich. *Poslovitsy russkogo naroda*. Moskva: Astrel', 2008. 751 pp.

3261. Dehio, Helmuth (ed.). *Russkie poslovitsy / Russische Sprichwörter*. Illustrations by Frieda Wiegand. München: Deutscher Taschenbuch Verlag, 1994. 96 pp.

3262. Demina, T.S. *Angliiskii s udovol'stviem. Frazeologiia poslovits i pogovorok. Uchebnoe posobie*. Moskva: GIS, 2001. 129 pp. With illustrations.

3263. Dubrovin, M.I. *A Book of Russian Idioms Illustrated*. Moscow: Russian Language Publishers, 1977 (2nd ed. 1980). 349 pp. (3rd ed. 1987). 328 pp. With illustrations.

3264. Dubrovin, M.I. *Russkie frazeologizmy v kartinkakh / Rusça Deyimler*. Illustrations by V.I. Tilman. Ankara: Ofset Fotomat, 1986. 419 pp.

3265. Dubrovin, M.I. *A Book of English and Russian Proverbs and Sayings – Illustrated. Angliiskie i russkie poslovitsy i pogovorki – v illiustratsiiakh*. Illustrations by V.I. Tilman. Moscow: "Prosveshchenie", 1993. 352 pp.

3266. Eyke, Wera von. *Russkie poslovitsy. Russische Sprichwörter*. Zürich: Europa Verlag, 1947. 111 pp.

3267. Felitsyna, Vera P., and Lurii E. Prokhorov. *Russkie poslovitsy, pogovorki i krylatye vyrazheniia*. Moskva: Izdatel'stvo "Russkii iazyk", 1979. 240 pp. (2nd ed. 1988) 272 pp.

3268. Fialkov, Lev, and Larisa Fialkova (eds.). *Narody mira o zhizni i smerti, zdorov'e i bolezniakh, bol'nykh i vrachakh. Poslovitsy i pogovorki*. Haifa: JKDesign, 2009. 166 pp.

3269. Fomina, Sinaida. *Die Welt der Emotionen: Deutsch-russische phraseologische Parallelen. Ein Lehrbuch für Studenten*. Woronesh: Universität Woronesh, 2003. 96 pp.

3270. Grodzenskaia, Tatiana. *Proverbi della Russia*. Milano: Aldo Martello, 1968. 107 pp. With illustrations.

3271. Grynblat, M.Ia. *Prykazki i prymauki*. Minsk: Navuka i Tekhnika, 1976. 560 pp.

3272. Gudkova, Olga, Stefan Henkel, Marcus Hoffmann, Ekaterina Nikitina, Marina Schröder, and Harry Walter. *Denezhki schet liubiat. Slovarnaia kopilka. Geld liebt Konto. Wörterbuch-Sparbüchse.* Greifswald: Ernst-Moritz-Arndt-Universität Greifswald, Institut für Fremdsprachliche Philologien – Slawistik, 2010. 149 pp.

3273. Guseinzade, A. *Krylatye slova. Poslovitsy i pogovorki.* Baku: Azerneshr, 1959. Rpt. as *Krylatye slova*. Baku: Azerneshr, 1985. 163 pp.

3274. Haldeman-Julius, E. *Proverbs of Russia*. Girard, Kansas: Haldeman-Julius Company, ca. 1925. 63 pp.

3275. Jaszczun, Wasyl, and Szymon Krynski. *A Dictionary of Russian Idioms and Colloquialisms. 2,200 Expressions with Examples.* Pittsburgh, Pennsylvania: University of Pittsburgh Press, 1967. 102 pp.

3276. Kokhtev, N.N., and D.E. Rozental'. *Russkaia frazeologiia.* Moskva: Russkii iazyk, 1986. 304 pp. With illustrations.

3277. Kolesnikova, Elizabeta. *Russkie poslovitsi Litvy.* Eds. Iu.A. Novikov and T.S. Shadrina. Vil'nius: Vaga, 1992. 255 pp.

3278. Krylov, Constantin A. *Russian Proverbs and Sayings in Russian and English.* New York: US Army Russian Institute, 1973. 280 pp.

3279. Kuz'min, S.S., and N.L. Shadrin. *Russko-angliiskii slovar' poslovits i pogovorok / Russian-English Dictionary of Proverbs and Sayings.* Moskva: Russkii iazyk, 1989. 352 pp.

3280. Langnas, Isaac A. *1200 Russian Proverbs.* New York: The Wisdom Library, 1960. 91 pp.

3281. Levin-Steinmann, Anke. *Thematisches phraseologisches Wörterbuch der russischen Sprache. Beschreibung und Charakterisierung des Menschen / Tematicheskii frazeologicheskii slovar' russkogo iazyka (opisanie i kharakteristika cheloveka).* Wiesbaden: Harrassowitz, 1999. 352 pp.

3282. Lubensky, Sophia. *Russian-English Dictionary of Idioms. Russko-angliiskii slovar' idiom.* New York: Random House, 1995. 1017 pp.

3283. Mal'tseva, Dina G. *Nemetsko-russkii frazeologicheskii slovar' s lingvostranovedcheskim kommentariem*. Moskva: Azbukovnik, 2002. 349 pp.

3284. Margulis, Alexander, and Asya Kholodnaya. *Russian-English Dictionary of Proverbs and Sayings / Russko-angliiskii slovar' poslovits i pogovorok*. Jefferson, North Carolina: McFarland, 2000. 487 pp.

3285. Martynova, A.N., and V.V. Mitrofanova. *Poslovitsy, pogovorki, zagadki*. Moskva: Sovremennik, 1986. 512 pp.

3286. Melerovich, A.M., and Valerii M. Mokienko (eds.). *Zhisn' russkoi frazeologii v khudozhestvennoi rechi. Shkol'nyi slovar'*. Kostroma: KGU im. N.A. Nekrasova, 2010. 730.

3287. Mel'ts, M. Ia., V.V. Mitrofanova, and G.G. Shapovalova. *Poslovitsy, pogovorki, zagadki v rukopisnykh sbornikakh, XVIII-XX vekov*. Moskva: Izdatel'stvo Akademii Nauk SSSR, 1961. 289 pp.

3288. Mertvago, Peter. *The Comparative Russian-English Dictionary of Russian Proverbs & Sayings. With 5543 Entries, 1900 Most Important Proverbs Highlighted, English Proverb Index*. New York: Hippocrene Books, 1995. 477 pp.

3289. Mertvago, Peter. *Dictionary of 1000 Russian Proverbs with English Equivalents*. New York: Hippocrene Books, 1998. 181 pp.

3290. Mikhel'son, M.I. *Russkaia mysl' i rech'. Svoe i chuzhoe. Opyt russkoi frazeologii. Sbornik obraznykh slov i inoskazanii*. 2 vols. S.-Peterburg: Obshchestvennaia Pol'za, 1892-1893. Rpt. ed. Valerii M. Mokienko. Moskva: Russkie slovari, 1994. I, 780 pp., II, 918 pp. (commentary II, pp. 1-98)

3291. Mitinia, I.E. *English Proverbs and Sayings and Their Russian Equivalents / Russkie poslovitsy i pogovorki i ikh angliiskie analogi*. Sankt-Peterburg: Kapo, 2003. 336 pp.

3292. Mokienko, Valerii M. *Shkol'nyi slovar' zhivykh russkikh poslovits. Dlia uchashchikhsia 5-11 klassov i srednikh spetsial'nykh uchebnykh zavedenii*. Sankt-Peterburg: Neva, 2002. Moskva: Olma-Press, 2002. 350 pp.

3293. Mokienko, Valerii M. *Novaia russkaia frazeologiia*. Opole: Uniwersytet Opolski – Instytut Filologii Polskiej, 2003. 168 pp.

3294. Mokienko, Valerii M., and T.G. Nikitina (eds.). *Slovar' pskovskikh poslovits i pogovorok*. Sankt-Peterburg: Norint, 2001. 176 pp.

3295. Mokienko, Valerii M., and T.G. Nikitina. *Bol'shoi slovar' russkikh narodnykh sravnenii*. Moskva: Olma Media Grupp, 2008. 800 pp.

3296. Mokienko, Valerii M., and T.G. Nikitina. *Bol'shoi slovar' russkikh pogovorok*. Moskva: Olma Media Grupp, 2008. 784 pp.

3297. Mokienko, Valerii M., and T.G. Nikitina. *Narodnaia mudrost'. Russkie poslovitsy*. Moskva: Olma Media Grupp, 2010. 415 pp.

3298. Mokienko, Valerii M., T. G. Nikitina, and E.K. Nikolaeva. *Bol'shoi slovar' russkikh poslovits*. Moskva: Olma Media Grupp, 2010. 1024 pp.

3299. Mokienko, Valerii M., O.P. Semenets, and K.P. Sidorenko. *Bol'shoi slovar' krylatykh virazhenii A.S. Griboedova („Gore ot uma")*. Moskva: Olma Media Grupp, 2009. 800 pp.

3300. Panin, I. M. *Alesha sobiraet poslovitsy i pogovorki*. Moskva: Russkii iazyk, 1989. 110 pp.

3301. Permiakov, Grigorii L'vovich. "75 naibolee upotrebitel'nykh russkikh sravnitel'nykh oborotov." *Proverbium*, no. 25 (1975), 974-975.

3302. Permiakov, Grigorii L'vovich. *300 allgemeingebräuchliche russische Sprichwörter und sprichwörtliche Redensarten. Ein illustriertes Nachschlagewerk für Deutschsprechende*. Moskau: "Russki jasyk", 1985. Leipzig: VEB Verlag Enzyklopädie, 1985. 160 pp. With illustrations.

3303. Permiakov, Grigorii L'vovich. *300 obshcheupotrebitel'nykh russkikh poslovits i pogovorok (dlia govorashchikh na bolgarskom iazyke)*. Moskva: Russkii iazyk, 1986. Sofiia: Narodna prosveta, 1986. 128 pp.

3304. Petermann, Jürgen, Renate Hansen-Kokoruš, and Tamara Bill. *Russisch-deutsches phraseologisches Wörterbuch*. Berlin: Langenscheidt, 1995. 946 pp.

3305. Politis, Vera, Alan A. Reich, and Richard Sheldon (eds.). *Russian Proverbs: 100 Favorites of Professor Nadezhda Timofeevna Koroton*. Hanover, New Hampshire: Dartmouth Triad Associates, 1998. 154 pp. With illustrations.

3306. Reller, Gisela. *Liebe auf Russisch: Sprichwörter*. Berlin: Buchverlag Der Morgen, 1990. 186 pp.

3307. Romadin, M.N. (ill.). *Russkie poslovitsy i pogovorki*. Ed. E.Ia. Prizent. Moskva: Sovetskii Khudozhnik, 1973. (12 postcards).

3308. Segal, Louis. *Russian Idioms and Phrases*. London: Kniga, 1933. 52 pp. 4th ed. London: Pitman, 1943. New York: Pitman, 1943. 46 pp.

3309. Shanskii, N.M., E.A. Bystrova, and V.I. Zimin. *Frazeologicheskie oboroty russkogo iazyka*. Moskva: Russkii iazyk, 1988. 389 pp.

3310. Shargorodskii, T. *Ateisticheskie poslovitsy i pogovorki narodov mira*. Moskva: Izdatel'stvo Polyticheskoi Literatury, 1965. 143 pp.

3311. Shejdlin, B. *Moskva v poslovitsakh i pogovorkakh*. Moskva: Nikitinskie Subbotniki, 1929. 76 pp.

3312. Skillen, Chris. *Russian Proverbs*. Illustrations by Vladimir Lubarov. San Francisco: Chronicle Books, 1994. 59 pp.

3313. Snegirev, I.M. *Russkie narodnye poslovitsy i pritchi*. Moskva: V Universitetskoi Tipografii, 1848. 503 pp. Rpt. ed. Evgenii Kostiukhin. Moskva: "Indrik", 1999. 624 pp.

3314. Tsvilling (Zwilling), M.Ia. *Russko-nemetskii slovar' poslovits i pogovorok. Sprichwörter – sprichwörtliche Redensarten. Russisch-deutsches Wörterbuch*. Moskva: Russkii iazyk, 1984 (3rd ed. 2002). 215 pp.

3315. Vitek, Alexander J. *Russian-English Idiom Dictionary*. Ed. Harry H. Josselson. Detroit: Wayne State University Press, 1973. 327 pp.

3316. Walshe, I.A., and V.P. Berkov. *Russko-angliiskii slovar' krylatykh slov / Russian-English Dictionary of Winged Words*. Moskva: Russkii Iazyk, 1988. 288 pp.

3317. Walter, Harry, and Valerii M. Mokienko. *Russisch-Deutsches Jargon-Wörterbuch*. Frankfurt am Main: Peter Lang, 2001. 579 pp.

3318. Walter, Harry, and Valerii M. Mokienko. *Wörterbuch russischer Anti-Sprichwörter. Lehrmaterial für Studenten der Slawistik*. Greifswald: Ernst-Moritz-Arndt-Universität, 2002. 153 pp. (German title only; entire text in Russian). (anti-proverbs).

3319. Walter, Harry, and Valerii M. Mokienko. *Antiposlovitsy russkogo naroda*. Sankt-Peterburg: Neva, 2005. 574 pp. (anti-proverbs).

3320. Walter, Harry, and Valerii M. Mokienko. *Bol'shoi slovar' russkikh prozvishch*. Moskva: Olma Media Grupp, 2007. 704 pp.

3321. Yokoyama, Olga T. "Proverbs and Sayings - Poslovitsi i pogovorki." *The Russian Context: The Culture Behind the Language*. Eds. Eloise M. Boyle and Genevra Gerhart. Bloomington, Indiana: Slavica Publications, 2002. 297-351. With illustrations.

3322. Zimin, V.I., S.D. Ashurova, V.N. Shanskii, and Z.I. Shatalova. *Russkie poslovitsy i pogovorki. Uchebnyi slovar'*. Illustrations by L.A. Aleksandrova. Moskva: Shkola Press, 1994. 318 pp.

3323. Zwilling (Tsvilling), M.J. *Sprichwörter und sprichwörtliche Redensarten. Russisch-deutsches und deutsch-russisches Wörterbuch. Slovar' poslovits i pogovorok russko-nemetskii i nemetsko-russkii*. Hamburg: Igor Jourist Verlag, 1997. Moskau: ETS Verlag, 1997. 247 pp.

Samoan

3324. Schultz, Erich. *Proverbial Expressions of the Samoans*. Wellington, New Zealand: Polynesian Society, 1953. Rpt. as *Samoan Proverbial Expressions. Alagā'upa fa'a – Samoa*. Auckland, New Zealand: Polynesian Press, 1980 (2nd ed. 1985). 140 pp.

Sanskrit

3325. Achappa, H.S. *A Book of Sanskrit Proverbs and Quotations*. Mysore, India: H.S. Achappa, 1983. 1196 pp.

3326. Wilkins, Charles. *Fables and Proverbs from the Sanskrit. Being the "Hitopadesa"*. London: George Routledge, 1886. 277 pp.

Sardinian

3327. Melis, Luisa. "Detti sardi su equini e bovini." *Paremia*, 3 (1994), 125-130.

Scottish

3328. Anderson, M.L. (ed.). *The James Carmichaell Collection of Proverbs in Scots [1628]*. Edinburgh: Edinburgh University Press, 1957. 149 pp. (same as #3332).

3329. Anonymous. *A Birthday Book of Scots Proverbs with Explanatory Glossary of Scottish Words*. Glasgow: H.B. Langman, ca. 1985. 122 pp.

3330. Anonymous. *Scottish Proverbs. Old Scots Proverbs.* Illustrations by John MacKay. Glasgow: Lang Syne Publishers, 1995. 74 pp. (based on Andrew Henderson, *Scottish Proverbs.* Glasgow: Thomas D. Morison, 1881).

3331. Anonymous. *Scottish Proverbs.* Illustrations by Shona Grant. New York: Hippocrene Books, 1998. 111 pp.

3332. Carmichaell, James. *The James Carmichaell Collection of Proverbs in Scots [1628].* Ed. M.L. Anderson. Edinburgh: Edinburgh University Press, 1957. 149 pp. (same as #3328).

3333. Cheviot, Andrew. *Proverbs, Proverbial Expressions, and Popular Rhymes of Scotland.* London: Alexander Gardner, 1896; rpt. Detroit: Gale Research Company, 1969. 434 pp.

3334. Henderson, Andrew. *Scottish Proverbs.* Edinburgh: Oliver & Boyd, 1832. 254 pp. New ed. as *Scottish Proverbs Collected and Arranged by Andrew Henderson with Explanatory Notes and a Glossary.* Ed. James Donald. London: William Tegg, 1876; rpt. Glasgow: Thomas D. Morison, 1881; rpt. Detroit: Gale Research Company, 1969. 204 pp.

3335. Hislop, Alexander. *The Proverbs of Scotland with Explanatory and Illustrative Notes and a Glossary.* Edinburgh: Alexander Hislop & Co., 1868; rpt. Detroit: Gale Research Company, 1968. 367 pp.

3336. Irving, Godron (ed.). *The Wit of Scots.* London: Leslie Frewin, 1969. 112 pp.

3337. Kelly, James. *A Complete Collection of Scotish [sicl Proverbs. Explained and Made Intelligible to the English Reader.* London: William and John Innys, 1721; rpt. Darby, Pennsylvania: Folcroft Library Editions, 1976. 420 pp.

3338. Kirkpatrick, Betty. *The Little Book of Scottish Wit and Wisdom.* London: Michael O'Mara Books, 2001. 96 pp. With illustrations (miniature book).

3339. Kirkpatrick, Betty. *Scottish Wit & Wisdom. The Meaning Behind Famous Scottish Sayings.* Edinburgh: Crombie Jardine Publishing, 2005. 128 pp.

3340. MacGregor, Forbes. *Scots Proverbs and Rhymes.* Illustrations by John MacKay. Edinburgh: Pinetree Press, 1976. 48 pp.

3341. Mackay, Aeneas James George. *A Century of Scottish Proverbs and Sayings, in Prose and Rhyme, Current in Fife and Chiefly of Fife Origin.* Cupar-Fife: A. Westwood, 1891. 55 pp.

3342. McDonald, Julie Jensen. *Scottish Proverbs.* Iowa City, Iowa: Penfield Press, 1987. 62 pp.

3343. Morrison, Allan. *"Haud Yer Wheesht!" Your Scottish Granny's Favourite Sayings.* Illustrations by Rupert Besley. Glasgow: Vital Spark, 1997 (2nd ed. 2001). 96 pp.

3344. Murison, David. *Scots Saws. From the Folk-Wisdom of Scotland.* Edinburgh: The Mercat Press, 1981. 92 pp.

3345. Raben, Joseph. *Proverbs in the Waverly Novels of Sir Walter Scott.* Diss. Indiana University, 1954. 521 pp. (proverb index, pp. 241-490).

3346. Ramsay, Allan. *A Collection of Scots Proverbs.* Edinburgh: Ramsay, 1737. 90 pp. Rpt. Edinburgh: W. Gordon, 1750; rpt. Edinburgh: Harris, 1979. 134 pp.

3347. Simpson, Charles, and Gladys Simpson. "Weather Sayings from Banffshire [Scotland]." *Tocher,* no volume given, no. 47 (Winter 1993-1994), 310-312.

3348. Stampoy, Pappity. *A Collection of Scotch Proverbs.* London: R.D., 1663. Rpt. ed. Archer Taylor. Los Angeles, California: Augustan Reprint Society, 1955. 58 pp. (introduction pp. i-vi).

3349. Walker, Colin S.K. *Scottish Proverbs.* Edinburgh: Birlinn, 1996. 128 pp.

3350. Wilson, James. "Proverbs and Sayings." In J. Wilson. *The Dialect of Robert Burns as Spoken in Central Ayrshire.* Oxford: Oxford University Press, 1923. 90-98.

3351. Wood, Nicola. *Scottish Proverbs.* Edinburgh: Chambers, 1989; rpt. Edinburgh: Chambers, 1994. 89 pp.

Serbian

3352. Karadžić, Vuk Stefanović. *Přisloví a pořekadla.* Ed. Irena Wenigová. Illustrations by Bogdan Kršić. Praha: Odeon, 1987. 85 pp.

3353. Turner, K. Amy. *National Proverbs: Serbia.* London: Cecil Palmer and Hayward, 1915. 91 pp.

Slovakian

3354. Dorotjaková, Viktória, Peter Ďurčo, Mária Filkusová, Magdaléna Petrufová, and Mária Olga Malíková. *Rusko-slovenský* *frazeologický slovník.* Bratislava: Slovenské Pedagogické Nakladatel'stvo, 1998. 664 pp.

3355. Profantová, Zuzana. *Dúha vodu pije. Slovenské l'udové pranostiky.* Bratislava: Tatran, 1986. 208 pp. With illustrations. (weather proverbs).

3356. Profantová, Zuzana. *Slovenské pranostiky!* Bratislava: Nestor, 1997. 344 pp. (weather proverbs).

3357. Záturecký, Adolf Peter. *Slovenské príslovia, porekadlá a úslovia.* Praze: Františka Josefa, 1894; rpt. Bratislava: Tatran, 1975. 760 pp.

3358. Záturecký, Adolf Peter. *Slovenské príslovia a porekadlá. Výber zo zbierky.* Praze: Česká Akademie Cisaře, 1896. 389 pp. Rpt. eds. Josef Mlacek and Zuzana Profantová. 2 vols. Bratislava: Nestor, 1996. I, 320 pp.; II, 319 pp.

Slovenian

3359. Jenko, Elizabeta M. *Sich auf die Socken machen / Vzeti pot pod noge: Deutsch-slowenisches Wörterbuch der Redewendungen.* Klagenfurt: Drava, 1994. 159 pp.

Sorbian

3360. Gardoš, Isolde. *Serbske přisłowa. Kajkiž ptačik – tajke hrónčko. Sorbische Sprichwörter. Wie der Vogel – so das Lied.* Bautzen: VEB Domowina, 1978 (2nd ed. 1982). 169 pp.

3361. Gardoš, Isolde. *Serbske přisłowa. Kajkiž ptačik – tajke hrónčko. Przysłowia łuzyckie. Jaki ptak – taka pieśń.* Wrocław: Wydawnictwo Ossolineum. 1984. 169 pp.

3362. Hose, Susanne. *Serbski přisłowny leksikon / Sorbisches Sprichwörterlexikon.* Bautzen: Lusatia Verlag, 1996. 382 pp.

3363. Hose, Susanne, and Wolfgang Mieder (eds.). *Sorbian Proverbs / Serbske přisłowa.* Illustrations by Hans Winkler. Burlington, Vermont: The University of Vermont, 2004. 149 pp.

3364. Ivčenko, Anatolij, and Sonja Wölke. *Hornjoserbski frazeolo-giski słownik. Obersorbisches phraseologisches Wörterbuch. Verkhne-luzhitskii frazeologicheskii slovar'.* Bautzen: Domowina, 2004. 572 pp.

3365. Mahling, Peter. *Worte wie Nüsse. Freches sorbisches Sprichwörterbuch mit vielen Bildern gefestigten Menschen ins*

Gepäck und ins Gedächtnis. Bautzen: Domowina, 1980 (2nd ed. 1983). 68 pp.

3366. Meschkank, Werner. *Mjedowa knižka. Serbske přisłowa / Das Honigbüchlein. Sorbische Sprichwörter.* Bautzen: VEB Domowina-Verlag, 1988. 111 pp. (miniature book).

3367. Michałk, Frido (ed.). *Wjedrowa knižka. Serbske burske kaznje. Das Wetterbüchlein. Sorbische Bauernregeln.* Bautzen: VEB Domowina, 1982. 113 pp. (miniature book). (weather proverbs).

3368. Michałk, Frido (ed.). *Wjedrowa knižka. Książeczka pogody. Serbske burske kaznje. Łużyckie chłopskie przykazania.* Budysin: Ludowe nakładnistwo Domowina, 1987. 113 pp. (miniature book). (weather proverbs).

Spanish

3369. Alvarez Díaz, Juan José. *El Ejército, las armas y la guerra en el lenguaje coloquial: Modismos, locuciones, frases proverbiales, adagios, refranes y algunos vocablos.* Madrid: Ministerio de Defensa, 2000. 625 pp.

3370. Aranda, Charles. *Dichos. Proverbs and Sayings from the Spanish.* Santa Fe, New Mexico: Sunstone Press, 1977 (2nd ed. 1991). 32 pp.

3371. Aulnaye, M. de. "Proverbes et sentences tirés de *l'Histoire de Don Quixote*." In M. de Aulnaye. *L'Ingénieux Chevalier Don Quixote de la Mancha.* Paris: Th. Desoer, 1821. IV, pp. 401-440.

3372. Beinhauer, Werner. *1000 idiomatische Redensarten Spanisch. Mit Erklärungen und Beispielen.* Berlin: Langenscheidt, 1939 (16th ed. 1978). 192 pp.

3373. Benavente Jareño, Pedro, and Xesús Ferro Ruibal. "A vaca como metáfora en galego." *Paremia*, 3 (1994), 107-114.

3374. Benítez Rodríguez, Enrique Manuel. *Sorbo a sorbo. Refranes y citas sobre el vino.* Madrid: CIE Inversiones Editoriales, 2003. 654 pp. With illustrations.

3375. Bizzarri, Hugo O. *Diccionario paremiológico e ideológico de la edad media (Castilla, siglo XIII).* Buenos Aires: SECRIT, 2000. 385 pp.

3376. Brandenberger, Erna. *Refranero Español – Spanische Sprichwörter*. München: Deutscher Taschenbuch Verlag, 1975. 96 pp.

3377. Buitrago Jiménez, Alberto. *Diccionario de dichos y frases hechas*. Madrid: Espasa Calpe, 1995. 515 pp.

3378. Buján Otero, Patricia. "El refrán y su sombra (*Faro de Vigo*) por José Sesto." *Cadernos de fraseoloxía galega*, 4 (2003), 345-369.

3379. Buján Otero, Patricia, Xesús Ferro Ruibal, Maria Carmen Paz Roca, Marta Rodríguez Añón, and Ana Vidal Castiñeira. "Refraneiro do Seminario de Santiago (1947-1958)." *Cadernos de fraseoloxía galega*, 4 (2003), 173-343.

3380. Burke, Ralph. *Sancho Panza's Proverbs*. London: Pickering, 1872. Later edition: *Spanish Salt. A Collection of all the Proverbs which are to be Found in Don Quixote*. London: Pickering, 1877; rpt Philadelphia: R.West, 1977. 99 pp.

3381. Campos, Juana G., and Ana Barella. *Diccionario de Refranes*. Madrid: Espasa Calpe, 1993 (2nd ed. 1995). 399 pp.

3382. Cantera Ortiz de Urbina, Jesús, and Julia Sevilla Muñoz (eds.). *Contribución al estudio del refranero judeoespañol de oriente*. Madrid: Fundación Universitaria Española, 1997. 118 pp. (= *Cuadernos para Investigación de la Literatura Hispánica*, 22 [1997], 207-324).

3383. Cantera Ortiz de Urbina, Jesús, and Julia Sevilla Muñoz. *El calendario en el refranero español*. Madrid: Guillermo Blázquez, 2001. 137 pp. (weather proverbs).

3384. Cantera Ortiz de Urbina, Jesús, and Julia Sevilla Muñoz. *Los 494 refranes del "Seniloquium"*. Madrid: Guillermo Blázquez, 2002. 129 pp.

3385. Cantera Ortiz de Urbina, Jesús, and Julia Sevilla Muñoz (eds.). *Libro de refranes y sentencias de Mosén Pedro Vallés*. Madrid: Guillermo Blázquez, 2003. 141 pp.

3386. Cantera Ortiz de Urbina, Jesús, and Julia Sevilla Muñoz. *Los 173 refranes que emplea Juan de Valdés en el "Diálogo de la lengua" (1535)*. Madrid: Guillermo Blázquez, 2004. 132 pp.

3387. Cantera Ortiz de Urbina, Jesús, and Julia Sevilla Muñoz and Manuel Sevilla Muñoz. *Refranes, otras paremias y fraseologismos en "Don Quijote de la Mancha"*. Burlington, Vermont: The University of Vermont, 2005. 200 pp.

3388. Carbajo, Antonio (ed.). *Spanish Proverbs. A Compendium of the Philosophy and Wisdom of the Spanish Race.* Miami Springs, Florida: Language Resaerch Press, 1964. 54 pp.

3389. Castillo de Lucas, Antonio. *Refranes de Medicina o relacionados con ella por el pueblo.* Madrid: Yagües, 1936. 225 pp.

3390. Caudet Yarza, Francisco. *Los mejores refranes españoles.* Madrid: M.E. Editores, 1994. 415 pp.

3391. Caudet Yarza, Francisco. *Los mejores refranes españoles.* Edición rústica. Madrid: M.E. Editores, 1996. 285 pp.

3392. Chen, Berta Alicia. *Diccionario práctico de expresiones y proverbios Español-Inglés / Inglés-Español.* Madrid: Espasa Calpe, 1994. 371 pp.

3393. Chen, Berta Alicia. *Dictionary of Proverbs and Sayings English-Spanish / Spanish-English. Diccionario de Proverbios y Refranes Inglés-Español / Español-Inglés.* Panama: CMC Publishing, 1998. 220 pp. With illustrations.

3394. Chen, Berta Alicia (ed.). *Proverbios Españoles.* Panamá: Management Development Corporation, 2002. 64 pp. With illustrations.

3395. Chen, Berta Alicia (ed.). *Proverbios Ingleses.* Panamá: Management Development Corporation, 2002. 64 pp. With illustrations.

3396. Chen, Berta Alicia (ed.). *Proverbios, refranes y pensamientos relativos al dinero.* Panamá: Management Development Corporation, 2002. 223 pp.

3397. Collins, John. *A Dictionary of Spanish Proverbs. Compiled from the Best Authorities in the Spanish Language, Translated into English; with Explanatory Illustrations from the Latin, Spanish, and English Authors.* London: S. Brooke, 1823; rpt. Darby, Pennsylvania: Folcroft Library Editions, 1977. 391 pp.

3398. Colombi, Maria Cecilia. *Los refranes en "Don Quijote".* Diss. University of California at Santa Barbara, 1988. 236 pp. Also as *Los refranes en el Quijote: texto y contexto.* Potomac / Maryland: Scripta Humanistica, 1989. 142 pp. (proverb index, pp. 111-136).

3399. Conca, Maria. *Els refranys catalans.* Valencia: L'Estel, 1988 (3rd ed. 1996). 285 pp.

3400. Concepción, José Luis. *Refranero tradicional canario: Antología del Saber.* Tenerife, Islas Canarias: Ediciones Graficolor, 1988. 76 pp.

3401. Correas Martínez, Miguel, and José Enrique Gargalla Gil. *Calendario romance de refranes.* Barcelona: Edicions de la Universitat de Barcelona, 2003. 423 pp. With illustrations. (weather proverbs).

3402. Correas, Gonzalo. *Vocabulario de refranes y frases proverbiales* (1627 manuscript). Madrid: Ratés, 1906; 2nd ed. Madrid: Tip. de la Rev. de Archivos, 1924. Rpt. ed. Louis Combet. Lyon: Institute d'Etudes Ibériques et Ibéro-Américaines de l'Université de Bordeaux, 1967. 797 pp.

3403. Correas, Gonzalo. *Vocabulario de refranes y frases proverbiales* (1627 manuscript). Madrid: Ratés, 1906; 2nd ed. Madrid: Tip. de la Rev. de Archivos, 1924. Rpt. ed. Victor Infantes. Madrid: Visor Libros, 1992. 662 pp.

3404. Costa Alves, Manuel. *"Mudam os ventos, mudam os tempos": O adagiário popular meteorológico.* Lisboa: Gradiva, 1996. 122 pp. (3rd ed. 2006) 165 pp. (weather proverbs).

3405. Ernouf, Anita Bonilla. *Proverbs and Proverbial Phrases in the "Celestina".* Diss. Columbia University, 1970. 743 pp.

3406. Etxabe Díaz, Regino. *Gran diccionario de refranes.* Barcelona: Larousse, 2001. 491 pp.

3407. Fernández, Mauro. *Diccionario de Refranes.* Madrid: Alderabán, 1994. 270 pp.

3408. Fernández Gonzáles, José Ramón. "Dichos y refranes del valle de Ancares (León)." *Revista de dialectologia y tradiciones populares.* 40 (1985), 191-217.

3409. Ferro Ruibal, Xesús. *Refraneiro galego máis frecuente.* Santiago de Compostela: La Voz de Galicia, 2002. 223 pp.

3410. Ferro Ruibal, Xesús, and Fernando Groba Bouza. "'Dichos y refranes en dialecto vianés' de Laureano Prieto (1951) (ms. RAG-C170/5)." *Cadernos de fraseoloxía galega*, 11 (2009), 259-282.

3411. Flonta, Teodor. *A Dictionary of English and Spanish Equivalent Proverbs.* Hobart, Tasmania: De Proverbio.com, 2001. 267 pp.

3412. Florian, Ulrich, and Fernando Martínez. *Spanische idiomatische Redewendungen*. Leipzig: VEB Verlag Enzyklopädie, 1988. 196 pp.

3413. Fuster, Joan. *Conseils, proverbis i insolències*. Barcolona: Editorial A.C., 1968; rpt. Barcelona: Edicions 62, 1992. 175 pp.

3414. Fuster, Joan. *Aforismes*. Ed. Isidre Crespo. Alzira: Bromera, 2000. 251 pp.

3415. Gella Iturriaga, José. "444 refranes de *La Celestina*." *La Celestina y su contorno social*. Ed. Manuel Criado de Val. Barcelona: Borrás, 1977. 245-268.

3416. Gonzales, Ralfka, and Ana Ruiz. *Mi Primer Libro de Dichos / My First Book of Proverbs*. With an introduction by Sandra Cisneros. San Francisco, California: Children's Books Press, 1995. 34 pp. With illustrations (children's book).

3417. Haller, Joseph. *Altspanische Sprichwörter und sprichwörtliche Redensarten aus den Zeiten vor Cervantes*. 2 vols. Regensburg: G.J. Manz, 1883. I, 652 pp. (collection), II, 304 pp. (bibliography).

3418. Hayes, Francis Clement. *The Use of Proverbs in the "Siglo de Oro" Drama. An Introductory Study*. Diss. University of North Carolina, 1936. 227 pp.

3419. Hermida Alonso, Anxos. "Fraseoloxía de Matamá (Vigo)." *Cadernos de fraseoloxía galega*, 11 (2009), 283-304.

3420. Hoyos Sancho, Nieves de. "Wellerismos agricolas de España." *Folklore* (Naples), 9, nos. 1-2 (1954), 57-62.

3421. Iribarren, José María. *El porqué de los dichos: Sentido, origen y anécdota de los dichos, modismos y frases proverbiales de España con otras muchas curiosidades*. Madrid: Aguilar, 1955. 603 pp. 8th ed. Pamplona: Gobierno de Navarra, 1995. 419 pp.

3422. Jaime Gómez, José de, and José María de Jaime Lorén. *Refranero Geográfico Turolense*. Calamocha: INO Reproducciones, 1995. 38 pp. With illustrations.

3423. Jaime Gómez, José de, and José María de Jaime Lorén. *Paremiología aragonesa / Refranero aragonés*. Valencia: Romeu, 1999. 254 pp. With illustrations.

3424. Jaime Gómez, José de, and José María de Jaime Lorén. *Paremiología médica española: Más de once mil refranes de Medici-*

na, Farmacia y Veterinaria. Calamocha: Artes Gráficas Manuel Tenas, 2001. 438 pp.

3425.   Jaime Gómez, José de, and José María de Jaime Lorén. *Refranero de la vida intelectual y de la enseñanza*. Calamocha: Artes Gráficas Manuel Tenas, 2001. 113 pp.

3426.   Jaime Gómez, José de, and José María de Jaime Lorén. *Refranero aragonés. Más de 5.500 refranes, aforismos, dichos, frases hechas, mazadas ..., originarios de Aragón*. Zaragoza: Institución "Fernando el Católico", 2002. 398 pp.

3427.   Jaime Lorén, José María de. *La Ensenanza y las Ciencias de la Salud en la literatura popular*. Valencia: Universidad Cardenal Herrera-CEU, 2003. 135 pp.

3428.   Johnson, James Henry. *The Proverb in the Medieval Spanish "Exempla"*. Diss. University of North Carolina, 1958. 246 pp.

3429.   Junceda, Luis. *Del dicho al hecho: Del origen y la historia de 800 refranes*. Barcelona: Ediciones Obelisco, 1991. 317 pp.

3430.   Junceda, Luis. *Diccionario de refranes*. Madrid: Espasa Calpe, 1996. 598 pp.

3431.   Krauss, Werner. *Die Welt im spanischen Sprichwort – spanisch und deutsch*. Wiesbaden: Limes, 1946. 4th ed. Leipzig: Philipp Reclam, 1988. 109 pp.

3432.   Leguiel, M. Émile. *"Tirant lo Blanch: Aphorismes et proverbes." Revue catalane*, 7 (1913), 90-92 and 122-124.

3433.   Martín, Juan José, and A. Merino. *El gran libro de los refranes*. Madrid: LIBSA, 2006. 607 pp.

3434.   Martín Sánchez, Manuel. *Diccionario del español coloquial. Dichos, modismos y locuciones populares*. Madrid: Tellus, 1997. 455 pp.

3435.   Martínez Kleiser, Luis. *Refranero general ideológico español*. Madrid: Real Academia Espanola, 1953; rpt. Madrid: Hernando, 1989. 783 pp.

3436.   Martíns Seixo, Ramón Anxo. *"108 fórmulas galegas." Cadernos de fraseoloxía galega*, 9 (2007), 235-246.

3437.   Mertvago, Peter. *Dictionary of 1000 Spanish Proverbs*. New York: Hippocrene Books, 1996. 147 pp.

3438. Núñez, Hernán. *Refranes o proverbios en romance.* Salamanca: Iuan de Canoua, 1555. 142 pp. Rpt. eds. Louis Combet, Julia Sevilla Muñoz, Germán Condé Tarrío, and Josep Guia i Marín. 2 vols. Madrid: Guillermo Blázquez, 2001. I, 454 pp., II, 286 pp.

3439. O'Donnell, Kathleen Palatucci. *Sentencias and Refranes in "La Celestina": A Compilation, Analysis, and Examination of Their Function.* Diss. University of California at Los Angeles, 1993. 322 pp.

3440. Ohara, Maricarmen. *Tesoro de refranes populares / A Treasure of Popular Proverbs.* Illustrations by Rubé D. Acevedo. Ventura, California: Alegria Hispana Publications, 1990. 144 pp.

3441. O'Kane, Eleanor S. *Refranes y frases proverbiales españolas de la edad media.* Madrid: S. Aguirre Torre, 1959. 267 pp.

3442. Olmos Canalda, Elías. *Los refranes del Quijote.* Valencia: J. Nacher, 1940; rpt. Madrid: CIE Inversiones Editoriales, 1998. 133 pp.

3443. Paz Roca, Maria Carmen. "Aportazón ao refraneiro. Coleición de refrás recollidos da tradizión oral por Lois Carré (1898-1965)." *Cadernos de fraseoloxía galega*, 4 (2003), 129-141.

3444. Paz Roca, Maria Carmen. "Aínda novos manuscritos paremiolóxicos de Vázquez Saco." *Cadernos de fraseoloxía galega*, 7 (2007), 247-293.

3445. Pérez de Castro, J.L. "Dialogismos en el refranero asturiano." *Revista de dialectologia y tradiciones populares*, 19, nos. 1-3 (1963), 116-138.

3446. Perry, Theodore A. (ed.). *Santob de Carrión. "Proverbios Morales".* Madison / Wisconsin: The Hispanic Seminary of Medieval Studies, 1986. 233 pp.

3447. Pottier, B. "Les noms de personnes dans la parémiologie espagnole." *Les langues modernes*, 41, no. 5 (1947), 428-435.

3448. Prieto Donate, Estefanía. "Refraneiro escolar galego do cambio de milenio." *Cadernos de fraseoloxía galega*, 11 (2009), 305-369.

3449. Rivas, Paco. *Fraseoloxía do mar na Mariña lugesa.* Santiago de Compostela: Xunta de Galicia, 2000. 92 pp. (= *Cadernos de fraseoloxía galega*, vol. 1).

3450. Rodríguez Marín, Francisco. *12.600 Refranes más no contenidos en las collecíon del Maestro Gonzalo Correas ni en "Más* *de 21.000 refranes castellanos"*. Madrid: Revista de Archivos, Bibliotecas y Museos, 1930. 345 pp.

3451. Romo Herrero, Lidia. "Refranes recopilados en Tresjuncos (Cuenca)." *Paremia*, 16 (2007), 157-163.

3452. Ruíz Leivas, Cristóbal, and Juan-A. Eiroa García-Garabal. "Fraseoloxía e terminoloxía dos cogomelos." *Cadernos de fraseoloxía galega*, 4 (2003), 371-387.

3453. Santilla, Iñigo López deMendoza, Marqués de. *Refranes que dizen las viejas tras el fuego [15th century]*. Ed. Hugo Oscar Bizzarri. Kassel: Edition Reichenberger, 1995. 187 pp.

3454. Sardelli, María Antonella, and Lourdes Achúcarro Fernández. "Florilegio aforistico." *Paremia*, 16 (2007), 165-168.

3455. Sbarbi, José María. *Florilegio o ramillete alfabético de fefranes y modismos comparativos y ponderativos de la lengua castellana*. Madrid: A. Gomez Fuentenebro, 1873; rpt. Medrid: Monserrat, 1980. 303 pp.

3456. Sbarbi, José María. *El refranero general espoñola*. 10 vols. Madrid: A. Gomez Funetenebro, 1874-1878; rpt. Madrid: Monserrat, 1980. I, 295 pp.; II, 295 pp.; III, 303 pp.; IV, 240 pp.; V, 197 pp.; VI, 351 pp.; VII, 255 pp.; VIII, 273 pp.; IX, 233 pp.; X, 296 pp.

3457. Selig, Karl-Ludwig. "An Important Seventeenth-Century List of Spanish Proverbs." *Proverbium*, no. 22 (1973), 847-849.

3458. Serrano, Juan, and Susan Serrano. *Spanish Proverbs, Idioms and Slang*. New York: Hippocrene Books, 1999. 196 pp.

3459. Sevilla Muñoz, Julia. "El refranero hoy." *Paremia*, 3 (1994), 143-150.

3460. Sevilla Muñoz, Julia. "El refranero hoy." *Paremia*, 5 (1996), 115-126.

3461. Sevilla Muñoz, Julia. "El refranero hoy." *Paremia*, 7 (1998), 141-152.

3462. Sevilla Muñoz, Julia. "El refranero hoy." *Paremia*, 9 (2000), 133-141.

3463. Sevilla Muñoz, Julia. "El refranero hoy." *Paremia*, 16 (2007), 149-156.

3464. Sevilla Muñoz, Julia. "El refranero hoy." *Paremia*, 19 (2010), 215-226.

3465. Soto Arias, María do Rosario. *Achegas a un dicionario de refráns galego-castelán, castelán-galego.* Santiago de Compostela: Xunta de Galicia, 2003. 347 pp. (= *Cadernos de fraseoloxía galega,* vol. 3).

3466. Stein, Leopold. *Untersuchungen über die "Proverbios morales" von Santob de Carrion mit besonderem Hinweis auf die Quellen und Parallelen.* Berlin: Mayer & Müller, 1900. 109 pp. (proverb index, pp. 45-108).

3467. Sturm, Harlan. *The "Libro de los buenos proverbios": A Critical Edition.* Lexington, Kentucky: University Press of Kentucky, 1970. 148 pp.

3468. Taboada Chivite, Xesús. *Refraneiro galego.* Ed. Xesús Ferro Ruibal et al. Santiago de Compostela: Xunta de Galicia, 2000. 194 pp. (= *Cadernos de fraseoloxía galega,* vol. 2).

3469. Thomas, Antoine. "Les *Proverbes* de Guylem [*sic*; Guillem] de Cervera. Poème catalan du XIIIᵉ siècle." *Romania,* 15 (1886), 25-110.

3470. Vázquez, Lois. "Refranero gallego. Colección hecha por el P. Gumersindo Placer López." *Cadernos de fraseoloxía galega,* 4 (2003), 143-171.

3471. Vázquez Saco, Francisco. *Refraneiro galego e outros materiais de tradición oral.* Ed. Xesús Ferro Ruibal et al. Santiago de Compostela: Xunta de Galicia, 2003. 1067 pp. (= *Cadernos de fraseoloxía galega,* vol. 5).

3472. Ventín Durán, José Augusto. *Fraseoloxía de Moscoso e outros materiais de tradición oral.* Ed. Xesús Ferro Ruibal et al. Santiago de Compostela: Xunta de Galicia, 2007. 469 pp.

3473. Vergara Martín, Gabriel María. *Refranero geográfico español.* Madrid: Hernando, 1936; rpt. Madrid: Hernando, 1986. 463 pp.

3474. Vidal Castiñeira, Ana. "Un manuscrito paremiolóxico de Murguía." *Cadernos de fraseoloxía galega,* 4 (2003), 117-128.

3475. Walsh, John K. *"El Libro de los doce sabios" o "Tractado de la nobleza y lealtad". Estudio y edicion.* Madrid: Real Academia Española, 1975. 179 pp.

Sumerian

3476. Alster, Bendt. *The Instructions of Suruppak. A Sumerian Proverb Collection.* Copenhagen: Akademisk Forlag, 1974. 167 pp. and 32 plates.

3477. Alster, Bendt. *Proverbs of Ancient Sumer: The World's Earliest Proverb Collections.* 2 vols. Bethesda, Maryland: CDL Press, 1997. 548 pp. and 133 plates.

3478. Alster, Bendt. *Wisdom of Ancient Sumer.* Bethesda, Maryland: CDL Press, 2005. 426 pp. and 72 plates.

3479. Gordon, Edmund I. *Sumerian Proverbs. Glimpses of Everyday Life in Ancient Mesopotamia.* Philadelphia: University of Pennsylvania Press, 1959. 556 pp. and 79 plates.

3480. Moll, Otto. "Über die ältesten Sprichwörtersammlungen [Sumerian]." *Proverbium*, no. 6 (1966), 113-120.

Swedish

3481. Asala, Joanne (ed.). *Swedish Proverbs.* Illustrations by Ezaline Boheman. Iowa City, Iowa: Penfield Press, 1994. 63 pp.

3482. Holm, Pelle. *Ordspråk och talesätt.* Stockholm: Albert Bonniers Förlag, 1965 (2nd ed. 1975). 394 pp.

3483. Holm, Pelle. *"Ett ord i rättan tid". 3530 Ordspråk och talesätt.* Illustrations by Fibben Hald. Stockholm: Bonnier Fakta, 1984. 260 pp.

3484. Kalén, Johan. "Några utbyggda ordstär från Halland." *Folkminnen och Folktankar*, 12, no. 2 (1925), 27-38 (wellerisms).

3485. Landgren, G.A. *Ordspråk, sanna språk. 6500 bevingade ord ur folkets mun.* Karlshamn: Sigrid Flodin, 1889; rpt. Stockholm: Rediviva, 1979. 183 pp.

3486. Palm, Christine, and Anders Odeldahl. *Tyska idiombok.* Berlings, Arlöv: Norstedts Förlag, 1993. 173 pp.

3487. Ström, Fredrik. *Svenskarna i sina ordspråk.* Illustrations by Ossian Elgström. Stockholm: Albert Bonniers Förlag, 1926. 352 pp.

3488. Ström, Fredrik. *Svenska ordspråk.* Stockholm: Albert Bonniers Förlag, 1929; rpt. Stockholm: Albert Bonniers, 1963. 374 pp.

3489. Ström, Fredrik. *Svenska ordstäv.* Stockholm: Tidens Förlag, 1931. Illustrations by Ossian Elgström. 274 pp. (wellerisms)

3490. Wahlund, Per Erik. *Osed och Ordsed. Det är 1234 oe-motsäliga ordspråk och kärnfulla talesätt, hämtade ur Sal. Hr. Christopher L. Grubbs "Penu Proverbiale" [1665]. Och här anyo atergivna med förklaringar, kommentares, ordlista samt andra gagneliga bihang.* Stockholm: Natur och Kultur, 1988. 207 pp.

Swiss

3491. Barras, Christine. *Les proverbes dans les patois de la suisse romande.* Diss. Université de Neuchâtel, 1984. Sierre: J. Périsset, 1984. 997 pp.

3492. Barras, Christine. *La sagesse des Romands: Proverbes patois de Suisse romande.* Lausanne: Editions Payot, 1997. 427 pp.

3493. Bätschi, J. *Der Davoser im Lichte seiner Sprichwörter und Redensarten.* Davos: Buchdruckerei Davos, 1937. 71 pp.

3494. Bürgin, Yvonne. *Alti und neui Schwiizer Schprüch.* Illustrations by Röbi Wyss. Niederteufen: Schellen, 1983. 79 pp.

3495. Dettli, Julius. "Davoser Redensarten und Sprüche sowie anderes aus der Sprachüberlieferung." *Walser Mitteilungen*, no volume given, no. 40 (1999), 28-35.

3496. Hauser, Albert. *Bauernregeln. Eine schweizerische Sammlung mit Erläuterungen.* Zürich: Artemis, 1973 (2nd ed. 1975). 710 pp. (weather proverbs).

3497. Kirchhofer, Melchior. *Wahrheit und Dichtung: Sammlung schweizerischer Sprichwörter.* Zürich: Orell, Füßli und Compagnie, 1824. Rpt. ed. Wolfgang Mieder. Hildesheim: Georg Olms, 1997. 366 pp. (introduction, pp. V*-XXX*).

3498. Kürz-Luder, Barbara. *Schwiizertütschi Sprichwörter.* Küsnacht: Edition Kürz, 1982. 59 pp.

3499. Laely-Meyer, Hans. "Bekannte und unbekannte Redensarten (und Redewendungen) [aus Davos]." *Davoser Revue*, 74, no. 1 (1999), 27-29 and 31.

3500. Lössi, Henri. *Proverbis da l'Engiadina e da la Val Müstair / Engadiner und Münstertaler Sprichwörter.* Schlarigna/Celerina: U-nium dals Grischs, 1987. 298 pp.

3501. Mieder, Wolfgang. *Das Sprichwort im Werke Jeremias Gotthelfs. Eine volkskundlich-literarische Untersuchung.* Diss. Michigan State University, 1970. 271 pp. Bern: Herbert Lang, 1972. 167 pp. (proverb index, pp. 101-156).

3502. Portmann, Paul F. (ed.). *"Di letschti Chue tuet's Törli zue":* *Schweizerdeutsche Sprichwörter.* Frauenfeld: Huber, 1983. Rpt. as *"Ohni Wii und Brot isch d'Liebi tod": Schweizerdeutsche Sprich-* *wörter.* Frauenfeld: Huber, 1999. 173 pp.

3503. Ruef, Hans. *Sprichwort und Sprache: Am Beispiel des* *Sprichworts im Schweizerdeutschen.* Berlin: Walter de Gruyter, 1995. 303 pp. (proverb index, pp. 85-293).

3504. Senti, Alois. *Reime und Sprüche aus dem Sarganserland* *[Switzerland].* Basel: G. Krebs, 1979. 232 pp.

3505. Singer, Samuel. "Alte schweizerische Sprichwörter." *Schweizerisches Archiv für Volkskunde,* 20 (1916), 389-419; and 21 (1917), 235-236.

3506. Singer, Samuel. "Schweizerische Sagsprichwörter." *Schweizerisches Archiv für Volkskunde,* 38 (1941), 129-139; and 39 (1941-1942), 137-139. (wellerisms).

3507. Sutermeister, Otto. *Die schweizerischen Sprichwörter der Ge-* *genwart in ausgewählter Sammlung.* Aarau: J.J. Christen, 1869. 152 pp.

3508. Waibel, Max. *Walser Weisheiten: Sprichwörter und Redens-* *arten.* Frauenfeld: Huber, 1998. 215 pp.

Tadzhik

3509. Bell, Evan Robert. *An Analysis of Tajik Proverbs [Tadzhiki-* *stan].* M.A. Thesis Graduate Institute of Applied Linguistics at Dal- las, Texas, 2009. 275 pp.

3510. Kalontarov, Iakub I. *Mudrost' trekh narodov. Chast' II.* *Tadzhikskie, uzbekskie i russkie poslovitsy, pogovorki i aforizmy v* *analogii.* Ed. Iosif Kalontarov. New York: Life Trans, 2002. 308 pp.

Taiwanese

3511. Chen, Chu-Hsien. *Tai-oan Siok-gan Gu-tian [The Interpret-* *er's Dictionary of Taiwanese Proverbs and Common Sayings].* 10 volumes. Taipei, Taiwan: Avanguard Publishing House, 1997-2009 (in Chinese). I, 234 pp.; II, 260 pp.; III, 448 pp.; IV, 419 pp.; V, 635 pp.; VI, 666 pp.; VII, 621 pp.; VIII, 415 pp.; IX, 785 pp.; X, 563 pp.

Thai

3512. Gühler, U. "Über Thai Sprichwörter." *Journal of the Thailand Research Society*, 34 (1943), 97-144.

3513. Otrakul, Ampha. *Perlen vor die Säue werfen oder Dem Affen einen Kristall geben. Thailändische-deutsche Sprichwörter im Vergleich mit Illustrationen.* Illustrations by Tongchai Burimchit. Bonn: Deutsch-Thailändische Gesellschaft, 1991. 129 pp.

3514. Peltier, Anatole-Roger (ed.). *Dictons et proverbes thai.* Bangkok: Travaux du centre d'histoire et civilisations de la peninsule indochinoise, 1980. 99 pp. With illustrations.

Tibetan

3515. Cüppers, Christoph, and Per K. Sørensen (eds.). *A Collection of Tibetan Proverbs and Sayings: Gems of Tibetan Wisdom and Wit.* Stuttgart: Franz Steiner, 1998. 444 pp.

3516. Naga, Acharya Sangye T., and Tsepak Rigzin. *Tibetan Quadrisyllabics, Phrases and Idioms.* Dharamsala: Library of Tibetan Works & Archives, 1994. 253 pp.

3517. Pemba, Lhamo. *Tibetan Proverbs.* Dharamsala: Library of Tibetan Works & Archives, 1996. 223 pp.

3518. Pemba, Lhamo. *Tibetische Sprichwörter. Zweisprachige Ausgabe.* Ed. Rainer Bull. München: Deutscher Taschenbuch Verlag, 2006. 320 pp.

3519. Read, A.F.C. "Balti Proverbs [Tibet]." *Bulletin of the School of Oriental Studies*, 7, no. 3 (1934), 499-502.

Tongan

3520. Māhina, 'Okusitino. *Tongan Proverbs.* Auckland, New Zealand: Reed Publishing, 2004. 224 pp.

Turkish

3521. Alikuli-Oglu, Ragimly Ragim. *Türk atasözleri ve Rusça eş değerleri.* Istanbul: Appinar, 1991. 90 pp.

3522. Atsiz, Bedriye, and Hans-Joachim Kissling. *Sammlung türkischer Redensarten.* Wiesbaden: Otto Harrassowitz, 1974. 186 pp.

3523. Barlas, Muhtar. *Almanca-Türkçe Deyimler ve Özel Anlatim Birimleri Sözlüğü.* Istanbul: ABC Kitabevi A.S., 1998. 220 pp.

3524. Başkan, Özcan. *Ingilizce Atasözleri*. Ed. by Metin Yurtbaşi. Istanbul: Ingilizce Ögretmeni, 1979 (2nd ed. 1985). 55 pp. With illustrations.

3525. Böhm, Richard. *Die Weisheit der Völker. III. Sprüche der Türken*. Wiesbaden: Wiesbadener Graphische Betriebe, 1962. 40 pp.

3526. Çekiç, A. Hulusi. *Karşilaştirmali atasözleri. Ingilizce-türkçe ve türkçe-ingilizce*. Ankara: Kalite Matbaasi, 1976. 286 pp.

3527. Dağpinar, Aydin. *Türkçe-ingilizce ingilizce-türkçe atasözleri ve deyimler sözlüğü. A Dictionary of Turkish-English English-Turkish Proverbs and Idioms*. Istanbul: Doyuran Matbaasi, 1982. 294 pp.

3528. Ermakova, Lilia, and Sevinç Üçgül. *Rusça-Türkçe Deyimler Sözlüğü*. Istanbul: (Sahaf) Kitabevi, 1998. 168 pp.

3529. Gökceoğlu, Aziz, and Roland Parton. *Deutsche Redewendungen: Deutsch-Türkisch / Almanca-Deyimler*. Illustrations by Hans-Jürgen Kathe. Oberhausen: Ortadoğu, 1988. 81 pp.

3530. Göknar, Hale. *Ispanyolca deyimler ve atasözleri sözlüğü / Diccionario de expressiones y proverbios en español*. Istanbul: ERA, 1993. 264 pp.

3531. Gültek, Vedat, and Buğra Gültek. *Atasözleri Sözlüğü: Türkçe-Rusça / Rusça-Türkçe*. Istanbul: Sosyal Yayinlar, 2000. 240 pp.

3532. Kuray, Gülbende. *Italyanca deyimler ve atasözleri sözlüğü*. Ankara: Sedir Yayinlari, 1990. 76 pp.

3533. Manioglu, Kemal, and Ludwig Scheuermann. *410 Türk Atalar Sözü / Türkische Sprichwörter*. Istanbul: Universum-Matbaasi, 1956. 82 pp.

3534. Muallimoğlu, Nejat. *Turkish Delights. A Treasury of Proverbs and Folk Sayings*. Illustrations by Laurie Webber. Istanbul: Avciol Matbaasi, 1988. 287 pp.

3535. Öndoğan, Erdem. *Türkçe-Ingilizce / Ingilizce-Türkçe Deyimler Sözlüğü*. Istanbul: Inkilâp Kitabevi, 1993. 351 pp. With illustrations.

3536. Özcan, Celal, and Rita Seuß (eds.). *Türk Atasözleri / Türkische Sprichwörter*. München: Deutscher Taschenbuch Verlag, 1996. 96 pp.

3537. Rybarski, Werner. *Kahle Henne und kahler Hahn / Kel tavuk ve Kel horoz: Eine vergleichende Sammlung deutscher und türki-*

scher Sprichwörter. Illustrations by Conny Schillo-Rybarski. Gelsenkirchen: Deutsch-Türkischer Freundeskreis, 1994. 129 pp.

3538. Sak, Ziya. *Türkçe-ingilizce deyimler sözlüğü / Dictionary of Turkish-English Idioms*. Istanbul: Ingilizce Öğretimi Yayinlari, 1988. 160 pp.

3539. Schlechta-Wschehrd, Ottokar Maria von. *Osmanische Sprichwörter / Proverbes Ottomans*. Wien: K.K. Hof- und Staatsdruckerei, 1865. 180 pp.

3540. Senaltan, Semahat. *Studien zur sprachlichen Gestalt der deutschen und türkischen Sprichwörter*. Diss. Universität Marburg, 1968. Marburg: Erich Mauersberger, 1968. 186 pp. (proverb index, pp. 138-162).

3541. Stein, Heidi. "Eine türkische Sprichwortsammlung des 17. Jahrhunderts." *Acta Orientalia Academiae Scientiarum Hungaricae*, 38, nos. 1-2 (1984), 55-104.

3542. Tekinay, Alev. *Pons-Wörterbuch der idiomatischen Redensarten: deutsch-türkisch, türkisch-deutsch*. Stuttgart: Klett, 1984. 170 pp.

3543. Yüksel, Azmi, and Lütfü Yilmaz. *Ingilizce-türkçe arapça sözlük (Atasözleri ve deyimler)*. Ankara: Birlesik, 1993. 96 pp.

3544. Yurtbaşi, Metin. *Ingilizce-türkçe halk deyişleri*. Yesilyurt/Istanbul: Hava Harp Okulu Yayinlari, 1987. 99 pp. With illustrations.

3545. Yurtbaşi, Metin. *A Dictionary of Turkish Proverbs*. Illustrations by Sadik Pala. Ankara: Turkish Daily News, 1993. 682 pp.

3546. Yurtbaşi, Metin. *Ingiliz ve amerikan atasözleri ve türkçe karşiliklari*. Istanbul: Türkiye Iş Bankasi Beylikdüzü, 1993. 128 pp. With illustrations.

3547. Yurtbaşi, Metin. *Türkisches Sprichwörterlexikon*. Illustrations by Sadik Pala. Ankara: Bilsev, 1993. 509 pp. and 130 pp. (index); (2nd ed. 1994) 522 pp.

3548. Yurtbaşi, Metin. *Turkish Proverbs and Their English Equivalents*. Illustrations by Sadik Pala. Istanbul: Türkiye Iş Bankasi Beylikdüzü, 1993. 120 pp.

3549. Yurtbaşi, Metin. *Siniflandirilmiş Türk Atasözleri: Geleneksel değer yargilarimizi 172 konuda sergileyen, aciklamali 10.000 türk* *atasözü. 1000 resim. Secme dizin.* Illustrations by Sadik Pala. Ankara: Özdemir Yayincilik, 1994. 377 pp. (student edition).

3550. Yurtbaşi, Metin. *Siniflandirilmis Türk Atasözleri: Geleneksel değer yargilarimizi 172 konuda sergileyen 30.000 türk atasözü. 172 resim.* Illustrations by Sadik Pala. Ankara: Özdemir Yayincilik, 1994. 311 pp.

3551. Yurtbaşi, Metin. *Eş ve karşit anlamlilar sözlüğü.* Illustrations by Sadik Pala. Istanbul: Birinci Baski, 1996. 451 pp.

3552. Yurtbaşi, Metin. *Örnekleriyle Deyimler Sözlüğü: Türkçenin zenginliğini ve yaraticiliğini kanitlayan 25.000 deyim. 30.000 örnek cümle. Binlerce resim.* Illustrations by Sadik Pala. Istanbul: Birinci Baski, 1996. 521 pp.

3553. Yurtbaşi, Metin. *Turks spreekwoordenboek.* Ankara: MEM Ofset Ltd., 1997. 123 pp.

3554. Yurtbaşi, Metin. *Türkische Redewendungen mit deutschen Entsprechungen / Türkçe-Almanca Deyimler Sözlüğü.* Illustrations by Sadik Pala. Istanbul: Bahar Verlag, 2000. 616 pp.

3555. Yurtbaşi, Metin. *Dictionnaire des proverbes et dictons turcs.* Illustrations by Sadik Pala. Istanbul: Türkiye Is Bankasi Beylikdüzü, 2002. 110 pp.

3556. Yurtbaşi, Metin. *Proverbes turcs et leurs équivalents en français.* Illustrations by Sadik Pala. Istanbul: Türkiye Iş Bankasi Beylikdüzü, 2002. 120 pp.

3557. Yurtbaşi, Metin. *Siniflandirilmiş türk atasözleri.* Illustrations by Sadik Pala. Istanbul: Türkiye Iş Bankasi Beylikdüzü, 2003. 213 pp.

3558. Yurtbaşi, Metin. *Vertailevia turkkilaisia ja suomalaisia sananlaskuja / Karşilaştirmali fin ve türk atasözleri.* Illustrations by Sadik Pala. Istanbul: Saritas, 2005. 340 pp.

3559. Yurtbaşi, Metin. *Proverbes turcs et français / Fransiz ve türk atasözleri.* Istanbul: Baris Matbaasi, 2007. 688 pp.

3560. Yurtbaşi, Metin. *Turkish and English Proverbs / Ingiliz ve türk atasözleri.* Istanbul: Bahar Yayinlari, 2007. 552 pp.

3561. Yurtbaşi, Metin. *Turetsko-russkie poslovitsy / Rus ve türk atasözleri.* Illustrations by Sadik Pala. Istanbul: Şahmat Matbaa, 2008. 1060 pp.

3562. Yurtbaşi, Metin. *Türkische und deutsche Redewendungen /
Almanca ve türkçe deyimler.* Istanbul: Şahmat Matbaa, 2008.
824 pp.

3563. Yurtbaşi, Metin. *Türkische und deutsche Sprichwörter / Alman ve türk atasözleri.* Istanbul: Bahar Yayinlari, 2008. 696 pp.

3564. Yurtbaşi, Metin. *Türkische Sprichwörter mit deutschen Entsprechungen / Almanca karşiliklari ile türk atasözleri.* Illustrations
by Sadik Pala. Istanbul: Bahar Yayinlari, 2009. 288 pp.

Udmurt

3565. Kralin, N.P. *Poslovitsy i pogovorki udmurtskogo o naroda
na udmurtskom iazyke.* Izhevsk: Tipografiia Ministerstva Kul'tury
UASSR, 1961. 188 pp.

Uigur

3566. Khamraev, M.K., and Iu. I. Levin. *Uigurskie poslovitsy i pogovorki na uigurskom i russkom iazykakh i s russkimi paralleliami.*
Moskva: Nauka, 1981. 182 pp.

Ukrainian

3567. Iurchenko, O.S., and A.O. Ivchenko. *Slovnik stiikikh narodnikh poriviian'.* Kharkiv: Osnova, 1993. 174 pp.

3568. Paziak, Mikhail Mikhailovich. *Pryslivia ta prykazky: Priroda, gospodars'ka diial'nist' liudini.* Kiev: Naukova Dumka, 1989.
479 pp.

3569. Plawiuk, Volodymyr S. *Ukrains'ki pripovidki / Ukrainian
Proverbs.* Eds. Bohdan Medwidsky and Alexander Makar. Edmonton, Alberta: The Huculak Chair of Ukrainian Culture and Ethnography, University of Alberta – Ukrainian Pioneers Association of
Alberta, Canada, 1996. 297 pp.

Uzbek

3570. Sarimsakov, B.L., and A.K. Musakulov. *Uzbekskie narodnye
poslovitsy.* Tashkent: Izdatel'stvo "Fan" Uzbekskoi SSR, 1983.
232 pp.

Vietnamese

3571. Hong, Luong Van. *Tuc ngu Viet Nam. Vietnamesische Sprichwörter*. Ho Chi Minh: Bibliothek der Universität Ho Chi Minh-Stadt, 1989. 58 pp.

3572. Hong, Luong Van. *Tuc ngu va caudo Duc-Viet. Sprichwörter und Rätsel Deutsch-Vietnamesisch*. Ho Chi Minh: Nha Xuat Ban Tre, 1992. 303 pp.

3573. Kinh, Nguyen Xuan, and Phan Hong Son. *Tuc ngu Viet Nam*. Ha Noi: Nha Xuat Ban Van Hoa, 1995. 200 pp.

3574. Thai Van Kiem, M. "Les proverbes vietnamiens et la sagesse des peuples." *Comptes rendus trimestriels des séances de l'Academie des Sciences d'Outre-Mer*, 39 (1979), 377-400.

Virgin Islands

3575. Petersen, Arona. *Herbs & Proverbs of the Virgin Islands*. St. Thomas, Virgin Islands: St. Thomas Graphics, 1974. 78 pp. With Illustrations.

3576. Seaman, George A. *Not So Cat Walk. The Philosophy of a People [from the Virgin Islands] and an Era Expressed by Proverbs*. With illustrations by J. Wells Champney. St. Croix, Virgin Islands: Crown Printing, 1975. 64 pp.

Welsh

3577. Evans, J.J. *Diarhebion Cymraeg / Welsh Proverbs*. Llandysul: Gwasg Gomer, 1965 (2nd ed. 1982). 59 pp.

3578. Vaughan, Henry Halford. *Welsh Proverbs with English Translations*. London: Kegan Paul, Trench, & Co., 1889; rpt. Detroit: Gale Research Company, 1969. 378 pp.

West Indies

3579. Valls, Rafael (Lito). *Ole Time Sayin's. Proverbs of the West Indies*. St. John: U.S.V.I., 1983. 96 pp.

Yiddish (Sephardic)

3580. Artmann, H.C. *Je länger ein Blinder lebt, desto mehr sieht er. Jiddische Sprichwörter*. Frankfurt am Main: Insel, 1965 (3rd ed.1986). 60 pp.

3581. Ayalti, Hanan J. *Yiddish Proverbs*. New York: Schocken Books, 1949 (5th ed. 1975). 127 pp.

3582. Bernstein, Ignaz. *Jüdische Sprichwörter und Redensarten*. Warschau: Kauffmann, 1908. Rpt. ed. Hans Peter Althaus. Hildesheim: Georg Olms, 1969; rpt. again Wiesbaden: Fourier, 1988. 734 pp. (introduction pp. IX*-XXVII*).

3583. Bernstein, Ignaz. *Proverbia Judaeorum Erotica et Turpia. Jüdische Sprichwörter erotischen und rustikalen Inhalts*. Als Manuskript gedruckt. Wien and Berlin: R. Löwit, 1918; rpt. Haifa: "Renaissance" Publishing, 1971. 70 pp.

3584. Bernstein, Ignaz. *Yiddish Sayinqs Mama Never Taught You*. Eds. Gershon Weltman and Marin S. Zuckerman. Van Nuys, California: Perivale Press, 1975. 99 pp.

3585. Danon, Abraham. "Proverbes judéo-espagnols de Turquie." *Zeitschrift für Romanische Philologie*, 27 (1903), 72-96.

3586. Dietzel, Volker (ed.). *Die ganze Welt steht auf der spitzen Zunge. Jüdische Sprichwörter*. Leipzig: Gustav Kiepenheuer, 1987; rpt. Wiesbaden: Fourier, 2003. 159 pp.

3587. Eno, Brenda Rae (ill.). *Jewish Proverbs*. San Francisco, California: Chronicle Books, 1989; rpt. London: Robert Hale, 1990. 58 pp.

3588. Kogos, Fred. *Book of Yiddish Proverbs and Slang*. Secaucus, New Jersey: Popular Books, 1967. 317 pp.

3589. Kogos, Fred. *1001 Yiddish Proverbs*. Secaucus, New Jersey: Castle Books, 1970; rpt. Secaucus, New Jersey: Citadel Press, 1990. 158 pp.

3590. Kogos, Fred. *The Dictionary of Popular Yiddish Words, Phrases, and Proverbs*. Secaucus, New Jersey: Citadel Press, 1997. 158 pp.

3591. Kolonomos, Žamila. *Poslovic i izreke sefardkikh jevreja Bosne i Herzegovine. Proverbs and Sayings of the Sephardic Jews of Bosnia and Herzegovina*. Beograd: Federation of Jewish Communities in Yugoslavia, 1976. 94 pp.

3592. Kolonomos, Žamila. *Poslovice. Izreke i priče sefardkikh jevreja makedonije. Proverbs, Sayings and Tales of the Sephardi Jews of Macedonia*. Beograd: Savez Jevrejskih Opština Jugoslavije, 1978. 192 pp. With illustrations.

3593. Kumove, Shirley. *Words Like Arrows. A Treasury of Yiddish Folk Sayings*. Illustrations by Frank Newfeld. Toronto: University of Toronto Press, 1984; rpt. New York: Schocken Books. 1985; rpt. New York: Warner, 1986. 268 pp.

3594. Kumove, Shirley. *Ehrlich ist beschwerlich. Jiddische Spruchweisheiten*. Berlin: Verlag Volk & Welt, 1991. 197 pp. (German translation of *Words Like Arrows. A Treasury of Yiddish Folk Sayings* Toronto: University of Toronto Press, 1984).

3595. Kumove, Shirley. "Words Like Arrows: Yiddish Proverbs." *Pakn-Treger: The Magazine of the National Yiddish Book Center*, no volume given, no. 24 (Spring 1997), 60-61.

3596. Kumove, Shirley. *More Words, More Arrows: A Further Collection of Yiddish Folk Sayings*. Detroit: Wayne State University Press, 1999. 313 pp.

3597. Landmann, Salcia. *Jüdische Anekdoten und Sprichwörter. Jiddisch und deutsch*. München: Deutscher Taschenbuch Verlag, 1965 (2nd ed. 1974). 252 pp. (proverbs, pp. 197-245).

3598. Landmann, Salcia. *Jüdische Weisheit aus drei Jahrtausenden*. Köln: Anaconda Verlag, 2010. 254 pp.

3599. Lévy, Iasaac Jack. *Prolegomena to the Study of the Refranero Sefardi*. New York: Las Americas Publications, 1968 (2nd ed. 1969). 232 pp. (proverbs, pp. 99-206).

3600. McCormick, Malachi. *A Collection of Yiddish Proverbs*. New York: The Stone Street Press, 1982. 49 pp. With illustrations.

3601. Nagy, Imre. *Zsidó közmondások: Jiddis és magyar nyelven*. Budapest: Az Ojság kiadása, 1995. 48 pp. (Yiddish proverbs).

3602. Neumann, Joseph. "Yiddish Proverbs." *Edoth*, 3 (1948), 98-104 (in Hebrew).

3603. Petrović, Luci. *Proverbs, Sayings and Tales of the Sephardic Jews of Macedonia*. Beograd: Federation of Jewish Communities in Yugoslavia, 1978. 192 pp.

3604. Romey, David, and Marc D. Angel. "The Ubiquitous Sephardic Proverb." *Studies in Sephardic Culture. The David N. Barocas Memorial Volume*. Ed. Marc D. Angel. New York: Sepher-Hermon, 1980. 57-64.

3605. Rubin, Ruth. "Yiddish Sayings and Some Parallels from the Sayings of Other Peoples." *New York Folklore Quarterly*, 22 (1966), 268-273.

3606. Saporta y Beja, Enrique. *Refranes de los judíos sefardíes y otras locuciones típicas de los judíos sefardíes de Salónica y otros sitios de Oriente recopilados*. Barcelona: Ameller Ediciones, 1978. 203 pp.

3607. Schack, Ingeborg-Liane. *Der Mensch tracht un Got lacht. 450 jiddische Sprichwörter. Auswahl, Umschrift, Übersetzung, Analyse und Einführung in die jiddische Sprache und Literatur*. Mainz: Hanns Krach, 1977. 128 pp.

3608. Schipper, Mineke, and Sabine Cohn. *De rib uit zijn lijf. Joodse spreekwoorden en zegswijzen over vrouwen*. Baarn: Ambo, 1996. 159 pp.

3609. Sitarz, Magdalena. *Yiddish and Polish Proverbs. Contrastive Analysis Against Cultural Background*. Kraków: Nakładem Polskiej Akademii Umiejetności, 2000. 161 pp.

3610. Strauss, Ruby G. (ed.). *If Grandma Had Wheels. Jewish Folk Sayings*. Illustrations by Richard Rosenblum. New York: Atheneum,. 1985. 32 pp.

3611. Swarner, Kristina (ill.). *Yiddish Wisdom / Yiddishe Chochma*. San Francisco: Chronicle Books, 1996. 80 pp.

3612. Tendlau, Abraham Moses. *Sprichwörter und Redensarten deutsch-jüdischer Vorzeit*. Frankfurt am Main: J. Kauffmann, 1860. Rpt. Hildesheim: Georg Olms, 1980. 425 pp. Rpt. as *Jüdische Sprichwörter und Redensarten*. Köln: Parkland, 1998. 666 pp.

3613. Tendlau, Abraham Moses. *Sprichwörter und Redensarten deutsch-jüdischer Vorzeit*. Berlin: Schocken Verlag, 1934; rpt. Heidelberg: Manutius Verlag, 1993. 112 pp. (shortened edition of previous entry).

3614. Vakhshteyn, Bernhard. "Dee Oysbreiterung fun Ignats Bernshteyn's Lebensverk." *Filologishe shriften fun Yivo*, 1 (1926), cols. 27-38; and 2 (1928), col. 516 (Yiddish proverbs).

Yugur

3615. Roos, Marti, Hans Nugteren, and Zhong Jìnwén. "On Some Proverbs of the Western and Eastern Yugur Languages." *Turkic Languages*, 3, no. 2 (1999), 189-214.

Name Index

Since the 3615 proverb collections listed in this international bibliography are arranged by linguistic groups, this name index will make it possible to find any collection by its author as well. The index includes both the names of individual authors and those of co-authors where they appear. The names of literary authors or politicians for whom collections of proverbial materials have been assembled are registered in the subject index. The numbers following the various names refer to the consecutively numbered collections and not to the pages of the bibliography.

310

Backer, Theodore B., 1219
Baerlein, Henry, 1034
Baggini, Julian, 1220
Bahar, Hadi, 3149, 3150
Bahder, Karl von, 7
Bahlmann, P., 1987
Bailey, Clinton, 926
Bailey, Karen, 2867, 2868
Bailey, Nathan, 1221, 1222, 1223
Bajewsky, Manfred, 1988
Baldwin, L. Karen, 529
Baldwin, Robert, 1224
Baller, Kurt, 1989
Ballesteros, Octavio A., 3115
Balling, Adalbert Ludwig, 153, 154
Balzer, Berit, 1990
Balzer, Hans, 1991
Bannister, Garry, 2869
Barakles, Charalampos, 2762
Baralt, Rafael María, 1877
Barber, David W., 1225
Barber, John W., 1226
Barbour, Frances M., 530, 531, 532
Bárdosi, Vilmos, 8, 1878, 2808, 2809, 2810, 2811, 2812
Barella, Ana, 3381
Bark, Melvin van den, 547
Barlas, Muhtar, 3523
Barman, Mrinal Deb, 2842
Barnes-Harden, Alene L., 533
Barnette, Martha, 1227
Barra, G, 365
Barras, Christine, 3491, 3492
Barrick, Mac E., 534, 535, 536, 537, 538, 539
Bartels, Klaus, 3029, 3030
Barten, John, 1228
Barth, Ludwig, 1992, 1993
Bartlett, John, 9, 540, 1229, 1230, 1231, 1232, 1233, 1234, 1235, 1236, 1237, 1238, 1239, 1240, 1241, 1242, 1243, 1244, 1245, 1246, 1247, 1248
Bartlett, John Russell, 540
Bartoszewicz, Iwona, 1994
Bartsch, Ernst, 155
Bartsch, Karl, 3031
Barwick, Dee Danner, 1249
Basile, Paola, 2915
Başkan, Özcan, 3524
Bates, William C., 2967
Bätschi, J., 3493
Baughman, Ernest W., 541
Baughman, M. Dale, 1250
Baumgartner, Ueli, 1995
Bayer, Karl, 3032
Baz, Petros D., 1251
Beal, George, 1252
Bear, John, 1253
Bebel, Heinrich, 1996
Beck, Harald, 1997
Becker, Sven, 1254
Beckwith, Martha Warren, 2968
Bedoya, Luis Iván, 1100
Beer, Ulrich, 1998
Beeton, Samuel Orchat, 1255
Behaghel, Otto, 1999
Beier, Brigitte, 2000
Beilenson, Evelyn L., 542, 543, 1256
Beilenson, John P., 1257
Beinhauer, Werner, 3372
Bekh, Wolfgang Johannes, 2001
Bekker, Leander J. de, 1794
Belck, Jack, 740
Bell, Evan Robert, 3509
Benardete, Doris, 544
Benavente Jareño, Pedro, 3373
Benawa, A.R., 3144
Bender, Andreas, 2002, 2003
Bender, Texas Bix, 545
Benham, W. Gurney, 156
Benítez Rodríguez, Enrique Manuel, 3374
Bennett, Gordon, 1619
Beran, Margret, 2004

Borneman, Ernest, 2032, 2033
Borovski, Conrad, 2034
Borowsky, Lothar, 2035
Borschette, Emile, 3101
Borua, Shri P.C., 2845
Bosch, Martha Maria, 2036
Boshears, Frances, 561
Boswell, George, 562
Bote, Hermann, 2037
Botha, R.P., 485
Böttcher, Kurt, 2038
Boudreaux, Anna Mary, 563
Bourgois, Lucien, 163
Boutina, Ekaterina, 2810
Bouza, Fernando Groba, 3410
Bowles, Colin, 968
Bozarth, George S., 2039
Bradley, F.W., 564
Bradley, John P., 1276
Brady, John, 1277
Braga, Theophilo, 3195
Bralczyk, Jerzy, 3161
Brandenberger, Erna, 3376
Brandreth, Gyles, 1278
Bratu, Ion, 3222, 3223
Bratu, Ion I., 12
Braude, Jacob M., 1279, 1280, 1281
Braun, Hermann, 2040
Brazão, José Ruivinho, 3196, 3197
Breatnach, R.A., 3108
Brecht, F. Albert, 2041
Bremen, Friedrich, 2042
Brendel, John, 565
Brendle, Thomas R., 566
Brennan-Nelson, Denise, 1282, 1283, 1284
Breton, Nicholas, 1285
Brewer, Ebenezer Cobham, 1286, 1287, 1288
Brewer, J. Mason, 568
Brewster, Paul G., 569
Brezin-Rossignol, Monique, 1880
Brings, Rolly, 2043

Brink, Karl-Erich, 2044
Brisolla, Thyrso, 2045
Brock, Suzanne, 164
Broek, Marinus A. van den, 1133, 1134, 1135
Broma, Adolph, 2046
Bronner, Michael A., 1289
Brooke, Kenneth, 2649
Brookhiser, Richard., 570
Brougham, Aileen E., 3109
Brown, H. Jackson, 1290, 1291, 1292, 1293
Brown, Marshall, 1294, 1295
Browning, D.C., 1296, 1297, 1298
Brozowska, Renata, 3160
Brückl, Reinhold, 2047
Brückner, A., 13
Brugger, Hans Peter, 2048
Brüllmann, Richard, 2049
Brunet, G., 14
Brunner, Hellmut, 929
Brunvand, Jan Harold, 571
Bryan, George B., 572, 573, 1299, 1300, 1301, 1302, 1303, 1304, 1305, 1579, 2870
Buchanan, Anne Christian, 1306
Buchanan, Daniel Crump, 2981
Büchmann, Georg, 2050, 2051, 2052, 2053, 2054, 2055, 2056, 2057, 2058, 2059, 2060, 2061, 2062, 2063, 2064, 2065, 2066, 2067, 2068, 2069, 2070, 2071, 2072, 2073, 2074, 2075, 2076, 2077, 2078, 2079, 2080, 2081
Buchna, Jörg, 993, 994, 995
Bücken, Hajo, 2082
Bücking, Johann Jacob Heinrich, 2083
Budde, Nadia, 2084
Budeus, Iris, 3249
Buehler, Allan M., 574
Bufienė, Giedrė, 3096
Bühler, Winfried, 2764, 2765, 2766
Buitrago Jiménez, Alberto, 3377

Chen, Chu-Hsien, 3511
Chernelev, Vsevolod, 3252, 3253, 3254, 3255, 3256
Chertok, Harvey, 583
Chesaina, Ciarunji, 371
Cheviot, Andrew, 3333
Chieger, Bob, 1320
Childers, Evelyn Jones, 1321
Chinnery, John D., 1067
Chiu, Kwong Ki, 1322
Chiu, Tony, 584
Christaller, Johann Gottlieb, 372
Christen, Jürgen, 2097
Christoffel, Karl, 2098
Christy, Robert, 1323
Chung, Chong-wha, 3019
Ciardi, John, 585
Cibot, Pierre Martial, 171
Cibotto, Giovanni Antonio, 2919, 3224
Cierpinski, Waldemar, 2213
Clairborne, Robert, 1324
Clark, J.D., 586
Clarke, John, 1325
Cleary, Kristen Marée, 587
Clemen, Otto, 2099
Clements, Jonathan, 1068
Cobos, Rubén, 588, 589
Cock, Alfons de, 1136
Coffin, Tristram P., 590
Coghlan, Evelyn, 591
Cohen, A., 2803
Cohen, Hennig, 590
Cohen, Israel, 172
Cohen, J.M., 1326, 1327
Cohen, M.J., 1326, 1327, 1328
Cole, Arthur H., 592
Cole, Sylvia, 1329
Colfescu, Silvia, 3225
Collins, John, 3397
Collis, Harry, 593, 594, 595
Collison, Mary, 1330
Collison, Robert, 1330
Collot, Joseph, 986
Colombi, Maria Cecilia, 3398

Colombo, John Robert, 1042, 1043, 1044
Combet, Louis, 1885
Combrink, Johan, 486
Conca, Maria, 3399
Concepción, José Luis, 3400
Conde, Germán, 308
Confucius, 1069, 1070
Conklin, George W., 1331
Conlin, Joseph R., 596
Conny, Beth Mende, 1332
Cook, Alexandra, 1333
Coonley, Prentiss L., 597
Cooper, Barbara, 2100
Cooper, Thomas C., 2100, 2101
Copeland, Lewis, 1334
Cordry, Harold V., 173
Cornette, James C., 2102
Correas Martínez, Miguel, 3401
Correas, Gonzalo, 3402, 3403
Corso, Raffaele, 2920
Corum, Ann Kondo, 2797
Costa Alves, Manuel, 3404
Costello, Robert B., 598
Coté, Jean, 1045
Cotgrave, Randle, 1335
Cotter, George, 1849, 1850, 1851
Coulon, Bettina, 2103
Couzerau, Béatrice, 174
Covell, Charles H., 599
Cowan, E., 1336
Cowan, Frank., 1337
Cowan, Lore, 2804
Cowan, Maurice, 2804
Cowie, Anthony P., 19, 1338, 1339
Cowie, Murray Aiken, 2104
Cox, Ernest., 600
Cox, H.L., 175, 176, 177, 178, 1137
Craig, Doris, 1340
Cramer-Klett, Elisabeth von, 2105
Crawley, Tony, 1341
Crépeau, Pierre, 373

Ewart, James, 1373
Ewart, Neil, 1374
Ewing, Ida, 632
Exley, Helen, 1375
Eyering, Eucharius, 2144
Eyke, Wera von, 3266
Eyre, Richard, 633

Faber, Harold, 1376
Faden, I.B., 634
Fadiman, Clifton, 1377
Fähnrich, Heinz, 1954
Fakih, Kimberly Olsen, 1378
Fallon, S.W., 2849
Fanany, Ismet, 3103
Fanany, Rebecca, 3103
Fanfani, Massimo, 27
Farkas, Anna, 1379
Farman, John, 1380
Farmer, John Stephen, 1381
Farø, Ken, 28
Farrell, Orin J., 635
Farries, Helen., 636
Farsi, S.S., 377, 378
Färver, Jupp, 2145
Farwell, Harold F.,, 637
Faselius, August, 3050
Fattakhova, Nailia N., 191
Fátunmbi, Fá'lókun, 379
Faust, Johann Heinrich, 2146
Fechner, Marco, 2147
Federer, William J., 638
Fehrenbacher, Don E., 639
Fehrenbacher, Virginia, 639
Feibleman, James Kern, 640
Feinsilber, Mike, 1805
Feistel, Peter, 2589, 2590, 2591, 2592, 2593
Feldman, David, 1382
Feldmann, Christa, 2148, 2149
Felitsyna, Vera P., 3267
Fendl, Josef, 2150, 2151, 2152, 2153
Ferguson, Charles A., 29
Fergusson, Rosalind, 1383, 1555

Fernández Gonzáles, José Ramón, 3408
Fernández Valledor, Roberto, 3218
Fernández, Lourdes Achúcarro, 3454
Fernández, Mauro, 3407
Ferro Ruibal, Xesús, 3409, 3410
Fialkov, Lev, 3268
Fialkova, Larisa, 3268
Fiedler, Sabine, 1836, 1837
Fieguth, Gerhard, 2154
Fielding, Thomas, 1384, 1385
Filatkina, Natalia, 3102
Filipenko, Tatjana, 30
Filkusová, Mária, 3354
Finbert, Elian-J., 192
Fink, Paul, 641
Fink-Henseler, Roland W., 2155, 2984
Finod, J. de., 1894
Fischer, J.L., 3193
Fischer, Katrin, 1386
Fitzhenry, Robert I., 1387
Flanagan, Laurence, 2874
Flavell, Linda, 1388, 1389
Flavell, Roger, 1388, 1389
Flechsig, Werner, 2156
Fleckenstein, Sister Mary Thecla, 2157
Flesch, Rudolf, 1390
Flexner, Doris, 1391
Flexner, Stuart Berg, 643, 644, 899, 900, 1391
Flonta, Teodor, 193, 194, 195, 196, 197, 198, 1895, 2922, 3202, 3227, 3228, 3411
Florian, Ulrich, 3412
Florinus, Henrik, 1855
Florio, John, 1392, 1393
Fogel, Edwin Miller, 645, 646
Fogg, Walter, 1394
Földes, Csaba, 31, 199
Fomina, Sinaida, 3269
Fonseca, José da, 1395

Forbes, Malcolm S., 1396
Forck, Ludwig, 2158, 2159
Ford, Paul Leicester, 647
Forgács, Tamás, 2815
Förster, Max, 1397
Förster, Waldtraut, 2235
Fort, Francesco, 2923
Foss, William O., 648
Frackiewicz, Iwona, 200
Fraenger, Wilhelm, 2160
Franceschi, Temistocle, 2924, 2925, 2926
Franck, Harry A., 2970
Franck, Sebastian, 2161, 2162, 2163, 2164
Frank, Ernst, 2165
Frank, Grace, 1896, 1897
Frank, Leonard Roy, 1398, 1399
Franke, David, 649
Franklin, Benjamin, 650
Franklyn, Julian, 1400
Franz, Angelika, 2166, 2167
Fraser, Betty, 1401
Frederiksen, Niels Werner, 1121
Fredrickson, Scott E., 2168, 2169
Freeman, Criswell, 651, 1402
Freier, George D., 1403
Frenzel, Herbert, 2927
Frenzel, Maria, 3163
Freund, Leonhard, 2170
Frey, Christa, 2171
Freya, Anis, 936
Freytag, Ernst Richard, 2172
Frick, R.O., 201
Friebertshäuser, Hans, 2173, 2174
Fried, Alfred Hermann, 2175, 2176
Friedenthal, Richard, 2177
Friederich, Wolf, 2178, 2179
Friedrich, Paul, 2180
Friesen, Victor Carl, 1052
Frieser, Walter, 1404
Friesland, Carl, 32, 33
Frijlink, H., 1141
Frischbier, Hermann, 2181, 2182

Fritz, Karl August, 202, 2183
Fritz, Klaus, 2184
Frome, Keith Weller, 652
Frost, Elizabeth, 653
Frost-Knappman, Elizabeth, 1405
Frye, Stanley N., 3123
Fulghum, Walter B., 998
Fuller, Edmund, 1406, 1407
Fuller, Thomas, 203
Fumagalli, Giuseppe, 34, 35, 3051
Funk, Charles Earle, 1408, 1409, 1410, 1411, 1412
Funk, Gabriela, 3203, 3204, 3205, 3206
Funk, Matthias, 3203, 3204, 3205, 3206
Fuster, Joan, 3413, 3414

Gabel, Marie., 654
Gabrielli, Michael, 2185, 2186
Gaffney, Sean, 2875
Galef, David, 2985, 2986
Gallo, Rudy, 1413
Gamber, Hans, 2187, 2188, 2189
Gárate, Gotzon, 985
García Moreno, Melchor, 36, 37, 38, 39
García, Carlos, 1101, 1102, 1103
García-Garabal, Juan-A. Eiroa, 3452
Gardoš, Isolde, 3360, 3361
Garmann, Bernhard, 2190
Garriott, Edward B., 1414
Garrison, Webb, 1415
Gash, Amy, 1416
Gates, John E., 558
Gaugler, Almut, 2191
Gehrmann, Maria, 3163
Geiger, Karola, 2192
Gella Iturriaga, José, 3415
Gennep, Arnold van, 1898, 1899, 1900
Gent, Nathaniel R., 204
Georgis, Takiss, 2768

Gérard, Jean Ignace Isidore, 1902
Gerbert, Manfred, 1417
Gerhard, Hartwig, 1418
Gering, Hugo, 3134
Gerke-Siefert, Hilde, 2193
Gerr, Elke, 2194
Gerritzen, Christian, 1275
Geyr, Heinz, 205
Gheorghe, Gabriel, 206
Ghitescu, Micaela, 207
Giebel, Marion, 2769
Gierlichs, Eleonore, 2195
Gil, José Enrique Gargalla, 3401
Giloi, Dietlinde, 655
Ginsburg, Susan, 1419
Glanze, Walter D., 1169
Glazer, Mark, 656, 657
Gleason, Norma, 208, 209, 210
Glick, David I., 658
Glickman, Ken, 659
Glismann, Claudia, 2189, 2196, 2197, 2198
Glock, Johann Philipp, 2199
Głuch, Wojciech, 3164
Gluski, Jerzy, 211
Goedeke, Karl, 40
Goethe, Johann Wolfgang von, 2200, 2201, 2202, 2203
Göhring, Ludwig, 2204
Goitein, S.D.F., 937
Gökceoğlu, Aziz, 3529
Göknar, Hale, 3530
Golden, Bernard, 1838, 1839
Goldin, Hyman E., 660
Goldman, Alex J., 661
Goldsmith, Warren H., 1420
Goldstein, Sharon, 1421
Golescu, Iordache, 3229
Gomes, Hélio, 1422
Gómez, Fermín de los Reyes, 58
Gonzales, Ralfka, 3416
Gööck, Alexandra, 2205
Gööck, Roland, 2206
Goodman, Ted, 1423
Gorbracht, Wernher, 2207

Gordon, Edmund I., 3479
Goris, Eva, 2208
Görner, Herbert, 2209
Gossel, J., 2210
Gossen, Gary H., 3116
Gossler, Erika, 2211
Göttert, Karl-Heinz, 2212
Gottschalk, Klaus, 2213
Gottschalk, Walter, 212, 1901
Gottschalk, Walter, 2674
Gottsched, Johann Christoph, 2214
Gowda, S., 2850
Graf, Adolf Eduard, 2215, 2216
Graf, Eduard, 2217
Graffagnino, J. Kevin, 662, 1424
Grandville, 1902
Gratet-Duplessis, Pierre-Alexandre, 41, 42
Grauls, Jan, 43, 1142, 1143
Gray, Ernest, 380
Gray, Martin, 1489
Green, Joanne, 1425
Green, Jonathon, 1426
Gregorich, Barbara, 1427, 1428
Griesbach, Heinz, 2218, 2219
Griessman, Gene, 663
Griffin, Albert Kirby, 213
Grigas, Kazys, 214, 3095, 3096
Gröbe, Volker, 2220, 2221, 2222
Grober-Glück, Gerda, 2223
Grocott, John C., 1429
Grodzenskaia, Tatiana, 3270
Groom, Winston, 664
Grose, Francis, 1430, 1431
Gross, Anthony, 665
Gross, David C., 2805
Gross, John, 1432
Grosshans, Rainald, 2224, 2225
Grothe, Mardy, 1433, 1434, 1435
Grove, Neil, 3111
Gruhle, Uwe, 2226, 2227
Grünberg, Paul, 999
Grundmann, Günter, 2228
Grunow, Alfred, 215, 216, 217

Grüterich, Tobias, 2229
Grynblat, M.Ia., 3271
Grzybek, Peter, 44
Guazotti, Paola, 2928
Gudkova, Olga, 2230, 3272
Guerlac, Othon, 1903
Gueye, Mamadou, 374
Gühler, U., 3512
Guinagh, Kevin, 1436
Guinzbourg, Lt. Colonel Victor S.M. de, 218, 219, 220
Guiterman, Arthur, 2876
Gulbransson, Olaf, 2231
Guli, Meri, 489
Gulland, Daphne M., 1437
Gültek, Buğra, 3531
Gültek, Vedat, 3531
Gundlach, Jürgen, 2232
Guntermann, Paul, 2233, 2234
Günther, Erika, 2235
Günther, Friederich Joachim, 2236
Guseinzade, A., 3273
Gutekunst, Dieter, 2237
Guthke, Karl S., 221, 222
Gutknecht, Christoph, 2238, 2239, 2240, 2241, 2242, 2243, 2244
Guzzetta-Jones, Angeline, 666, 667
Gvardzhaladze, I.S., 1438

Ha, Tae Hung, 3020
Haan, Marina N., 668
Habeck, Reinhard, 2245, 2246, 2247
Hacke, Axel, 2248
Hackmann, Bärbel, 2249
Haddenbach, Georg, 2250, 2251
Haefeli, Leo, 1000
Haek, D., 2252
Hagen, Edmund von, 2253
Hahnemann, Helga, 2254
Haidle, Julius, 2036
Hakamies, Pekka, 1862

Haldeman-Julius, E., 3274
Hale, Sarah Josepha, 1439
Halemba, Andrzej, 381
Halén, Harry, 3028
Hall, Joan Houston, 581
Hall, Terry, 669
Halldórsson, Halldór, 2839, 2840
Haller, Joseph, 45, 3417
Hallstein, Reinhard, 2255
Halpert, Herbert, 561, 670, 671, 672
Hamacher, Gustav, 2256
Hamilton, A.W., 3104
Hamilton, Kim, 673
Hammerstrom, Richard B., 668
Hand, Wayland D, 46, 674, 1440
Hanford, G.L., 675
Hanger, Charles Henry, 1441
Hangin, John Gombojab, 3124
Hankí, Joseph, 938
Hannaford, Peter, 676
Hansen-Kokoruš, Renate, 3304
Hanuš, Ignace Jan, 47
Harder, Kelsie B., 782
Hardie, Margaret, 677
Hardwick, Michael, 1442, 1443
Hardwick, Mollie, 1442, 1443
Hargrave, Basil, 1444
Harmon, Marion F., 678
Harnsberger, Caroline Thomas, 679
Harrebomée, Pieter Jacob, 1144
Hars, Wolfgang, 2257
Hart, Clive, 2877
Hart, Henry H., 1073, 1074
Harter, Jim, 1445
Harvey, Sir Paul, 1446
Hassell, James Woodrow, 1904
Hattery-Beyer, Lynn, 2424
Hau, Willi, 2258, 2259
Hauschka, Ernst R., 2260
Hauser, Albert, 3496
Häussler, Reinhard, 3052
Hayes, Francis Clement, 3418

Hayward, Arthur L., 1447
Hazard, Harry W., 921
Hazlitt, W. Carew, 1448
He Jing-jiang, Zhang Xiu-Fang, 1075
Healey, Joseph G., 382, 383, 384, 385, 386, 387, 388
Hearn, Lafcadio, 1108
Heimann, Gabi, 3053
Heimeran, Ernst, 3054
Heinlein, Robert A, 680
Heinser, Bernhard, 2283
Helbing, Franz, 2261
Helfer, Christian, 3055
Heller, Karin, 2262
Hellwig, Gerhard, 2263
Hemelryck, Tania Van, 1931
Henderson, Alfred, 3056
Henderson, Andrew, 3334
Henderson, B.L.K., 1449
Henderson, George Surgeon, 1450
Hendricks, George D., 681, 682, 683
Hendrickson, Robert, 684, 685, 686, 687, 688, 689, 1451, 1452, 1453
Hendyng, 1454
Henisch. Georg, 2264
Henkel, Stefan, 3272
Henley, William Ernest, 1381
Hennes, William R., 3057
Henry, Lewis C., 1455
Henschel, F., 1456
Henschelsberg, Wolf von, 2265
Herbert, George, 1457, 1458
Herg, Emmi, 223
Herkt, Matthias, 2000
Hermann, Leonard, 2266
Hermida Alonso, Anxos, 3419
Herrmann, Konrad, 1076
Herrmann-Winter, Renate, 2267
Herskovits, Melville J., 389
Hertslet, William Lewis, 2268
Hertzog, Phares H., 690, 691

Herzig, Horst, 692
Herzig, Tina, 692
Herzog, Annelies, 2171, 2270, 2271, 2335
Herzog, George, 390
Herzog, Heinrich, 2269
Hesse, Günter, 2272
Hesse, Heinz, 2273
Hesse, Margret, 2273
Hessky, Regina, 8, 2274, 2275, 2276
Hettinger, Eugen, 1077, 2987, 3058
Hetzel, S., 2277
Heuber, Hans-Georg, 1459, 1928
Heuseler, J.A., 2278
Heusinkveld, Holly Flame, 1145
Hewetson, Cecil, 2878
Heyd, Werner P., 2279
Heyen, Asmus Geerds, 2280
Heyse, T., 1985
Heywood, John, 1460, 1461, 1462
Hiemer, Ernst, 224
Hilgers, Heribert A., 2281, 2282
Hill, Wayne F., 1463
Hindermann, Federico, 2283
Hinds, Arthur, 1001
Hinds-Howell, David G., 1437
Hines, Donald M., 693
Hinrichsen, Helmut, 3135
Hințescu, I.C., 3230
Hirsch, E.D., 694, 695
Hirson, Christina, 2284
Hisa, Michitaro, 2988
Hislop, Alexander, 3335
Hiss, Albert, 2285
Hockings, Paul, 2851
Hoefer, Edmund, 2286, 2287
Hoefnagels, Peter, 1146
Hoffman, W.J., 696
Hoffmann von Fallersleben, August Heinrich, 1147, 2289, 2290
Hoffmann, Alexander F., 2389
Hoffmann, Detlef, 2288

Hoffmann, Marcus, 3272
Hofmann, Michel, 3054
Hofmann, Winfried, 2291
Holbek, Bengt, 225, 1120
Holcomb, Dana, 673
Holder, R.W., 697, 1464
Hollenbach, Ida V., 698
Holm, Hans Henning, 2292
Holm, Pelle, 3482, 3483
Holt, Alfred H., 1465, 1466
Holt, Daniel D., 3021
Hönes, Winfried, 2293, 2294
Hong, Luong Van, 3571, 3572
Hood, Edwin Paxton, 1467
Hook, Donald D., 1468
Hopf, Andreas, 2295
Hopf, Angela, 2295
Hore, Herbert F., 2879
Hörmann, Ludwig von, 973, 974
Horne, Abraham Reeser, 699, 700, 701
Horstmann, Rudolf, 2296
Hose, Susanne, 3362, 3363
Hoskins, Lotte, 702
Houghton, Patricia, 226
House, Jack, 1469
Howard, Philip, 1470
Howell, James, 227
Hoyos Sancho, Nieves de, 3420
Hoyt, Jehiel Keeler, 1471, 1472
Hronek, Jiri, 1115
Hruschka, Rudolf, 2297
Huanyou, Huang, 1078
Hubbard, Elbert, 703
Huber, Ludwig, 3030
Hucke, Helene, 2298, 2299, 2300
Hügen, Ludwig, 2301
Hughes, Arthur John, 2880
Hughes, Muriel J., 705, 706, 707, 708
Hughes, Shirley, 1473, 1474
Hülsemann, Kurt, 2302
Humes, James C., 1475
Hummerding, Pearl, 709

Humphreys, William Jackson, 1476
Hunfeld, Hans, 2303
Hunsinger, Walter W., 1786
Hunzaye, Nasir Uddin, 391
Hurd, Charles, 710
Hürlimann, Martin, 228
Hussar, A., 1841
Huth, Mari [sic] Luise, 2304
Hutter, Claus-Peter, 2208
Huzii, Otoo, 2989
Hyamson, Albert M., 1477
Hyatt, Harry Middleton, 711
Hyman, Dick, 1478, 1479
Hyman, Robin, 1480

Ibele, Gisela, 2305
Ichikawa, Sanki, 1481
Idström, Anna, 1856
Igwe, G.E., 392
Ikeda, Yasaburo, 2990
Ilg, Gérard, 229
Ilgenstein, Erhard, 2306
Inchley, Valerie M., 3128
Inui, Ryoichi, 1481
Inwards, Richard, 1482
Iribarren, José María, 3421
Irving, Godron, 3336
Irwin, Godfrey, 712
Iscla, Luis, 230
Isil, Olivia A., 1483
Iurchenko, O.S., 3567
Ivčenko, Anatolij, 3364
Ivchenko, A.O., 3567

Jack, Albert, 1484
Jackson, Pastor L.A., 2971
Jacobson, John D., 1485
Jagendorf, Moritz A., 1486
Jaime Gómez, José de, 48, 49, 50, 3422, 3423, 3424, 3425, 3426
Jaime Lorén, José María de, 48, 49, 50, 3422, 3423, 3424, 3425, 3426, 3427
Jaimoukha, Amjad, 1060

James, Ewart, 1487
Jannen, Reinhard, 2307
Jaszczun, Wasyl, 3275
Javna, John, 1583
Jay, Antony, 1488
Jeep, John M., 2308, 2309
Jeffares, A. Norman, 1489
Jelali, Adnan, 1254
Jellinek, Ad., 231
Jenko, Elizabeta M., 3359
Jensen, Herman, 2852
Jente, Richard, 51, 713, 1148, 1490
Jernigan, Kenneth, 1491, 1492
Jeromin, Rolf, 2310, 2311
Jetter, Monika, 2312
Jockel, Gabriele, 2313
Jogschies, Rainer, 2314
John, Johannes, 2315
Johnson, Albert, 1493, 1494
Johnson, James Henry, 3428
Johnson, Sterling, 1495
Jona, Hokojiro, 2990
Jónasson, Björn, 3136
Jones, Hugh Percy, 232
Jonsen, Helen, 969
Jordan, Gilbert J., 714
Jósa, Iván, 2816
Joseph, Michael, 715
Jüchen, Aurel von, 1002
Judd, Henry P., 2798
Jührs, Carola, 2316
Julliani, Le Seur, 233
Junceda, Luis, 3429, 3430

Kabale, Sim Kilosho, 393
Kabira, Wanjiku Mukabi, 394
Kacirk, Jeffrey, 716
Kadler, Alfred, 1905
Kahn, Lothar, 1468
Kainis, Dr., 2317
Kaiser, Dietlind, 2318
Kaiser, Stephan, 2318
Kalén, Johan, 3484
Kalma, Maurice, 234

Kalontarov, Iakub I., 3510
Kammerer, Kristen, 717
Kammerman, Roy, 718
Kandel, Howard, 719
Kapchits, Georgi L., 395, 396
Karadžić, Vuk Stefanović, 3352
Karagiorgos, Panos, 235, 2770
Karapetiana, G.O., 964
Kariuki, Joseph, 397, 398, 399
Kašėtienė, Rasa, 3095, 3096
Kasper, Muriel, 3059
Kastner, Georges, 1906
Katabarwa, Calvin C., 400
Kaufman, Lois L., 1496
Kawanabe, Kusumi, 2991
Kay, Joe, 1538
Kebbede, Eshetu, 1853
Keene, Donald, 2990
Keil, Reinhold, 2319
Keim, Anton Maria, 2320
Keitges, John, 1497
Kellermann, Dieter, 2321
Kelley, Edmond Morgan, 2322
Kelly, Fergus, 2881
Kelly, James, 3337
Kelly, Joan Larson, 2882
Kelly, Walter K., 236
Kelly-Gangi, Carol, 720
Kenin, Richard, 1498
Ker, John Bellenden, 1499
Kerler, Christine, 2323, 2324
Kerler, Richard, 2323, 2324
Kern, Christine, 2325
Kern, Heike, 2325
Kerschen, Lois, 721
Keszeg, Vilmos, 2817
Kett, Joseph, 695
Keyes, Ralph, 722, 1500, 1501
Khamraev, M.K., 3566
Kholodnaya, Asya, 3284
Kidner, Frank Derek, 1003
Kieffer, Jarold, 723
Kiess, Arthur, 2326, 2327
Kihara, Kenzo, 1481

Kim, Yong-il, 3022
Kim-Werner, Samhwa, 3023
Kin, David, 724, 725
King, John, 1502, 1503
King, Kevin, 1504
Kingsbury, Mildred E., 1505
Kingsbury, Stewart A., 782, 1505, 1580
Kinh, Nguyen Xuan, 3573
Kipfer, Barbara Ann, 1506
Kirchberger, Joe H., 2328, 2329
Kirchhofer, Melchior, 3497
Kirchner, Mark, 3016
Kiriş, Mehmet, 1149
Kirkpatrick, Betty, 1507, 3338, 3339
Kirkpatrick, E.M., 1508
Kispál, Tamás, 52
Kiss, Gábor, 2811, 2812
Kissling, Hans-Joachim, 3522
Kitamura, Yoshikatsu, 2992, 2993
Kjaer, Iver, 1119, 1120, 1121
Klančar, Anthony J., 53
Klapper, Joseph, 2330
Klein, Allen, 1509
Klein, Hans Wilhelm, 237, 1907
Kleiser, Grenville, 1510, 1511
Klepsch, A., 1985
Klingsporn, Debra K., 1306
Kloberdanz, Rosalinda, 726
Kloberdanz, Timothy J., 726
Klöker, Ralf, 727
Knape, Rose-Marie, 2331
Knapp, Elisabeth, 238
Knappert, Jan, 401, 402, 403, 404
Knecht, George, 728
Kneen, Maggie, 1512
Knoop, Ulrich, 2332
Knorr, Stefan, 2333
Knortz, Karl, 729, 730
Knowles, Elizabeth, 1513, 1514, 1515
Knowles, James Hinton, 2853
Knox, D.B., 1516

Koch, Mary, 2334
Koch, William E., 731, 732
Kocher, Christian Friedrich, 3060
Kogos, Fred, 3588, 3589, 3590
Kohl, Ida, 1517
Kohl, J.G., 1517
Köhler, Carl Sylvio, 2771
Köhler, Claus, 2335
Kohn, Alfie, 1518
Kokare, Elza, 3093, 3094
Kokhtev, N.N., 3276
Kolatch, Alfred J., 2806
Kolesnikova, Elizabeta, 3277
Kolonomos, Žamila, 3591, 3592
Komarov, A.S., 1519
Komorowska, Ewa, 1026
Konstantinova, Anna, 54
Kopp, Thomas, 2336
Korach, Myron, 1520
Korhonen, Jarmo, 55, 1857
Korpiola, Kyösti, 2994, 2995
Korse, Piet, 405
Körte, Wilhelm, 2337
Kośka, Lidia, 3165
Kossman, Leonid, 733, 734
Kossmann, L.S., 2338
Koster, Monika, 2339
Köster, Rudolf, 2340
Kösters-Roth, Ursula, 1908
Kövecses, Zoltán, 1521
Krack, Karl Erich, 2341
Kradolfer, J., 2930
Kralin, N.P., 3565
Krämer, Julius, 2342
Krämer, Walter, 2343
Krauss, Heinrich, 1004
Krauss, Werner, 3431
Krebs, Gotthold, 2344, 2345
Kremer, Edmund Philipp, 2346
Kreuzer, Peter, 2347
Krienke, Eberhard, 2348
Krikmann, Arvo, 1841, 1842, 1843, 1844, 1845, 1846, 1847, 1848
Kroes, G., 485

Krohn, Axel, 239
Kroker, E., 2349
Krolop, Kurt, 2038
Krone, Sabine, 2350
Kronenberger, Louis, 1211
Krueger, John R., 3124
Krüger-Lorenzen, Kurt, 2351,
2352, 2353, 2354
Krumbholz, Eckart, 2355
Kruyskamp, C., 1150
Krylov, Constantin A., 3278
Krynski, Szymon, 3275
Krzanowska, Agnieszka, 1026
Krzyżanowski, Julian, 3166, 3167
Kuchmann, Dieter, 2356
Kuckertz, Beate, 2357
Kudirkienė, Lilija, 3095, 3096
Küffner, Georg M., 1522, 2358
Kuip, Frederik Johan van der,
1951, 1952
Kul'kova, Mariia A., 191
Kulišič, Spiro, 56
Kumove, Shirley, 3593, 3594,
3595, 3596
Kunin, A.V., 1523
Kunitskaya-Peterson, Christina,
240
Kunkel-Razum, Kathrin, 98
Kuntz, Lieselotte, 2101
Kunze, Horst, 2359
Küpper, Heinz, 2360, 2361, 2362
Kuray, Gülbende, 3532
Kuria, Elizabeth Nafula, 406
Kursitza, Waltraud, 2335
Kurzer, Michael, 2363, 2364
Kürz-Luder, Barbara, 3498
Kuskovskaya, S., 1524
Küttner, W.P., 2365
Kuusi, Matti, 241, 242, 407, 408,
1858, 1859, 1860, 1861
Kuz'min, S.S., 3279

L'Aulnaye, M. de, 1912
La Mesangère, Pierre de, 1909
Laan, K. ter, 1151

Lábadi. Károly, 2818
Laber, Harry G., 2366
Lacey, Gary, 1053
Laely-Meyer, Hans, 3499
Lafleur, Bruno, 1910
Lafuente Niño, Carmen, 57, 58
Lahn, Wilhelm, 2137
Låle, Peder, 1122
Lall, Kesar, 3129
Lamb, G.F., 1525
Lambert, James, 970
Landgren, G.A., 3485
Landmann, Salcia, 3597, 3598
Landy, Eugene E., 1526
Lane-Poole, Stanley, 939
Lang, Ewald, 2367
Langdon, S., 982
Lange, Kofi Ron, 409
Langer, Howard J., 735
Langnas, Isaac A., 3280
Lapucci, Carlo, 2914, 2931
LaRoche, Nancy, 1786, 1787
Larsen, Judith Clark, 1911
Lass, Abraham H., 1329
Latendorf, Friedrich, 2368
Latsch, Günter, 2369
Lau, Theodora, 1079
Lauchert, Friedrich, 2370
Laukkanen, Kari, 1862
Lauri, Achille, 2932
Lautenbach, Ernst, 2371, 2372,
2373
Lawson, James Gilchrist, 243
Lawson, JonArno, 1060
Lazarus, John, 2854
Le Roux de Lincy, Adrien Jean
Victor, 1913, 1914
Lean, Vincent Stuckey, 1527
Leaver, K.D., 410
Lebe, Reinhard, 2374
Lechleitner, Franz, 2375
Lederer, Richard, 1528
Lee, Albert, 1529
Lee, Charles, 1586
Leedy, Loreen, 1530

Loubens, Didier, 1916
Louis, Cameron, 63
Loukatos, Démétrios, 1005, 1006, 1007, 2776, 2777
Lourenço, Tomás, 3208
Loux, Françoise, 1917
Lovelace-Käufer, Cicely, 1369
Lover, Samuel, 2883
Lubensky, Sophia, 64, 3282
Lucas, Edward Verrall, 1542
Luciani, Vincent, 2933
Ludwig, Gerda, 248
Lunde, Paul, 940
Luomala, Katharine, 65, 3024
Lupande, Joseph M., 415, 416
Lupande, Makoye, 415
Lupande, Wilbard J., 416
Lüpkes, Wiard, 2401
Lupson, J.P., 2402
Lurie, Charles N., 1543
Luther, Martin, 2403, 2404, 2405, 2406
Lutz, H.F., 983
Lux, Günter, 2407, 2408
Lyman, Darryl, 1544, 1545
Lytle, Clyde Francis, 1546

Maas, Herbert, 2409
Maaß, M., 1547
Maaß, Winfried, 2410
Mabry, Edward Loughlin, 754
Mac Con Iomaire, Liam, 2884
MacDonald, Flora, 2885
MacGregor, Forbes, 3340
Machač, Jaroslav, 1115
Machado, José Pedro, 3209
MacHale, Des, 1548
Mackay, Aeneas James George, 3341
Mackensen, Lutz, 2411
Mackin, R., 1338, 1339
Macon, John Alfred, 755
Macrone, Michael, 1549, 1550, 2778, 3062
Madaus, Christian, 2412

Madumulla, J.S., 417
Maess, Thomas, 2413
Magg, Wotan Wolfgang, 2414, 2415
Maggio, Rosalie, 1551
Mahgoub, Fatma Mohammed, 941
Māhina, 'Okusitino, 3520
Mahling, Peter, 3365
Mahoney, Kathleen, 756
Mai, Manfred, 2416
Mair, James Allan, 1552
Maitland, James, 757
Major, Clarence, 758, 759
Major, John, 1328
Makkai, Adam, 760, 761
Malberg, Horst, 2417
Małdzyjewa, Wiara, 3171
Malíková, Mária Olga, 3354
Mälk, Vaina, 249, 250, 251
Mall, Iosephus, 3063
Malone, Kemp, 762
Maloux, Maurice, 1918
Mal'tseva, Dina G., 3283
Mancini, A.M., 2926
Mandos, Hein, 988
Mandos-van de Pol, Miep, 988
Mang, A., 1985
Manioglu, Kemal, 3533
Mann, Leonard, 1553
Mannai, Ali Shabeeb al-, 942
Manruhf, Heinrich, 2418
Manser, Martin H., 1554, 1555
Manuelian, P.M., 965
Manwaring, Alfred, 2855
Mapletoft, John, 252
Mapplebeck, Elizabeth L., 1057
Marangoni, Giovanni, 2934
Marbach, Gotthard Oswald, 2419
Marcus, Eric, 763
Margalits, Ede, 2823
Margolin, Robert, 1556
Margulis, Alexander, 3284
Marketos, B.J., 2779

Marques da Costa, José Ricardo, 3210

Marsh, John B., 1557

Martín Sánchez, Manuel, 3434

Martin, Johannes, 1919

Martín, Juan José, 3433

Martin, Nancy, 743

Martin, Pat, 1116

Martin, Thomas L., 1558

Martin, Walter, 253

Martínez Kleiser, Luis, 3435

Martínez, Fernando, 3412

Martíns Seixo, Ramón Anxo, 3436

Martynova, A.N., 3285

Marvin, Dwight Edwards, 254, 1559

Maschke, George W., 3152, 3154

Masłowscy, Danuta, 3172, 3173

Masłowscy, Włodzimierz, 3172, 3173

Massa, Gaetano, 2935

Massebeuf, Albert, 1920

Massing, Jean Michel, 3064

Massobrio, Lorenzo, 2917

Mateaux, Clara, 1560

Mathews, Mitford M., 764, 765

Mathews, Norris, 66

Matković, Dinko, 1110

Matras, Daniel, 255

Matthewman, Lisle de Vaux, 1561

Matzek, Robert, 2420, 2421

Matzinger-Pfister, Regula, 2422

Mauritz, Christina, 2423

Mawr, E.B., 256

Mayotte, Ricky Alan, 1008

Mayr, Fr., 418

Mayreder, C., 67

Mbonde, John P., 419

McCaig, I. R., 1339

McCann, Sean, 2886

McCleary, John Bassett, 766

McCormick, Malachi, 1562, 3600

McCunn, Ruthanne Lum, 1082, 1083

McDonald, James, 1563

McDonald, Julie Jensen, 257, 1123, 2424, 3342

McDonnell, A.F., 3110

McFadden, Tara Ann, 1564

Mchedlishzili, D.I., 1438

McIntyre, Gail, 767

McKenzie, Carol, 1565

McKenzie, E.C., 1566

McKernan, Maggie, 1567

McKillroy, John, 2425

McKnight, Robert K., 3141

McLellan, Vern, 1568, 1569

McMahon, Sean, 1570

McNeal, Doris Schuckler, 1921

McNeil, William K., 20, 768

McPhee, Nancy, 1571

McShane, Marjorie, 64

Mead, Frank, 1009

Mead, Hirini Moko, 3111

Mead, Jane Thompson, 769

Meaini, Amado M., 943

Meech, Sanford B., 3065

Mehring, Margit, 2426

Meier, John, 68

Meier-Pfaller, Hans-Josef, 2427

Meisinger, Othmar, 2428

Meitsch, Rudolf, 2429, 2430

Mejsner, Ernst, 2431

Mel'ts, M. Ia., 3287

Melerovich, A.M., 3286

Melis, Luisa, 3327

Mellado Blanco, Carmen, 2432

Melnick, Sharon, 1256

Melo, Verissimo de, 2936

Mencken, H.L., 1572

Menzel, Hans, 2433

Merbury, Charles, 2937

Meredith, Mamie, 770

Merford, Oliver, 796

Merino, A., 3433

Merriam, Alan P., 420

Merriam, Barbara W., 420
Merrick, Captain G., 421
Mertvago, Peter, 1922, 2434, 2938, 3288, 3289, 3437
Merwin, W.S., 1084
Meschkank, Werner, 3366
Mesner, Susan, 613
Mesotten, Bart, 3007
Mesters, G.A., 1153
Meyer, Gérard, 422
Meyer, Hans Georg, 2435
Meyer-Werfel, Fred, 1573
Michael, Roland, 2436, 2437
Michałk, Frido, 3367, 3368
Michel, Arthur, 2171, 2270, 2271
Mickenberg, Risa, 771
Micu, Anamaria, 258
Middlemore, James, 259
Mieder, Wolfgang, 69, 70, 71, 72, 73, 74, 75, 76, 77, 78, 79, 80, 81, 82, 83, 84, 85, 86, 87, 88, 89, 90, 91, 92, 93, 94, 111, 260, 261, 262, 263, 264, 572, 573, 772, 773, 774, 775, 776, 777, 778, 779, 780, 781, 782, 1010, 1505, 1540, 1574, 1575, 1576, 1577, 1578, 1579, 1580, 1581, 1727, 2438, 2439, 2440, 2441, 2442, 2443, 2444, 2445, 2446, 2447, 2448, 2449, 2450, 2451, 2452, 2453, 2454, 2455, 2456, 2457, 2458, 2459, 3363, 3501
Miholek, Vladimir, 1111
Mikhel'son, M.I., 3290
Mikić, Pavao, 265
Militz, Hans-Manfred, 1925
Miller, Arthur Maximilian, 2460
Miller, Cynthia L., 1011
Miller, Donald L., 783
Miller, Peter, 784, 785
Mine, Takuji, 1481
Miner, Dorothy, 1897
Miner, Margaret, 822, 1582
Mingo, Jack, 1583
Mintz, Morton, 786

Miruka, Okumba, 423
Mitchell, Roger, 787
Mitchener, Joseph J., 788
Mitchison, Naomi, 424
Mitelli, Giuseppe Maria, 2940
Mitinia, I.E., 3291
Mitrofanova, V.V., 3285, 3287
Mizner, Addison, 796
Mokienko, Valerii M., 30, 346, 1012, 1027, 2706, 3247, 3286, 3292, 3293, 3294, 3295, 3296, 3297, 3298, 3299, 3317, 3318, 3319, 3320
Mokitimi, 'Makali I., 425
Molera, Frances M., 789
Moll, Otto, 95, 3480
Möller, Ferdinand, 2942
Molnár, Judit, 2461
Montana, Gladiola, 790
Montapert, Alfred Armand, 1584
Monteiro, George, 791, 792, 1031, 1585
Montreynaud, Florence, 1923, 1924
Monye, Ambrose A., 426, 427
Mooijaart, Marijke, 1154
Mook, Maurice A., 793
Moon, Rosamund, 96
Moore, Gary, 794
Moorhead, J.K., 1586
Morawski, J., 97
Mordock, John B., 1520
Moreira, António, 3211
Moreno, Consuelo, 1990
Morgan, Frances Elnora Williams, 1587
Morgen, Christian, 2462
Mori, Yoko, 2996
Morin, Yves-Charles, 391
Morison, O., 1054
Moritz, Lukas, 266
Moriz, Eduard, 2463, 2464, 2465, 2466, 2467
Morottaja, Hans, 1856
Morris, Mary, 1588

Morris, William, 1588
Morris-Brown, Vivien, 2972
Morrison, Allan, 3343
Morwood, Vernon S., 2793
Moya, Ismael, 962
Mrozowski, Teresa, 3174
Muallimoğlu, Nejat, 3534
Müldner-Nieckowski, Piotr, 3175
Mullane, Deirdre, 795
Müller, Gunter, 2331
Muller, H. Nicholas, 662
Müller, Kathrin, 944
Müller, Klaus, 2468
Müller, Maler [Friedrich], 2961
Müller, Peter O., 98
Müller-Hegemann, 2469
Müller-Thurau, Claus Peter, 2470, 2471
Mumford, Ethel Watts, 796
Munro, Angus, 1589
Munro, Pamela, 797
Muntean, George, 3231
Munzar, Jan, 1117
Muranga, Manuel John Kamugisha, 428
Murison, David, 3344
Murphy, Colin, 2887
Murphy, Edward F., 1590, 1591
Murphy, William Peter, 429
Muş, Ali Osman, 2997
Musakulov, A.K., 3570
Mushi, Michael, 430
Mustaeva, L.I., 1739
Mutahi, Karega, 394
Muth-Schwering, Ursula, 267
Mwela-Ubi, Kalunga, 431
Mweseli, Monica Nalyaka, 432
Myers, Robert, 268, 741

Naga, Acharya Sangye T., 3516
Nagel, Ulrich, 2472
Nagy, Gábor O., 2824, 2825
Nagy, Géza, 2826
Nagy, Imre, 3601
Nares, Robert, 1592

Ndunguru, Egino, 433
Neaman, Judith S., 1593
Neander, Michael, 2473
Necker, Claire, 1594
Nehry, Hans, 2474
Nelson, Timothy C., 2475
Nestor, Hellen Byera, 434
Netaob, Alema, 435
Neumann, Gisela, 2476
Neumann, Joseph, 3602
Neumann, Manfred, 2943
Neumann, Renate, 2477
Neumann, Siegfried, 2476, 2478, 2479, 2480
Newbern, John, 269
Newlin, George, 1595
Ngoy Kasongo Kata, Mfum-wa-Mangi, 436
Nicholas, J. Karl, 637
Nicoloff, Assen, 1035
Nicolson, Alexander, 2888
Nieter, Christoph Georg Heinrich, 2481
Nikitina, Ekaterina, 3272
Nikitina, T. G., 3298
Nikolaeva, E.K., 3298
Nikolaiéva, I., 99
Nissen, Moritz Momme, 2482
Nissen, Peter, 2107
Nitecki, Jan, 3176
Nitsch, Thomas, 2483
Nitsche, Franz, 2484
Nkafu Nkemnkia, Martin, 100
Nkumbulwa, Joseph, 437, 438, 439, 440
Nolte, Andreas, 2459, 2485, 2486
Nolte, Therese, 2305
Nopitsch, Christian Conrad, 101
North, Maurcie, 1965
Notley, David, 1596
Noueshi, Mona Rashad, 945
Novak, Richey, 1741
Nowakowska, Alicja, 3164
Nowlan, Gwendolyn L., 1597
Nowlan, Robert A., 1597

Nugteren, Hans, 3615
Nuh, Omar Au, 1173
Nulman, Macy, 2807
Nunes, Manuela, 3201
Núñez, Hernán, 3438
Nussbaum, Stan, 798, 799
Nyakundi, Evans K., 441, 442
Nyandwi, Jean, 443
Nyczaj, Stanisław, 3177
Nyembezi, Cyril L. Sibusiso, 410, 444

Ó Corráin, Ailbhe, 2889
Ó Muirithe, Diarmaid, 2890
O'Rahilly, Thomas F., 2896
O'Byrne, Lorraine, 1598
O'Connor, Gemma, 1599
O'Dea, Donal, 2887
O'Donnell, James, 1059, 2891
O'Donnell, Kathleen Palatucci, 3439
O'Donoghue, D.J., 2892
O'Donoghue, Jo, 2893
O'Farrell, Padraic, 2894
O'Griofa, Mairtin, 2895
O'Kane, Eleanor S., 3441
O'Leary, C.F., 1600
Odaga, Asenath Bole, 445
Oddera, Maria Federica, 2929
Odeldahl, Anders, 3486
Odell, Ruth, 800
Ohara, Maricarmen, 3440
Ohrbach, Barbara Milo, 1601
Ojoade, J. Olowo, 446, 447, 448, 449
Okutsu, Fumio, 2998
Olivier, René, 1925
Olmos Canalda, Elías, 3442
Olschansky, Heike, 2487
Öndoğan, Erdem, 3535
Opalenko, M.E., 1602
Opoku, Kofi Asare, 450
Orben, Robert, 1603
Orsini, Stéphanie, 2944
Ortabaeva, R., 3014

Osten, Alexander, 2488
Osterbrauck, Cornelia, 1085
Otis, Harry B., 801
Otrakul, Ampha, 3513
Öttchen, Cynthia J., 1463
Otto, August, 3066, 3067, 3068, 3069, 3070, 3071, 3072, 3073, 3074
Otto, Luise, 2469
Otto, Manfred, 2489
Ottow, A.M., 102
Ould Mohamed-Babá, Ahmed-Salem, 946, 947, 948, 949
Owens, Paul T., 499
Owomoyela, Oyekan, 451, 452
Özcan, Celal, 3536

P., 3075
p'Bitek, Okot, 453
Pachocinski, Ryszard, 454
Paczolay, Gyula, 103, 270, 271, 272, 273, 274, 275, 276, 277, 278, 279, 2827, 2828, 2829, 2830, 2831, 2832
Page, Robin, 1604
Pagliaro, Marcelo A., 963
Pagter, Carl R., 617, 618, 619, 620, 621
Palitta, Gianni, 2921
Palm, Christine, 3486
Palmatier, Robert A., 1605
Pamies, Antonio, 104
Pampalk, José, 455
Panati, Charles, 1606
Panin, I. M., 3300
Papadopoullos, Theodore, 2780
Paqué, Ruprecht, 456
Paris, Ruth, 1224
Parkinson, Judy, 1607
Parks, Lois F., 802
Parks, Taylor E., 802
Partington, Angela, 1608
Partnow, Elaine, 1609, 1610
Parton, Roland, 3529
Partridge, Angela, 2897

Partridge, Eric, 1611, 1612, 1613, 1614, 1615
Paschales, Demetrios P., 2781
Pasetti-Bombardella, Gisela, 2962
Pastor, Eilert, 2490
Paz Roca, Maria Carmen, 3443, 3444
Paziak, Mikhail Mikhailovich, 3568
Pe, Hla, 1039
Peake, Mervyn, 1616
Pearce, Helen, 803
Pearce, T.M., 804
Pearl, Anita, 1617
Pearson, Rosemary, 1618
Pechau, Jochem, 2491
Peers, John, 1619
Peixoto, Alfrânio, 1032
Peltier, Anatole-Roger, 3514
Peltzer, Karl, 2492
Pemba, Lhamo, 3517, 3518, 3519
Penfield, Joyce, 457
Percival, Peter, 2856
Pereira Ginet, Tomás, 280
Péret, Benjamin, 1891, 1892, 1893
Peretz, Bernhard, 1926
Pérez Bugallo, Rubén, 963
Pérez de Castro, J.L., 3445
Pérez, Soledad, 805
Perkins, Anne E., 806
Permiakov, Grigorii L'vovich, 105, 281, 282, 283, 3301, 3302, 3303
Perry, Theodore A., 3446
Persch, Franz, 2106
Person, Henry, 807
Peter, Laurence J., 1620
Petermann, Jürgen, 3304
Petersen, Arona, 3575
Peterson, Eugene H., 1013
Peterson, Gail, 1621, 1622
Petlevannyi, G.P., 2493
Petri (Peters), Friedrich, 2494
Petro, Makuru S., 458

Petroselli, Francesco, 2945
Petrov, P., 2857
Petrović, Luci, 3603
Petrufová, Magdaléna, 3354
Petschel, Günter, 2495
Petty, Jo, 1623
Peyerl, Elke, 975
Pfauntsch, Michael, 2496
Pfeffer, J. Alan, 1014, 2497
Pfeffer, Karl, 1624
Pfeffer, Wendy, 1927
Pfeiffer, Herbert, 2498
Philippi, Jule, 2499
Phillips, Bob, 1625
Phythian, B.A., 1626
Piątkowska, Renata, 3178
Pickering, David, 1627
Pierron, Agnès, 1923, 1924
Pierron, Louis, 808
Pietsch, Barbara, 2000
Pignolo, Marie-Thérèse, 1928
Piirainen, Elisabeth, 2500
Pilane, Amos Kgamanyane, 424
Pine, L.G., 1628
Piñel, Rosa, 1990
Pinette, Roger G., 1629, 1630
Pinkney, Maggie, 971
Piø, Iørn, 225
Pitrè, Giuseppe, 106, 2946, 2947
Pitts, Arthur William, 1631
Płaskowicka-Rymkiewicz, Stanisława, 107
Platt, Suzy, 809
Plaut, M., 2501
Plawiuk, Volodymyr S., 3569
Plesovskii, Fedor Vasilevich, 3017
Plopper, Clifford Henry, 1086
Plotkin, David George, 724, 725
Pohlke, Annette, 2502
Pohlke, Reinhard, 2502, 2503
Politis, Vera, 3305
Pollmann, Bernhard, 2000
Pollock, Carl Arthur, 1632

Polt-Heinzl, Evelyne, 2504, 2505, 2506
Polve, Adella, 810
Ponette, Pierre, 2858
Popovich, R.I., 284
Porter, Kenneth, 811
Porter, Mary Gray, 2507
Portmann, Paul F., 3502
Potter, David, 1536
Pottier, B., 3447
Pound, Louise, 812, 813
Powell, Michael, 1633
Powers, George W., 1634
Powers, Nick, 814
Prahl, August, 2508
Prahlad, Sw. Anand, 815, 816
Prędota, Stanisław, 108, 109, 110, 1138, 1154, 1155, 1156, 3179, 3180
Prenzel, Eberhard, 2509
Preston, Dennis R., 817
Préval, Guerdy, 2796
Price, Barbara Wells, 818
Price-Thompson, Tracy, 819
Priest, William L., 1635
Prieto Donate, Estefanía, 3448
Primrose, Arthur John, 2859
Prinz, Friedrich, 2510
Pritchard, Ilka Maria, 2511
Probst, Alfred, 2512
Prochnow, Herbert V., 1636, 1637, 1638, 1639
Prochnow, Jr., Herbert V., 1638, 1639
Profantová, Zuzana, 3355, 3356
Prokhorov, Lurii E., 3267
Prossliner, Johann, 2513, 2514
Proteau, Lorenzo, 1055
Provenzano, Renata, 2799
Pruys, Karl Hugo, 2515
Puchner, Günter, 2516, 2517
Puetzfeld, Carl, 2518
Pukui, Mary Kawena, 2800
Puntsch, Eberhard, 2519
Pusko, Gábor, 2833

Pusposaputro, Sarwono, 2864
Pyczewska-Pilarek, Jadwiga, 3181

Quadbeck-Seeger, Hans-Jürgen, 2520, 2521
Quin, E. G., 2898
Quintão Duarte Silva, Helena Maria, 285
Quintão, José Luís, 285
Quitard, Pierre-Marie, 1929, 1930

Raab, Heinrich, 2522
Rabe, Hubertus, 2582
Raben, Joseph, 3345
Raders, Margit, 1990
Radić, Tomislav, 286
Radvilas, Gediminas, 3095, 3097
Rak, Pavel, 1837
Ramage, Craufurd Tait, 2523
Rambow, Susan, 738
Ramirez, Manuel D., 820
Ramsay, Allan, 3346
Ramsey, Betty Jo, 1640
Randolph, Vance, 821
Rao, N. Venkata, 2844
Rao, Narasinga, 2860
Rashidonduk, Sh., 3125
Rassart-Eeckhout, Emmanuelle, 1931
Rat, Maurice, 1932
Ratcliffe, Susan, 1641, 1642
Rattray, R. Sutherland, 459
Raub, Julius, 2524
Rauch, Karl, 287
Rauchberger, Karl Heinz, 2525
Rawson, Hugh, 822, 1582, 1643, 1644, 1645
Ray, John, 1646
Raymond, Alain, 1935
Raymond, Janice, 3126
Read, Allen Walker, 823
Reagan, Michael, 824
Reed, Alexander W., 3109
Rees, Nigel, 1647, 1648, 1649, 1650, 1651, 1652, 1653, 1654,

1655, 1656, 1657, 1658, 1659, 1660, 1661, 1662, 1663, 1664, 1665, 1666, 1667, 1668

Rehbein, Detlev, 288, 1157, 2526

Reich, Alan A., 3305

Reichert, Heinrich G., 3076

Reichhart, Bogusław, 3182

Reidel, Marlene, 2527

Reiners, Ludwig, 2528

Reinirkens, Hubert, 2999

Reinsberg-Düringsfeld, Otto von, 188, 289, 290, 291, 292

Reiser, Karl, 2529

Reisner, Robert, 1669, 1670

Reitman, Judith, 825

Reller, Gisela, 2530, 3139, 3306

Rey, Alain, 1933

Reynolds, Joe, 2899

Rhodes, Richard, 742

Ricapito, Joseph, 2948

Richard, Philippe, 1917

Richey, Werner, 2228, 2531, 2532, 2663

Richmond, Arthur, 1671

Richter, Alan, 1672

Richter, Albert, 2533

Richter, Manfred, 2741, 2742

Richter, Renate, 1853

Ridout, Ronald, 1673, 1674

Riedel, Herbert, 2270, 2271

Riege Rudolf, 2534

Ries, Hubert, 460

Riesenberg, Saul H., 3193

Riffl, Karoline, 2535

Rigzin, Tsepak, 3516

Riley, Cindy, 293

Riley, Murdoch, 3112

Ringo, Miriam, 1675

Risse, Anna, 2536

Rittendorf, Michael, 2537

Ritter, Michael, 1676

Rittersbacher, Christa, 1677

Rittgasser, Stefan, 26

Rivas, Paco, 3449

Roback, Abraham Aaron, 294

Robbins, Ceila Dame, 1788, 1789

Robea, Mihail M., 3232, 3233

Roberts, Kate Louise, 1678

Roberts, Warren, 1061

Robertson, James I., 826

Roche, Reinhard, 2538

Rodas Estrada, Haroldo, 2790

Rodebaugh, P.M., 269

Rodegem, F., 461

Roderich, Albert, 2539

Rodríguez Marín, Francisco, 3450

Rogak, Lisa, 827

Roger, E.G., 828

Rogers, James, 1679

Röhl, Klaus Rainer, 2540

Rohlfs, Gerhard, 2782

Röhrich, Lutz, 111, 2541, 2542, 2543

Rohsenow, John S., 1087, 1088

Rölleke, Heinz, 2026, 2544

Romadin, M.N., 3307

Roman, Christian, 1680, 1681, 2545, 2546, 2547

Romero, Elena, 16

Romey, David, 3604

Romo Herrero, Lidia, 3451

Ronner, Markus M., 2548, 2549

Room, Adrian, 1682

Roos, Marti, 3615

Rosen, Heinrich, 2550

Rosenberger, Jesse Leonard, 829

Rosenstock, Gabriel, 2900, 2901

Rosenthal, Beatrice, 1683

Rosenthal, Peggy, 1684

Rosenzweig, Paul, 295

Rosié, Paul, 2551

Ross, H.R., 2902

Ross, W.A., 2902

Rössing, Roger, 2552

Rosten, Leo, 830, 1685

Roth, Herb, 831

Rother, Karl, 2553

Rotondo, Antonio, 2949

Rottauscher, Anna von, 1089

Rottgardt, Hans-Heinrich, 2554
Rottmann, Johannes, 2555
Rowinski, Kate, 1686
Rowsome, Frank, 832
Roylance, William H., 1687
Royle, Trevor, 1688
Rozental', D.E., 3276
Rozycki, William V., 3124
Rübesamen, Anneliese, 950
Rubin, Bonnie Miller, 1689
Rubin, Ruth, 3605
Rueda de Taylor, Evelia, 3142
Ruef, Hans, 3503
Ruelius, Hermann, 2556
Ruffins, Reynold, 1696
Ruffner, Frederick G., 1790
Rühmkorf, Peter, 2557
Ruibal, Xesús Ferro, 3373, 3379
Ruíz Leivas, Cristóbal, 3452
Ruiz Moreno, Rosa María, 112,
951
Ruiz, Ana, 3416
Ruiz-Zorrilla Cruzate, Marc, 346
Runes, Dagobert D., 1690
Rupprecht, Karl, 113
Russell, Thomas Herbert, 833
Rutledge, Leigh W., 1691
Rybarski, Werner, 3537

Safian, Louis A., 834, 1692, 1693
Safir, Leonard, 1695
Safire, William, 1694, 1695
Sahado, Karaba, 465
Saiga, Yohei, 3000
Sailer, Johann Michael, 2558,
2559
Sainéan, L., 1934
Sak, Ziya, 3538
Sakayan, Dora, 966, 967
Sakharova, Marfa Aleksandrovna,
3018
Sallinen, Pirkko, 296
Salvante, A. Raffaele, 2950
Sampson, John, 2794
Sánchez Bringas, Ángeles, 3118

Sanchez-Boudy, José, 1112
Sandburg, Carl, 835
Sanders, Daniel, 2560
Sandtner, Hilda, 2561
Sandvoss, Franz, 2562, 2563,
2564
Santi, Antonio, 2951
Santilla, Iñigo López deMendoza,
Marqués de, 3453
Saporta y Beja, Enrique, 3606
Sardelli, María Antonella, 114,
3454
Sarimsakov, B.L., 3570
Sarnoff, Jane, 1696
Sarv, Ingrid, 1841, 1843, 1844,
1845, 1846, 1847, 1848
Sattler, Johann Rudolph, 2565
Sauer, Wolfgang, 2343
Sbarbi, José María, 115, 3455,
3456
Schack, Ingeborg-Liane, 3607
Schaeffler, Julius, 2566
Schäfer, Jochen, 2537
Schaible, Karl Heinrich, 2567
Schalk, Leonard, 1080
Schambach, Georg, 2568
Schanda, Eva, 2834
Schattenhofer, Monika, 2569
Schaufelbüel, Adolf, 2570
Scheffel, Fritz, 2571
Scheffler, Axel, 297
Scheffler, Heinrich, 2572
Schellbach-Kopra, Ingrid, 1864,
1865, 1866
Schellhorn, Andreas, 2573
Schemann, Hans, 1935, 2574,
2575, 2576, 2577, 2578, 3212
Scherer, Burkhard, 2579
Scheuermann, Ludwig, 3533
Scheven, Albert, 462, 463
Schewietzek, Udo P., 2579
Schilling, María Luisa, 1990
Schindler, Eva, 2580
Schindler, Franz, 1114
Schinke-Llano, Linda, 865

Sellner, Alfred, 304, 1939, 2784, 2954, 3079
Semenets, O.P., 3299
Senaltan, Semahat, 305, 3540
Senti, Alois, 3504
Seoighe, Mainchín, 2903
Sereno, Maria Helena Sampaio, 117, 3213
Serrano, Juan, 3458
Serrano, Susan, 3458
Service, R.G., 3124
Serz, Georg Thomas, 3080
Sethi, Narendra K., 2862
Settel, T.S., 840
Seuß, Rita, 3536
Sevilla Muñoz, Julia, 58, 118, 119, 120, 121, 122, 306, 307, 308, 1884, 1885, 1940, 3382, 3383, 3384, 3385, 3386, 3387, 3459, 3460, 3461, 3462, 3463, 3464
Sevilla Muñoz, Manuel, 58, 3387
Shadrin, N.L., 3279
Shaffer, J. Frank, 841
Shafritz, Jay M., 1702
Shankle, George Earlie, 842
Shanskii, N.M., 3309
Shanskii, V.N., 3322
Shapiro, Fred R., 1703, 1704
Shapovalova, G.G., 3287
Shargorodskii, T., 3310
Shatalova, Z.I., 3322
Shaw, Henry Wheeler, 549, 550
Shaw, Susanna, 843
Shearer, William J., 309
Sheba, Laide, 467
Shehab El-Din, Tahia, 954
Shejdlin, B., 3311
Sheldon, Richard, 3305
Shelton, Ferne, 844, 845
Sheng-qing, Gu, 1091
Shepard, Priscilla, 1705
Sherrin, Ned, 1706
Sherry, Kevin, 1707
Shoemaker, Henry Wharton, 846

Shoemaker, William P., 847
Shongolo, Abdullahi A., 468
Shrager, David S., 1405
Shurgaia, Tea, 123, 1955
Shvydkaia, L.I., 1739
Sick, Bastian, 2635
Sidorenko, K.P., 3299
Siebenkees, Johann Christian, 2636
Sielicki, Franciszek, 3183
Sillner, Leo, 2637
Silver, Carole G., 1593
Sima, Alexander, 955
Simeonova, Ruska, 1036
Simmons, Donald C., 469, 470
Simon, Irmgard, 2638
Simpson, Charles, 3347
Simpson, Gladys, 3347
Simpson, James B., 1708
Simpson, John A., 1214, 1709, 1710, 1711
Simrock, Karl, 2639, 2640, 2641, 2642
Sinapius-Horčička, Daniel, 3081
Singer, Samuel, 310, 311, 312, 313, 314, 315, 316, 317, 318, 319, 320, 321, 322, 323, 324, 3505, 3506
Sitarz, Magdalena, 3609
Škara, Danica, 265
Skeat, Walter W., 1712, 1713
Skillen, Chris, 3312
Skipwith, Ashkhain, 925
Skorupka, Stanisław, 3163
Skriabin, Agnieszka, 3184
Skupy, Hans-Horst, 976, 2643, 2692
Skuza, Sylwia, 325
Slung, Michele, 848, 849, 850
Smith, Arthur H., 1092
Smith, Charles G., 1714, 1715
Smith, Cornelia Marshall, 1716
Smith, Diann Sutherlin, 851
Smith, Elmer L., 854, 855
Smith, Joan, 613

338

Smith, John B., 1717, 1718, 1719
Smith, John R., 1720
Smith, Lloyd E., 1721
Smith, Logan Pearsall, 1722
Smith, Morgan, 852
Smith, Norman A., 853
Smith, William George, 1723
Smitherman, Geneva, 856, 857
Smoliakovas, Grigorijus, 3098
Smyth, Alice Mary, 1724
Snapp, Emma Louise, 858
Snavely, Elmer S., 859
Snegirev, I.M., 3313
Snow, Richard F., 1725, 1726
Snyder, Bridget, 717
Soares, Rui J.B., 326, 327, 328, 3214
Sobieski, Janet, 93, 94, 1727
Sochatzy, Klaus, 2644, 2645
Socin, Albert, 956
Söhns, Franz, 1020, 2646
Soler i Marcet, Maria-Lourdes, 2647
Solman, Joseph, 977
Sommer, Elyse, 1728, 1729
Sommer, Mike, 1728
Sommer, Robin Langley, 3082
Sommerfeldt, Josef, 3185
Son, Phan Hong, 3573
Sørensen, John Kousgård, 1121, 1124
Sørensen, Knud, 1730
Sørensen, Per K., 3515
Sotavalta, Arvo, 3028
Soto Arias, María do Rosario, 3465
Soto Posada, Gonzalo, 1104, 1105
Soukhanov, Anne H., 644
Sowa, Michael, 2248
Soyter, G., 2785
Spaan, Gerrit van, 1158
Spalding, Henry D., 860
Spalding, Keith, 2648, 2649
Speake, Jennifer, 1731

Spears, Richard A., 861, 862, 863, 864, 865, 1264, 1265, 1732
Speck, Charles H., 3120
Spector, David A., 1733
Speight, E.E., 3137
Speirs, James, 2791
Sperber, Hans, 866
Sperenza, Adriana, 963
Sperling, Susan K., 1734
Speroni, Charles, 2955, 2956, 2957
Spicker, Friedemann, 329, 2650
Spink, Kathryn, 1735
Spörl, Gerhard, 2651
Sporschil, Johann, 1736
Spurgeon, Charles Haddon, 1737, 1738
Stambaugh, Ria, 2652
Stampoy, Pappity, 3348
Stanciulescu-Bîrda (Bârda), Alexandru, 3234, 3235, 3236
Stark, Judith, 867
Stauffer, Charles, 2653
Stebben, Gregg, 669
Stechow, Walter, 2654
Steenackers, Francis, 3001
Stefanovich, G.A., 1739
Steger, Heribert, 1021, 1022, 1023, 1024
Steiger, Karl, 2655
Stein, Heidi, 3541
Stein, Ingo, 2656
Stein, Leopold, 3466
Steindl-Rast, David, 1740
Steiner, Arpad, 3083
Steiner, Paul, 868
Steinmeyer, Beate, 2657
Stenstrom, Oscar Sten Paul, 471
Stepanova, Liudmila, 3247
Sterkenburg, P.G.J. van, 1156
Stern, Henry R., 1741
Sternbach, L., 124
Steuck, Udo, 1742
Stevens, James S., 1743

Stevenson, Burton Egbert, 1025, 1744, 1745
Stewart, Roy L., 1746
Stibbe, Claudia A., 1139
Stibbs, Anne, 1747
Still, James, 869
Stirling-Maxwell, Sir William, 125
Stöber, August, 2658, 2659
Stoett, F.A., 1159, 1160
Stoikova, Stefana, 1037
Stölting, Cécile, 1878, 2810
Stoltze, Friedrich, 2660
Stone, Jon R., 330, 3084, 3085
Stoudt, John Baer, 870
Stovall, TaRessa, 819
Strafforello, Gustavo, 331
Straniero, Michele L., 2952
Straubinger, Otto Paul, 2661
Strauss, Emanuel, 332, 333
Strauss, Maurcie B., 1748
Strauss, Ruby G., 3610
Street, Pat, 1530
Strich, Christian, 2662
Strich, Michael, 2228, 2532, 2663
Ström, Fredrik, 3487, 3488, 3489
Strömberg, Reinhold, 2786, 2787
Strutz, Henry, 2664, 2665
Stul'nikova, S.V., 1749
Stundžiene, Brone, 3099
Sturm, Harlan, 3467
Stypuła, Ryszard, 3186
Su, Lim, 3025
Sudau, Günter, 3002
Sugar, Bert Randolph, 1750
Suksov,Valentin, 152
Suljkić, Hifzija, 1029
Sullivan, Andrew, 871
Sullivan, Pat, 1320
Sumbwa, Nyambe, 472
Summerfield, Anne, 2865
Summerfield, John, 2865
Sumner, Claude, 1854
Sumrall, Amber Coverdale, 1751
Sun, C.C., 1093

Sundwall, McKay, 126
Sunners, William, 872
Suringar, Willem Hendrik Dominikus, 127, 128, 334
Susan, S., 2666
Sutermeister, Otto, 3507
Suwarno, Peter, 3003
Suzuki, Tozo, 3004
Suzzoni, François, 1923, 1924
Swainson, Charles, 1752
Swarner, Kristina, 3611
Swenson, Ann H., 335
Świerczyńska, Dobrosława, 336, 337
Świerczyński, Andrzej, 336, 337
Swirko, Stanisław, 3187
Swope, Pierce E., 873
Syv, Peder, 1125
Szałas, Roman, 3188
Szelinski, Victor, 3086
Szemerkényi, Ágnes, 2835
Szydłowska, Natalia, 3189

Taboada Chivite, Xesús, 3468
Taft, Michael, 874
Tagbwe, Sie, 389
Taggart, Caroline, 1753
Tair, Mohammad Nawaz, 3145
Takaha, Shiro, 1481
Takashima, Taiji, 338
Takeda, Katsuaki, 2993
Tan, Situ, 1094
Tange, Ernst Günter, 2667, 2668, 2669, 2670, 2671, 2672
Tanttu, Erkki, 1867, 1868, 1869, 1870, 1871, 1872
Tappe, Eberhard, 339
Tard, Françoise, 2673
Taubken, Hans, 2190
Taylor, Archer, 129, 130, 131, 340, 875, 876, 877, 878, 879, 880, 881, 882, 883, 884, 1756, 1757, 1758, 1759, 3005
Taylor, Jefferys, 1754
Taylor, Joseph, 1755

Taylor, Ronald, 2674
Teichmann, Jo, 2675
Tekinay, Alev, 3542
Templeton, John Marks, 1760, 1761
Tendlau, Abraham Moses, 3612, 3613
Tenenbaum, Ann, 542, 543
Tenzler, Gisela, 2676
Tenzler, Wolfgang, 2677, 2678
Terban, Marvin, 1762, 1763, 1764, 1765
Tereshchenko, O.E., 1739
Tertrais, Max, 438, 439, 440
Thai Van Kiem, M., 3574
Thal, Hella, 341
Theissen, Siegfried, 1155
Thiele, Johannes, 978, 2582
Thiessen, Jack, 1056
Thiselton-Dyer, T. F., 1766
Thomas, Antoine, 3469
Thomissøn, Hans, 1126
Thompson, Harold W., 885, 886
Thomsen, Bernd, 2679, 2680, 2681, 2682, 2683
Thomsett, Michael C., 1767
Thurston, Helen M., 887
Tibau, Georges, 989
Tidwell, James N., 888
Tiffou, Etienne, 391, 3140
Tilles, Sally Simon, 2684
Tilley, Morris Palmer, 1768, 1769, 1770
Titcomb, Timothy, 1771
Titelman, Gregory Y., 1772
Titus, Charles H., 889
Tobias, Anton, 132
Tobler, Adolf, 1941
Tokarczuk, Olga, 3190
Tokita, Masamizu, 3006
Tokunosuké, Véda, 3001
Tomasek, Tomas, 2132
Tonn, Maryjane Hooper, 342
Torge, Martha, 583

Tosi, Renzo, 3087
Tóth, Marianne, 1521
Treffry, Elford Eveleigh, 1774
Trefil, James, 695
Trenkle, Bernhard, 2685
Trenkler, Robert, 2686
Trent, D.C., 1775
Treskow, Irene von, 2687
Tripp, Rhoda Thomas, 1776
Trittschuh, Travis, 866
Trivedi, Devkumar, 2863
Trofimkina, O.I., 1012
Trojer, Johann, 979
Troxell, William S., 566
Troxler, H.J., 1942
Troyer, Lester O., 890
Trusler, John Rev., 1777
Tschachler-Roth, Elisabeth, 2005, 2006
Tschinkel, Wilhelm, 2688
Tsvilling (Zwilling), M.Ia., 3314
Tucci, Giovanni, 2958, 2959, 2960
Tuleja, Tad, 891, 1778, 1779, 1780
Tulloch, Tom, 1781
Tunnicius, Antonius, 2689
Tupper, Martin Farquhar, 1782
Turner, K. Amy, 3353
Turnitz, Georg von, 1095
Tüshaus, Friedrich, 2690

Ua Cnáimhsi, Pádraig, 2904
Ua Donnchadha, Tadhg, 2905
Üçgül, Sevinç, 3528
Uhlenbruck, Gerhard, 2691, 2692
Uhlig, Gudrun, 2219
Uí Bhraonáin, Donla, 2906
Ulrich, Karl-Heinz, 2693
Umurova, Gulnas, 2694
Ungar, Frederick, 2695
Unterweger, Ursula, 2696, 2697
Unterweger, Wolf-Dietmar, 2696, 2697

Urdang, Laurence, 1783, 1784, 1785, 1786, 1787, 1788, 1789, 1790
Ustinov, Peter, 1791
Uthe-Spencker, Angela, 1792

Väänänen-Jensen, Inkeri, 1873
Vakhshteyn, Bernhard, 3614
Valle, Alvaro, 1033
Vallés, Pilar, 3118
Valls, Rafael, 3579
Vande Walle, Willy, 3007
Vanoni, Marvin, 1793
Vargha, Katalin, 2820, 2821, 2822
Varrini, Giulio, 2961
Vartier, Jean, 1943
Vasconcellos, José Leite de, 133
Vasconcelos, Carolina Michaëlis de, 3215
Vasselli, Robert, 745
Vasvári, Lajos, 2836
Vaughan, Henry Halford, 3578
Vázquez Saco, Francisco, 3471
Vázquez, Lois, 3470
Vedder, H., 474
Velasco Valdés, Miguel, 3121
Ventín Durán, José Augusto, 3472
Ventzel, T.V., 2795
Vergara Martín, Gabriel María, 3473
Veth, Klemens, 1539
Vidal Castiñeira, Ana, 3474
Vidal, O.E., 475
Viellard, Stéphane, 134
Viitso, Tiit-Rein, 3100
Virkkunen, Sakari, 1874
Vitek, Alexander J., 3315
Viterbo, Sousa, 3216
Vizetelly, Frank H., 1794
Vlakhov, Sergei, 343, 1038
Vliet, Rietje van, 1161
Völker, Peter, 2112
Vollmann, Herbert, 2698

Volxem, Dö Van, 2226, 2227
Vöö, Gabriella, 2837
Voss, Karl, 1795, 1944, 2962

Wachler, Ludwig, 2699
Wächter, Oskar Eberhard Siegfried von, 2700
Waeger, Gerhart, 2701
Wagener, Samuel Christoph, 2702
Wagenfeld, Karl, 2703
Wager, Wulf, 2704
Wagner, Joh. Jacob, 892
Wagner, Paul, 135
Wahl, Moritz Callman, 344, 345
Wahlund, Per Erik, 3490
Waibel, Max, 3508
Wakefield, Edward, 893
Walker, Colin S.K., 3349
Wallace, A., 1796
Walley, Dean, 1797
Walsh, John K., 3475
Walsh, William, 1798
Walshe, I.A., 3316
Walter, Elizabeth, 1799
Walter, Harry, 346, 1026, 1027, 2705, 2706, 3272, 3317, 3318, 3319, 3320
Walther, Hans, 3088, 3089, 3090
Walther, Helmut, 2350
Walther, Richard, 2788
Wanamaker, John, 1800
Wandelt, Oswin, 1945
Wander, Karl Friedrich Wilhelm, 136, 137, 2707, 2708, 2709, 2710, 2711, 2712, 2713
Wanjohi, Gerald Joseph, 476, 477, 478
Ward, Anna L., 1801, 1802
Ward, Caroline, 347
Warewicz, Barbara, 3191
Warren, D.M., 479
Warren, Mary S., 479
Wathelet, Jean-Marc, 1946
Watkins, Dana, 1803

342

Watson, G. Llewellyn, 2973
Watson, Seosamh, 2907
Watts, Alan S., 1355
Watts, Karen, 1804
Weaver, Nevilee Maass, 894
Webber, Elizabeth, 1805
Webster, Sheila K., 957
Weckmann, Berthold, 1028
Wegener, Hans, 2714
Weidinger, Birgit, 2715
Weier, Hans-Ingolf, 480
Weigel, Lawrence A., 895
Weininger, Simon, 348
Weisberg, Jacob, 871, 896
Weise, Oskar, 2716
Weise, Wilhelm, 2717
Weiss, Carl Theodor, 2718
Weiss, Dorrie, 1729
Weitnauer, Alfred, 2719, 2720
Weller, Tom, 897
Welsch, Roger L., 898
Welzig, Werner, 980
Wentworth, Harold, 899, 900
Werkner, Turi, 2721
Werner, Elyane, 2722
Werner, Jakob, 3091
Werner, Jürgen, 138, 2789
Wertheimer, Hans Stefan, 2723, 2724
Wessels, Antje, 2631
Westermarck, Edward, 958
Wettig, Knut-Hannes, 2725
Weyers, Susan Paramore, 488
White, Rolf B., 1806
White, Vallie Tinsley, 901
Whiting, Bartlett Jere, 884, 902, 903, 904, 905, 906, 907, 908, 1807, 1808, 1809, 1810, 1811, 1812, 1813, 1814, 1815, 1816, 1817, 1947, 1948, 1949
Whitting, Charles Edward Jewel, 481
Whymant, Neville J., 3127
Widdowson, John D.A., 1425, 1818, 1819

Widmer, Walter, 1950
Wiese, Joachim, 2726
Wigand, Paul, 2727, 2728
Wilcke, Karin, 2729
Wilcox, Frederick B., 1820
Wilder, Roy, 909
Wildner, Ödön, 2838
Wilgus, D.K., 910
Wilkes, G.A., 972
Wilkins, Charles, 3326
Wilkinson, P.R., 1821
William, Tony Catherine Antoine, 2908
Williams, Fionnuala Carson, 2871, 2909, 2910, 2911, 2912, 2913
Williams, Rose, 3092
Willnat, Wolfgang, 2730
Willson, Frederick Newton, 913
Wilson, April, 2731
Wilson, F.P., 139, 1822
Wilson, George P., 821
Wilson, James, 3350
Wilstach, Frank J., 1823
Wilts, Ommo, 1953
Winckler, C.H., 485
Winick, Stephen D., 914
Winkler, Leonhard, 2732
Winstedt, Richard Olof, 3105
Winter, Fritz, 2733
Winter, Georg, 2734
Winter, Klaus, 2733
Winters, Jonathan, 1824
Wintle, Justin, 940, 1498
Witt, Rainer, 2333
Witte, P.A., 482, 483, 484
Witting, Clifford, 1673, 1674
Wittstock, Albert, 2735
Wiznitzer, Manuel, 349
Woeste, Friedrich, 2736
Wolf, Judith, 2737
Wölke, Sonja, 3364
Wolle, Helmut, 2738
Wood, Frederick T., 1825
Wood, James, 1826

Subject Index

Even though the 3615 proverb collections listed in this international bibliography are arranged by linguistic groups and thus easily to locate, this subject index should be of considerable value to make this bibliographical resource even more accessible. For example, bilingual collections obviously had to be placed into the group of one of the two languages. However, its number has also been registered under the second language. Specialized collections of proverbs dealing with certain geographical regions and cities, alcohol, business, children, humor, law, love, medicine, obscenity, sexuality, weather, women, etc. have also been recorded in this index. The same is true for such special genres as anti-proverbs, aphorisms, graffiti, proverbial comparisons, slurs, stereotypes, twin formulas, wellerisms, etc. Collections of proverbial materials found in the works of certain literary authors or politicians are cited under their names, and the titles of anonymous collections of earlier times have been included as well. It should also be noted that even though African, Arabic, and Indian language collections are listed under the general terms of "African Languages," "Arabic Languages," and "Indian Languages" so that they can be grouped together, all the various languages of these areas are included in this comprehensive subject index. The numbers following the various index words refer to the consecutively numbered collections and not to the pages of the bibliography.

Alsatian, 1942, 2653
Amandebele, 410
American, 5, 20, 24, 156, 202,
216, 221, 222, 301, 304, 341, 355,
369, 489, 490-922, 1360, 1429,
1439, 1498, 1611, 1615, 1677,
1703, 1801, 1802, 2100, 2101,
2512, 3546
American English, 223, 581,
593-595, 644, 862, 863
American Midwest, 677, 709,
770, 787
American Northeast, 739, 775,
776, 784, 785
American Northwest, 693
American South, 355, 586, 637,
684, 687, 821
American Southwest, 588
American West, 492, 495, 496,
538, 685
Americanism, 540, 609, 764, 765,
876, 878
Amish, 890
Amrum, 2307
Ancares, 3408
Ancren Riwle, 1810
Andrews, Oscar, 1131
Anglicism, 1456
Anglo-American, 489, 1360
Anglo-German, 2512
animal, 262, 1178, 1227, 1344,
1451, 1525, 1530, 1544, 1545,
1550, 1597, 1605, 1742, 1946,
2119-2121, 2207, 2377, 2389,
2480, 2594, 2597, 2675, 2676,
2701, 2771, 2918, 3327
Aniocha, 426, 427
Anna Sophia, Countess, 2620
anti-proverb, 498, 509, 510, 514,
548, 605, 633, 640, 659, 674, 680,
719, 745, 747, 751, 753, 754, 763,
767, 788, 796, 830, 834, 835, 841,
848-850, 867, 897, 912, 913, 921,
1036, 1131, 1172, 1253, 1291,
1336, 1380, 1536, 1537, 1540,

1556, 1568, 1573, 1578, 1581,
1633, 1680, 1681, 1971, 1978,
1988, 2002, 2003, 2016, 2117,
2118, 2166, 2167, 2188, 2189,
2196, 2197, 2198, 2211, 2233,
2234, 2245-2247, 2254, 2258,
2259, 2265, 2303, 2316, 2357,
2365, 2366, 2391, 2407, 2408,
2418, 2439, 2440, 2446, 2447,
2448, 2449, 2453, 2455, 2456,
2463-2467, 2477, 2478, 2525,
2538, 2539, 2541, 2545-2547,
2579, 2600, 2635, 2656, 2657,
2679-2683, 2730, 2737, 2755,
2820-2822, 3208, 3318, 3319
anti-quotation, 1969, 2445, 2457,
2458, 2541, 2551, 2723
anti-Semitic, 224, 231, 2009,
2627, 2684, 3185
Antioquia, 1101-1103
Anzengruber, Ludwig, 2438
aphorism, 329, 597, 680, 754,
755, 788, 841, 848-850, 912, 915,
976, 1211, 1261, 1268, 1281,
1432, 1435, 1820, 1881, 2106,
2118, 2123, 2154, 2184-2186,
2200-2203, 2229, 2253, 2283,
2293-2295, 2356, 2396, 2416,
2433, 2436, 2449, 2451, 2453,
2455, 2456, 2461, 2489, 2510,
2520, 2548, 2587, 2589-2593,
2599, 2650, 2685, 2691-2693,
2695, 2738, 2757, 2760, 2849,
3150, 3182, 3191, 3219, 3254,
3256, 3413, 3414, 3432, 3454,
3510
Appalachian, 637, 641, 673, 687,
869
apple, 1486
Apulia, 2948
Arabic, 6, 17, 29, 112, 144, 156,
278, 307, 923-959
Aragon, 3423, 3426
Aramaic, 344, 960, 961
Aranyosszék, 2817

Brioude, 1920
British Columbia, 1054
Brivadois, 1920
Browning, Robert, 1716
Bruegel, Pieter, the Elder, 1139,
1142, 1143, 2160, 2183, 2224,
2225, 2364, 2996
Buckley, William F., 649
building, 2472
Bukusu, 406
Bulgarian, 343, 1034-1038, 3171,
3303
Burma-Shave signs, 832
Burmese, 1039
Burns, Robert, 3350
Burundi, 443, 461
Busch, Wilhelm, 1991, 1998
Bush, George H.W., 871
Bush, George W., 896
business, 750, 794, 1281, 1396,
1423, 1767, 1800, 1806, 2418,
2520, 2588, 2739, 3396
Bussemacher, Johann, 2288

Cairene, 941
Cairo, 930, 931, 941
California, 490, 491, 516-518,
576, 713, 748, 789, 875, 879, 883
Calitrano, 2950
Campania, 2958-2960
Canadian, 1040-1057
Canarian, 3400
Canetti, Elias, 2449
Caribbean, 301
Carmichaell, James, 3328
Carré, Lois, 3443
Carrión, Santob de, 3446, 3466
cartoon, 914, 1537, 2231, 2457,
2458, 3006
Castilian, 115, 280, 1877, 3375,
3455, 3465
cat, 1597, 2597, 2676, 2701
Catalan, 306, 308, 3399, 3469
Cato, Marcus, 2748
Cats, Jacob, 1133

celebrity, 1368
Celestina, 3405, 3415, 3439
Celtic, 904, 1058, 1059
Central American, 355
Cervantes Saavedra, Miguel de,
3371, 3380, 3387, 3398, 3442
Cervera, Guillem de, 3469
Chagga, 430
Chamula, 3116
Chan, Charlie, 583
Chargaff, Erwin, 2449
Chaucer, Geoffrey, 1808
Chechen, 1060
Cheremis, 270, 271, 1061
chiasmus, 1433
children, 292, 767, 867, 1163,
1282-1284, 1293, 1401, 1416,
1419, 1427, 1428, 1473, 1496,
1512, 1516, 1560, 1707, 2016,
2032, 2033, 2325, 2499, 2527,
3178, 3416
Chinese, 274-276, 278, 351, 1062-
1097, 1674, 2984, 2988
Christie, Agatha, 1299
Churchill, Winston S., 1166,
1345, 1469, 1475, 1579, 1596
Chuvash, 1098, 1099
clock, 2123
cloth, 384-386, 388, 636, 2535,
2696
coin, 2619
collecting, 1
college, 622, 668, 797, 2975
Cologne, 1975, 1980, 1986, 2010,
2024, 2025, 2028, 2043, 2145,
2220-2222, 2256, 2281, 2282,
2392
Colombian, 1100-1105
color, 1180, 2753
comics, 837
communication, 1629, 1630, 2590
Condé, Baudouin de, 1949
Condé, Jean de, 1949
Confucius, 1069, 1070
cook, 1686

Emerson, Ralph Waldo, 652
Emsland, 2190
Enevoldsen, Poul, 1118, 1126
Engadine, 3500
Engelbreit, Mary, 630
English, 19, 24, 51, 63, 66, 77,
125, 129, 131, 139, 141-144, 146,
147, 150, 151, 156, 158, 160, 162,
163, 172, 174-177, 184-186,
193-195, 197, 204, 211, 214, 223,
227, 229, 230, 232, 235, 252, 256,
258, 270, 271, 276, 279, 280, 285,
302, 304, 306-308, 326-328, 334,
335, 338, 341, 343, 349, 354, 552,
574, 581, 593-595, 644, 757, 846,
862, 863, 892, 925, 938, 966, 991,
992, 997, 998, 1001, 1003,
1008-1011, 1013, 1019, 1025,
1038, 1059, 1067, 1070, 1087,
1088, 1093, 1094, 1108, 1132,
1142, 1163-1835, 1849, 1879,
1880, 1890, 1893, 1895, 1922,
1955, 1957, 1965, 2004, 2034,
2096, 2109, 2129, 2168, 2169,
2346, 2399, 2402, 2424, 2434,
2570, 2577, 2578, 2632, 2649,
2664, 2665, 2674, 2721, 2731,
2770, 2829, 2831, 2832, 2834,
2836, 2856, 2901, 2902, 2922,
2972, 2990, 2993, 2998, 3019,
3022, 3037, 3056, 3065, 3128,
3133, 3146, 3188, 3190, 3202,
3227, 3228, 3244, 3248, 3250,
3262, 3263, 3265, 3278, 3279,
3282, 3284, 3288, 3289, 3291,
3315, 3316, 3337, 3363, 3392,
3393, 3395, 3397, 3411, 3416,
3437, 3440, 3524, 3526, 3527,
3535, 3538, 3543, 3544, 3546,
3548, 3560, 3569, 3578, 3593,
3596, 3611
epic, 1905, 1911, 1937, 2132,
2654
epitaph, 1657, 2396, 2757
Erasmus of Rotterdam,

Desiderius, 128, 334
Esperanto, 163, 1836-1840
essay, 2236, 2484
Estienne, Henri, 1921
Estonian, 242, 249-251, 270-272,
279, 328, 1841-1848, 2832
ethics, 459
Ethiopian, 1849-1854
ethnicity, 591, 624, 666, 667,
1043
euphemism, 697, 813, 1213, 1464,
1593, 1645, 1667, 1732
European, 190, 196, 198, 202,
216, 221, 222, 272-274, 276, 277,
278, 288, 298, 299, 303, 310-328,
332, 333, 336, 337, 340, 344-348,
350, 352, 353, 428, 1471, 1472,
1527, 1916, 2170, 2176, 2226,
2227, 2911
Even, 3028
Ewe, 359, 482
explanation, 70, 77, 131

Fabri, Johannes, 2289
fairy tale, 944, 2026, 2108, 2441,
2544
family, 803, 1419, 1658
Fante, 372
farm, 787
Fife, 3341
Filey, 1818
film, 1341
Finnish, 55, 242, 249, 257, 271,
279, 296, 326, 1855-1874, 2832,
2994, 2995, 3558
Finno-Ugric, 277
first line, 1599
Fischart, Johann, 2193, 2322,
2508
Flemish, 178, 989, 1900, 2010
Fletcher, John, 1757-1759
Florida, 820
flower, 1216
flying, 2185
folk etymology, 2487

folk song, 2785
Fon, 376
food, 406, 553, 894, 1205, 1485, 1601, 1686, 2242, 2249, 2385, 2420, 2421, 2585, 2678, 3070
Franck, Sebastian, 2699
François I, 3064
Franconian, 1985
Frankfurt, 2047, 2660
Franklin, Benjamin, 505, 508, 532, 647, 650, 831, 833, 838, 918
Freidank, 1926, 2330, 2375
French, 15, 32, 33, 41, 42, 60, 67, 97, 118, 119, 122, 142, 143, 146, 151, 156, 158, 160, 162-164, 174-177, 184, 185, 186, 193, 204, 207, 211, 214, 223, 227, 229, 230, 232, 233, 235, 240, 252, 255, 256, 258, 280, 284, 285, 302, 304, 306-308, 334, 335, 338, 341, 343, 349, 354, 356, 563, 991, 1108, 1335, 1381, 1646, 1807, 1812, 1814, 1840, 1875-1950, 1957, 2103, 2570, 2673, 2810, 2942, 3001, 3010, 3133, 3539, 3555, 3556, 3559, 3574
Fried, Erich, 2442
friendship, 1199
Frisian, 177, 178, 1951-1953, 2113, 2307, 2623, 2625
Friulian, 2923
Froissart, Jean, 1948
Fulani, 481

Gaelic, 1051, 2869, 2880, 2885, 2888, 2902, 2904
Galician, 280, 306, 308, 3373, 3378, 3379, 3409, 3410, 3419, 3436, 3443, 3444, 3448, 3449, 3452, 3465, 3468, 3470-3472, 3474
Gallicism, 1877
García Moreno, Melchor, 4
garden, 264, 1258, 1259
Geechee, 916

Gelnhausen, 2630
geography, 3067
Georgia, 814
Georgian, 1954, 1955
German, 7, 25, 31, 40, 47, 52, 68, 74, 79, 83, 89, 95, 98, 101, 102, 111, 132, 135, 136, 138, 140, 143, 146, 150, 151, 156, 158, 160, 162, 163, 172, 174-177, 185, 186, 191, 199, 200, 205, 211, 214, 229, 232, 235, 240, 242, 255, 256, 270, 271, 276, 279, 285, 299, 302, 303, 307, 310, 334, 338, 339, 341, 343, 345, 346, 349, 350, 354, 356, 376, 503, 521, 522, 539, 566, 574, 645, 646, 654, 696, 699, 700, 701, 713, 714, 726, 743, 808, 829, 836, 870, 894, 895, 927, 945, 990, 991, 993-995, 999, 1000, 1002, 1004, 1015-1018, 1020-1024, 1026-1028, 1036, 1056, 1142, 1148, 1228, 1274, 1275, 1369, 1381, 1386, 1417, 1456, 1459, 1502, 1503, 1517, 1522, 1539, 1589, 1718, 1736, 1741, 1792, 1795, 1832, 1840, 1848, 1857, 1864-1866, 1878, 1907, 1908, 1925, 1926, 1928, 1935, 1939, 1942, 1944, 1954, 1956-2761, 2828, 2830, 2832, 2927, 2930, 2941-2943, 2954, 2961, 2962, 2999, 3016, 3023, 3033, 3049, 3060, 3077, 3080, 3094, 3133, 3139, 3163, 3168, 3174, 3180, 3192, 3198, 3201, 3212, 3246, 3249, 3261, 3266, 3269, 3283, 3302, 3304, 3314, 3317, 3323, 3359, 3360, 3362, 3364-3367, 3372, 3376, 3412, 3431, 3486, 3494, 3497, 3498, 3500, 3502-3504, 3507, 3508, 3513, 3518, 3523, 3529, 3533, 3536, 3537, 3539, 3540, 3542, 3554, 3563-3564, 3571, 3572, 3580, 3582, 3583, 3586, 3594, 3597, 3598, 3607, 3612,